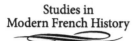

Studies in
Modern French History

Nobility and patrimony in modern France

Manchester University Press

Studies in
Modern French History

Edited by
David Hopkin and Máire Cross

This series is published in collaboration with the UK Society for the Study of French History. It aims to showcase innovative short monographs relating to the history of the French, in France and in the world since c.1750. Each volume speaks to a theme in the history of France with broader resonances to other discources about the past. Authors demonstrate how the sources and interpretations of modern French history are being opened to historical investigation in new and interesting ways, and how unfamiliar subjects have the capacity to tell us more about the role of France within the European continent. The series is particularly open to interdisciplinary studies that break down the traditional boundaries and conventional disciplinary divisions.

Recently published in this series

The Society for the
Study of French History

Nobility and patrimony in modern France

ELIZABETH C. MACKNIGHT

Manchester University Press

The right of Elizabeth C. Macknight to be identified as the author of this work
has been asserted by her in accordance with the Copyright, Designs and Patents
Act 1988.

Published by Manchester University Press
Altrincham Street, Manchester M1 7JA

www.manchesteruniversitypress.co.uk

British Library Cataloguing-in-Publication Data
A catalogue record for this book is available from the British Library

ISBN   978 1 5261 2051 9   hardback

First published 2018

Typeset by
Servis Filmsetting Ltd, Stockport, Cheshire
Printed in Great Britain by
TJ International Ltd, Padstow

For Campbell, Lorraine, and Thomas, and for Jacques

Contents

Tables

Acknowledgements

My commitment to write this book grew from love of working with the sources deposed in the Archives départementales of France. I am indebted to owners who gave me permission to consult nobles' private collections of papers. Staff and interns in the archives have helped me in my research with utmost consideration. For expert assistance on archival matters I thank Ségolène de Dainville-Barbiche, Isabelle Brunet, Camille Buzon, Martin de Framond, Samuel Gibiat, Olivier Gorse, and Claude Petit. Advice on heritage valorisation in rural areas came from Marilyne Avont, Aurore Jarry, Daniel Labarthe, and Simone Sauges. I am especially grateful to my father Campbell Macknight, to the editors of Studies in Modern French History, and to the anonymous peer reviewers who gave generously of their time to read and comment on drafts. It has been a delight to work with the team at Manchester University Press.

Sebastian Percival, an inspiring Australian teacher, first introduced me to the wonderful freedoms of travelling on European railways and exploring the French countryside. Fortunate are the researchers like me who travel by train and on foot in France. For joyful moments along the way I thank Elaine Adams, Frances and Ian Black, Luc Boudon, Pauline Brassier, Pierre Brillard, Suzanne Brustel, Giorgia and Sarah Bulli, Annick Caro, Pierre-Paul Castelli, Josette Clauzier, Valérie Cros, David Davatchi, Hélène Doré, Tatiana and Raphaël Dumas, Patrick Durand, Michel Fournier, Guillaume and Agathe Hazebaert, Marie Heyraud, Hélène Hiquily, Caroline and Michael Hubbard, Jérôme Jouve, Louise Leates, Bernard Lepère, Henriette Loiseau, Francine Martinaud, Frédérique Palaccio, Marcelle Portalier, Maria Pulvéric, Valérie Rapaud, Nathalie and

Franck Raymond, Philippe Rigaud, Isabelle Romano-Philippon, Marie-Thérèse and Vincent Roubaud, Corine and Alain Rouleau, Claire Simon, Jean-Pierre and Marie-Thérèse Soulier, Christine Varagne, and Raymond Vigoureux.

Journeys like book projects are made sustainable by the patience and thoughtfulness of particular people. Of special mention are my wonderful neighbours Catherine Brustel and her family. I also deeply appreciate the kind welcome from Père Pierre Badon and his helpers. For words of encouragement thanks to Béatrice Bronnert, Mariem Dali, Juliet Flesch, James Graham, Von Harrington, Scott and Gina Harrington, Ben and Sylvia Harrington, Christian Kapteyn, Maximiliano Lorenzi, John and Jan Macknight, Tiger and Deb Macknight, and Kirsty Munro. Through adventures in dark and light Luke Gartlan provides boundless support. Daniel Nethery brings to our long conversation his insights that I cherish. Jacques Denhez keeps life sparkling with humour and wisdom. Most importantly my father, mother, and brother showed faith in me to imagine and to complete this book on the opposite side of the world from Australia. Their love and the happy spirit of Agnès Galand bring me home.

Haute-Loire, 2017

Abbreviations

AD	Archives départementales
AN	Archives nationales
ANF	Association d'entraide de la noblesse française
AP	Archives privées
UNESCO	United Nations Educational, Scientific, and Cultural Organisation

Introduction

Neither the frost nor the autumn rain brought damp into the houses that day. Beneath the jutting cliff that peered over the river Tarn the smell of smoke, so familiar to the villagers of La Malène, began to arouse fear. Armed men who had crossed into the department of Lozère from neighbouring Ardèche had drunk all of the wine in the village and slaughtered all of the pigs. Now this 'band of assassins, known as the revolutionary army' set out to destroy what remained. 'They tied up our inconsolable women and subjected them to constant terror and mortal threat in front of the horrible spectacle of flames engulfing their homes.' La Malène, inhabited by some eighty people, was razed on 4 November 1793. Those who survived the calamity described how 'nothing was spared, neither our belongings, nor our livelihoods. Everything was reduced to ash.'[1]

Gabriel de Brun de Montesquiou, *seigneur* of La Malène, was among those whose possessions were consumed by the fire. He and his wife Marie-Catherine du Pont de Ligonnès owned the château de La Malène and two of the houses in the village along with various stables and barns. The couple had raised three children and employed four servants in the household. Produce that had been harvested from their lands by peasants or bartered locally to store for nourishment over the winter caught alight and burned. Among the losses were twenty *cartes* of wheat, sixteen of barley, twenty-four of oats, and sixty of chestnuts; forty pounds of butter, thirty of lard, and twenty-four of cooking fat; one pig, one ewe, twenty pounds of rice, and two *cartes* of lentils.[2] The fire also took colanders, pots, casseroles, and a cauldron; beds and linen; mirrors, chairs, chests, and tables; chimney guards, pails for wood, bedroom tapestries, and a large leather tapestry depicting the grape harvest in the style of Louis XIII. Most distressing for the noble *seigneur* was the destruction of some of his family papers in the blaze.[3]

The damage wrought by the fire at La Malène forms part of a wider picture of material loss for the Brun de Montesquiou family and other nobles during the French Revolution.[4] In 1797 Gabriel de Brun de Montesquiou tried to calculate the financial sums involved for his own family using the debased paper currency that had been in circulation. The decrees of 4 August 1789 deprived him of seigneurial dues worth around 1,500 *assignats* each year. Gabriel's eldest son, Jean-Baptiste de Brun de Montesquiou, had participated in the 1789 assembly of nobles of the province of Gévaudan and was married to the daughter of another noble of the province, Gilberte de Pons de la Grange. The dowry brought to the marriage in 1784 was to have been worth some 60,000 *assignats*, but around half the dowry was still owed to the Brun de Montesquiou when the Pons de la Grange family properties were seized and sold as *biens nationaux*. Jean-Baptiste fathered three children by his wife before her death in 1790. The forty-year-old widower decided to emigrate and join the princes' army, leaving his three infants in the care of their paternal grandparents, Gabriel and Marie-Catherine. On 12 October 1793 Gabriel, aged seventy-two, was placed under arrest as a suspect because of Jean-Baptiste's emigration. He and Marie-Catherine were imprisoned until 1795, which meant they did not witness the fire at La Malène. Their townhouse in Mende was ransacked then sold. The couple lost 12,000 *assignats*' worth of linen, clothing, and other goods from this townhouse as well as 5,000 *assignats*' *worth* of annual *rentes* from land they owned in the diocese of Mende. Gabriel estimated that over an eight-year period from 1789 to 1797 he and his family had realised losses of property and income totalling some 134,000 *assignats*.[5]

A fundamental question that this book sets out to answer is how nobles like the Brun de Montesquiou re-established themselves as landowners and maintained patrimony. At its origin the concept of 'patrimony', a word derived from the Latin words *patrimonium* and *pater*, was designed to enable the ensemble of a father's goods to be transmitted to his children. Hence, the Roman jurist Gaïus distinguished between goods subject to private appropriation (*res in patrimonio*) and goods that were not (*res extra patrimonio*). Two nineteenth-century legal theorists in France, Aubry (1803–83) and Rau (1803–77), developed the concept of patrimony within French law where property ownership is understood as a universal right for every legal individual. In theory the emphasis on universality makes the value of what is owned irrelevant: a street beggar with just a few belongings has patrimony, and legal rights associated with it, in exactly the same way that a millionaire with countless belongings does. The notion that patrimony derives from a legal individual, never a group, family, or company, is also significant in French jurisprudence. Within the ensemble of goods making up a legal individual's patrimony there are both tangible and intangible items. The Civil Code (article 516) distinguishes two kinds of tangible property: movable goods (*meubles*) and immovable goods (*immeubles*). Intangible property includes such things as names, traditions, inventions, mottoes, brands, and creative works.[6]

The Civil Code is the legal instrument most often invoked in France on matters concerning an individual's patrimony. In the twenty-first century, however, there is also the Code du patrimoine for the protection of the nation's cultural, artistic, and architectural heritage. The Code du patrimoine builds upon earlier French legislation, notably the Loi sur les monuments historiques (31 December 1913), the Loi Malraux (31 December 1968), and the Loi sur les archives (3 January 1979).[7] France is one of the countries to feature within the European Heritage Network, a resource for conservators, researchers, and policy-makers established under the auspices of the Council of Europe. National heritage policies vary within the European Union but there is a common context created through the European Cultural Convention (1954), the Convention for the Protection of the Architectural Heritage of Europe (1985), and the European Convention on the Protection of Archaeological Heritage (1992).[8]

To investigate nobles' maintenance of patrimony thus requires close attention to the nobility's relations with the State, which has been a crucial theme in medieval and early modern French history but remains under-explored for the post-revolutionary period.[9] Nobles' roles and activities after 1789 have tended to be subsumed within studies of male 'notables'. André-Jean Tudesq argued that by the middle of the nineteenth century nobles and haut bourgeois were largely united in their outlook and behaviour. Concentrating on the decade of the 1840s, Tudesq developed the notion of 'a single social psychology' characteristic to the men of his study, *les grands notables*. These large-scale property owners experienced some decline in their economic power and political influence in the final quarter of the nineteenth century. An agricultural crisis triggered a fall in land prices, whilst growing popular support for the Third Republic regime meant that increasing numbers of middle-class men with professional careers, such as doctors and lawyers, were elected to parliament. In Daniel Halévy's interpretation the 1870s marked 'the end of the notables'.[10]

This book presents a new reading of landed elites that for the period from 1789 to the 2000s aims at radical reversal of 'nobles' disappearance from modern French historical thought'.[11] Patrimony that originally belonged to the nobility provides evidence not only of nobles' experiences but also of the impact their existence had on people of lower social strata. Since the 1960s historians have devoted much effort to writing history 'from below', raising awareness of sources about the experiences of people accustomed to oppression. One of the paradoxes of historians shunning the study of nineteenth- and twentieth-century nobility has been to leave gaps in understanding of why and how and which sources have survived from an elite minority historically accustomed to rule.

In documenting nobles' interactions with the State, I argue for the distinctiveness of nobles' lived experiences that is downplayed by those historians who accept the notion of 'a single social psychology' shared by noble and bourgeois property owners. That is not to say that nobles and bourgeois were necessarily in conflict, or that there were no similarities at all. It was a symbiotic relationship. Yet the nobility's persistent concern to protect noble identity meant there were contrasts between the social strata in practices and attitudes with regard to inheritance and the cultivation of collective memory. Those contrasts appear in sharpest definition when analysed over a period of time longer than a single decade or a single political regime. This book adopts a longer chronological range, looking back to the watershed of the French Revolution and just as importantly continuing beyond the fall of the Second Empire. My choice of a *longue durée* perspective reflects the influence of innovative approaches and concepts introduced to the field of nobility studies by scholars of the Middle Ages and early modern era.[12]

Historians as well as archivists, curators, and specialists in art and architectural conservation have abiding professional interests in how notions of 'national' patrimony developed and continue to evolve in France. In the wake of the French Revolution abbé Grégoire and Alexandre Lenoir are credited with recognising that important traces of the *ancien régime* should be preserved; the beginnings of a systematic approach to identification and documentation of heritage date from the July Monarchy. In 1830, at François Guizot's instigation, the Ministry of the Interior hired art historian Ludovic Vitet and author Prosper Mérimée as inspectors of historic monuments to identify and catalogue France's most significant sites and structures. From 1840 the newly created Commission des monuments historiques appointed architects, notably Eugène Viollet-le-Duc, to supervise the restoration of structures on the list of classed monuments. Victor Hugo lobbied for a system of quality control by experts and influenced the drafting of the first law on historic monuments adopted on 30 March 1887. Across the nineteenth century conservators and curators in public museums, archives, and galleries were working to refine policies and pursue strategies for augmenting national collections.[13]

Alongside these initiatives by State bodies and by male 'pioneers of patrimony' numerous lesser-known citizens were also making contributions to the preservation and interpretation of cultural property. After 1789 a diverse range of groups in French society were engaged in nurturing collective memories of the revolutionary and Napoleonic decades, for which all kinds of artefacts and intangibles like dances and songs were useful.[14] Learned societies, academies, and institutes that flourished from the 1830s catalogued and studied patrimony in the provinces. These associational networks were comprised mostly of men of the middling bourgeoisie who embraced liberal values, although nobles and clerics also joined some of the societies. Under the July Monarchy (1830–48) the associational networks gained support from central authorities for their promotion of patrimony and the Minister of Public Instruction, François Guizot, created a Comité des travaux historiques. But the French State grew increasingly ambivalent about associational networks advancing local or provincial causes and fostering sentiments and interpretations of the past deemed to be dangerous to national unity.[15]

Meanwhile noble families in post-revolutionary France were interacting with the State over patrimony in private ownership. There were only some 5,033 of these families by 1900, and numbers fell to 4,075 families by 1975.[16] In this predominantly Catholic milieu most nobles maintained longstanding political allegiances to empire or monarchy. During the early decades of the Third Republic the State introduced new laws to protect 'national' patrimony (1887, 1913) and government policy on many fronts was geared toward embedding republicanism and promoting republican interpretations of the past. It was precisely in this period of consolidation for France's republican regime that the nobility was strengthening its participation in heritage and arts bodies. Cultural patronage committees were presided over by nobles. Aristocratic collectors donated particular items or whole private collections to public museums and galleries. Across the twentieth century nobles set up, presided over and joined organisations such as La Demeure historique,

La Sauvegarde de l'art français, Le Comité Vendôme, Vieilles maisons françaises and SOS Paris.[17] These types of initiatives have meant that, whilst the number of nobles serving as elected representatives in national politics has declined since the 1870s, the nobility has sustained significant influence in France's cultural sector as the meanings attached to the term '*le patrimoine*' have evolved.[18] In France patrimony has never lost its legal definition in the Civil Code for an individual's rights over property. Under the Fifth Republic, however, patrimony gained a further definition in government circles and among the French people as a way of conceiving of public cultural assets. Nobles have been vitally engaged with all of the shifts in legislation and in political and cultural interpretations of patrimony from 1789 right up to the present day.

On the other side of the English Channel there has been contemporaneous growth of aristocratic influence in the arts and heritage sector.[19] This can be explained by certain commonalities between the British and French upper classes in their preservationist instincts and pecuniary concerns for tax relief, as well as participation in transnational social networks, leisure, and travel.[20] The impact of 1789 upon society in France, however, meant that French nobles' stake in the elaboration of 'national' patrimony did not evolve in precisely the same way as the evolution of English peers' stake in the heritage industry of Britain. The ebb and flow of anti-aristocratic sentiment and the aristocracy's parliamentary representation were patterned differently in the two countries.

During the first half of the twentieth century the context for negotiations between private owners and the French State about 'national' patrimony was profoundly shaped by the destruction that took place during the two world wars. In the wake of revolutions and wars people in all parts of the world find that the existence of cultural property helps to restore quality of life and sense of community; such property may also be the subject of legal claims or efforts to establish legal rights.[21] After the Second World War international efforts led to the Hague Convention for the Protection of Cultural Property in the Event of Armed Conflict (1954). The increasing commercialisation within museums and the wider heritage industry has sharpened attention to the ways in which sites, objects and intangibles can be marketed for the benefit of national and local economies.[22] As custodians of archives, paintings, furniture, jewellery, and *objets d'art* noblewomen and noblemen have been continuously involved in decisions over what happens to such items. In France properties historically owned by nobility attract tourism that remains vitally important for communes across the country.

Given the range of reasons for which patrimony holds 'value' then, it is a curious paradox that among academic historians the subject of life at the château after 1789 has been regularly dismissed, neglected, and pushed to the margins of modern French history. For, if France is proud of its revolutionary heritage symbolised by the Bastille, visitors today will see that older forms of heritage associated with noble identity are hardly suppressed or missing from the matrix of images the nation presents of itself to the world.

Origins, lifestyles, and challenges

We can never know precisely the size of the noble population in France on the eve of the French Revolution. The most reliable historical estimates suggest between 17,000 and 26,000 families; the number of noble individuals is thought to have been between 110,000 and 120,000.[23] Who were these people and how did they live?

In eighteenth-century France the nobility was a very diverse social group in which differences in families' origins and material circumstances encouraged a sense of internal hierarchy among members. At the top of the social ladder were some two hundred ancient and illustrious families who had greatest access to the court by virtue of their pedigree. These were nobles who could trace their aristocratic ancestry back to 1400 or further, which meant they were eligible for presentation to the monarch. Among them was a smaller elite of court nobility (*la noblesse de la cour*) who regularly attended upon the royal family. Members of this select group had to attract favour from the king in the form of lucrative pensions, court offices, high commands, and governorships to enable them to pursue court habits. Incomes at this level of French society were generally in the order of 50,000–200,000 *livres* per year, reaching to 500,000 *livres* for dukes and into the millions for princes.[24] Expenses were large in scale, and so were many rich nobles' debts. Constant jockeying to secure one's position as a favourite in the eyes of the king and queen gave rise to the verbal jousting and slights that peppered social interaction. Elsewhere in eighteenth-century France there were plenty of nobles of very ancient lineage who did not participate in court rituals or visit the capital because they could not afford the expense. There were also families who had attained recent ennoblement, most commonly through purchase of a heritable office.[25]

Provincial nobility, those who lived year-round in the countryside, had smaller fortunes than nobles who lodged at Versailles or in Paris, and their expenditure was configured rather differently from that of *les grands*. Around three and half thousand families with incomes of 10,000–50,000 *livres* per year represented the most affluent segment living in sumptuous style away from the capital. Elegance and finery mattered to these nobles, but for them the desire for social advancement was hedged by concerns about the pecuniary risks of chasing superiors' favour and, for some, distaste for Parisian mores.[26] There were around twice as many nobles, or seven thousand families, living very comfortably on incomes of 4,000–10,000 *livres* per year. Like their wealthier counterparts, these nobles tailored their expenditure to create an impression of ease and *bon ton*. Then there was a considerably larger group of perhaps eleven thousand families whose incomes were less than 4,000 *livres*. These nobles led a frugal existence, avoiding outlay for new clothes or entertaining, but they could still afford to employ a few servants. Finally some five thousand families had incomes of less than 1,000 *livres* per year, which meant they were subject to financial hardship bordering on poverty.[27]

Members of the provincial nobility, even those who enjoyed considerable luxury, were often looked down upon for their 'country manners' by the *habitués* of Versailles and Paris. But within rural communities such nobles were the local lords who owned the château, *maison de maître*, manor, or *castel*, and who exercised control over key resources, notably land but also mills, presses, ponds, orchards, and forests. In practice, the manner in which they exercised control depended on frequency and length of residency. It was customary for most nobles to divide their time between different estates and spend part of the year in a townhouse in a regional urban centre. With greater amounts of absenteeism came greater reliance on local agents, especially the steward (*le régisseur*). Marital alliances combined with frequent purchases or exchanges of property within and between families meant that nobles' socio-economic networks crisscrossed the country. Nevertheless, the majority of nobles, whilst known for a peripatetic lifestyle, tended to identify with one province in which to a considerable extent they were socially and economically embedded.

One set of challenges to 'living nobly' arose out of France's physical geography and the ways in which environmental change interacted with political and economic change. On an everyday basis, as well as at times of crises such as food shortage or natural disaster, those challenges contributed to shaping the dynamics of nobles' relationships with other inhabitants of rural communities. Historians have long debated the transformative effects of the French Revolution for the cultivation of land.[28] The abolition of the seigneurial system meant that over time peasants became more likely to own their own land and even those who rented plots had greater autonomy to decide which crops to grow and how to grow them. With the steady improvement of transport infrastructure and communications, new opportunities collided with age-old environmental constraints.[29] The nobility, like the rural bourgeoisie, leased portions of land to lower-middle-class and working-class cultivators on a tenant farming or sharecropping basis. Cultivation practices were extremely diverse. Many noble landowners were also engaged in farming, not in the sense of tilling the soil with their own hands, but rather by employing labourers to carry out their instructions about which crops to sow and which animals to breed for market demand; on some estates there were tracts of forest and mineral reserves, which when exploited brought further income through sales of timber, clay, iron and other substances important to manufacture. Environment and economy were not simply in the backdrop of social relations in rural communities; rather they formed a motor in human interaction because livelihoods depended upon natural resources.

A second set of challenges stemmed from the law. In the 1789 Declaration of the Rights of Man and Citizen, and much subsequent legislation, property ownership was upheld as a basic right of citizens subject to legal protection. Whilst the nobility and bourgeoisie faced some similar issues with regard to property there was more divergence in their experiences (but not in their standing as citizens) before the law than is generally recognised. Nobiliary law is a branch of the legal discipline no longer taught in French law faculties today. Yet it still operates to regulate transmission of nobiliary titles and there is extensive jurisprudence from the nineteenth, twentieth, and twenty-first centuries demonstrating how these rules have been applied in court. At France's highest judicial level, the Conseil d'État made explicit reference to the 'rules of French nobiliary law' in a decision handed down on 25 February 1983.[30] Nobiliary law is complex because its sources are a mix of constitutional texts, decisions taken by different sovereigns, parliamentary acts, and foreign legislation applying to territories that have shifted into another nation's possession. This branch of the law exists within the legal systems of other European countries too, which can be relevant in jurisprudence because of transnational ties among the nobility. The complexity in France is further increased because each change of political regime through the nineteenth century was accompanied by an overhaul to the legalities associated with nobiliary titles. Modifications to family and property law could have profound ramifications for nobles whose rights to titles, related possessions, and forms of income were all bound up in nobiliary law. In particular, Napoleon's introduction of the entail system known as the *majorat* in 1808 sealed for the recipients of imperial titles, as well as for the *ancienne noblesse*, a singular fate with regard to experiences of the legal system that were never shared by bourgeois property owners to whom nobiliary law did not apply.[31]

Sources and approach

This book is based principally on empirical research carried out in *archives privées* produced by nobility.[32] The very creation of these collections (*fonds*) of nobles' private papers deposited in public repositories is a form of marking and preserving patrimony – a core issue explored in following chapters. For information on certain topics it has been helpful to investigate public archives as well, particularly the M series (Administration and economy 1800–1940) and Q series (Property). Supplementing these archival sources, I have drawn on newspapers and on published reports from a range of government and non-government bodies that provided quantitative and qualitative data to establish a national overview of property.

Whilst this is original research for the history of France, there do exist models for such a study treating similar themes. One of the purposes of placing the post-1789 French nobility at the centre of enquiry is to show how the wealth of source material available in France can be gathered and exploited for the type of research on nobles, country houses, and landed estates undertaken for other countries of continental Europe and Britain.[33] The broad range of complex institutions and practices relevant for understanding the nobility's relationship to family property are brought together and surveyed here, in the hope that researchers in the future will give each phenomenon deeper attention in articles, monographs, and dissertations. The list of archival sources is intended to serve as a finding aid to stimulate research, and many of the collections could become the basis for a doctoral thesis. In the 2000s scholars continue to call for more empirical and more comparative work on European nobilities, especially for the twentieth century.[34]

Why choose private archives scattered across the country as sources of historical evidence? To date, there have been few efforts to investigate nobles' circumstances using a national representative sample for the post-revolutionary period. From the starting point of research he conducted in the department of Dordogne, Ralph Gibson sought 'to try and collate material from other areas, and to set [his] own as far as possible in the national context.'[35] Keenly aware of the difficulties created by varying definitions of nobility in the historical literature, Gibson nonetheless sought to make some comparisons between departments, bringing together information on nobles' geographic distribution across France, with details on levels of tax payment and amounts of land owned derived from the cadastre.[36] In a similar way, but as part of a larger study for the decades 1800–70, David Higgs presented quantitative findings on nobles' landowning for different departments, such as could be drawn from electoral rolls and tax records. He also tackled issues such as the evolving influence of aristocratic landowners in national and local politics.[37]

Both Gibson and Higgs pointed to some of the problems of working from public records for nobles. Both these historians recognised that there were major aspects of nobles' post-revolutionary experiences on which speculation was possible but which really needed further historical investigation. Patterns of residency, cultures of estate management, and levels of involvement in agriculture were among those aspects that remained 'hidden' from the researcher using public archives.[38] Equally obscure to historians consulting such records was information about family strategies to transmit property, the aesthetics of 'home' for nobility, and social interaction. In what ways did noblewomen participate in the running of an estate? How were aristocratic children taught about financial matters including ways to exercise thrift and keep track of debt? When and why were nobles' properties 'modernised', turned into heritage sites for tourist consumption, or left to fall into ruin? Where did nobles look for ideas on how to decorate the interiors of châteaux and townhouses or what to plant in parks and gardens? What were the hiring procedures and wages for servants and outdoor labourers? How much interaction did nobles have with stewards, tenants, neighbouring landowners, and residents of local towns and villages? In what ways did such relationships evolve?

Questions like these about key aspects of nobles' daily life would remain impossible to resolve if, as Robert Forster argued in 1963, evidence in the form of personal correspondence, diaries, business letters, receipts and accounts, notary records, memoirs, wills and other legal documents was 'extremely rare'.[39] In fact, the evidence is not lacking at all. It exists in spectacular abundance but is dispersed all over France in nobles' *archives privées*.[40]

Increasingly, these types of archives are being sought out and used by historians, most often for micro-histories focusing on a single family or a cluster of families.[41] Studies of nobles in particular regions of France have also been produced.[42] However, questions about nobles' lived experiences in post-revolutionary France deserve to be answered for more than one family or one region at a time. Many of the questions treated in this book are not amenable to statistical enquiry by their very nature. But that does not mean that one cannot establish what is typical or what is exceptional by drawing upon a wide array of archival material from across France. This book is intended to be not a quantitative study but rather an effort to enter into understanding nobles' emotions and motivations regarding patrimony, to bring out how they perceived the threats and opportunities that pertained to its ownership in the modern world.

The conceptual tools used in my interpretation come from the social sciences.[43] Pioneering work by Pierre Bourdieu and Monique de Saint Martin on conversions and reconversions of capital, cultural field, gift exchange, and habitus underpins my approach to the study of class and power.[44] Application of these theoretical concepts in a study of modern French history requires grounding in the laws that defined both the constraints and the room to manoeuvre for families seeking to protect different forms of capital (economic, social, cultural, and symbolic).

Chapters 1 to 4 form a sequence in which social history is combined with history of law to investigate the effects of legal reform upon nobles' transmission of tangible and intangible patrimony. New laws originating in the French Revolution (for example on partible inheritance, marriage and divorce, and adoption) as well as the introduction of Napoleon's Civil Code, the *majorat*, and other legal innovations are examined using archival case studies. I draw attention to the challenges as well as to the possibilities for nobles to benefit from the French Revolution. Chapters 5 to 8 also form a sequence in which social history is combined with cultural and political history to investigate how nobles' tangible and intangible patrimony has been managed and communicated to the public. Here and in some earlier chapters novels and art are brought in to the discussion for the light they shine on matters of preoccupation to French society. Archival documentation provides the empirical base for analysing the nobility's repertoire of techniques for upholding its identity.

Equally important to this book's analytic aims and resonating through the whole work are Maurice Halbwachs's writings on the social frameworks of memory, those 'instruments used by the collective memory to reconstruct an image of the past which is in accord, in each epoch, with the predominant thoughts of the society'. When analysing the traditions of groups, such as families and social classes, Halbwachs argued: 'It is not sufficient, in effect, to show that individuals always use social frameworks when they remember. It is necessary to place oneself in the perspective of the group.'[45] Both before and after 1789, it was very important to the French nobility to try to keep its 'framework for family memory' intact because this constituted families' 'traditional armour' for protecting noble identity.[46] Noble families' elaboration of collective memory took place privately through the aristocratic tradition of educating children in the home and rituals of sociability. As noble families constructed collective memory over time, out of selective myth-like versions of real events, they bequeathed these fictions to the next generation. Stories about ancestors repeatedly told to children were essential to maintain collective memory, and were often written down in the form of memoirs, whether or not intended for publication. Oral traditions formed part of noble families' intangible patrimony together with names and titles, coats of arms, livery colours, hunting fanfares, and family mottoes.[47]

Combining theoretical insights with an archival research strategy provides an opportunity to be very clear about who is being identified as 'noble' and why.[48] Historians, sociologists, and anthropologists have long insisted on rigour in defining 'peasant'.[49] Yet, as Gibson and others have pointed out, imprecision in identifying nobility continues to be a problem in the much smaller academic literature on landowning elites, which impacts on historical study of the ways in which landowners exercised power.[50] Unless care is taken to address landowners' identities, historians will remain handicapped when investigating aspects of social authority and responses to it. This includes fundamental patterns of human behaviour such as deference, paternalism, patronage, and mediation.

In drawing upon archival material I have sought to enable the voices of individuals to emerge frequently throughout the book. Letters and other personal writings allow access to nobles' preoccupations and also to the experiences of the bourgeoisie and of the working class who lived in rural and urban communities. An imponderable amount can never be 'heard' by us today, of course, and it should not be imagined that the ways in which villagers and townsfolk used language in writing to nobles at the château, or to the mayor, or the curé, or to national authorities, were the ways in which villagers and townsfolk spoke among themselves. But by examining the evidence that we have of interaction among these people of differing backgrounds we begin to interpret the nuances, and to identify the gaps and the silences.

The strongly centralised nature of the modern French State means that a proportion of the bureaucratic and legislative paperwork in the archives emanated from the capital. Paris itself, however, does not feature a great deal in the following pages.[51] My research has been concerned with identifying how the laws and bureaucratic instructions were received and responded to in communes situated away from Paris. Eighteenth-century nobles who lived year-round in the provinces held a variety of attitudes toward the capital that were often informed by generational differences.[52] The same was true of nineteenth- and twentieth-century nobles. In 1888 the princesse Cécile de Béarn wrote to her son Henri: 'Grandfather cannot understand how one can live outside Paris and especially not in the Midi. I do not share his opinion at all.'[53] By contrast, in January 1909, the comtesse Adeline de Raymond received a note from her niece Sabine who yearned to experience Parisian social life: 'Bastia is especially dull this winter. Nobody dances, nobody has fun.'[54]

In commencing this history with the French Revolution, the archival documentation for the opening chapters contains signs of the State's transition to new administrative structures and territorial divisions. On 4 March 1790 Louis XVI signed the letters patent ordering the establishment of departments; shortly afterwards a committee within the Constituent Assembly began the awesome task of carrying out the work involved.[55] 'The creation of a new idea of France was the work of urban elites with a distinctive vision of spatial organization and institutional hierarchy. It was designed to give reality to two of their keywords: to "regenerate" the nation while cementing its "unity".'[56]

Provincial nobility, including the Brun de Montesquiou family in Gévaudan, did not have much to celebrate in this 'important victory of the new State'; they were far too preoccupied and alarmed. For them, and for many other people, older forms of spatial awareness, older hierarchies, and older province-based and territorial loyalties – including to languages or dialects – did not disappear. Yet nobles had no choice but to engage with the State, as well as with rural and urban inhabitants, for the recovery, defence, and maintenance of cultural property. Theirs was a long-term project, bequeathed by ancestors, to ensure descendants maintained the legal rights to ownership and enjoyment of patrimony.

One may always regret what has been destroyed or lost. The great fortune for historians, however, is that so much archival evidence has survived about how successive generations of nobility fared on their estates. It is to that evidence, of destruction and survival in a gradually modernising France, which we now turn.

Notes

1 'Petition au Conseil de cinq cents', November 1793, in AD Lozère 7J/7 Fonds de Saint Amand.

2 The term *carte* refers to a measure of grain or, in some regions, a measure of other products such as wine or salt. In Lozère one *carte* of chestnuts was equivalent to 30.98 litres. See '*carte*' in M. Lachiver, *Dictionnaire du monde rural* (Paris, 2006). On the persistence of barter by the muleteers of Gévaudan in the nineteenth century see E. Weber, *Peasants into Frenchmen: The Modernization of Rural France 1870–1914* (London, 1976), p. 35.

3 'Mémoire de ce que nous avons perdu' in AD Lozère 7J/7 Fonds de Saint Amand.

4 R. Forster, 'The survival of the nobility during the French Revolution', *Past and Present* 37 (1967), 71–86; D. Higgs, *Nobles in Nineteenth-Century France: The Practice of Inegalitarianism* (Baltimore, 1987), pp. 51–4; L. Boisnard, *La Noblesse dans la tourmente 1774–1802* (Paris, 1992); P. Bourdin (ed.), *Les Noblesses françaises dans l'Europe de la Révolution* (Rennes and Clermont-Ferrand, 2010).

5 'Etat et mémoire des pertes' in AD Lozère 7J/7 Fonds de Saint Amand.

6 R. Encinas de Munagorri, *Introduction générale au droit* Revised ed. (Paris, 2006), pp. 77–80, 85–91.

7 C. Nougaret and P. Even (eds), *Les Archives privées: manuel pratique et juridique* (Paris, 2008), pp. 21–8, 178–9; *Code du patrimoine: partie legislative* (Paris, 2004).

8 European Commission, *Getting Cultural Heritage to Work for Europe: Report of the Horizon 2020 Expert Group on Cultural Heritage* (Brussels, 2015). On global developments in heritage legislation, see, for example, D. Poulot (ed.), *Patrimoine et modernité* (Paris, 1998); D. Poulot, *Patrimoine et musées: l'institution de la culture* (Paris, 2003); H. Deacon, L. Dondolo, M. Mrubata, and S. Prosalendis, *The Subtle Power of Intangible Heritage* (Cape Town, 2004); C. Bortolotto (ed.), *Le Patrimoine culturel immatériel: les enjeux, les problématiques, les pratiques* (Paris, 2011); M. Hall (ed.), *Towards World Heritage: International Origins of the Preservation Movement* (Aldershot, 2011); L. Bernie, M. Dormaels, and Y. Le Fur, *Le Patrimonialisation de l'urbain* (Paris, 2012); A. Swenson, *The Rise of Heritage: Preserving the Past in France, Germany, and Britain 1789–1914* (Cambridge, 2015).

9 See, for example, W. Beik, *Absolutism and Society in Seventeenth-Century France: State Power and Provincial Aristocracy in Languedoc* (Cambridge, 1985); J. R. Major, *The Monarchy, the Estates and the Aristocracy in Renaissance France* (London, 1988); P. Contamine (ed.), *L'État et les aristocraties (France, Angleterre, Écosse) XIIe–XVIIe siècle* (Paris, 1989); A. Jouanna, *Le Devoir de révolte: la noblesse française et la gestation de l'État moderne, 1559–1661* (Paris, 1989); J. B. Collins, *The State in Early Modern France* (Cambridge,

1995); D. Bohanan, *Crown and Nobility in Early Modern France* (New York, 2001).

10 A.-J. Tudesq, *Les Grands Notables en France (1840–1849): étude historique d'une psychologie sociale* 2 vols (Paris, 1964); D. Halévy, *La Fin des notables* (Paris, 1930).

11 J. Dewald, 'French nobles and the historians, 1820–1960' in J. M. Smith (ed.), *The French Nobility in the Eighteenth Century: Reassessments and New Approaches* (University Park, 2006), p. 306.

12 J. Dewald, *Pont-St-Pierre 1398–1789: Lordship, Community, and Capitalism in Early Modern France* (Berkeley, 1987); J. Dewald, *Aristocratic Experience and the Origins of Modern Culture: France, 1570–1715* (Berkeley, 1993); J. Dewald, *The European Nobility, 1400–1800* (Cambridge, 1996); H. M. Scott (ed.), *The European Nobilities in the Seventeenth and Eighteenth Centuries* 2 vols (London, 1995); L. Bourquin, *La Noblesse dans la France moderne (XVIe–XVIIIe siècles)* (Paris, 2002); J. Pontet, M. Figeac, and M. Boisson (eds), *La Noblesse de la fin du XVIe au début du XXe siècle: un modèle social?* 2 vols (Anglet, 2002); D. Crouch, *The Birth of Nobility: Constructing Aristocracy in England and France, 900–1300* (London, 2005); J. Dumanowski and M. Figeac (eds), *Noblesse française et noblesse polonaise: mémoire, identité, culture XVI–XXe siècles* (Pessac, 2006); M. Figeac, *Châteaux et vie quotidienne de la noblesse: de la Renaissance à la douceur des Lumières* (Paris, 2006); A. Livingstone, *Out of Love for My Kin: Aristocratic Family Life in the Lands of the Loire, 1000–1200* (Ithaca, 2010).

13 L. Courajod, *Alexandre Lenoir, son journal et le Musée des monuments français* (Paris, 1878–87); P. Verdier, *Le Service des Monuments historiques, son histoire, son organisation, administration, législation* (Paris, 1936); J.-P. Bady, *Les Monuments historiques en France* (Paris, 1985); P. Preschez, *Cours de droit: législation et monuments historiques* (Paris, 1994); D. Sherman, *Worthy Monuments: Art Museums and the Politics of Culture in Nineteenth-century France* (Cambridge, 1994); J.-P. Babelon and A. Chastel, *La Notion de patrimoine* (Paris, 1994); M.-A. Sire, *La France du patrimoine: les choix de la mémoire* (Paris, 1996); F. Bercé, *Des Monuments historiques au patrimoine, du XVIIIe siècle à nos jours* (Paris, 2000); R. Recht (ed.), *Victor Hugo et le débat patrimonial* (Paris, 2003); R. Thomson, *The Troubled Republic: Visual Culture and Social Debate in France 1889–1900* (New Haven, 2004); J. S. Milligan '"What is an archive?" in the history of modern France' in A. Burton (ed.), *Archive Stories: Facts, Fiction and the Writing of History* (Durham and London, 2005), pp. 159–83; F. Choay, *L'Allégorie du patrimoine* 4 ed. (Paris, 2007); A. Stara, *The Museum of French Monuments 1795–1816: 'Killing Art to Make History'* (Farnham, 2013).

14 M. Agulhon, *Marianne into Battle: Republican Imagery and Symbolism in France, 1789–1880*, translated by J. Lloyd (Cambridge, 1981); L. Mason, *Singing the French Revolution: Popular Songs and Revolutionary Politics in*

Paris (Ithaca, 1996); J. D. Harden, 'Liberty caps and liberty trees', *Past and Present* 146 (1995), 66–102; S. Hazareesingh, 'Conflicts of memory: republicanism and the commemoration of the past in modern France', *French History* 23 (2009), 193–215; S. Hazareesingh, 'Memory, legend, and politics: Napoleonic patriotism in the Restoration era', *European Journal of Political Theory* 5 (2006), 71–84; T. Stammers, 'The bric-à-brac of the old régime: collecting and cultural history in post-revolutionary France', *French History* 22 (2008), 295–315; M. C. Nussbaum, 'Teaching patriotism: love and critical freedom', *University of Chicago Law Review* 79 (2012), 213–50.

15   J.-P. Chaline, *Sociabilité et érudition: les sociétés savantes en France, XIXe–XXe siècle* (Paris, 2001), pp. 206–12, 218–20, 242–52, 271; S. Gerson, *The Pride of Place: Local Memories and Political Culture in Nineteenth-Century France* (Ithaca, 2003); O. Parsis-Barubé, *La Province antiquaire: l'invention de l'histoire locale en France (1800–1870)* (Paris, 2011); F. Ploux, *Une mémoire de papier: les historiens de village et le culte des petites patries rurales (1830–1930)* (Rennes, 2011).

16   A. Texier, *Qu'est-ce que la noblesse?* (Paris, 1988), pp. 137, 409.

17   A. M. Spies, *Opera, State and Society in the Third Republic 1875–1914* (New York, 1998); P. Assouline, *Le Dernier des Camondo* (Paris, 1999); A. de Cossé Brissac, *La comtesse Greffulhe* (Paris, 1991); M. Pinçon and M. Pinçon-Charlot, *Les Ghettos du gotha: au cœur de la grande bourgeoisie* (Paris, 2007).

18   On the evolving meanings of the term in ancient and modern contexts see Babelon and Chastel, *La Notion de patrimoine*, pp. 11–12, 14, 27, 49, 72, 109; A. Desvallées, 'A l'origine du mot patrimoine' in Poulot, *Patrimoine et modernité*, pp. 89–106; Poulot, *Patrimoine et musées*, p. 3.

19   P. Mandler, *The Fall and Rise of the Stately Home* (New Haven, 1997); G. Jackson-Stops (ed.), *The Treasure Houses of Britain: Five Hundred Years of Private Patronage and Art Collecting* (New Haven and London, 1985); M. Hunter (ed.), *Preserving the Past: The Rise of Heritage in Modern Britain* (Stroud, 1996).

20   É. Mension-Rigau, *Aristocrates et grands bourgeois: éducation, traditions, valeurs* (Paris, 1994), ch. 6; D. Cannadine, *The Decline and Fall of the British Aristocracy* (London, 1992).

21   T. Caravella, 'The laws of war and the destruction of cultural property in the Iraq War 2003', *Archives and Manuscripts* 32 (2004), 106–36.

22   Poulot, *Patrimoine et musées*; Deacon et al., *The Subtle Power*; F. Haskell, *The Ephemeral Museum: Old Masters and the Rise of the Art Exhibition* (New Haven, 2000); M. Alivizatou, 'Museums and intangible heritage: the dynamics of an "unconventional" relationship', *Papers from the Institute of Archaeology* 17 (2006), 47–57.

23   Texier, *Qu'est-ce que la noblesse?*, pp. 78–9; G. Chaussinand-Nogaret, *The French Nobility in the Eighteenth-Century: From Feudalism to Enlightenment*, translated by W. Doyle (Cambridge, 1985), pp. 28–30.

24 Chaussinand-Nogaret, *The French Nobility*, pp. 53–8; P. Mansel, *The Court of France 1789–1830* (Cambridge, 1988), ch. 1; S. Kettering, *Power and Reputation at the Court of Louis XIII: The Career of Charles d'Albert, duc de Luynes (1578–1621)* (Manchester, 2008), ch. 4.

25 F. Bluche and P. Durye, *L'Anoblissement par charges avant 1789* (Paris, 1965); W. Doyle, *Venality: The Sale of Offices in Eighteenth-Century France* (Oxford, 1996).

26 R. Forster, *Merchants, Landlords, Magistrates: The Depont Family in Eighteenth-Century France* (Baltimore, 1980), ch. 2. Case studies illustrate the financial risks for middling nobles seeking to improve status. See R. Descimon and É. Haddad (eds), *Épreuves de noblesse: les expériences nobiliaires de la haute robe parisienne (xvi–xviii siècle)* (Paris, 2010).

27 Chaussinand-Nogaret, *The French Nobility*, pp. 52–3. Brittany had a high proportion of poor nobility, see J. Meyer, *La Noblesse bretonne au XVIIIe siècle* 2 vols (Paris, 1966); M. Nassiet, *Noblesse et pauvreté: la petite noblesse en Bretagne aux XVe–XVIIIe siècles* (Rennes, 2005). For comparative discussion using evidence from different countries see M. L. Bush, *Rich Noble Poor Noble* (Manchester, 1988), pp. 111–52.

28 The rich historiography is detailed in P. McPhee, 'The French Revolution, peasants, and capitalism', *American Historical Review* 94 (1989), 1265–80; R. Forster, 'Obstacles to agricultural growth in eighteenth-century France', *American Historical Review* 75 (1970), 1600–15; T. W. Margadant, 'Tradition and modernity in rural France during the nineteenth century', *Journal of Modern History* 56 (1984), 667–97.

29 P. Simoni, 'Agricultural change and landlord–tenant relations in nineteenth-century France: the canton of Apt (Vaucluse)', *Journal of Social History* 13 (1979), 115–35. On land use see H. D. Clout, *The Land of France 1815–1914* (London, 1983), pp. 18–28, 117–23. On infrastructure and environmental constraints see R. Price, *An Economic History of Modern France, 1730–1914* Revised ed. (London, 1981), pp. 41–2, 54–71; R. Price, *The Modernization of Rural France: Communications Networks and Agricultural Market Structures in Nineteenth-Century France* (London, 1983), pp. 95–196.

30 Texier, *Qu'est-ce que la noblesse?* pp. 186–7.

31 A. Levesque, *Du droit nobiliaire français au XIXe siècle* (Paris, 1866); P. Tournade, *Du nom de famille et des titres de noblesse* (Paris, 1882); G. Guérin and E. Guérin, *Législation et jurisprudence nobiliaires* 5 ed. (Limoges, 1978).

32 The J series is for *archives privées* deposed in the Archives départementales; a few *fonds* produced by noble families were located in the E and F series. Nougaret and Even, *Les Archives privées*, pp. 12–15.

33 F. M. L. Thompson, *English Landed Society in the Nineteenth Century* (London, 1963); L. Stone and J. C. Fawtier Stone, *An Open Elite? England 1540–1880* (Oxford, 1984); H.-U. Wehler (ed.), *Europäischer Adel 1750–1950*

(Göttingen, 1991); E. Conze and M. Wienfort (eds), *Adel und Moderne: Deutschland im europäischen Vergleich im 19. und 20. Jahrhundert* (Cologne, 2004); D. Lancien and M. de Saint Martin (eds), *Anciennes et nouvelles aristocraties de 1800 à nos jours* (Paris, 2007); Y. Kuiper, N. Bijleveld, and J. Dronkers (eds), *Nobilities in Europe in the Twentieth Century: Reconversion Strategies, Memory Culture and Elite Formation* (Leuven, 2015).

34 K. Urbach (ed.), *European Aristocracies and the Radical Right 1918–1939* (Oxford, 2007), Foreword by H. Schulze and pp. 1–4; E. Wasson, *Aristocracy and the Modern World* (New York, 2006), p. 119.

35 R. Gibson, 'The French nobility in the nineteenth century – particularly in the Dordogne' in J. Howorth and P. G. Cerny (eds), *Elites in France: Origins, Reproduction and Power* (London 1981), p. 7. See also R. Gibson and M. Blinkhorn (eds), *Landownership and Power in Modern Europe* (London, 1991). Gibson's concern for the 'national' picture contrasts with Forster's advocacy of analyses focusing on one geographic region or one family. R. Forster, 'The provincial noble: a reappraisal', *American Historical Review* 68 (1963), 681–91; Forster, *Merchants, Landlords, Magistrates,* preface; R. Forster, *The House of Saulx-Tavanes: Versailles and Burgundy, 1700–1830* (Baltimore, 1971), preface; R. Forster, *The Nobility of Toulouse in the Eighteenth Century* (Baltimore, 1960), R. Forster, 'The noble wine producers of the Bordelais in the eighteenth century', *Economic History Review* second series 14 (1961), 18–33.

36 Gibson showed, for example, how the error of taking the particle *de* as a sign of nobility produced very distorted statistics. See table 1.1 in Gibson, 'The French nobility', p. 7. Unfortunately, use of the particle as a sign of nobility is likely to have marred the results presented in T. Beck, 'The French Revolution and the nobility: a reconsideration', *Journal of Social History* 15 (1981), 219–33. On other uses of the cadastre see H. D. Clout and K. Sutton, 'The "cadastre" as a source for French rural studies', *Agricultural History* 43 (1969), 215–24.

37 Higgs, *Nobles,* ch. 2. See also D. Higgs, 'Politics and landownership among the French nobility after the Revolution', *European Studies Review* 2 (1971), 105–71. Scholars of the French nobility in the early modern period have done most to work at the national level or comparatively in the context of Europe. See for example Dewald, *The European Nobility*; Bourquin, *La Noblesse dans la France moderne.*

38 Higgs, *Nobles,* pp. 39, 62.

39 Forster, 'The provincial noble', 690.

40 J. Favier (ed.), *La Pratique archivistique française* (Paris, 2008), pp. 76–9; J. Sablou, 'Les Archives privées dans les Archives départementales', *La Gazette des Archives* 85 (1974), 89–103; S. d'Huart, 'Les Archives privées aux Archives Nationales', *La Gazette des Archives* 85 (1974), 79–88. The Association des archivistes français has produced a guide for owners: *Archives privées: un patrimoine méconnu* (Paris, 2005).

41 See for example, F. Lalliard, *La Fortune des Wagram: de Napoléon à Proust*
     (Paris, 2002); B. Goujon, 'Le grand domaine aristocratique dans le monde
     rural en France et en Belgique au 19e siècle: l'exemple de trois propriétés de
     la famille d'Arenberg (1820–1919)', *Ruralia* 14 (2004), 45–74; M. Hamard,
     *La Famille La Rochefoucauld et le duché-pairie de la Roche-Guyon au XVIIIe
     siècle: reconnaissance royale et puissance locale* (Paris, 2008); É. Haddad,
     *Fondation et ruine d'une 'maison': histoire sociale des comtes de Belin (1582–
     1706)* (Limoges, 2009).

42 See for example, C.-I. Brelot, *La Noblesse réinventée: les nobles de Franche-
     Comté de 1814 à 1870* 2 vols (Paris, 1992); J.-M. Wiscart, *La Noblesse de la
     Somme au dix-neuvième siècle* (Amiens, 1994); L. Bourquin, *Noblesse seconde
     et pouvoir en Champagne au XVIe et XVIIe siècles* (Paris, 1994).

43 F. Braudel, 'Histoire et sciences sociales: la longue durée', *Annales: economies,
     societies, civilisations* 17 (1958), 723–53; F. Braudel, *Écrits sur l'histoire* (Paris,
     1969).

44 P. Bourdieu, L. Boltanski, and M. de Saint Martin, 'Les Stratégies de reconver-
     sion', *Social Science Information* 12 (1973), 61–113; P. Bourdieu, *Outline of
     a Theory of Practice*, translated by R. Nice (Cambridge, 1977); P. Bourdieu,
     The Field of Cultural Production: Essays on Art and Literature, translated by
     R. Johnson (New York, 1993); P. Bourdieu, *The State Nobility*, translated by
     L. C. Clough (Stanford, 1996); P. Bourdieu, *Distinction: A Social Critique of
     the Judgement of Taste*, translated by R. Nice (London, 2000); M. de Saint
     Martin, *L'Espace de la noblesse* (Paris, 1993); M. de Saint Martin, 'Towards
     a dynamic approach to reconversions', *Social Science Information* 50 (2011),
     429–41.

45 M. Halbwachs, *On Collective Memory* (*Les Cadres sociaux de la mémoire*,
     1925), ed. and translated by L. A. Coser (Chicago, 1992), p. 40, chs
     5 and 7. M. Halbwachs, *The Collective Memory* (*La Mémoire collective*,
     1950), translated by F. J. Didder Jr and V. Yazdi Ditter (New York, 1980).
     For application and interpretations see for example N. Russell, 'Collective
     memory, before and after Halbwachs', *The French Review* 79 (2006), 792–804;
     D. Middleton and S. D. Brown, *The Social Psychology of Experience: Studies
     in Remembering and Forgetting* (London, 2005), pp. 118–37; A. Radley,
     'Artefacts, memory and a sense of the past' in D. Middleton and D. Edwards
     (eds), *Collective Remembering* (Newbury Park, 1991), pp. 46–59; J. Assmann,
     'Collective memory and cultural identity', *New German Critique* 65 (1995),
     125–33; G. Izenberg, *Identity: The Necessity of a Modern Idea* (Philadelphia,
     2016).

46 Halbwachs, *On Collective Memory*, p. 59.

47 E. C. Macknight, *Aristocratic Families in Republican France, 1870–1940*
     (Manchester, 2012); N. L. Paul, *To Follow in Their Footsteps: The Crusades and
     Family Memory in the High Middle Ages* (Ithaca, 2012).

48 Documents that constitute *preuves de noblesse* are variously located in

the Archives nationales, Archives départementales, Archives de la guerre, Bibliothèque nationale, and private collections. See the reference works in the List of families.

49 S. W. Mintz, 'A note on the definition of peasantries', *Journal of Peasant Studies* 1 (1973), 91–106; S. C. Rogers, 'Good to think: the "peasant" in contemporary France', *Anthropological Quarterly* 60 (1987), 56–63; P. McPhee, 'A reconsideration of the "peasantry" of nineteenth-century France', *Peasant Studies* 9 (1981), 5–25; C. Tilly, 'Did the cake of custom break?' in J. M. Merriman (ed.), *Consciousness and Class Experience in Nineteenth-Century Europe* (New York, 1979), pp. 17–44.

50 Gibson and Blinkhorn, *Landownership and Power*, p. 2; R. Gibson, 'The Périgord: landownership, power and illusion' in Gibson and Blinkhorn, *Landownership and Power*, pp. 79–98.

51 M. Marraud, *La Noblesse de Paris au XVIIIe siècle* (Paris, 2000); A. Martin-Fugier, *La Vie élégante ou la formation du Tout-Paris 1815–1848* (Paris, 1990); P. Mansel, *Paris between Empires 1814–1852* (London, 2001).

52 Forster, *Merchants, Landlords, Magistrates*, ch. 2.

53 8 December 1888 in AD Charente J 1093 Fonds Galard, Brassac, Béarn, Chalais.

54 8 January 1909 and undated note in AD Lot-et-Garonne 1J/1009 Fonds Gavini de Campile.

55 A. Fierro-Domenech, *Le Pré carré: géographie historique de la France* (Paris, 1986), pp. 101–11; G. Dupont-Ferrier, 'Sur l'emploi du mot "Province" notamment dans le langage administratif de l'ancienne France', *Revue historique* 160 (1929), 241–67.

56 P. McPhee, *Living the French Revolution, 1789–99* (New York, 2006), p. 58.

1

Protecting property during revolution

We have the misfortune to be born at the moment of one of these big revolutions: whatever the happy or unhappy result of it shall be for the people born in future, the present generation is lost.[1]

'Among the many letters I write to you, my dear mother, there must be some that reach you. Finally I can breathe again! Your letter of 25 August [1793] restored me to life. I thought you were ill, God knows what I feared ...'[2] The twenty-nine-year-old Julie de Théas had not seen her mother Émilie de Montgrand or her husband François de Théas, comte de Thorenc, for over a year. France was at war against the coalition forces of Europe and in a bid to curtail military crisis the National Convention had issued a decree for mass conscription. It was an unpopular move among a population bitterly divided over the direction the French Revolution had taken. For four years communities across France had grappled with colossal change to the structures that underpinned daily life. Now in the west Vendéen rebels, angered by reforms to the Catholic Church that attacked traditions they prized, engaged in guerrilla fighting against republican troops. Whilst postal communication was often slow and unreliable, people's hunger for information sped the pace of verbal gossip. Rumour thrived on fears of conspiracy and invasion.[3] During the days and weeks that passed without word from her loved ones, Julie's mind was plagued by uncertainty.

For the comte de Thorenc and the widow Montgrand anxiety about Julie was compounded by the frustration of trying to clarify her civil status with the republican authorities. In numerous letters addressed to

the *citoyens administrateurs* of the department of Var, and also to deputies of the National Convention, François explained the circumstances
that had led Julie to leave their home near Grasse in August 1792 with
the couple's two children, Jean-Baptiste and Flore. 'Everyone in Grasse
knew that an exchange of property for 221,000 *livres* between the Théas
family and *citoyenne* Albert [François's niece] had been put into arbitra-
tion in Nice.' After signing a contract with *citoyenne* Albert, which gave
her rights of use to the estate of Caille, François had perceived too late
that this would jeopardise the rights of his own children to the same
estate when they attained their majority. Confident that the mediators
would look favourably on his efforts 'to return the land of Caille to the
Théas family' François had in mind a negotiated solution with *citoyenne*
Albert. But the weakening eyesight and frail health of this seventy-year-
old made him indisposed for travel. François had therefore decided to
send his young wife to Nice, as the Théas family's representative. Their
seven-year-old son and five-year-old daughter 'from whom she had never
been separated' were to travel with her. 'It could never be imagined,' he
argued, that Julie had solicited a passport for this trip as 'a pretext in order
to cover plans for emigration.'[4]

In the eyes of the republican authorities, however, Julie de Théas's
absence from her home could hardly have looked more suspicious.
The legislation and public opinion regarding emigration had changed
dramatically since the summer of 1789 when a first wave of *émigrés*,
including the king's brother the comte d'Artois, and cousins the prince de
Condé and the prince de Conti, had departed France legally and without
concern for reprisal.[5] After Louis XVI's flight to Varennes in June 1791,
deputies of the Assembly were all too aware of the counter-revolutionary
threat posed by male *émigré* troops joining the armies of foreign sovereigns. Although the king had opposed the decree that made emigration a
crime, his arrest on 10 August 1792 enabled the Assembly to override his
veto. *Émigrés* who returned to France faced punishment by death; priests
who refused to take the oath required by the Civil Constitution of the
Clergy faced deportation. François de Théas's frantic appeals about Julie,
Jean-Baptiste, and Flore were in vain. To the republican officials, his wife
and children might as well have been dead.

The dilemma facing this Provençal family fits within a richly complex
picture of the ways in which people throughout France experienced
the French Revolution. At all levels of society, the events of 1789–99
provoked passionate conflicting responses. People's attitudes towards
the Revolution continually evolved as circumstances changed and new

demands were made of them on behalf of the nation.[6] Whilst the urgency of reform was sharply apparent when the Estates General met in 1789, the full ramifications of new laws passed by successive governing bodies became apparent only gradually, and sometimes not for years or even decades later. Even those closest to the political action could find it difficult to distinguish fact from hearsay. People who lived in communities distant from Paris and Versailles sometimes doubted what they heard was happening or maintained a state of denial until it became impossible to do so any longer.[7]

For the men and women of the Second Estate the decrees of 4 August 1789 began the process of tearing apart the structures on which their privileges had rested. The thundering blow came on 19 June 1790 when the deputies of the National Assembly voted in the decree that abolished the legal status of nobility.[8] Precisely because nobles had exercised such authority and control over resources in French society, this group – alongside the monarchy and the Catholic Church – seemed poised to lose the most. How can we understand what the upheavals of the French Revolution meant to those nobles who lived through it? What were their immediate priorities and concerns? When and how did they realise that nothing was ever going to be the same again?

Donald Greer estimated that around 17 per cent of the total numbers of people who emigrated were members of the Second Estate. Of those 16,400 noble persons perhaps 35 per cent were officers and 15 per cent were women.[9] Nobles' accounts of emigration, often published as memoirs and novels, reveal diverse experiences. Whilst some of the wealthier aristocratic émigrés were able to maintain a comfortable lifestyle, and even relished their time abroad, many other people from modest social backgrounds had to make do with meagre resources and faced significant hardship.[10]

In his discussion of Chateaubriand's writing about the French Revolution, Halbwachs defined memoir as 'a description created long afterward by a writer' and drew attention to the selective process of its composition as well as its resemblance to fiction. 'The person who tells the story is obliged to translate his recollections so as to communicate them; what he writes may not correspond exactly to all he calls to mind.' A memoir serves as 'a summary of collective reflections and feelings' and 'projects a singularly vivid image on the screen of an obscure and unclear past'.[11] The word 'summary' points to Halbwachs's concern to explain how an individual's memories are reconstructed through mutual elaboration between the individual and other people with whom they are connected.

'Family recollections in fact develop as in so many different soils, in the consciousness of various members of the domestic group.'[12]

Memoirs and novels that were written by nobles testify to a vibrant oral culture that operated in the families of nobility during the nineteenth century. Authors recounted stories that filtered down through generations and were told to them as children, as well as stories of moments that were significant in their own lives; all of these they passed on to their children, and to their children's children. What appeared in written form was only one version of an ongoing oral narrative.[13] In that narrative, memory and myth were frequently combined, and the selective manner in which that happened tells us how certain memories and certain myths assumed power in the domestic environment. We will return to this subject of collective memory later in the chapter but first we need to consider what has been left in the way of archival documentation.

Less commonly studied than the *émigrés* are those provincial nobles who remained in France. These women and men had to respond to the series of laws passed by revolutionary governing bodies that affected the safety of their loved ones and their rights to property. Materials in *archives privées* document the types of decisions and actions that nobles took in bewildering and sometimes life-threatening circumstances. The agency of individuals, their networks and sources of help, are critical for understanding how the nobility emerged from the French Revolution and where the future priorities of these families lay. It mattered to nobles to keep a record wherever possible and by returning to the sources we can better understand why that was so.

Those who stayed and those who left

In August 1789 Béraud, *régisseur* to the comte and comtesse Saint-Paul du Chayla, was in Paris trying to sort out legal and financial matters relating to an inheritance on behalf of his employers. On 4 August, when the National Assembly voted to abolish seigneurial privileges, he wrote to the comtesse expressing concern for her safety and that of her daughter in the château de Beauregard near Sauges on the border of Velay and Gévaudan. The comte Saint-Paul du Chayla had accompanied Béraud to Paris and both men were anxious to receive word from the comtesse. The *régisseur* wrote: 'To reassure you Monsieur le comte has written to you twice a week since the troubles began here, but we hear from every direction that there is unrest across the whole kingdom … All the bad news being reported daily is hardly reassuring and makes me fear that the Revolution will have reached as far as home.'[14] Amidst the political turmoil, Béraud was pressing the lawyers to finish the paperwork about the inheritance. He fretted about the delay as the business extended into the autumn and assured the comtesse, who was becoming impatient, that he was doing his best under the circumstances. On 5 October: 'Paris is in a state of alarm. There has been no bread for several days, or at any rate one can obtain it only with great difficulty and it tastes horrible … All the shops have been closed. Five or six thousand people, more women than men, are going to march on Versailles this evening.'[15]

Fearful of the violence, those members of nobility who normally resided in the capital over the winter to participate in the dinners, balls, and other entertainment of the Season moved to other locations, hoping for security. From Nancy on 9 February 1790 the comte Charles de La Tour wrote to François Hyacinthe d'Oryot, comte d'Apremont:

> Our domestic arrangements and first visits to make and receive have kept us busy, my dear cousin. We have contented ourselves to hear of your news from the chevalier whom we see often with pleasure … There are many people here from the *beau monde* of Paris. The marquis de Mirpoix [sic], Monsieur de Taillerand [sic] and others have come to take refuge in our town, which is very calm, especially since Monsieur the marquis de Bassompierre accepted and arrived to take up the command of the military.[16]

Amidst the social distractions of Nancy, there were various matters that preoccupied the comte de La Tour. 'How are your affairs going?' he enquired of d'Oryot, 'Rather badly, no doubt, since cash is hard to come by and the farmers and vassals pay little or nothing at all. Everywhere I feel the effects. I cannot obtain money from anywhere, neither Brittany, nor Paris, nor many other lands.' Happily, he reported, his wife the comtesse de La Tour was six months pregnant. 'I try to amuse her as best I can. She is always charming, full of good sense and affection for me, in short we love one another even more than the first days [of our marriage].'[17]

On the same day that La Tour wrote this letter, another nobleman, the baron Augustin-Alexandre de Faramond, was enjoying the festive atmosphere of the annual Carnival in Rodez. Faramond was *seigneur* of Jouqueviel in Albigeois and of Le Fraysse in Rouergue. He spent parts of the year on each of these estates and at other times lived in his townhouse in Rodez. Towards the evening on 9 February, as the costumed townsfolk made merry in the streets, peasants from some eight villages that made up the *seigneurie* of Jouqueviel, joined by residents from neighbouring parishes, took advantage of Faramond's absence to attack his château. At around 6 p.m. 'armed with guns, tools, and other objects' the peasants climbed on to the roof of the château and forced their way in, 'pillaging and carrying off goods and provisions of all kinds … tapestries, mirrors, beds, linen, tables, chests, chairs, men's clothing, arms, musical instruments and generally all the furnishings … some hoisting the objects on to their shoulders and others using carts.' The *seigneur's* 'numerous and tidily arranged' papers were tossed into the courtyard and burned whilst the peasants danced around the flames. Then the château de Jouqueviel and all its surrounding buildings were set on fire.[18]

Faramond's brother in Clairevaux, after hearing what happened at Jouqueviel, sent commiserations to his sibling and vowed his support: 'We are in a very dangerous crisis, the public being especially hostile toward the nobility. Our destiny would be infinitely less perilous if we stood perfectly united and commit to giving one another all the mutual assistance possible. Therefore I offer mine, even at risk to my life.'[19] There was no time for these fraternal sentiments to be put into effect for already Augustin-Alexandre de Faramond had been dealt a second blow. At around 2 p.m. on 13 February peasants from the village of Le Fraysse and a cluster of other villages nearby used mallets and iron tools to smash their way into the château du Fraysse. A terrified servant tried to remonstrate as the peasants ripped shrubs and flowers from the garden, threw furniture through the windows, and torched the tapestries. After this attack, which unlike the one at Jouqueviel was conducted in broad daylight, arrests were made quickly. The identified perpetrators included men, women, and children from Le Fraysse, Masgarnit, Truels, and Boussac.

Letters from the priest Viala at Boussac reveal the tensions he felt as those members of his parish who had been arrested for the attack on the château du Fraysse turned against the local clergy. 'Some have even gone to the point of accusing us to be on your side and favouring your claim to the detriment of their interests.' The peasants' determination to destroy every sign of Faramond's seigneurial privileges had extended to removing his family's pew from the church at Boussac. According to Viala, a 'so-called lawyer' had intimated to the peasants that whilst the administrators in Rodez awaited a response from the National Assembly about the attack on Faramond's properties 'they [the peasants] were not obliged to put back your church pew, and that they could not be forced to do so, because, he said, this seigneurial right was abolished.' The priest praised Faramond's leniency in consenting to the release of those arrested. 'If you do not hold an insurmountable horror for this land [*pays*] my brother prays, and I join in his prayer, that you will accept a room in his presbytery whilst awaiting the repairs to be carried out on your château.'[20]

Faramond's ownership of different seigneurial properties, less than one hundred kilometres apart but in separate provinces, reminds us that in eighteenth-century France nobles were very accustomed to regular travel. Their peripatetic lifestyle resembled that of their ancestors from the sixteenth and seventeenth centuries.[21] Nobles made trips to visit relatives and friends living within their own province or in a different one. There was often business to attend to that might require meeting with a notary. They liked to shop for luxury goods and garments, as well as enjoy theatre, concerts, and socialising in town.[22] Travel, however, became less straightforward from the summer of 1789. It was also more closely scrutinised following the creation of the committees of surveillance by law of 21 March 1793. The numerous passports and certificates of residency preserved in nobles' *archives privées* testify to the authorities' concern for identification of persons moving about the country.

A passport issued to François de Rozières on 1 September 1789 by the Comité Permanent des Trois Ordres in Nancy specified that he wanted to travel by carriage to Saint Dié, in the province of Lorraine, with a suitcase containing some of his belongings. Rozières lived in Saint Dié and on this occasion was travelling with his uncle's widow Madame Rostaing whom he was helping with her affairs.[23] This particular passport was one of many that Rozières had to obtain, along with certificates of residency in Saint Dié, over the next few years. These types of documents detailed some of the physical characteristics of the individual to whom they were issued. Rozières, a former soldier, was described as: 'forty-two years old, 5'4" in height, quite plump, an aquiline nose that is slightly crushed, grey eyes, small mouth, blond hair and eyebrows, crippled in the left arm'. Similarly, on 19 August 1793, in the department of Meuse the municipal officers of Étain issued a passport to Anne Françoise Henriette de Briey so that she could travel to 'Bar-sur-Ornin' (the new name to replace the aristocratic sounding 'Bar-le-Duc') for her affairs. She was described as: 'thirty-one years of age, 4'4" in height, light chestnut hair and eyebrows, grey eyes, long aquiline nose, medium-sized mouth, high forehead, round chin, long thin face'.[24]

For François de Rozières and Anne Françoise Henriette de Briey the possession of passports and certificates of residency became critically important in the defence of their personal rights. Archival documents detailing what happened to these individuals and thousands of others like them provide insight into difficulties that arose for nobles who did not emigrate, as well as the varied, sometimes contradictory, views of authorities with whom they had dealings.

On 19 March 1793, the National Convention defined the crime of emigration and placed all former nobles, their agents and servants (as well as refractory priests) outside the protection of the law. On 28 March 1793 an *émigré* was declared to be any French person absent from their home since 1 July 1789 who had not returned there before 8 April 1792. Article 2 of the Law of Suspects, passed on 17 September 1793, allowed for the arrest of 'those former nobles, including husbands, wives, fathers, mothers, sons or daughters, brothers or sisters, and agents of *émigrés* who have not constantly demonstrated their loyalty to the Revolution.'[25]

In February 1793, François de Rozières's name was added to the list of *émigrés* alongside that of his younger brother, Charles-Joseph, who was a sub-lieutenant in the royal cavalry of Lorraine and had disappeared from his normal place of residence at Euvezin (Meurthe). François de Rozières appealed against the inclusion of his own name on the list, arguing that he had left France only temporarily in order to take a cure in the German spa town of Baden, which he had done on medical advice owing to a longstanding illness. The law of 12 September 1792 on the seizure and sale of *émigré* property said nothing about absence for medical reasons; the Minister for Justice recommended the sale of François de Rozières's property should not go ahead.[26] On 19 April 1793, however, François was arrested. Just eight days later the Conseil Général of Saint Dié (Vosges) reconsidered the arrest, which had been made '*not because the actions of Rozières had caused us alarm* but because he is a nobleman and his brother [Charles-Joseph] is presumed to have emigrated'. On 27 April the surveillance committee in Nancy authorised François's release from imprisonment: 'the said Rozières has his real home in Saint Dié [and] has done nothing to make him appear suspect to the council of the commune'.[27] He was granted a certificate of non-emigration by the department of Vosges in September.[28]

Anne Françoise Henriette de Briey went to the expense and trouble of putting her case forward in a printed pamphlet. '*Citoyens administrateurs*,' she announced, 'I am perhaps the first example of a woman of your jurisdiction who has followed the letter of the law.' Madame de Briey had taken advantage of the newly introduced divorce law of 20 September 1792 to end her marriage to Jean Baptiste Claude Achille de Nettancourt, former captain of the fourth regiment.[29] Nettancourt had emigrated in 1791 and Madame de Briey was seeking to sell some property. She had presented marriage and residency certificates to the authorities, but as for the required evidence of estate management: 'It has not been possible to obtain either rents or arrears payments … I haven't received a sou.' Madame de Briey had resigned herself to a long wait for a response from the authorities about the property sale. On 29 September 1793, however, she was arrested as a suspect. The estate of Nubécourt, part of which belonged to her exclusively, as well as farms in the district of Verdun, were sold 'as if everything belonged to my husband'. Upon her release from imprisonment she petitioned for the return of these properties and described their sale as illegal. Citing the Constitution and article 8 of the Declaration of the Rights of Man and Citizen, she declared to the administrators: 'No-one, under any pretext, was permitted to deprive me of [those properties].'[30]

Other noblewomen too were quick to try to secure fiscal benefit through rights afforded by the divorce law and by changes in the laws of inheritance (discussed in Chapter 2). Charles-François-Casimir, first duc de Saulx-Tavanes, died in January 1792 after his eldest surviving son Charles-Marie-Casimir had married a Choiseul-Gouffier and emigrated with her. The *émigré* duc's two sisters the comtesse de Castellane and the comtesse de Kercado each chose to renounce their rights to a share of their father's fortune under partible inheritance. They submitted instead claims for the full payment of their dowries to which they were entitled under a 1794 decree. The comtesse de Castellane was at the same time pursuing divorce. The dowry claims made both sisters privileged creditors eligible to receive 200,000 *livres* each, when their deceased father's entire estate was not worth much more than 500,000 *livres*.[31]

All over France, departmental administrators received petitions from nobles seeking removal from the lists of *émigrés*, release from imprisonment as a suspect, and return of seized property. Copies and drafts in the archives reveal remarkable persistence in petitioning. Far from sitting out the Revolution quietly on their estates, and not seeking to draw attention to their situation, nobles in the provinces asserted themselves boldly and repeatedly as they tried to force a response from the local administration. Still more significantly, archival documents also show nobles' shrewd and rapid adaptation to the 'language of the law' created by the French Revolution. Noblewomen and noblemen used the French republic's own rhetoric about *liberté* and *égalité* to defend their personal rights.

In the context of war nobles often drew upon on the notion of 'service' to France in their appeals for justice.[32] Léopold Charles Claude des Pilliers from the department of Vosges was a retired army major and chevalier of the royal and military order of Saint Louis. Imprisoned for the third time by the surveillance committee of Saint Mihiel, on the accusation of displaying counter-revolutionary attitudes, Pilliers came before the revolutionary tribunal in late September 1794. He prepared notes for his defence:

> Forty-four years of my life consecrated to the nation's service, the loss of one of my limbs, my blood spilled on its behalf, should have been an indisputable pledge of my fidelity. Fate has deemed that titles so honourable have turned to my prejudice! I have only done my duty, citizens, and place those titles before your eyes only to ask if whether having thus passed my youth I would wait until this late stage of my life to contradict a past I regarded as glorious … Citizens, you may be forgiven; you do not know me; I have been portrayed before you as a dangerous foreigner. I trust that with light now shed upon my conduct you will grant me justice, convinced that I have never ceased to be faithful, and in consequence restore me to my family, my children, my fellow citizens and let me finally enjoy that priceless possession that is liberty.[33]

We cannot know precisely what determined the jury's decision on the fate of this self-described 'old soldier condemned by slander'. Perhaps it was Pilliers's eloquent declarations of innocence, or perhaps the evidence brought against him was as thoroughly inadequate and prejudiced as he made out. By unanimous verdict on 15 October 1794 the jury of twelve including a baker, postmaster, *pâtissier*, bailiff, and locksmith, acquitted Pilliers of complicity in emigration and the judge ordered his release.[34]

Soldiers' wives and widows evoked their husband's military service. Émilie de Montgrand had received notice to pay the collector in the district of Grasse a contribution to the costs of war, which she believed was because of her daughter Julie's presumed emigration. The widow Montgrand was charged a single lump payment of 369 *livres* 18 *sols* for the uniforms and equipment of two army volunteers, and also a daily tax of 1 *livre* 10 *sols* for the pay of two army volunteers, backdated to 1 January 1792. Émilie gave three reasons why she should not be obliged to pay these sums. First, she argued, 'the law of 12 September [1792] only applies to the fathers and mothers of *male émigrés* … the preamble to this law clearly indicates the harm [male] *émigrés* can do to the nation, by augmenting the number of its enemies … However, *citoyenne* [Julie] Théas, being of the female sex, is not able to bear arms'. Second, her daughter was a married woman and therefore 'her mother has no authority over her'. Finally, the widow Montgrand noted that 'she does not blush to admit that she has no financial means to pay the tax required of her.

All her resources for subsistence lie in a modest pension, paid because her husband had *risked his life many times in service to the State.*[35]

Important questions, which remain difficult or impossible to answer in a precise way for many families, concern the influence of relatives in decision-making about emigration. To what extent did wives put pressure on husbands to emigrate, or the reverse? How much control did parents or other senior relatives wield over younger members of the family in ordering them to leave or to stay? Did children who had attained their majority feel able to resist elders' authority?

In the case of the Nettancourt family of Lorraine, the piecing together of records from public archives (series Q) sheds light on how and when eight different members of this family came to the notice of departmental authorities that were compiling the lists of *émigrés*.[36] The authorities' information on these eight family members is represented in Table 1.

From the records in public archives, the fate of Marc-Pierre de Nettancourt appears the most shadowy; he was added to the list of *émigrés* on 1 July 1793 but there is nothing further to indicate what happened to this nobleman. However, a handwritten document in the *archives privées* provides an account of the movements of Marc-Pierre, his wife Jeanne Charlotte des Roys, and their five children. It is not clear who wrote this document, although it certainly seems to have been a member of the Nettancourt family. The document is particularly interesting for the suggestive remarks on who exercised authority over whom in decision-making.

The writer notes that Marc-Pierre 'left France after having received the order of M. de Vaubecourt who had emigrated before him'. This was an order from Charles-Jean de Nettancourt-Haussonville, comte de Vaubecourt, marquis de Nettancourt, listed as person 1 in Table 1. Marc-Pierre went to Trèves in Germany, where he gave the order for his wife and children (four sons and a daughter all under the age of seven) to join him. When Marc-Pierre rejoined the prince de Condé's army his family could no longer stay at Trèves, so following the King of Prussia's entry into France Jean Charlotte made her own return with the children. They went to Étain (Meuse). Jeanne Charlotte was arrested at Étain as the wife of an *émigré* and during the eighteen months of her imprisonment the couple's children remained with a servant. On 8 *nîvose*, an III Jeanne Charlotte was released, only to discover that two of her five children had died.[37] Her former home the château de Dorevant had been sold by the nation along with all the furniture it contained, so she took refuge with the remaining three children in the village of Brainville near Doncourt

(Meurthe-et-Moselle). In 1796, with the assistance of Charles-Jean de Nettancourt-Haussonville, Jeanne Charlotte purchased the château de Choiseul. This property was occupied at the time by peasants 'whom she had a great deal of difficulty in evicting'. Marc-Pierre managed to travel to Choiseul for reunion with his wife and remaining children, but upon arrival he was tipped off that the authorities were planning to arrest him the following day and he fled during the night to Basel. He then spent several more years in hiding, during which a member of his wife's family, the des Roys, sent him financial aid. Marc-Pierre finally returned to France ten years after he emigrated.[38]

This account depicts both the exercise of authority based on seniority and gender, and also the ties of kinship that facilitated financial aid to relatives in need. The provision of loans was already customary among the eighteenth-century provincial nobility, but this practice could result in a death sentence during the Revolution.[39] Jeanne Charlotte des Roys was never placed on a list of *émigrés*, although she had definitely emigrated at the order of her husband Marc-Pierre – just one example of the kinds of omissions that complicate any historian's attempt to give precise statistics on emigration.

Of course it fell to those nobles who remained in France to explain their family's dispersal and absence to the authorities. Given that such explanations often happened at the point of arrest as a suspect, with the prospect of imprisonment or execution, it is not surprising that the tone of the written records should be angry and defensive as nobles hammered back at claims launched against them. Interestingly, too, nobles often corrected inaccuracies regarding personal details, suggesting that the time-poor administrators of the department, overwhelmed by reforms of all kinds, either made a guess or relied on word of mouth rather than bother to check birth or marriage certificates.

Adélaïde Celeste de Nagu, placed under arrest with her daughter at Yvetôt in 1793, responded point-by-point to the justifications listed for her imprisonment by the administrators of Seine-Inférieure. Her husband, '*citoyen* Mortemart', had emigrated at the end of 1791 and in April 1792 Madame de Nagu had initiated legal separation. Mortemart had taken with him their eleven-year-old son whom the authorities erroneously described as a sixteen-year-old. 'Could I have opposed their departure? Is the *citoyen* Mortemart not the master of his son? Moreover, what could a boy of that age do against the republic? I kept my daughter with me who was only six-and-a-half years old, not eight.'[40]

We do not know whether the eleven-year-old Mortemart took up

Table 1 Emigration records for the Nettancourt family

	Date added to the list of émigrés	Removal from the list of émigrés	Certificate of amnesty	Decree of definitive removal from the list of émigrés	Indemnity (francs)
1. Charles-Jean de Nettancourt-Haussonville, comte de Vaubecourt, marquis de Nettancourt	16 Oct. 1792 and 5 Feb. 1793			8 germinal, an X	23,301.81 rentes
2. Marie-Claude de Nettancourt, wife of Claude-François-Adrien de Lezay-Marnésia	23 ventôse, an II, died 30 June 1794			5 fructidor, an IX	61,104.79 proposed by the director of the Domaines de la Meuse
3. Jean-Baptiste-Claude-Achille de Nettancourt, son of the émigré Marie-Anne Magot, widow Nettancourt	5 Feb. 1793		17 ventôse, an XI		4,897.56 rentes
4. François-Dominique de Nettancourt	16 Oct. 1792 and 5 Feb. 1793, died at Rastadt on 1 Jan. 1794		10 germinal, an XI		827.45 rentes to share with sister Marie-Anne-Louise (5. below)

5. Marie-Anne-Louise de Nettancourt, sister of persons 3 and 4 above, wife of the *émigré* Charles George Christophe d'Hoffelize	1 July 1793			9 *vendémiaire, an* X	see 4. above
6. Anne-Thérèse de Nettancourt, sister of the persons 3, 4, and 5 above, wife of Antoine-Louis-Joseph Renaud, comte de Sagonne	list for Allier, 30 *ventôse, an* II	11 *ventôse, an* IV by the department of the Marne	23 *fructidor, an* X		
7. Joseph-Claude-Charles de Nettancourt, comte de Vaubecourt, brother of the persons 3, 4, 5, and 6 above, abbé at Saint-Pierre aux Monts de Châlons, vicaire-général at Châlons-sur-Marne	list for Marne, 30 *ventôse, an* II	24 *ventôse, an* III			
8. Marc-Pierre de Nettancourt	1 July 1793				

arms, but certainly there were very young noble 'recruits' to the counter-revolutionary armies. Strength of military tradition and loyalty to the crown meant that in many families boys trained at the court's *école des pages* from the age of eight, or at the École Royale Militaire, were thrust into active service.[41] Jean-Jacques-Hyacinthe Dondel followed his father into the military, serving as sub-lieutenant in the grenadiers and participating in the failed Quiberon expedition in 1795. Jean-Jacques-Hyacinthe was captured by the republican army but managed to escape from the prison at Auray only to be rearrested at Rieux (Morbihan). When executed at Férel on 30 *prairial, an* IV he was just seventeen-years-old.[42] The archives of the Courson family, of which there were numerous branches, similarly contain details of the armed service of men and boys. Alexandre de Courson de la Villehelio, Armand de Courson de la Villeneuve, and Placide de Courson de la Villeneuve were appointed colonel, lieutenant colonel, and *sous-chef d'état major* respectively in Georges Cadoudal's army. Auguste de Courson de la Villehelio was a lieutenant and commander of troops at Quiberon where François de Courson de Kernescop and François de Courson de la Belleissue served as cadets. Louis de Courson de Lessac was commander in chief in Andigné's army and there were a dozen more Coursons who led small bands of *chouans* in the Côtes-du-Nord. After the failure at Quiberon, and just a few hours before his execution, Auguste de Courson de la Villehelio wrote a final letter to his father Jean-René living at Plouha: 'Goodbye, I love you with all my heart. Please pray for me. When you receive my letter I hope that I will be in perfect happiness.'[43]

For noble *émigrés* as well as those nobles who remained in France worry about their money supply in the short term was compounded by a growing realisation of permanent losses to income. Letters to their *régisseur* or local notary were essential for obtaining information and advice. From Orléans, Jean de Bournazel wrote to the notary Herail for help. He stressed that the departmental administrators of Aveyron were wrong to include his own name on the list of *émigrés* for he had sent them his certificates of residency at Orléans (Loiret). 'I would like to know the condition in which my father left to me [the estate of] Bournazel [Aveyron] and the other lands nearby ... I have the greatest need of funds ... Might you know where the title deeds for Belcastel are to be found?' Jean asked Herail to send him letters via the care of M. de La Combe at Villefranche: 'he will forward them securely to me.'[44]

Taxation developments also provoked reactions among the nobility whose representatives had stubbornly resisted proposals for a new land tax on the eve of the Revolution. From the 1790s nobles' antipathy was manifest by requesting reductions and frustrating the authorities' attempts to sort out the registers and collect payments.[45] A decree of 23 September 1791 authorised communes to gather current information on landownership and use it to draw up new maps, but this decree proved impossible to implement.[46] Nobles' archives reveal that such information was hard to obtain. In December 1791, the mayor of Saux (Lot) informed Madeleine de Montagu-Fayols, widow of Pierre de Gozon, of the need for her to provide up-to-date information on the extent of each of her landholdings within a fortnight. This mayor had longstanding knowledge of the Gozon family's control of local resources and probably relished writing his imperious message to the former *seigneur's* widow. 'You tell me that I am perfectly aware of your possessions from the cadastre, but one must point out that, because there have been so many changes in the two hundred years or so since the cadastre was made, only a very small number of holdings are recognisable … You will be obliged to have surveyed all of the plots of land for which you do not know the measurements. You must conform to the law in timely fashion … the era of privileges is no more.'[47]

It could be difficult for nobles to hide their disdain for these kinds of orders, issued by people who the Revolution brought to positions of local authority but who in nobles' eyes continued to be social inferiors. Before 1789 the degree of seigneurial domination over village affairs had varied across the country. When democratic processes replaced seigneurial authority villagers embraced the opportunity to control their affairs by electing mayors and council members much faster than most seigneurs' attitudes changed.[48] The widow Gozon protested against the contributions required of her in the commune of Carjac where she lived, citing reasons grounded in longstanding socio-economic hierarchy. To the commune administrators she wrote that it was quite impossible for her to pay them twenty-one *quintaux* of grain, which she considered 'exorbitant' in the circumstances. She had a household of ten or eleven persons to feed, not counting the men she hired daily to work her lands; her estate of Andressac and its mill was exposed to flooding of the river Lot that necessitated frequent and costly repairs; and she had to make charitable donations to the poor inhabitants of the area. Appealing to the administrators' sense of justice the widow closed her petition with the request that, instead of the twenty-one *quintaux* of grain, she be allowed to make an equivalent payment in *assignats*.[49]

Historians investigating the sale of *émigrés'* property as *biens nationaux* from 1794 have remarked upon the contrasts between departments and also between districts within the same department. There are some difficulties with establishing comparisons because not all historians use the same type of source for the quantitative data.[50] Nevertheless conclusions have been drawn about some of the effects for nobles' landholdings. A comparison of the department of Gironde with the department of Cher, for example, shows that properties of 228 *émigré* nobles were sold in the former but only 84 in the latter. The nature of the land was a contributing factor because the vineyards around Bordeaux were far more appealing to buyers than the poorer-quality plots on offer in Cher.[51] As for nobles buying *biens nationaux* there were many who did make purchases, although the practice became discouraged and declined because of negative attitudes that emerged within the nobility about it.[52] Long after the end of the Revolution the buying of *biens nationaux* remained associated with bourgeois speculators in nobles' collective memory.

Keeping records

A further cause of interaction between nobles and local authorities was the legislative requirements that estate paperwork, which documented the seigneurial structures of the *ancien régime*, be handed over for destruction. The law of 17 July 1793, which abolished without indemnity all seigneurial rights, also stipulated that relevant title deeds be burned. In 1794 the first archivist of the Republic, Armand-Gaston Camus, drafted the law of 7 *messidor, an* II to legitimate the act of destroying such documents.[53] But, from nobles' perspective, if in the future the monarchy should be restored to France and some compensation given for damages caused by the French Revolution, how would their families be able to lodge claims without the papers proving estate ownership? What measures were available to them, either by design or by luck, to safeguard their archives?

The law of 17 July 1793 inspired a struggle for control over estate paperwork between the widow Rose Isoard and the mayor of the commune of Vauvenargues (Bouches-du-Rhône). Rose's husband, Jean Antoine Isoard, had obtained the ennobling office of secretary in the Parlement of Provence in 1774; the couple had five children together before Jean Antoine's death in 1781. Ambitious for the family's social ascension, Rose purchased the château de Vauvenargues from the marquis de Clapiers who, in June 1791, was anxious to sell this estate in order to pay his creditors.[54] Vauvenargues was a *marquisat* (from 1722) and Rose's desire to secure for her sons the title of marquis that was linked to this property made it crucial that she keep hold of the estate papers. Rose appended the property name to her husband's surname and added the particle *de* – creating 'd'Isoard-Vauvenargues' – to make the Isoards, a family of recent robe nobility, appear a more ancient landowning lineage. In November 1793 the mayor insisted that *citoyenne* Isoard hand over to him all of the title deeds relating to the estate, and reminded her that refusal to comply would mean punishment according to the terms of article 7 of the law of 17 July. Three months went by before the mayor received Rose's response: 'Locks were placed on my son's apartment. The locks are still there and the nation has sequestered all the properties in my belonging … I am not in a position to hand over anything.'[55] The mayor tried again, ordering Rose on 4 February 1794 to give up the title deeds that were 'to be burned in the presence of the Conseil Général of the commune'. By late May the locks had been removed from her son's apartment, but Rose maintained that the sequestration of her various properties meant she was still unable to provide the required documents. Cheekily she suggested that the mayor contact the district administration to end the sequestration.[56]

Delay in responding to administrators, deliberate obfuscation, and playing one authority off against another featured among nobles' tactics to avoid handing over estate paperwork for destruction. Nor did nobles want to give up the evidence of personal honours such as letters patent conferring the cross for the royal and military order of Saint Louis, which by law of 28 *brumaire, an* II were supposed to be handed over to the municipal authorities. Historians have long found it difficult to judge from public archives just how much burning of seigneurial records really took place in the summer of 1793.[57] The fact that so much documentation is preserved in families' *archives privées* does confirm archivists' observation that the campaign to eradicate traces of feudalism was poorly implemented owing to a lack of personnel and resources.[58] It also reflects the unease expressed in the deliberations of the committees on feudal rights that in destroying the title deeds of a *seigneur* one also destroyed evidence of property for his tenant. A further reason documents have survived is that nobles at the time of the French Revolution wanted to keep hold of their papers so found ways to resist the implementation of the law.

When a family's archives were forcibly removed during the Revolution the owners made persistent efforts to have them returned. In 1793 Cérice-François-Melchior de Vogüé's property was sequestered. The *tuteurs* appointed to look after the rights of his children, Philippe and Charles de Vogüé, who were minors, managed to have the sequestration lifted by *arrêté* of 17 *messidor, an* V but the family had to wait an additional four years for the restitution of the archives. Archivists believe the revolutionary sequestration was responsible for the disorder in the Vogüé papers that were deposed in the Archives départementales de la Côte-d'Or in 1958.[59]

Family archives that escaped the flames, or were returned to their owners after sequestration, remained vulnerable to other human and environmental threats, and we shall see in later chapters examples of deliberate destruction that show not all nobles were conscientious about the safe keeping of records. A classic illustration of how papers of the nobility have fared since the French Revolution – and the types of risks pertaining to this patrimony – is found in the charter of Clérac, now conserved in the Archives départementales de la Charente-Maritime.

In the spring of 1788 an inventory was made of the furniture and effects of the château de Callières in the parish of Clérac, province of Saintonge. The purpose of the inventory was to itemise goods for a sale owing to the death of the château's owner, the *seigneur* Charles de Callières, on 11 March. The inventory records that, on 27 March after climbing the stairs to the upper floor of the château, one found in a small antechamber adjoining a central room 'an old wooden chest that has not been valued, being designed to pack and store papers'. Upon opening the chest it was discovered that those papers, comprising title deeds, were at risk of being eaten by rats. There was also the problem of pervading damp for, in May 1788, the floorboards of the upper rooms in the unoccupied château were 'rotten and full of gaps' while the roof was 'dilapidated and covered in moss'.[60] The sale of the furniture and effects of the château took place from 5 May to 18 June, but shortly beforehand Raphaël de Callières, the brother of the deceased owner, had arranged for the wooden chest of papers comprising the charter of Clérac to be transported to a secure place, probably his residence at Vallade.

When Raphaël died on 21 *brumaire, an* VII, his widow Jeanne Marie de Villatel gave the charter to her brother-in-law, Charles de Callières the younger, who kept it for only a short while before he died on 29 January 1802. This latter Charles's grandson, Frédéric-Charles, inherited the charter of Clérac but because his own children died prematurely Frédéric-Charles gave the charter to his younger brother, Stanislas Fortuné de Callières, who in turn gave it to his son Arthur. Since Arthur de Callières had no children, the charter passed to Arthur's two sisters, Marie-Caroline ('Tullia') and Madeleine, who lived together in the commune of Clérac. These two sisters, in 1888, loaned the charter to a Dr

Vigen in order for him to write up the genealogy of the Callières family. Around 1909 the charter was also loaned to another local historian and teacher, Monsieur David, who drew on it to write his book *Le Canton de Montguyon à travers l'Histoire*. Then, in 1917, Dr Vigen again consulted the charter in an attempt to establish whether there was any connection between the Callières family established in the province of Saintonge and a certain François de Callières, sixteenth-century ambassador and *conseiller secrétaire* to the king.[61]

When Tullia de Callières died on 29 August 1923 the charter, which at some point had been taken out of the wooden chest and placed into a more easily portable trunk, was taken back to the château de Callières by a Madame Poineau and entrusted temporarily to a member of the Callières family living in the château. Madame Poineau collected the trunk again in June 1924 and took it to the château de la Madeleine where she lived with her daughter and son-in-law Bernard de Callières. In 1959, the château de la Madeleine was sold and Bernard de Callières and his wife moved to Bordeaux. This couple had no children, so they gave the trunk and its contents to a cousin, Camille Bertrand. In 1973 Camille Bertrand's son-in-law, Jean Godefroy, kept the contents of the trunk in Nantes. An archivist, Monsieur Liebel, inventoried those contents and, realising that the material represented only a fraction of the charter used by the historian David around 1909, set about some detective work to locate the rest.

Liebel suspected, correctly as it turned out, that during its time at the château de Callières in 1923–4 the charter had been divided into two lots. The bigger one had remained at the château de Callières, while the smaller lot went in 1924 to the château de la Madeleine. On 22 December 1945 Charlotte de Callières sold the château de Callières, containing part of the charter, to a Monsieur Fleurian, and Fleurian subsequently sold the property to a Madame Massier (née Devienne). Madame Massier had various pieces of the charter examined by an antiquarian and she kept what she had of the charter upon selling the château de Callières on 27 May 1969. In the summer of 1973 the archivist Liebel met Madame Massier at her new home and found 'numerous pieces of the charter, alas not making up the totality of what was missing'. The reunion of the two lots – one from Madame Massier and one from Jean Godefroy – was brought about thanks to Liebel's efforts. Liebel handed the resulting archival collection, known as the charter of Clérac, to the Archives départementales de la Charente-Maritime on 31 July 1975. In this way a charter that, in Liebel's view, had probably never been taken out of the château de

Callières prior to 1788 because the title deeds were those of the *seigneurs* of Clérac was subjected to numerous peregrinations over the nineteenth and twentieth centuries. Like scores of other *archives privées* of nobility, located across France, the charter of Clérac, by its very contents and state of preservation, gestures toward a 'back story' of deaths, sales, researches, divisions, speculations, and donations.

The history of this charter contains a generic element that applies to any type of archive, namely the risk of material degradation through human neglect and environmental causes.[62] It also contains all the particular elements characteristic to nobles' *archives privées* across France. There is the marked preference for transmitting the family archive to a son or other male relative. There is the tendency since the Middle Ages to store the archive in a château (*castrum sine armario est quasi castrum sine armamentario* – 'a castle without an archive is a castle without equipment'). There is the use of the archive for genealogical or community history research by family members and local *érudits*. There is the possibility of individual pieces, usually parchments of special beauty, being sold on the private market thus depriving the collection of some of its historical value. Finally there is the effort of archivists liaising with owners in the twentieth and twenty-first centuries to ensure the collection enters a public repository.

Conclusion

The material condition of nobles' *archives privées* stands as a continual reminder to historians of the argument for a long-term perspective on French history that allows for connections rather than partitions to be drawn between eras.[63] There were threats to such archives before the French Revolution, as well as after it, so the notion that revolutionary legislation was mostly to blame for the destruction of nobles' papers is, as archivists point out, too simplistic. It is symptomatic of a broader mythology from the perspective of the nobility that 'everything' was lost in 1789–99. That mythology has grown from the way the nobility maintains its social frameworks of collective memory, including through oral story telling and memoirs.

In fact, the extent of damage to aristocratic property differed from one area to another in France, and from family to family. The losses were particularly resented among the generation of adult nobles who were obliged to take stock. In Robert Forster's estimation the average income of a provincial noble family declined from 8,000 to 5,200 francs. While seigneurial dues had represented only 5 per cent of noble income near Bordeaux, they had amounted to 63 per cent in the provinces of Aunis and Saintonge. Compounding the loss of those dues, up to one half of all noble families lost some lands and a few families lost virtually all. The State introduced a uniform land tax levied at around 16 per cent. Although nobles responded to the land tax by charging higher rents to tenants and sharecroppers, the steady erosion of deferential behaviour toward nobility meant an increase in litigation and other forms of protest against these landowners. The fiscal impact of revolutionary legislation was experienced neither all at once nor in a uniform way among the nobility but even the wealthiest families felt the effects.[64]

Nobles' rhetoric of loss, developed in published memoirs and novels by the generation most keenly affected, is informed by the emotional distress provoked by the violence and disruption of the revolutionary years. Families' collective memory of relatives' suffering was transmitted orally to noble children who learned of how their ancestors confronted danger, were killed, or forced to cope with dramatic ruptures to their way of life.[65] In the mid-nineteenth century, the duchesse de Saulx-Tavanes, by then an elderly woman reflecting on the France to which she had returned after emigration, described a painful sense of disorientation that inspired feelings of regret and retreat: 'All the ties which hold me to life have been successively broken. Only a few traces of what I have known remain. Ideas, opinions, mores have changed; and like the daughters of Jerusalem, I mourn the miseries of Zion in a strange land.'[66] Such vivid sentiments in published memoirs do not tell the whole story any more than does the language of eighteenth-century pamphlets launching 'attacks on the principles and practices of nobility in the public sphere'.[67]

Behaviours during the nineteenth and twentieth centuries point to the persistence of certain ideas about the French Revolution within the collective memory of noble families.[68] Legitimists among the *ancienne noblesse* participated in commemoration of guillotined 'martyrs' at the Chapelle Expiatoire constructed by Louis XVIII and at a special commemorative garden at 35 rue de Picpus in Paris. Nobles donated funds for a monument at Quiberon to honour the memory of the *chouans* and gathered in other urban and rural settings for commemorative events.[69] Responses to Mension-Rigau's questionnaire in the 1980s reveal the sentiments that guided such activities, which echo sentiments uncovered in Wylie's research. Rejection of the Revolution was expressed in families where grandparents 'closed the shutters of the house on the 14 July' and where granddaughters were clothed 'in mourning for Marie-Antoinette'.

The impact was felt by successive generations: 'For us the Revolution was yesterday. We had six ancestors beheaded or shot' or 'In my family we were still traumatised by the violence and executions'. The Revolution was 'always associated with the Convention's assassinations and the genocide of the Vendée war'. Respondents to the questionnaire had reservations about the role of the marquis de Lafayette. One descendant of Lafayette recalled: 'My father said that there was no reason to be proud of it because he had been one of the promoters of the 1789 Revolution.' Another described how Lafayette 'was a controversial figure in my mother's family that did not accept liberal ideas'. There was aloofness toward 'buyers of biens nationaux'.[70]

As Figeac argues it is not accurate to apply the term 'genocide' to nobles' experiences of the French Revolution.[71] On this point, as well as on other issues relating to strategies for the protection of property, we can see the ways in which family stories functioning like myth have left complicated patterns in their wake. Those patterns have affected nobles' relationship with the history of their own family and with the history of France. They form a part of the social atmosphere in a milieu associated with old landed estates, ties to the Church, and connections to royal and imperial courts.[72]

Many (not all) of the collections of archives privées that have come down to us contain compelling evidence of nobles' actions and attitudes during the decade of 1789–99. Letters, wills, receipts, account books, certificates, passports, and petitions reveal how the effects of multiple decrees played out in personal and familial histories. The Revolution unquestionably changed patterns of ownership and control in many parts of the French countryside, engendering new sensibilities, aggravating old antipathies, and sowing the seeds of later struggles. For the nobility the rapid evolution of legislation meant that the consequences of any one revolutionary law became entangled with the consequences of another.

Attention to both sexes is crucial to deepen our understanding of nobles' experiences during the French Revolution. The numerous female voices expressing views to local authorities in archival documentation show that noblewomen played a very active role in property affairs.[73] Some 85 per cent of the noble émigrés were of the male sex, so their wives, mothers, sisters, and daughters who remained in France very often bore huge responsibilities in trying to defend the material interests of kin. These noblewomen's perspectives bring fresh insights and understanding to issues often overlooked in historical writing weighted toward aristocratic male military and political involvement. A generation of noblewomen in their adult prime during the revolutionary decade had to employ skills and assertiveness that we shall see had implications for the tripartite power relations of ownership, management, and labour on estates. In 1789–99 the nobility who had long enjoyed a privileged legal status saw the law repeatedly turned into a weapon used against their families. What nobles did not yet know in that decade was how far they could manoeuvre within a range of new laws to protect their interests. Some of their experiments indicated that reforms could swing back to shield them.

Notes

1 F.-R. de Chateaubriand, *Oeuvres complètes* vol. 1 *Essai historique sur les révolutions* (Paris, 1830), pp. 160–1.

2 19 September 1793 in AD Alpes-Maritimes 25J/255 Archives du château de Mouans Sartoux.

3 T. Tackett, 'Conspiracy obsession in a time of Revolution: French elites and the origins of the Terror, 1789–1792', *American Historical Review* 105 (2000), 691–713. In the 1780s the fastest coach travelling from Paris took eight days to reach Toulouse or Marseille. H. D. Clout, *The Land of France 1815–1914* (London, 1983), p. 39.

4 18 January 1793 in AD Alpes-Maritimes 25J/255 Archives du château de Mouans Sartoux.

5 Laws on emigration are detailed in D. Greer, *The Incidence of the Emigration during the French Revolution* (Gloucester, MA, 1966), pp. 10–12.

6 For a masterful study of factors that shaped people's responses see R. Cobb, *Reactions to the French Revolution* (Oxford, 1972).

7 On disbelief about revolutionary change see R. Forster, *The House of Saulx-Tavanes: Versailles and Burgundy 1700–1830* (Baltimore, 1971), pp. 143–4.

8 For an account of the Assembly vote see W. Doyle, *Aristocracy and its Enemies in the Age of Revolution* (Oxford, 2009), pp. 233–8.

9 Greer, *The Incidence,* pp. 84–5, 127; J. Dunne, 'Quantifier l'émigration des nobles pendant la Révolution française: problèmes et perspectives' in J.-C. Martin (ed.), *La Contre-révolution en Europe, XVIIIe-XIXe siècle: réalités politiques et sociales, résonances culturelles et idéologiques* (Rennes, 2001), pp. 133–41.

10 F. Baldensberger, *Le Mouvement des idées dans l'émigration française* (Paris, 1924); J. Vidalenc, *Les Émigrés français, 1789–1825* (Caen, 1963); G. de Diesbach, *Histoire de l'émigration (1787–1814)* (Paris, 1975); M. H. Darrow, 'French noblewomen and the new domesticity, 1750–1850', *Feminist Studies* 5 (1979), 41–65; K. Carpenter and P. Mansel (eds), *The French Émigrés in Europe and the Struggle against Revolution 1789–1814* (London, 1999);

C. Chappell Lougee, 'Emigration and memory: after 1685 and after 1789' in R. Dekker (ed.), *Egodocuments and History: Autobiographical Writing in Its Social Context since the Middle Ages* (Hilversum, 2002), pp. 89–106; S. Kale, *French Salons: High Society and Political Sociability from the Old Regime to the Revolution of 1848* (Baltimore, 2004), ch. 2; C. Jaquier, F. Lottier, and C. Seth (eds), *Destins romanesques de l'émigration* (Paris, 2007); K. Carpenter, *The Novels of Madame de Souza in Social and Political Perspective* (Bern, 2007); S. Genand (ed.), *Romans de l'émigration* (Paris, 2008); D. P. Harsanyi, *Lessons from America. Liberal French Nobles in Exile 1793–1798* (Philadelphia, 2010); B. Dumons and H. Multon (eds), *'Blancs' et contre-révolutionnaires en Europe: espaces, réseaux, cultures et mémoires* (Rome, 2011).

11 M. Halbwachs, *On Collective Memory* (*Les Cadres sociaux de la mémoire*, 1925), ed. and translated by L. A. Coser (Chicago, 1992), pp. 54, 60.

12 M. Halbwachs, *The Collective Memory* (*La Mémoire collective*, 1950), translated by F. J. Didder Jr and V. Yazdi Ditter (New York, 1980), pp. 23, 118; Halbwachs, *On Collective Memory*, pp. 40, 54.

13 A. S. Byatt, *On Histories and Stories: Selected Essays* (London, 2000), pp. 123–50, 165–71; J. D. Niles, *Homo Narrans: The Poetics and Anthropology of Oral Literature* (Philadelphia, 1999).

14 4 August 1789 in AD Haute-Loire 23J–24J/194 Archives Langlade du Chayla et Familles Apparentées.

15 5 October 1789 in AD Haute-Loire 23J–24J/194 Archives Langlade du Chayla et Familles Apparentées.

16 9 February 1790 in AD Meuse 39J/40 Archives de la famille Nettancourt.

17 9 February 1790 in AD Meuse 39J/40 Archives de la famille Nettancourt.

18 'Pillage et destruction du château de Jouqueviel' 28 avril 1790 in AD Aveyron 60J/41 Fonds de Faramond. For analysis of peasant attacks in the preceding year, see G. Lefebvre, *La Grande Peur de 1789* (Paris, 1932), pp. 48, 50, 114, 116, 128, 131. On violence at Carnival see J. R. Ruff, *Violence in Early Modern Europe 1500–1800* (Cambridge, 2001), pp. 164–6, 178–80.

19 13 February 1790 in AD Aveyron 60J/39 Fonds de Faramond.

20 21 March 1790 in AD Aveyron 60J/39 Fonds de Faramond.

21 K. B. Neuschel, 'Noble households in the sixteenth century: material settings and human communities', *French Historical Studies* 15 (1988), 595–622, esp. 605–7; J. Dewald, *Pont-St-Pierre 1398–1789: Lordship, Community, and Capitalism in Early Modern France* (Berkeley, 1987), pp. 196–7.

22 On consumerism see Dewald, *Pont-St-Pierre 1398–1789*, pp. 193–9.

23 Passport 1 September 1789 in AD Vosges 41J/30 Fonds de la famille de Rozières.

24 Passport 19 August 1793 in AD Meuse 38J/38 Chartrier de Nettancourt.

25 Law of Suspects, 17 September 1793, translated in P. G. Dwyer and P. McPhee (eds), *The French Revolution and Napoleon: A Sourcebook* (London, 2002), pp. 103–4.

26 Minister's letter of 16 February 1793 in AD Vosges 41J/30 Fonds de la famille de Rozières.
27 27 April 1793 in AD Vosges 41J/30 Fonds de la famille de Rozières.
28 Certificate of non-emigration 27 September 1793 in AD Vosges 41J/30 Fonds de la famille de Rozières.
29 Divorce certificate in AD Meuse 38J/38 Chartrier de Nettancourt.
30 Pamphlet printed in Bar-sur-Ornin in AD Meuse 38J/38 Chartrier de Nettancourt.
31 Forster, *The House of Saulx-Tavanes*, p. 194; On divorce, S. Desan, *The Family on Trial in Revolutionary France* (Berkeley, 2004), ch 3.
32 On conceptions of service in early modern aristocratic thought see J. M. Smith, *The Culture of Merit: Nobility, Royal Service, and the Making of Absolute Monarchy in France, 1600–1789* (Ann Arbor, 1996), ch. 1.
33 Response to the observations of the Comité de Surveillance in AD Vosges 134J/36 Fonds des Pilliers.
34 Judgement of the criminal tribunal in AD Vosges 134J/36 Fonds des Pilliers.
35 31 December 1792 in AD Alpes-Maritimes 25J/255 Archives du château de Mouans Sartoux.
36 A list of Nettancourts and members of related families who emigrated during the Revolution appears in the inventory of AD Meuse 38J Chartrier de Nettancourt from J. Dubois, 'Liste des émigrés, des prêtres déportés et des condamnés pour cause révolutionnaire du department de la Meuse', *Bulletin de la Société des Lettres, Sciences et Arts de Bar-le-Duc* (1910), pp. 5–136. On the Nettancourt family in the sixteenth and seventeenth centuries see L. Bourquin, *Noblesse seconde et pouvoir en Champagne aux XVIe et XVIIe siècles* (Paris, 1994), pp. 126–7, 130, 142, 162–3, 207, 214.
37 The fourth child (Louis-Chrétien) born on 3 November 1788, died at Étain on 30 March 1793. The eldest son (Charles-Gabriel-Étienne) born on 22 May 1785, died at Bar-le-Duc on 18 August 1793.
38 'Notes sur l'émigration' in AD Meuse 38J/39 Chartrier de Nettancourt.
39 M. Trévisi, 'Solitudes et solidarities dans une famille noble du XVIIIe siècle, les d'Estourmel' in J.-P. Bardet, É. Arnoul, and F.-J. Ruggiu (eds), *Les Écrits du for privé en Europe* (Pessac, 2010), pp. 227–46. One noblewoman was executed for sending money to her son in Spain. D. Higgs, *Ultraroyalism in Toulouse: From Its Origins to the Revolution of 1830* (Baltimore, 1973), p. 39.
40 'Relevé du tableau de la citoyenne Nagu Mortemart' in AD Seine-Maritime 203J/33 Chartrier de l'ancien marquisat de La Mailleraye.
41 Smith, *The Culture of Merit*, pp. 196–202.
42 AD Morbihan 50J Chartrier de Kergonano.
43 29 July 1795 in AD Côtes-d'Armor 19J/15 Archives de Courson.
44 8 November 1793 in AD Aveyron 13J/11 Fonds du château de Bournazel.
45 For examples of the reasoning in pleas for reductions see 'Demande de baisse

d'impôt foncière (1792–3)' in AD Bouches-du-Rhône 103J/3 Archives de la famille d'Isoard-Vauvenargues.

46 G. Duby and A. Wallon (eds), *Histoire de la France rurale* vol. 3 *Apogée et crise de la civilisation paysanne de 1789 à 1914* by M. Agulhon, G. Désert, and R. Specklin (Paris, 1976), pp. 118–20.

47 20 December 1791 in AD Lot 13J/1A5 Fonds Camy-Gozon.

48 I. Woloch, *The New Regime: Transformations of the French Civic Order, 1789–1820s* (New York, 1994), pp. 35, 129; M. Agulhon, L. Girard, J.-L. Robert (eds), *Les Maires en France du Consulat à nos jours* (Paris, 1986), pp. 7–17, 35–55.

49 Undated petition in AD Lot 13J/3E Fonds Camy-Gozon.

50 A. Gain, *La Restauration et les biens des émigrés* 2 vols (Nancy, 1929); C. Girault, *La Noblesse émigrée et ses pertes foncières dans la Sarthe* (Laval, 1957); M. Bouloiseau, *Étude sur l'émigration et la vente des biens d'émigrés (1792–1830)* (Paris, 1963); P. Bossis, 'Recherches sur la propriété nobiliaire en pays vendéen avant et après la Révolution', *Bulletin de la Société d'émulation de la Vendée* (1973), 123–47; B. Bodinier and É. Teyssier, *L'Événement le plus important de la Révolution: la vente des biens nationaux* (Paris, 2000).

51 M. Figeac, *Destins de la noblesse bordelaise (1770–1830)* 2 vols (Bordeaux, 1996), vol. 1, pp. 420–45.

52 J. Tulard, *Napoléon et la noblesse d'Empire* (Paris, 1979), p. 121; Figeac, *Destins*, vol. 1, pp. 458–66; B. Bodinier, 'Une noblesse ruinée par la Révolution?' in P. Bourdin (ed.), *Les Noblesses françaises dans l'Europe de la Révolution* (Rennes and Clermont-Ferrand, 2010), pp. 69–86.

53 J.-P. Gérard, *Répertoire des ressources généalogiques et héraldiques du Départment des Manuscrits de la Bibliothèque Nationale de France* (Versailles, 2003), p. 38; S. Coeuré and V. Duclert, *Les Archives* (Paris, 2001), p. 17.

54 7 June 1791 in AD Bouches-du-Rhône 103J/3 Archives de la famille d'Isoard-Vauvenargues. Rose Pin purchased Vauvenargues on 15 July 1791.

55 Mayor's letter 22 November 1793 and Rose's reply in AD Bouches-du-Rhône 103J/5 Archives de la famille d'Isoard-Vauvenargues.

56 Vauvenargues belonged to the Isoards from 1791 to 1943 when it was sold to industrialists from Marseille. In 1958 Pablo Picasso bought the property and he was buried there in 1973.

57 A. Soboul, 'Le brûlement des titres féodaux (1789–1793)' in *Problèmes paysans de la revolution (1789–1848)*, pp. 135–46, esp. 142.

58 M. Duchein, 'Requiem pour trois lois défuntes', *La Gazette des Archives* 104 (1979), 12–16; P. Santoni, 'Archives et violence: à propos de la loi du 7 messidor an II', *La Gazette des Archives* 146–7 (1989), 199–214.

59 Various documents pertaining to lands, which properly belonged to the Vogüé *fonds*, had been mixed up with the papers of another family classed separately. On Charles and Philippe de Vogüé see AD Côte d'Or 32F/291, 292, and 297 Fonds Vogüé. For the request to the prefect (12 *pluviôse, an X*)

and *enlèvement* (22 *ventôse, an* IX) see AD Côte d'Or Q 1139 and Q695 fol. 413–21.

60 'Historique du chartrier de 1788 à 1973' in AD Charente-Maritime 19J Chartrier des seigneurs de Clérac.

61 Vigen's research was published in *Bulletins des Archives Historiques de la Saintonge* vol. 37.

62 H. Grousson, H. Michon, B. Poinas, and C. Poirson, *Blessures d'archives, rêve d'éternité* (Valence, 2004).

63 A. de Tocqueville, *The Old Regime and the French Revolution*, translated by S. Gilbert (New York, 1955).

64 R. Forster, *The Nobility of Toulouse in the Eighteenth Century* (Baltimore, 1960), pp. 47–119; R. Forster, 'The survival of the nobility during the French Revolution', *Past and Present* 37 (1967), 71–86; Forster, *The House of Saulx-Tavanes*, ch. 5 and conclusion; Higgs, *Ultraroyalism in Toulouse*, pp. 32–3, 51; D. Higgs, *Nobles in Nineteenth-Century France: The Practice of Inegalitarianism* (Baltimore, 1987), pp. 51–4.

65 R. de La Croix de Castries, *Papiers de famille* (Paris, 1977), pp. 237–8; R. de Saboulin Bollena, *Liberté, égalité, fraternité ou la mort* (Saint-Chély d'Apcher, 1988). Stories about the 1848 revolution were also recounted to children: see I. de Paris, *Mon bonheur de grand-mère* (Paris, 1995), p. 18.

66 Duchesse de Saulx-Tavanes, *Mémoires*, translated by Forster in, *The House of Saulx-Tavanes*, p. 201.

67 Doyle, *Aristocracy and Its Enemies*, p. 341.

68 On the variety of collective memories see M. Agulhon, *Marianne into Battle: Republican Imagery and Symbolism in France, 1789–1880*, translated by J. Lloyd (Cambridge, 1981); R. Huard, 'La Révolution française, événement fondateur: le travail de l'histoire sur l'héritage et la tradition', *Cahiers d'histoire de l'Institut de recherches marxistes* 32 (1988), 54–71; M. Yalom, *Blood Sisters: The French Revolution in Women's Memory* (New York, 1995); E. Hobsbawm, *Echoes of the Marseillaise: Two Centuries Look Back on the French Revolution* (New Brunswick, 1990); S. L. Kaplan, *Farewell Revolution: Disputed Legacies, France 1789/1989* (Ithaca, 1995).

69 P. Mansel, *Paris between Empires 1814–1852* (London, 2001), pp. 170–1, 193–4; A. Texier, *Qu'est-ce que la noblesse?* (Paris, 1988), p. 465; R. Jonas, *France and the Cult of the Sacred Heart: An Epic Tale for Modern Times* (Ewing, 2000), pp. 158–68; J. Goldhammer, *The Headless Republic: Sacrificial Violence in Modern French Thought* (Ithaca, 2005), pp. 5, 71; B. Dumons, 'Ainay, le quartier "blanc" de Lyon' in Dumons and Multon, *'Blancs' et contre-révolutionnaires*, pp. 105–31.

70 É. Mension-Rigau, *Aristocrates et grands bourgeois: éducation, traditions, valeurs* (Paris, 1994), pp. 138–41, 153, 467–9; L. Wylie (ed.), *Chanzeaux: A Village in Anjou* (Cambridge, MA, 1966).

71 Figeac, *Destins*, vol. 1, pp. 395–418.

72 A. J. Mayer, *The Persistence of the Old Regime: Europe to the Great War* (New York, 1981), pp. 3–15, 329. See also Higgs, *Nobles*, pp. xv, 223.

73 Forster, *The House of Saulx-Tavanes*, p. 196. For perspectives on women and gender see, for example, S. Reynolds (ed.), *Women, State and Revolution: Essays on Power and Gender in Europe since 1789* (Brighton, 1986); O. Hufton, *Women and the Limits of Citizenship in the French Revolution* (Toronto, 1992); L. Hunt, *The Family Romance of the French Revolution* (Berkeley, 1992); J. W. Scott, *Only Paradoxes to Offer: French Feminists and the Rights of Man* (Cambridge, 1996).

2

Divisions of inheritance

All patrimony is a material and moral responsibility.[1]

Everything lay before them. It was 1 February 1800 when Joseph-Raymond de Bonald and his wife Marie-Régis (née de Séguret) began to prepare for the division of patrimony among their three children. Deeds and accounts had been assembled for scrutiny. Calculations of annual revenue were made and compared. The couple already knew in broad terms what these documents confirmed in detail: that the value of what they owned in that first year of the nineteenth century was around 20 per cent less than the value of what they had owned sixteen years before. Their chief real estate holdings were the estate and château de Vielvayssac near the village of Flavin (Aveyron) and the townhouse in the rue de Bonald, Rodez. 'Striking degradations' wrought to these buildings during the Revolution had stripped them of monetary value. The château, estimated to be worth around 100,000 *assignats* in 1784, was valued at just 35,000 in 1800. Heading a list of other reasons for the depreciation of fortune was 'the abolition of *rentes, champarts, charrois* and other *corvées, droit de lods* and other useful and honorific rights, the loss of all the arrears'. Also to blame were the 'greatly increased taxes', 'the very sharp rise in servants' wages', 'considerable costs of farming and harvesting', and 'excessive inflation affecting expenditure of all kinds'.[2]

Little wonder, then, at the start of the new century that Joseph-Raymond and Marie-Régis felt 'already bowed down with the weight of years that the revolutionary humiliations have made heavier'. In 'wanting to free themselves entirely of the administration of their affairs', and at the same time ensure a comfortable existence for themselves in old age, the couple had to plan carefully how best to transfer responsibility for property to the next generation. On 28 November 1801 the Bonalds met with their three children and son-in-law in Rodez to conclude the process and to obtain formal agreement on arrangements for the division of patrimony.[3]

There was a critical unknown element. Notwithstanding the scrupulous care taken with arrangements in 1800–1, no one in the Bonald family or any person advising them could confidently say that there would not be a return to what the French by then referred to as the 'ancien régime'. It is clear from the Bonalds' written considerations that the possibility of seigneurialism being re-established was prominent in their thinking. 'The rents, benefits, charges and other former seigneurial rights abolished by various revolutionary laws, notably that of 17 July 1793, were also estimated according to different title deeds and other documents that were produced and examined … *the re-establishment of these dues is possible*.'[4]

This statement from nobles grappling with the uncertain potential for reversal of revolutionary outcomes provides a reminder of the gulf between their world and our perspective in hindsight on that world. In 1800–1 France remained in a state of flux after political volatility and disaffection for the Directory regime had culminated in the 1799 *coup d'état* and installation of the Consulate. Across the nation communities were lumbered with social and economic problems made worse by a decade of war. Distanced from Paris, the bulk of the population heard only partial reports and rumours of proposed Napoleonic reforms that would roll out over the next decade to shape French society in lasting ways.

Considerations of patrimony in this context were complicated by the multiplicity of changes set in train by the Revolution. The decree of 20 October 1800 lifted the sequestration of *émigré* lands. Those lands that had not been sold as *biens nationaux* were returned to owners in 1800–2. Beyond the immediate uncertainties about calculating 'net worth', owing to losses and gains, nobles now had to navigate new legislation on the transmission of property. The Assembly had abolished primogeniture on 15 March 1790 and introduced the law on partible inheritance on 8 April 1791. Henceforward, all siblings regardless of sex had the right to inherit an equal share of the family estate. Under the *ancien régime* nobles had benefited from more flexible arrangements with a welter of possibilities for allocating patrimony. The legal systems varied across the country with written law operating in most of the south and local customary systems in the north.[5] Decision-making on inheritance was also influenced by social status, for example in the pre-revolutionary tradition of *le partage noble* based on the principle of *le droit d'aînesse*.[6] In *le partage noble* a father with numerous offspring might leave the bulk of his property to the eldest male child, provide a dowry for daughters who married, and place other unmarried daughters and sons in the Church. When there was no direct heir the legal mechanism known as substitution had enabled titles and land to be transmitted to another relative such as a nephew.[7] The revolutionaries wanted to break the nobility's capacity for holding on to its estates and this was a prime motive for sweeping away a great jumble of old laws and customs. When the legal requirement for partible inheritance was introduced across the whole country it both sharply increased the potential for conflict between children and was regarded as detrimental to the interests of nobility.

Archives privées contain evidence not only of revolutionary upheaval to nobles' arrangements for succession but also of the ways in which nobles during earlier centuries had confronted longstanding challenges that accompanied transmission of property. Consider the Vassal family from the province of Quercy whose name is first known to appear in two late tenth-century charters recording donations made to the abbey of Beaulieu. This family celebrated one thousand years of recorded existence with a special gathering in the department of the Lot in 1987. In the Vassal archives are documents produced across the period 1276–2000.[8] Both in breadth of chronological coverage and in depth of content, nobles' *archives privées* show how behaviours and attitudes toward property have tended to be informed by mixes of long and short periods of ownership in a particular geographic territory; a legacy of real estate ownership is that family papers are deposed in the department that corresponds most closely to the territory. When exploring archival evidence from different eras within a single collection, information and clues emerge about how legal customs were used to keep noble titles and land in a family's ownership. There is also information about the circumstances that surrounded the selling of estates, and about why, sometimes, a family's determined efforts to maintain property failed.

This chapter focuses on the apportioning of tangible patrimony in aristocratic successions. As in medieval and early modern family strategies, succession remained a profoundly significant matter for the nobility during the post-revolutionary era. Historians of the France of the Middle Ages have long been accustomed to studying aristocratic lineages and the mechanisms by which land and titles were accumulated, lost, or transferred from one generation to the next.[9] For the early modern

period, too, a good deal is known about nobles' approaches to property
transmission through their encounters with the law, structures of households, and purchase of heritable office.[10] When we consider the evolution
of aristocratic succession after the French Revolution there continues to
be a mix of contrasts and similarities between what nobles were doing
and the practices among people of lower classes. By presenting new
evidence on inheritance practices among the nobility this chapter helps
to explain how nobles manoeuvred within the post-revolutionary legal
system. Overall the nobility had considerable success, even though by
the twentieth century fewer nobles figured within the very top bracket of
the wealthy.[11] This chapter shows how solidarity between kin was tested
continually both by external forces and by internal family dynamics of
power, interest, and emotion.

Ties of affection and the law

Scholars of the Middle Ages have opened various paths of investigation
into aristocratic succession where there were not only material interests
involved but also emotions toward kin. Georges Duby was a proponent
of the argument that a model of family dynamic developed in the eleventh century that favoured patrilineage. The male line, especially the
first-born son, was supported to the detriment of other lines; families
shifted from an inclusive approach to an exclusive approach in organising succession.[12] Amy Livingstone's study of the charters of aristocratic
families in the area surrounding Blois and Chartres has revealed for the
eleventh and twelfth centuries how primogeniture and partible inheritance were not separate exclusive systems, but rather strategies that could
be implemented concurrently for different properties within the same
succession. The medieval nobility living in the vicinity of Blois and
Chartres took full advantage of the malleability and diversity of legal
options for transmitting patrimony, and parents openly expressed affection in making bequests 'out of love for my kin'. From what survives of
the charters for the period 1000–1200, Livingstone argues for an inclusive model of aristocratic family life where harmony and recognition
prevailed over conflict and alienation.[13]

To what extent do such inclusive practices and affectionate sentiments appear in the post-revolutionary writings of nobles about the
apportioning of patrimony? How did changes to inheritance law at the
end of the eighteenth century affect siblings whose relations with one
other remained naturally informed by birth order and gender? Before

approaching the archival evidence left by nobles we need to situate such questions within the context of an evolving legislation.

The principle of equality between heirs introduced by the partible inheritance law of 8 April 1791 continued to be upheld after the revolutionary decade of 1789–99. Under the Consulate regime some flexibility was introduced for parents of all social classes to apply the principle less strictly. By the law of 4 *germinal, an* VII (25 March 1800) a parent could allocate a disposable share of his or her estate (not less than one-quarter and not more than one-half) to one heir, with all the heirs having equal rights to the remainder. The provision of the disposable share (*la quotité disponible*) was incorporated into the Civil Code in 1804.[14]

A further initiative, which contradicted the principle of equality between heirs, was the *majorat* introduced by Napoleon I's decree of 1 March 1808. The *majorat* was applicable only to families of nobility; this form of entail for male heirs based on *le droit d'aînesse* had long facilitated the transmission of noble titles and real estate in other European countries (discussed in Chapter 3). From 1817 the restored Bourbon monarchy made the *majorat* obligatory for transmission of the peerage. In the favourable environment of Louis XVIII's reign there was also an increase in requests for *majorats sur demande* by nobles who were not members of the Chamber of Peers.[15] When Charles X succeeded to the throne in 1824 a campaign to reintroduce primogeniture led to debates on the Succession Laws Bill tabled by Villèle's government. A return to primogeniture was ultimately rejected.[16] These various imperial and royal offensives against the principle of equality between heirs were reined in after the 1830 Revolution. The creation of new *majorats sur demande* was forbidden by law of 12 May 1835 and their suppression was achieved by law of 11 May 1849. Yet *majorats de propre mouvement* continued to exist for the transmission of nobiliary titles and property during the Third Republic.[17]

In sum, the France that had made the transition from multiple local customs to a national law on partible inheritance, and then implemented the Civil Code under Napoleon, still left open a range of options for organising succession through the nineteenth century and into the twentieth. Nobles continued to exploit the potential to implement concurrently a form of primogeniture for some property, and partible inheritance for remaining property, within the same succession.

In practice, families' inheritance strategies at all levels of French society were more complex than the articles of the Civil Code suggest. This is because not only could a parent decide whether or not to use the provision for a disposable share but also there was parental control over the timing of succession.[18] Four opportunities stood out for exercising this control at different points in the sequence of parent–child relations. First, at the point of the parents' marriage, it was possible in a marriage contract to make stipulations about succession, including whether or not a portion of the bride or groom's estate would be left after his or her death to the surviving spouse. Second, at the point when the parents' child was old enough to marry, an advance donation of that child's portion (*donation en avance d'hoirie*) could be given as dowry. Third, at the point when parents wanted to retire from the duties of managing property, a *donation entre vifs* allowed for the transfer of property ownership to younger kin. Finally, at the point of making a will, a parent apportioned his or her estate, choosing whether or not to make a preferential legacy (*le préciput*). The preferential legacy was a type of donation made to one heir separately and in addition to that heir's ordinary share from the partition of inheritance; hence it was described as *par préciput et hors part*.[19]

A key factor in any succession was the interaction between parental control over timing and the heirs' ultimate decisions over the property transferred.[20] At the legal opening of a succession the first step under the Civil Code was to make an inventory of patrimony and provide copies to all the heirs (article 503). Upon receipt of the inventory the heirs had various alternatives open to them as individuals. A first option was renouncement of their personal share in the estate. A second option was inaction for any part or item of the estate not allocated to an individual (left 'undivided') so that that part or item would remain equally owned by all heirs. A third option was to seek agreement with other heirs to buy out their shares of an undivided part or item in order to gain sole ownership of it. Finally there was the option of liquidating one's personal share.

Provisions were made during the French Revolution for cases of contestation pertaining to inheritance; a decree of 16 August 1790 established the family tribunals (*les tribunaux de famille*). When disputes arose and could not be resolved between the heirs alone the contesting parties were each required to name two relatives, or in the absence of relatives 'friends or neighbours', to represent them. If the four members of a family tribunal reached a deadlock in deliberations then a fifth person would be named.[21]

Implementing a *donation entre vifs* represents a very particular situation in which to consider how the apportioning of patrimony worked within families so we will investigate this method before turning to nobles' wills and marriage contracts.[22] The *donation entre vifs* enabled parents who wanted to retire from the duties of owning property to pass on those responsibilities and rights of ownership to the next generation while the parents remained alive. Parents' choice of this method might be read as a sign of familial harmony and intergenerational trust among nobles. An alternative interpretation is to see it as motivated by parents' worry over how, in practice, relations would evolve among offspring once the parents were dead.

Let us return to the Bonalds of Rodez to examine how nobles' approach to *donation entre vifs* is addressed in the archive. The account of the family reunion on 28 November 1801 states that Joseph-Raymond and Marie-Régis felt 'equal tenderness' toward and 'equally satisfied of the good conduct' of their two sons, Auguste and René, and daughter Marie-Victoire. Their stated parental aim in dividing property with all parties present (including Marie-Victoire's husband, Monsieur de Bourran) was to guard against any potential dispute among the children after the parents died:

> Since the discussion of these kinds of interests was too often a source of disagreement [*une pomme de discorde*], even in the most united families, and [the Bonalds] held nothing closer to heart than the eternal maintenance of the peace, friendship and good harmony that have reigned without shadow among them since childhood, [Joseph-Raymond and Marie-Régis] wished to establish by consent [with their children] their rights respective to their position.[23]

The account of this reunion goes on to record the children's 'joy and gratitude' for the arrangements made. On reading the terms of the Bonalds' arrangements, however, it is strikingly apparent that there was an unequal distribution of responsibilities. The responsibilities fell heavily upon the eldest child, Auguste, but comparatively lightly upon his siblings René and Marie-Victoire.

René's rights as the younger son, 'even in the case of re-establishment of all the abolished former seigneurial rights', were 'irrevocably fixed at the sum of 39,500 *livres* including a gift of 500 *livres* made to him by the abbé Lenormand, archdeacon of Commings'. From this total, René had already received 3,000 *livres* by way of advance donation (*la hoirie*). Of the remaining 36,500 *livres* a sum of 17,500 *livres* was to be paid before his father's death, and 19,000 *livres* after both parents had died. As the only daughter, Marie-Victoire's rights were aligned with René's, so fixed at 39,000 *livres*, of which Marie-Victoire's husband, Monsieur de Bourran, had already received 10,000 by way of advance donation. Of the remaining 29,000 *livres* for Marie-Victoire a sum of 10,000 *livres* was to be paid in two annual instalments of 5,000 before her father's death and 19,000 *livres* after both parents had died.

In accepting their respective fixed sums, René and Marie-Victoire forfeited 'the value of their quota of the rents, rights and seigneurial dues previously abolished and of which the re-establishment may take place in part or in full. As a result, it is explicitly understood that even if this re-establishment should never occur there will be no deduction from the sum of 39,000 at any point in time.' Furthermore, the two siblings had to promise on their honour never to press their elder brother Auguste for a part in his share. They 'formally gave consent that their father and mother make to [Auguste de Bonald] a universal bequest of each and every one of their present and future goods, rights, and shares in favour of the marriage he will be able to contract'.

Auguste de Bonald, then, received a very differently configured share of patrimony in comparison with his brother and sister. To him, the eldest son, passed the estate and château de Vielvayssac and the townhouse in the rue de Bonald, Rodez, together with all the furnishings and effects of those properties, plus all other parental possessions in the form of names, rights, and shares. The marriage mentioned in the 28 November 1801 account was realised, for in that same year Auguste wed Joséphine de Peyrot-Restaurand. This newly wed couple thus began conjugal life in charge of the Bonald family estate, previously the responsibility of Auguste's parents.

Joseph-Raymond and Marie-Régis attached certain conditions to Auguste's share to protect their own way of life in old age. First, they were 'to be lodged, fed, served, and maintained in sickness or in health by their eldest son in the house in which they live [rue de Bonald, Rodez]; and in addition he will pay them annually a pension of 1,000 *livres* of which 600 *livres* for father Bonald and 400 *livres* for his wife dame de Séguret'. Second, 'in the case where the parents would like to live independently [from Auguste and Joséphine], they would have for themselves and for their servants their choice of habitation in suitable apartments in the same house [rue de Bonald, Rodez] with the use of linen, silverware and other furnishings for them to select at their discretion; they would also have the enjoyment of the garden beside the house'. All three children signed up to these arrangements, which in effect marked the retirement of Joseph-Raymond and Marie-Régis as landowners. The parents were to hand over all the deeds and contracts pertaining to the properties and their exploitation to Auguste, who was about to marry Joséphine de

Peyrot-Restaurand, and they promised to assist their successor in taking over the estate 'even to lend him their name for all sales and acquisitions' in future.[24]

The Bonald documents illustrate the interaction between parental control over timing and the heirs' ultimate decisions over the property transferred. Because Joseph-Raymond and Marie-Régis began to plan succession on 1 February 1800, shortly before the law on a disposable share (25 March 1800) and concluded arrangements with their children on 28 November 1801, it may be that their decisions were informed by the disposable share initiative, or by older traditions of the Rouergue, a province on the border between customary law territory and written law territory; the archive does not provide a conclusive answer. In this particular case what survives of the documentation suggests the heirs happily accepted the parental wishes. During the nineteenth century there were other families of nobility in which a parent or parents made early transfer of rights and responsibilities for property to children in arrangements similar to those outlined above for the Bonalds. A case that illustrates how such arrangements could go wrong, and fracture relations between heirs, is found in the archives of the Vacher de Tournemire family.

For the first three decades of the nineteenth century, in a career that spanned from the Consulate to the July Monarchy, Jean-Charles Vacher de Tournemire was an imposing figure in the administration and local politics of the arrondissement of Mauriac (Cantal). He received the title of baron during the Bourbon Restoration and, like his father before him, served as mayor of Escorailles. The office of mayor, although subject to election, stayed within this same family and passed from relative to relative from 1800 to 1865. Whilst consolidating their local political power, the Vacher de Tournemires had gradually augmented their landholdings through alliances with other wealthy families of the Auvergne. Jean-Charles married Mademoiselle de Lollier who bore him three daughters (Emilie, Rose, and Agathe) and two sons (Bernard and Étienne).

In June 1820, Jean-Charles's younger son, the chevalier Étienne Vacher de Tournemire, wed Louise Chasteau. Under the terms negotiated for the marriage contract, Étienne was to receive from his father and mother a preferential legacy (*le préciput*) comprising one-quarter of all the movable and immovable goods that they would leave at their death. The baron de Tournemire's real estate holdings included an *hôtel particulier* with terraces, stables and gardens in the town of Mauriac, plus the château and estate of Tournemire, situated in the communes of Escorailles and Drignac with some land on the mountain of Jacques-Soubs in the commune of Saint Bonnet (Cantal).

Jean-Charles, who was sixty-five years old in 1820 when Étienne married, 'hoped for repose [so] authorised his son to take charge of the household and its affairs [*se mettre à la tête de la maison*], to receive the income and receipts, to manage all the expenses'. It was understood that Étienne must meet the expenses and needs of the extended household, not just the family he would raise with Louise but his parents and siblings as well. This meant keeping the Tournemire family in the honourable state to which it was accustomed, 'living in the town of Mauriac during the winter and in the countryside of Escorailles during the summer, having always at its service many servants and two or three horses for riding or for the carriage'. The annual income from the properties was roughly estimated at 12,000 francs. 'In these circumstances, and out of deference and obedience toward his father, Étienne took over his father's responsibilities for the management and administration of the household.'[25]

Expenses were considerable, soaking up not only the income from Jean-Charles's estate but also the income from a property Étienne and Louise purchased with part of Louise's dowry.[26] When the baron Jean-Charles de Tournemire died a widower on 20 September 1840 (his wife had passed away in 1834) all five children and their spouses gathered to make an inventory of household goods. During this gathering Étienne informed his siblings that their father Jean-Charles had kept locked away in one of his bedroom wardrobes a sum of 4,215 francs in gold coin, distributed between several wallets. Étienne had been invited by his father to see and to count this sum while Jean-Charles was alive. Immediately after Étienne's announcement the wardrobe was opened and the money counted, but 1,500 francs worth was missing along with the wallet that held it. No amount of searching led to its discovery. Arguments then broke out among the siblings who were already divided against one another 'by different circumstances that there is no point recounting'. The tension mounted so much that on 17 November, some eight weeks after their father Jean-Charles's death, Agathe obtained a legal writ of summons against Étienne. It was demanded of Étienne that he furnish a report on the annual household income and receipts since 1820, and he was held responsible for the missing 1,500 francs.

Agathe led the coalition of her two sisters, elder brother, and in-laws against Étienne in 1840. They claimed that the agreement for the 1820 marriage contract, by which Étienne was to receive a preferential legacy (*donation par préciput et hors part*), was invalid and to this end 'the principle of equality in dividing inheritance' was invoked. In response Étienne pointed out that one of the holdings (Fignac) was not suitable for partition because of its mountainous location, far from towns and villages, which meant the land could not readily be sold in small lots. The Tournemire estate in Escorailles, by contrast, could be divided up into lots, but this would be to contradict the formal wishes of their father Jean-Charles to respect the interest of agriculture by avoiding the parcelling of land (*la morcellement*).[27]

There are some clues in the archive to a source of bitterness in this sibling quarrel, and in particular why Agathe should contest Étienne's authority. Six years earlier, on 14 February 1834, a concerned relative wrote to Étienne from Paris:

> Agathe's fate neither can nor should leave you cold and yet you do nothing that might show her you take the least bit of interest. You have left her without a sou and obliged to live by borrowing. You owe her arrears from 1833 and we are now in the second month of 1834 without any funds having been sent. Must she renounce the pension that was promised to her? Do not hope by denying her that to cut her down and force her to return to Auvergne … She no longer wants to return there … She has retired to a convent to live in her own fashion, without pressure, without obligation to anyone: getting up, going to bed, eating, drinking, praying when it suits her. She wants this independence … As to becoming cloistered, she is very disposed to the idea and this would have happened already had the amount of her pension, which is too modest, allowed. She tried and was forced to abandon the plan [so] she looked for a convent where she could afford to live … She is much thinner and I noticed the difference myself. She has scarcely the girth of an orange.[28]

This letter provides tantalising insights into a noblewoman's sense of her own agency within the family, and the motives that might inspire her adult retreat to a convent in the nineteenth century. Girls of noble birth were often educated in convents by nuns to whom the family had to provide proof of nobility and pay a dowry if the girl joined the community permanently.[29] During the nineteenth century France witnessed exponential growth in the numbers of religious orders, especially female ones, which helped the Church to recover from the blows of 1789–91.[30] Christian faith and the conviction of responding to God's call to religious life were no doubt the main reasons noblewomen took the veil. But Agathe's desire for 'independence' and refusal to return to her family in Auvergne illustrates a different set of motivations. It is possible that piety was a factor, for the weight loss referred to in the letter may have been the result of religious fasting; her straitened circumstances probably also made it difficult for her to eat regular meals.[31] From a position of limited economic power, Agathe was protesting against her brother Étienne's control over the household and its finances. For her the convent provided escape from the terrain of subjugation and familial tension.

The two cases of *donation entre vifs* discussed so far point to parental concern about the potential for dispute between siblings, and to latent sibling tensions that escalated into open conflict after parents' death. There is a methodological problem in trying to find answers about family dynamics by enumerating contestations. Records were more often made and kept when disagreement among heirs ended in legal proceedings. A lack of recorded dispute might be interpreted as a sign of acceptance about property division. On the other hand, it might be the case that an unhappy member of the family simply held their tongue rather than challenge a perceived injustice. Techniques for quantitative analysis serve for research questions in which humans or other subjects under study can be represented as numbers. But such methods are less helpful for the history of emotions and family dynamics where we need instead to use the archives differently to try to understand how individuals saw a situation.

Wills and marriage contracts

Although nobles' wills 'governed the money flow between generations', difficulties quickly arise when trying to interpret them for economic information.[32] Nineteenth-century wills often lacked any mention of the financial value of legacies and were written in the hand of the testator then signed and dated (*le testament olographe*). This means that for many nineteenth-century successions it is impossible to attach a monetary estimate to any share. Twentieth-century wills were more likely to be drawn up by a notary and witnessed (*le testament public*) and these do contain financial figures that give insight into families' economic circumstances.

The preponderance of wills is one of the features that make aristocratic successions distinctive compared with successions among the lower classes.[33] Intestacy was common in nineteenth-century France. It predominated in small rural communities such as Marlhes (Loire) where 67 per cent of inhabitants died intestate in 1850–65 and 71 per cent in 1883–98. Urban communities followed a similar trend; in the industrial city of Lille (Nord), where the population increased by 40 per cent from the mid-1850s to the 1870s, the numbers of adults leaving wills declined from 32 per cent to 25 per cent.[34] For a noble, however, not to make a will was exceptional; intestacy ran entirely contrary to the spirit of nobles' education. Conditioned from birth to see themselves as temporary guardians of patrimony that was to be passed on to the next generation, nobles were inclined to see the making of a will as a duty to maintain the reputation of the 'house'.

In marriage contracts, as with wills, we find that aristocratic practices are distinctive when compared with practices among lower classes.[35] A sample of 374 noble marriage contracts (1801–70) from the departments of Cher, Haute-Garonne, Hautes Pyrénées and Eure-et-Loire showed the nineteenth-century nobility's increasing preference for *le régime dotal*. Such contracts gave the husband authority to manage dotal funds and property but specified that neither spouse could dispose of dotal property; upon death that property had to devolve to the heirs. Nobles' preference for *le régime dotal* (chosen in two-thirds of the sampled marriages in the 1860s) was the direct opposite of the national trend in marriage contracts. The norm in France was the community of acquisitions (*la communauté*) that meant spouses' equal sharing of profit or losses from the management of joint fortunes including the dowry. In practice *la communauté* could damage the wife's interests. The *régime dotal*, although it implied a wife's subservience, acted as a brake on risky speculation by her husband.[36]

In her handwritten will of 29 June 1876, Louise de Laurière de Moncaut, marquise de Saint-Exupéry, refers to a legal process under way to end the *communauté* contract between her and her husband, Balthazar-Joseph de Saint-Exupéry. She hoped that a house at 14 cours de la Plateforme, Agen (Lot-et-Garonne) would be attributed to her as a result. There were two surviving children from the marriage: a son Guy who held a diploma in law and a daughter Térésa who was married to the comte Adhémar de Lusignan. No financial figures appear in the marquise's will, but Guy was left his mother's property by preferential legacy and not subject to division (*par préciput et hors part*). He was to exercise his rights as heir over 'the château d'Arasse with all its outbuildings, small and large furnishings (*les meubles et meubles meublants*), silverware of all kinds, linen, jewels, and all titles and papers, all the diverse objects that are found in the buildings of the said château at the time of my death … as well as the surrounding lands and *métairies* in short, everything that comprises my hereditary rights in the said estate'. In the event that the house in Agen was attributed to the marquise, when the annulment of the *communauté* was concluded, then that, too, was to pass to Guy along with everything that the house contained. The marquise concluded her will with exhortations that the two children should stay 'united' and that Guy, 'my heir', should 'uphold the good traditions of his name'.[37]

A more complex example of a nineteenth-century succession can be seen in the Ligne family, whose origins and prestige can be traced back to twelfth-century Hainaut.[38] On 20 May 1880, His Highness Eugène-François-Charles Lamoral, ninth prince de Ligne, d'Amblise, d'Épinoy died leaving a will made out on 24 December 1871 in which he appointed as executor the notary and senator Alphonse-Joseph Hubert, who was also the late prince's intendant and personal adviser. Hubert was under no illusion concerning the challenges of the 'huge and delicate mission' invested in him that required insight to the late prince's intentions, observance of issues arising from the location of properties on both sides of the Franco-Belgian border, and absolute impartiality in establishing the revenues to be received by the heirs in accordance with French law. He had to honour 'the trust of the *père de famille*'. The prince de Ligne had married three times and on each occasion the contract was one of *communauté* for property purchased during the marriage. The prince had children by each of his three wives during the time he was married to them so all of the half-brothers and half-sisters were legitimate heirs. In the succession the first two contracts of *communauté* did not present too many problems, partly because the second marriage had been of short duration. But the prince's third marriage (to Hedwige, princesse Lubomirska) lasted for forty-four years and involved more purchases than the preceding unions.[39]

A first task for the executor was land valuation and here we can see Hubert's painstaking efforts to establish the worth of properties variously located in France and Belgium. Table 2 shows two sets of estimates he prepared for lands on either side of the border. Set A was based on taxable revenue assessed from the cadastre and an official multiplier used by the Belgian government (Hubert noted this was problematic for the lands in France). Set B was based on actual revenue and a calculation to establish annual revenue to the nearest fortieth or 2.5 per cent. Some lands were left off the list (Uccle, Forêt, and some land in Flanders) because the intention was to sell them to pay inheritance taxes and resolve debts.

At the time he finished the provisional land valuation the executor still had before him the task of estimating the worth of the other movable and immovable goods. The prince de Ligne had made a bequest to his third wife Hedwige (who outlived him by fifteen years) that included their *hôtel particulier* in Brussels and half the furniture. Major items that remained, for which the executor had to organise valuation and

Table 2 Land valuation in the succession of the prince de Ligne

Name of property	Extent of lands (hectares, ares, centiares)	Set A valuations (francs)	Set B valuations (francs)
Amblise	303h 37a 23ca	1,750,000.00	1,719,810.19
Antoing	1,022h 13a 26ca	5,620,504.14	5,671,434.03
Beloeil	1,575h 18a 86ca	7,471,208.46	7,204,970.46
Boussu	51h 17a 91ca	265,114.20	260,845.60
Fagnolles	727h 80a 24ca	705,454.34	705,454.34
Gallicie	15,573h 93a 15ca	3,926,391.30	3,926,391.30
Jeumont-Hestrud	1,073h 11a 24ca	2,589,484.23	2,632,229.43
Ligne	181h 71a 22ca	1,139,506.25	1,206,709.25
Montroeul-sur-Haine	105h 68a 97ca	677,138.55	620,529.20
Neuville sous Huy	542h 71a 10ca	1,266,966.00	1,123,434.00
Paris	—	525,000.00	525,000.00
Rumpts	81h 67a	490,091.00	1,094,333.60
Silly	531h 04a 27ca	2,543,959.45	2,650,112.60
Sirault	367h 20a 28ca	1,957,817.00	1,825,520.00
Ville-Pommeroeul	952h 64a 81ca	3,217,313.30	3,262,553.95
Totals	24,657h 10a 09ca	39,708,013.35	39,946,586.94

partition, were the château de Beloeil with its appendages and furniture, the château d'Antoing with its appendages and furniture, and the château de la Neuville with its appendages and furniture. Hubert observed to the heirs: 'Apart from the bequests of some furnishings, on which we are now in agreement, the will only contains one principal clause: one-quarter by preferential legacy of the properties in Belgium and France to prince Louis representing the eldest of the family [the late prince's grandson who became the tenth prince de Ligne, d'Amblise, d'Épinoy] and to prince Charles, too, one-quarter by preferential legacy in half of the estates of Gallicie.'[40]

Twentieth-century successions similarly show how a preferential legacy (*le préciput*) typically given to the eldest male child could be used to keep a certain amount of aristocratic estate outside division, whilst remaining property was divided up following valuation. The château des Bordes in the commune of Pontlevoy (Loir-et-Cher) has been in the hands of the Bodard de La Jacopière family since 1878. Léopold Bodard de La Jacopière (1830–99), mayor of Pontlevoy, left the château to his son Louis Marie Diégo, who in turn left it to his son Jean (1883–1953), and so it has passed down through the direct male line of succession to the owner in 2013.[41]

Jean Bodard de La Jacopière died a widower on 17 November 1953 leaving behind four adult children (Michel, Gaston, Pierre, and Jeanne) from his marriage to Renée Marie Geneviève Yvert de Saint Aubin. Table 3 gives the partition of real estate (*immobilier*) between Jean's four children and shows hectares and acres for land where known. The château des Bordes valued at 4 million francs was left by preferential legacy to Michel, the eldest son. In addition to the château, Michel received a share of *immobilier* valued at 12.5 million francs bringing his total value of *immobilier* to 16.5 million. Each of the other three children received a share of *immobilier* valued at 12.5 million.[42]

Other forms of investment that appear in Jean's succession were shares in real estate and energy companies and bonds from Romania, Yugoslavia, and Serbia. There were membership shares in the Crédit Mutuel Agricole and Union des Coopératives des Associations Agricoles du Loir-et-Cher. All of these movable goods (*mobilier*) together were estimated at 41.23 million francs in total and their partition followed a similar pattern to the *immobilier*. Michel, the eldest, received a part worth just over 13.45 million. His brothers and sister each received a part worth just over 9.25 million.

The Bodard de la Jacopière family can be distinguished from the

Table 3 Real estate in the succession of Jean Bodard de La Jacopière (hectares, ares, centiares, million francs)

	Preferential legacy	Lot 1	Lot 2	Lot 3
Michel	château des Bordes and appendages (13h 74a 86ca) 4 million francs	Farm 'La Basse-cour' (28h 21a 87ca) 3.5 million francs	Farm 'Les Petites Bordes' (65h 17a 73ca) 8 million francs	Woods of Maré (12h 41a 25ca) 1 million francs
Gaston	n/a	Farm 'Les Grands Anglées' (47h 35a 10ca) 5 million francs	Pond 'Sudaie' (81h 24a 43ca) 7.4 million francs	Coppice 'Les Petits Anglées' (1h 37a) 0.1 million francs
Pierre	n/a	Manor of Maré and appendages (2h 84a 82ca) plus land 'La Sablier des Bordes' (3h 34a 82ca) 2 million francs	Farm 'La Patte du Loup' (55h 4a 49ca) 4.5 million francs	Farm 'La Thibau' (61h 30a 27ca) plus woods of Defroc (8h 53a 62 ca) and isolated land parcels 'Vallières les Grandes' (41a 68ca) 6 million francs
Jeanne	n/a	Farm 'Les Petits Anglées' (47h 86a 22ca) 4 million francs	Farm 'Laizerie' (63h 37a 20ca) 7 million francs	Woods of 'Les Anglées' and pond 'Taille des Anglées' (9h 20a 73ca) 1.5 million francs

vast majority of French families in the mid-twentieth century not only by its wealth but also by its size. Four children (born 1918, 1920, 1923, and 1927) was a higher number than most French couples had in the two decades immediately after the First World War when nationally the number of divorces doubled and the birth rate remained low (2.05 being the average number of offspring for French couples in 1935). The Bodard de La Jacopières' strong fertility continued in the next generation born after the Second World War: Michel had four children, Gaston had three children, Pierre had three children, and Jeanne had two children. With many offspring, common for families of the nobility but less so in the French population as a whole, the partition of real estate into lots had unfavourable consequences for the exploitation of land for income.

Childlessness

As sources of historical evidence the wills and correspondence of nobles who did not marry or have children, or who married but produced no offspring, are particularly valuable both for the study of upper-class kin relations and for the study of religion.[43] For centuries the nobility deployed controls on exogamy in order to guard various forms of capital, especially the family name. Many noblewomen, especially eldest daughters, never married because an endogamous match could not be made, and the alternative – to marry a commoner and assume his family's name – was 'unthinkable'.[44] For these single nobles, as well as for married nobles without offspring, lateral kin ties (siblings, nephews and nieces) rather than vertical kin ties (sons and daughters) served for the transmission of property to the next generation.

Testators thought deeply about the relative personal circumstances of those to whom property was to be given. In a codicil to her will dated 19 January 1865 Eléonore de Châteauneuf-Randon, vicomtesse de La Rochnégly, who had no surviving children from her marriage to Charles-Amable de La Rochnégly, explained the basis of her decision-making about the property she apportioned between her nephews and niece.

> I apologise to dear Adhémar [comte de Châteauneuf-Randon] if I have not assigned to him a share equal to that of Adelbert [marquis de Châteauneuf-Randon] and that of Mathilde [wife of Jules Gabriel de Vinols]. He [Adhémar] is not married, has no responsibilities and will always be more at his own leisure. Espérance [vicomte de Châteauneuf-Randon] in spite of his large family is also in a better position. I would have liked to be able to

leave to all the comfortable existence that my heart wished for them since their birth.[45]

Relatives consulted with one another to obtain or to share information on the personal circumstances of legatees. On 15 August 1891, from her convent in Rouen, Blanche de Béarn, Soeur Vincent Supérieure de la Miséricorde, wrote to her brother Gaston de Béarn about amendments made to her will which he had asked her to make: 'I altered my will that, as you know, had been made out in favour of your eldest son alone. What you have told me about the financial position of Jean [their younger brother] has made me change my mind [so that] I am giving an equal share to [Jean's] eldest son ... and to Jean *for his daughters*.'[46]

Unmarried nobles often entered religious orders through the nineteenth and twentieth centuries, just as their ancestors had done since the Middle Ages.[47] These nobles' holy vows to renounce the secular world did not prevent their engagement in legal transactions on property.[48] For historians this opens up questions about the circumstances and proportions in which these religious men and women bequeathed their share of an estate to the Church. As Constance Bouchard has demonstrated, the desire to perpetuate family traditions often lay behind nobles' decisions on medieval bequests to monastic institutions.[49]

An illustration of the manner by which a noble in a religious order might dispose of material wealth gradually, and with control over the timing, is found in the archives of the Ripert d'Alauzier family. Born in Carpentras (Vaucluse) in 1810, Marie-Josephine grew up at the château de Saint Roman near Bedarrides with her brothers, sisters, and parents the marquis and marquise Ripert d'Alauzier. Following her education at Saint Sacrement in Carpentras, Marie-Josephine consulted a Jesuit priest Père Renaud regarding her feelings of a religious vocation. The marquis Ripert d'Alauzier initially opposed his daughter's wish to enter a Carmelite order in Avignon, but he relented and gave permission in September 1832. Marie-Josephine took the veil on 7 December 1832, and was henceforward known by her religious name, Marie-Louise de Sainte Thérèse. After a decade in the Carmelite order she was appointed its prioress at the age of thirty-one. Whilst her father the marquis remained alive he made financial gifts to Marie-Louise de Sainte Thérèse, a few hundred francs at a time. Because she did not wish to keep these sums Marie-Louise de Sainte Thérèse gave them to her Carmelite order. When the marquis died, Marie-Louise de Sainte Thérèse sought permission from her superiors to dispose of what came to her from her father's estate.

A handwritten biography of Marie-Louise de Sainte Thérèse by another Carmelite nun outlines the results of how this noblewoman, between the 1830s and her death in 1885, made the religious order in Avignon the beneficiary of her fortune.

> Thanks to our Mère [Marie-Louise] and to the generosity of her noble family, many important repairs were made in the community and we felt a certain wellbeing after the greatest poverty ... The monastery's church that had previously been only a modest chapel was rebuilt and decorated with many precious things ... [By the 1850s] there remained for Mère Marie-Louise still one great work to do ... it was the complete restoration (the reconstruction) of this monastery that the superiors requested of her. Our Mère Marie-Louise gave a sum of 60,000 francs for the new building of the Lord's house, not to mention the accessories and particular donations that she added afterwards.[50]

Conclusion

In matters of inheritance France's transition from the *ancien régime* to the post-1789 era was full of paradoxes. Faced with the undesirable effects of the law on partible inheritance, including fragmentation of landholdings and increased likelihood of conflict between brothers and sisters, French people from different regions and different social backgrounds responded with strategies and practices reflecting class-based priorities. The results of parents' decision-making can be seen demographically. For example the pattern among nineteenth-century peasant couples was to reduce the numbers of children they had in order to keep smallholdings intact. Continuities in regional and local customs could support parental strategies. For example in the Auvergne parents left the farmhouse (*houstau*) to the child whom they identified was most likely to marry, settle, and perpetuate the family's stake in the land, but on condition that the *houstau* remain a shelter for all the children until they established their own households.[51]

Unlike the common patterns of intestacy and *la communauté* marriage contracts in the nineteenth-century French population as a whole, the patterns among nobility were to make a will and to form marriages based on *le régime dotal*. The birth rate among nobility remained higher than the national average through to the twentieth century because of the imperative to maintain the bloodline and transmit the distinctive aristocratic patrimony of names and titles. A great range of documents in nobles' private archives demonstrate that after the French Revolution, although partible inheritance was a matter nobles had to grapple with, there were ways and means of ensuring it need not be applied in absolute fashion. Nobles' attention to natural differences of birth order and gender acted as a curb on equality. Using a preferential legacy to concentrate a larger share of patrimony in the hands of one child (typically male) was one method to limit the drain on resources caused by fragmentation of an aristocratic estate. Furthermore, the nobility's longstanding strategy of having at least one child enter the Church carried on through the nineteenth century into the twentieth. Noblewomen and noblemen, who often rose to senior influential positions in religious orders, had autonomy to dispose of personal wealth and property in pious donations and charitable action. Benefactions to monastic institutions were made at the donor's discretion and often resembled charitable patterns previously established by medieval or early modern ancestors.

As in the families of Blois-Chartres in the Middle Ages, sentiments of affection were very commonly expressed in the wills and letters of late modern nobles. 'Love of kin' was a common refrain for parents who wished their children to succeed and experience happiness in life. Nevertheless, as we have seen from archival documents, the loving 'inclusive' model of aristocratic family life proposed by Livingstone for the eleventh and twelfth centuries cannot fully capture the spectrum of emotional relations among noble kin in the modern period. Feelings such as anger, resentment, envy and belittlement that were temporarily manifest between siblings could build into longer-term tensions and give rise to acrimonious struggles.

Divisions of inheritance in families of nobility meant that nobles maintained correspondence with non-noble professionals such as notaries and lawyers over many months or years at a time. Exhortations to offspring to uphold 'unity' appear frequently in the closing lines of nobles' wills and in the letters that parents addressed to their children. But parents' desire to prevent legal contests among heirs could be ineffective or ignored when it came to heirs' reactions to wills and the procedures for succession. Inheritance was not necessarily the direct or only cause of friction for there were many causes of disputes. But, as the concept of equality increasingly penetrated the language of the French nation, so it became more difficult in families of nobility to reconcile the collective interests of the 'house' with the individual interests of each member within it.

Notes

1 Duchesse de Sabran-Pontevès, *Bon sang ne peut mentir* (Paris, 1987), p. 306.
2 The couple's total wealth was estimated at 203,000 *assignats* in 1784, dropping to 162,000 *assignats* by 1800. 1 February 1800 in AD Aveyron 71J/12 Fonds de Bonald de Vielvayssac.
3 28 November 1801 in AD Aveyron 71J/12 Fonds de Bonald de Vielvayssac.
4 28 November 1801 (emphasis in original) in AD Aveyron 71J/12 Fonds de Bonald de Vielvayssac.
5 J. Yver, *Égalité entre héritiers et exclusion des enfants dotés: essai de géographie coutumière* (Paris, 1966); R. E. Giesey, 'Rules of inheritance and strategies of mobility in pre-revolutionary France', *American Historical Review* 82 (1977), 271–89; M. H. Darrow, *Revolution in the House: Family, Class, and Inheritance in Southern France, 1775–1825* (Princeton, 1989); G. Hanlon and E. Carruthers, 'Wills, inheritance and the moral order in seventeenth-century Agenais', *Journal of Family History* 15 (1990), 149–61; S. Desan, *The Family on Trial in Revolutionary France* (Berkeley, 2004), pp. 144–5.
6 L. Bourquin, 'Partage noble et droit d'aînesse dans les coutumes du royaume de France à l'époque moderne', *L'Identité nobiliaire: dix siècles de metamorphoses, IX–XIXe siècle* (Le Mans, 1997), pp. 136–65; J.-M. Berton, *Des majorats et substitutions et de la pairie héréditaire* (Paris, 1831), pp. 13–15.
7 P. Nicole, *Substitutions et majorats* (Paris, 1861), pp. 11–14.
8 *Maison de Vassal 987–1987: mémoire du millénaire* (Paris 1987) in AD Lot 40J/1 Fonds de la famille Vassal et familles alliées. The Vassal family had four main branches (Frayssinet, Rignac, Nozac, and La Tourette) of which the eldest branch, represented by Sicard de Vassal, seigneur de Frayssinet, in the thirteenth century, lived in what is now the arrondissement of Gourdon.
9 On dower and dowry see A. Livingstone, *Out of Love for My Kin: Aristocratic Family Life in the Lands of the Loire, 1000–1200* (Ithaca, 2010), ch. 5. Much research on the ninth to the twelfth centuries has been geared toward explaining the 'birth' of nobility and origins of feudalism. G. Duby, *Qu'est-ce que la société féodale?* (Paris, 2002); C. B. Bouchard, 'The origins of the French nobility: a reassessment', *American Historical Review* 86 (1981), 501–32; K. F. Werner, *Naissance de la noblesse, l'essor des élites politiques en Europe* (Paris, 1998); D. Crouch, *The Birth of Nobility: Constructing Aristocracy in England and France, 900–1300* (London, 2005).
10 F. Bluche and P. Durye, *L'Anoblissement par charges avant 1789* (Paris, 1965); R. Descimon and É. Haddad (eds), *Épreuves de noblesse: les expériences nobiliaires de la haute robe parisienne (XVI–XVIII siècle)* (Paris, 2010); É. Haddad, *Fondation et ruine d'une 'maison': histoire sociale des comtes de Belin (1582–1706)* (Limoges, 2009); M. Gerber, *Bastards: Politics, Family, and Law in Early Modern France* (Oxford, 2012); S. Desan and J. Merrick (eds), *Family, Gender, and Law in Early Modern France* (University Park, 2009); J. Hardwick, *Family*

Business: Litigation and the Political Economies of Daily Life in Early Modern France (Oxford, 2009).

11 A. Daumard, *Les Fortunes françaises au XIXe siècle* (Paris, 1973), pp. 257–67; T. Picketty, *Les Hauts Revenus en France au XXe siècle: inégalités et redistributions 1901–1998* (Paris, 2001).

12 G. Duby, *The Chivalrous Society*, translated by C. Postan (Berkeley, 1978); G. Duby, *The Knight, the Lady and the Priest: The Making of Modern Marriage in Medieval France*, translated by B. Bray (New York, 1983); G. Duby, *Medieval Marriage: Two Models from Twelfth-Century France*, translated by E. Forster (Baltimore, 1978).

13 Livingstone, *Out of Love for My Kin*, p. 3.

14 Desan, *The Family on Trial*. For sociological analyses see P. Steiner, 'L'Héritage égalitaire comme dispositive social', *European Journal of Sociology* 46 (2005), 127–49; J. Beckert, 'The "longue durée" of inheritance law: discourses and institutional development in France, Germany and the United States since 1800', *European Journal of Sociology* 48 (2007), 79–120.

15 F. de La Gaulayrie, *Les Majorats depuis le premier Empire jusqu'à nos jours* (Rennes, 1909); J. Descheemaeker, *Les Titres de noblesse en France et dans les pays étrangers* vol. 1 (Paris, 1958), pp. 13–15, 26–7.

16 A. de Dijn, 'Aristocratic liberalism in post-revolutionary France', *Historical Journal* 48 (2005), 661–81.

17 E. C. Macknight, *Aristocratic Families in Republican France, 1870–1940* (Manchester, 2012), ch. 3.

18 Timing was also significant under the *ancien régime*; for example, in the region of the Midi, Roman law had allowed fathers to wait until sons were far into adulthood before emancipating them. Desan, *The Family on Trial*, pp. 144–5. On transmission of property during parents' lifetime in the Middle Ages see Livingstone, *Out of Love for My Kin*, pp. 102–3.

19 J. R. Lehning, *The Peasants of Marlhes: Economic Development and Family Organization in Nineteenth-Century France* (London, 1980), ch. 8. See also J. Shaffer, *Family and Farm: Agrarian Change and Household Organization in the Loire Valley, 1500–1900* (Albany, 1982). A helpful glossary of the legal terms can be found in *Héritage et Succession: Notre Temps* (Montrouge, 2014), pp. 118–20.

20 Lehning, *The Peasants of Marlhes*, p. 117; T. Leopold and T. Schneider, 'Family events and the timing of intergenerational transfers', *Social Forces* 90 (2011), 595–616.

21 J. F. Traer, 'The French family court', *History* 59 (June 1974), 211–28; R. Phillips, *Family Breakdown in Late Eighteenth-Century France: Divorces in Rouen, 1792–1803* (Oxford, 1980), pp. 17–33; S. Desan, '"War between brothers and sisters": inheritance law and gender politics in revolutionary France', *French Historical Studies* 20 (1997), 597–634.

22 A. Laferrère, 'Inheritances and gifts Inter Vivos: the use of the disposable

portion for the purpose of unequal division between siblings in France', *Continuity and Change* 7 (1992), 377–404.

23 28 November 1801 in AD Aveyron 71J/12 Fonds de Bonald de Vielvayssac.

24 28 November 1801 in AD Aveyron 71J/12 Fonds de Bonald de Vielvayssac.

25 'Mémoire' in AD Cantal 19J/44 Fonds Vacher de Tournemire.

26 Étienne and Louise had four daughters who were educated at boarding schools first in Clermont-Ferrand then Paris. There were dowries to pay for the sisters (21,000 francs in the case of Emilie's marriage to Monsieur Cabanes). Bernard, the eldest son, was in the army. For the household accounts and loans see 19J/45–7 Fonds Vacher de Tournemire. On Bernard see 19J/48 Fonds Vacher de Tournemire.

27 'Mémoire' in AD Cantal 19J/44 Fonds Vacher de Tournemire.

28 14 February 1834 in AD Cantal 19J/44 Fonds Vacher de Tournemire.

29 Desan, *The Family on Trial*, pp. 31–3, 113.

30 C. Langlois, *Le Catholicisme au féminin: les congrégations françaises à supérieure générale au XIXe siècle* (Paris, 1984).

31 On religious women fasting see P. Kilroy, *The Society of the Sacred Heart in Nineteenth-Century France, 1800–1865* (Cork, 2012), pp. 173–4, 184–5.

32 D. Higgs, *Nobles in Nineteenth-Century France: The Practice of Inegalitarianism* (Baltimore, 1987), pp. 199–201.

33 On the significance of class see J. Goody, E. P. Thompson, and J. Thirsk (eds), *Family and Inheritance in Western Europe, 1200–1800* (Cambridge, 1976); J. Addy, *Death, Money and the Vultures: Inheritance and Avarice, 1660–1750* (London, 1992); J. Finch, L. Hayes, J. Mason, J. Masson, and L. Wallis, *Wills, Inheritance and Families* (Oxford, 1996).

34 Lehning, *The Peasants of Marlhes*, pp. 120–1; F.-P. Codaccioni, *De l'inégalité sociale dans une grande ville industrielle: le drame de Lille de 1850 à 1914* (Lille, 1976); A. Owens, 'Property, will making and estate disposal in an industrial town, 1800–1857' in J. Stobart and A. Owen (eds), *Urban Fortunes: Property and Inheritance in the Town, 1700–1900* (Aldershot, 2000), ch. 4.

35 On marriage contracts and class in England, America, and Canada see E. Spring, *Law, Land and Family: Aristocratic Inheritance in England 1300–1800* (Chapel Hill, 1990); J. Habbakuk, *Marriage, Debt and the Estates System: English Landownership* (Oxford, 1994); T. Stretton and K. Kesslering, *Married Women and the Law: Coverture in England and the Common Law World* (Montreal, 2014); N. Basch, *In the Eyes of the Law: Women, Marriage and Property in Nineteenth-Century New York* (Ithaca, 1982); M. Salmon, *Women and the Law of Property in Early America* (Chapel Hill, 1986); C. B. Backhouse, 'Married women's property law in nineteenth-century Canada', *Law and History Review* 6 (1988), 211–57. On Italy and Scandinavia see P. Macry, *Ottocento: famiglia, élites e patrimoni a Napoli* (Torino, 1988); M. Ågren and A. Erickson (eds), *The Marital Economy in Scandinavia and Britain 1400–1900* (Aldershot, 2005).

36 Higgs, *Nobles*, pp. 199–201; Lehning, *The Peasants of Marlhes*, pp. 125–6.

37 'Testament olographe' in AD Lot-et-Garonne 83J/41 Fonds du château d'Arasse.

38 In 1923, by Belgian decree, members of the direct line of succession from the 9th prince de Ligne were accorded the right to be known as 'Highness' and authorised to continue to carry the titles of prince d'Amblise (1608) et d'Epinoy (1592). The *Almanach de Gotha* contains historical details of the house of Ligne.

39 'Rapport' in AD Nord 26J (E2508)/3 Papiers de la famille de Croÿ. This document is in the Croÿ family papers owing to marital connection between the Ligne and Croÿ families.

40 'Rapport' in AD Nord 26J (E2508)/3 Papiers de la famille de Croÿ.

41 The Bodard de La Jacopière family became owners of the château des Bordes through marriage. In 1878 Guillaume Théodat de Belot left the château to his daughter Pauline de Belot who was the second wife of Léopold Bodard de La Jacopière. When the archive was classed in 2013 the owner was Léopold's great-great-grandson, Xavier Bodard de La Jacopière born in Pontlevoy in 1948. AD Loir-et-Cher 113J Fonds du château des Bordes.

42 AD Loir-et-Cher 113J/42 Fonds du château des Bordes.

43 On the property of single persons and widows in other contexts see O. Hufton, 'Women without men: widows and spinsters in Britain and France in the eighteenth century', *Journal of Family History* 9 (1984), 355–76; M. Anderson, 'The social position of spinsters in mid-Victorian Britain', *Journal of Family History* 9 (1984), 337–93; B. B. Diefendorf, 'Women and property in ancien régime France: theory and practice in Dauphiné and Paris' in J. Brewer and S. Staves (eds), *Early Modern Conceptions of Property* (London, 1995) pp. 170–93; D. R. Green, 'Independent women, wealth and wills in nineteenth-century London' in Stobart and Owens (eds), *Urban Fortunes*, ch. 9; M. Lamarche Marrese, *A Woman's Kingdom: Noblewomen and the Control of Property in Russia, 1700–1861* (Ithaca, 2002); A. Schmidt, 'Generous provisions or legitimate shares? Widows and the transfer of property in seventeenth-century Holland', *History of the Family* 15 (2010), 13–24.

44 Demographic research shows that intermarriage between nobles and haut bourgeois in post-revolutionary France remained limited. C. Grange, *Les Gens du Bottin Mondain: y être c'est en être* (Paris, 1996), pp. 104, 376; M. de Saint Martin, 'Les stratégies matrimoniales dans l'aristocratie', *Actes de la Recherche en Sciences Sociales* 59 (1985), 74–7; D. Merllié and J.-Y. Cousquer, 'Mariage et relations familiales dans l'aristocratie rurale: deux entretiens', *Actes de la Recherche en Sciences Sociales* 31 (1980), 22–34.

45 'Codicile' 19 January 1865 in AD Haute-Loire 24J/6 Archives Langlade du Chayla.

46 15 August 1891 in AD Charente J1084 Fonds Galard, Brassac, Béarn, Chalais.

47 In rare cases nobles who were married joined religious orders. See E. C.

Macknight, 'In memory of myriad selves: the baronne Mathilde de Mackau (1837–1886)', *Magistra* 12 (2006), 46–72.

48 Livingstone, *Out of Love for My Kin*, pp. 110, 114, 136–7, 189–91; A. Livingstone, 'Brother monk: monks and their family in the Chartrain, 1000–1200' in D. Blanks, M. Frassetto, and A. Livingstone (eds), *Medieval Monks and Their World: Ideas and Realities* (Leuven, 2006), pp. 93–118; J. Baker, 'Female monasticism and family strategy: the Guises and Saint Pierre de Reims', *Sixteenth-Century Journal* 28 (1997), 1091–108.

49 C. Bouchard, *Sword, Miter, and Cloister: Nobility and the Church* (Ithaca, 1987), pp. 130–49.

50 'La Révérende Mère Marie-Louise de Sainte Thérèse' in AD Vaucluse 43J/9 Fonds Ripert d'Alauzier. Bequests to the Church feature prominently in the wills of married Catholic nobles as well as unmarried ones. C. Biquard, 'Piété et foi dans le Faubourg Saint-Germain au XIXe siècle', *Histoire, économie et société* (1993), 299–318.

51 Lehning, *The Peasants of Marlhes*, p. 115; P. McPhee, *A Social History of France 1789–1914* 2 ed. (New York, 2004), p. 104.

3

———

Adoption for transmission

The beneficiary of the majorat, the first-born son, belongs to the land.[1]

Over the centuries in Europe and other parts of the world numerous bloodlines of nobility have ceased to exist when the last member of a family passes away. In Halbwachs's view these extinctions hold far-reaching ramifications for society and for historical memory. 'Names and titles evoke the past of families, the geographical location of their belongings, their personal relations with other noble families, and their proximity to princes and to the court ... When a noble family dies out a tradition dies along with it; part of history falls into oblivion.'[2] The psychological effects created by class in nobles' responses to the risk of extinction were bound up with the understanding of names and titles as 'a spiritual and inalienable inheritance'. These forms of symbolic capital received from ancestors were inextricably linked with collective memories.[3] The mnemonic associations between names and events from the past were passed on through oral and literary traditions of story telling. Following ideas that in the West stretch back to Aristotle, 'nobility' connotes illustrious ancestors, virtue, and sustained excellence of lineage.[4]

For nobles, names were the most crucial element of this intangible patrimony that connected the living members of families to preceding generations.[5] In order to preserve names it has been a tradition among the nobility to give sons and daughters the same *prénom* as a distinguished ancestor.[6] The tradition was practised in France among the *ancienne noblesse* before 1789 and taken up as well by Napoleonic *titrés* in the nineteenth century. An ancestral *prénom*, normally incorporated within a hyphenated series of *prénoms*, could be in either masculine or feminine form. For example, the *prénom* Victurnien or Victurnienne has consistently been given to offspring in the Mortemart line of the noble house of Rochechouart. It thus appears in the full name of Marie-Adrienne-Anne-Victurnienne de Mortemart, who upon marriage took the surname of her husband and corresponding title, the duchesse d'Uzès.[7] Similarly the *prénom* Gonzague is given to offspring in the noble house of Broglie; the *prénom* Urbain in the noble house of Keroüartz; the *prénom* Sosthène in the noble house of La Rochefoucauld and so on. These *prénoms* link with familial legend and may refer to a saint, for example Saint Elzéar (1285–1323) and his wife the Blessed Delphine in the house of Sabran-Pontevès.[8] One of the sons of prince Joachim Murat I and Caroline Bonaparte was given the *prénom* Achille because his uncle, Emperor Napoleon I, wanted the child's name to be drawn from ancient mythology; Joachim and Achille are the *prénoms* passed down in the elder and cadet branches respectively of the house of Murat.[9]

Naming serves a linguistic function to link individual remembrances into the common framework of collective memory. In a family, when one sibling utters the proper name of their brother or sister, the name itself invokes a rich pattern of prior knowledge and relationships, 'locating' the named person in the kinship structure.[10] As with *prénoms*, there has been the same concern for strategic preservation of surnames among the French nobility, which explains why married noblewomen often incorporated the surname they were given at birth, as well as their husband's surname, in their signature on documents. Noblewomen's use of natal names shows they maintained their own identity and the maternal line mattered in families.[11] Some nobles' marriage contracts included conditions on naming designed to ensure rehabilitation of a surname at risk of disappearing because there was no male to carry it on.[12]

Titles were of secondary importance to nobles in France. The majority of French nobility was untitled (*la noblesse simple*) and there was no relationship between the bearing of a title and the antiquity of the lineage. Originally a title of nobility was a rank attached to certain pieces of land. Titles were a mark of recognition from a sovereign or pope for some form of service performed by a noble, often on the battlefield or in politics. 'All their value resided in the number and quality of glorious or honourable recollections that sustained the nobles and which they perpetuated. One could hence not think of a title without calling to mind those who were first in attaining it. They had stamped this title with their imprint and had possessed it before its current bearer.'[13]

The numbers and density of nobles have varied considerably between European countries. So too the legal criteria for the heritability of noble status, and the specific procedures for formal transmission and recording of titles, have evolved over time through changes of sovereignty, governance, and territorial boundaries. Natural extinction, where there is a failure to continue biological reproduction and the last member of a house dies, is only one factor that has led the number of noble families to fall. When the sovereign within a country no longer performs acts of ennoblement there is a faster rate of demographic decline. 'Without new creations no nobility can remain dynamic or numerous in the long term.'[14]

In France transmission of nobility is virtually always restricted to the male bloodline. As a tiny fraction of the French population, which saw itself as a 'race', the nobility in the nineteenth and twentieth centuries pursued family strategies to try to promote a high birth rate. Noblemen sought a young fertile woman for marriage in the hope of quickly producing lots of sons. The hire of a wetnurse to feed a newborn meant the father and mother of that child could recommence conjugal sex without the mother's breastfeeding causing delay to a further pregnancy. Among twentieth-century nobles pronatal strategies were perceived to help the numbers of noble individuals in France to remain comparatively steady, which to their minds offered some compensation for the fact that the numbers of families fell.[15]

Nobiliary law regulates how titles of nobility may be transmitted. An individual must apply to the Garde des Sceaux for verification of the title in order to include it next to the name on official documents. Only possessors of an *arrêté d'investiture* may use the title, and the *arrêté* is strictly personal. Twentieth-century investitures for titles of the First Empire include: the duc Régnier de Massa (1949), the baron Suisse de Saint-Claire (1962), the comte Daru (1971), the comte Portalis (1984), and the baron Pinoteau (1993). Investitures for *ancien régime* titles include: the marquis de Terraube (1986), the marquis de la Charce (1993), the vicomte de Quincy (1993), the duc de Mortemart (1995), and the duc de Lorge (1999). Only three ducal titles of the Empire exist in the 2000s: Montebello (originally awarded to Maréchal Lannes in 1808), Rivoli (originally awarded to Maréchal Massena in 1808) and Albufera (originally awarded to Maréchal Suchet in 1812).[16]

In the history of French law, there have been two mechanisms – substitution and adoption – that allowed nobles to transmit a name and title when there was no biological heir. Analysis of these mechanisms allows for more long-term benefits from the French Revolution for the nobility to come into focus. The innovation of a law on adoption, introduced after the legislators abolished substitution in 1792, was profoundly significant for the nobility for it provided a route for transmission of names and titles that would otherwise have been eliminated. As with the revolutionary divorce law, and the possibilities for buying property sold as *biens nationaux*, nobles adjusted to the changing legal landscape and took advantage where they saw it. Adoption was a major advantage for the nobility built into family strategies when needed.

This chapter adds further struts to the bridge that connects the pre-1789 and post-1789 periods in modern French history. The subject of adoption for transmission among nobility links with other subjects such as illegitimacy and kinship treated in the historical literature on families, gender and law in early modern France.[17] It also links with the historical literature on masculinity and fatherhood in the France of the nineteenth and twentieth centuries.[18] Politics and culture intersect with the social and legal history because of the significance of names and titles in social frameworks of collective memory. In modern French history the best-known example of a person whose name is connected with a tradition is Napoleon Bonaparte, who 'became a role model for successive generations', 'a legend, a figure of mythical proportions'.[19] It is not surprising that we should find the *prénoms* Napoléon or Napoléone incorporated within the names of children in families with attachment to the political and cultural heritage of Empire.

Substitution

Substitution was a legal mechanism for transmitting property that nobles relied upon prior to 1789, at least in the territories of France where written law applied. When a nobleman had no child to receive the inheritance another person was identified as a substitute heir. In territories that followed customary law substitution was not permitted, although Brittany was unusual because in that province a legislative exception was made in favour of substitution for the noblemen Rohan and Rieux who descended from the *princes de Bretagne*.[20]

Key to the system of substitution is the notion of *parenté* – that is, the relationship between two individuals in a family where proximity is determined by degree. Measurement of *parenté* operates in direct line (known as *l'échelle simple*) or in collateral line (known as *l'échelle double*) and 'each generation is called a degree'. To give some examples: a father-and-son relationship is one degree of *parenté*, a grandfather-and-grandson relationship is two degrees, and an uncle-and-nephew relationship is three degrees.[21]

The ordinance of Orléans in January 1560, issued by the king at the request of the Estates General, had stipulated that, in the future, two degrees of separation were the limit for a substitution. Because this ordinance left open the issue of what limit applied to a pre-1560 substitution, a further ruling in the ordinance of Moulins in February 1566 reaffirmed two degrees of separation in the future and made four degrees of separation the limit for subsitutions prior to 1560. The Daguesseau ordinance of August 1747 confirmed two degrees of separation as the limit.[22] In practice this last ruling meant that a name and title of nobility could be passed by substitution from brother to brother (two degrees of *parenté*), for example, but not from first cousin to first cousin (four degrees).

Transmission by substitution had a fiduciary aspect in law; that is to say, the property was considered as held 'in trust' so that the 'trustee' in one generation had an obligation to conserve and to transmit the property to the next trustee. Substitution *simple* was a transmission that occurred once only between one *fiduciaire* (the giver) and one *fidéicommissaire* (the receiver). Substitution *perpétuelle* was meant to continue in perpetuity so that a name and title passed from one trustee to the next until the extinction of males. Letters patent were registered with the parlements. Substitution for *duché-pairies* under the *ancien régime* was perpetual and if there were no remaining male descendants in the noble house then daughters became eligible (a title that devolved by substitution to a female was said to have fallen *en quenouilles*). Ducal houses such as the Rohan, Chabannes, and Luynes are recorded as having substitution *perpétuelle* and the legal terms that applied were set out in an edict of 21 May 1711.[23]

Early modern evolutions in substitution occurred because of two interrelated debates: first, about the 'quality' or 'authenticity' of the nobility and, second, about the rules of inheritance and how those rules applied to illegitimate children. Since the sixteenth century *la noblesse d'épée* had staunchly defended heredity and racial purity. The defensiveness was a sign of anxiety about *mésalliances* and about the rising status and wealth of *la noblesse de robe*. Gilles-André de la Roque wrote in a treatise on nobility: 'the mixture of a commoner's blood always taints a noble family'. The Edict on the Taille (1600) excluded bastards from nobility. The Bourges versus Roussel case (1656) established limits on the amount of property extramarital offspring could inherit from parents.[24]

Illegitimacy was seen as a source of shame and bastards could be identified as such by their arms in some cases.[25]

The National Convention abolished substitution by the law of 14 September 1792. In the 1804 Civil Code (article 896) 'substitutions are prohibited'. Yet the rule of law was not quite that straightforward because, in practice, exceptions were allowed in certain narrowly defined circumstances. Substitution was brought back in during the Bourbon Restoration but the criteria imposed in the law of 17 May 1826 meant its use was restricted. In the nineteenth and twentieth centuries, substitution *fidéicommissaire* continued to operate in extremely rare cases in France as permitted by the Civil Code (article 896 note 2 and article 897).[26]

From substitution to adoption

As the technicalities of substitution became increasingly difficult to navigate, let alone to reconcile with the general prohibition stated in the Civil Code, nineteenth-century nobles began to use instead the second mechanism of adoption. There were historical precedents for adoption by nobles and not only within France. In early modern Poland-Lithuania, groups of noble families had formed clans and shared a common coat of arms that gave to each clan a unifying focus of identity. 'Adoption into a clan remained a way into the nobility until the sixteenth century'.[27]

There had been few legally recognised adoptions in France since the sixteenth century because a change in social attitudes meant the practice fell into disuse; adoption became perceived as 'unnatural' and contrary to the Christian faith. Even though childlessness was common and there was a high rate of child mortality the disinclination of couples to adopt, rather than to accept 'God's will', was linked to fear of investigation into reasons for a barren marriage as well as to practical concerns about succession. Jurists acknowledged that adoption had operated in ancient Rome and during the early Middle Ages but from the 1500s 'the institution was no longer commensurate with the structure and goals of the early modern family'.[28]

The idea for a law on adoption when it was introduced to legislative debates during the French Revolution opened up to all classes in society the prospect of a new route for transferring property from one generation to the next. But its implications were also understood far more broadly in terms of social justice, part of radical change 'to break with the monarchical and aristocratic past'.[29] On 18 January 1792 adoption was welcomed in principle and a committee was tasked with examining proposals for legislation in more detail. Cambacérès, a jurist from a *noblesse de robe* family of Montpellier, presented various projects for a law to the Convention in 1793. On 6 December 1794 a decree was issued confirming that adopted children were recognised as legitimate heirs.[30] In the context of the 1790s the merits of adoption were proclaimed in terms of challenging social inequalities. 'Those among the old nobility who cherish the New Constitution, if they wish to adopt children, let them do so without regard for social class. A citizen holding a one-time illustrious name could then give it to the son of an artisan or merchant,' wrote Madame de Brulart, ex-governess of the Dauphin.[31]

Adoption of minors was not acceptable to the Convention because of the value placed on individual liberty. In the France of the 1790s it was understood to be the adoptee's right 'to choose'.[32] This meant the adoptee had to have reached the age of majority and give their consent to be adopted – it was not a decision that could be taken by anyone else on their behalf. The same scruples of legislators applied in the debates leading to the Civil Code of 1804. Official *tutelle* of a minor (discussed in Chapter 4) could be changed to a relationship of adoption only when the person under *tutelle* attained majority and if they gave consent.

By the early 1800s the tone of legislators' discussions on adoption had become more cautious and conservative; indeed in the initial drafts of the Civil Code adoption was not even included. Berlier reintroduced it in 1803. The availability of adoption was restricted in the 1804 Civil Code, on the adopter side, to infirm bachelors or couples aged over fifty and without children. There was a minimum age of twenty-five years for a female adoptee and a minimum age of thirty years for a male adoptee; adoptees had to be single and without children of their own.[33]

Legislation on adoption, and the interconnections set up thereby with other areas of civil law, had consequences for the nobility that were at once demographic, social, and cultural. Nicholas Paul argues that story telling among nobility of the Middle Ages was 'a continuous conversation between and about members of a family that helped to define that family's identity and to inform the behaviour and decisions of its members over the course of succeeding generations'.[34] Adoption could be seen as a disruptive act to an identity based on blood lineage, 'unnatural' and against Christian belief to seventeenth-century eyes. Nineteenth-century nobles therefore had to work out a strategy for incorporating a new member by act of adoption without destabilising the family's identity.

One option was to build a narrative around the adoptee, and an example of that in practice will be explored later in the chapter using an archival case study. The alternative option was to create a pact of silence on the background to the adoption, and we will see examples of that too. Tactical use of silence in a noble family could be extremely powerful and it was used in various circumstances involving the binary of honour and shame.[35] Silence on an adoptee's biological origins is discouraged by psychologists and in France there was no way of 'hermetically sealing' the secret that a person was adopted because the act of adoption had to be legally registered.[36]

Imperial models

Scholars have argued that Emperor Napoleon I's own personal and family circumstances help to explain why adoption was retained in the Civil Code of 1804. During his marriage to his first wife, Joséphine, Napoleon I did not father any children by her. Joséphine already had two children (Eugène and Hortense) who were the offspring resulting from marriage to her first husband Alexandre de Beauharnais.[37] In May 1805 Joséphine was crowned queen of Italy and Napoleon I made his Eugène de Beauharnais his own viceroy. Then, on visit to Milan 1807, Napoleon I accorded Eugène the title of prince of Venice. The emperor's adoption of Eugène sealed the special quality of this relationship. Napoleon I addressed Eugène as '*mon fils*' in letters. Engravings with a caption to explain the image of adoption show Napoleon I with Eugène, and Eugène is depicted paying homage to the emperor. Another element in the Bonaparte family history is Napoleon I's adoption of Stéphanie de Beauharnais (a niece of Joséphine) on 2 March 1806. This adoption was undertaken in the context of arranging Stéphanie's marriage with Crown Prince Charles Frederick of Baden. By adopting Stéphanie, Napoleon I made her a princesse of France and thereby raised her aristocratic rank to match that of the bridegroom.[38]

Once incorporated into the Civil Code, the advantages of adoption specific to nobility can next be seen in Napoleon I's decree on the *majorat* of 1 March 1808. By this decree a person to whom the emperor granted a nobiliary title had to own property that would bring an income appropriate to his status. That title and associated property were transmissible to a male heir in the form of hereditary entail, known as the *majorat*.[39] In the history of law the origins of the *majorat* can be traced back to fourteenth-century Spain.[40] The 1808 decree on the *majorat* explicitly mentions adoption as one of the routes available for noblemen to honour primogeniture. Article 2 on ducal titles contains the relevant phrase which was repeated elsewhere in the decree for other nobiliary titles: 'This title and this *majorat* will be transmissible to direct and legitimate descendants, natural or adoptive, from male to male by order of primogeniture.'[41]

A key point then about the functioning of the *majorat* lies in the link it established between intangible patrimony (name and title) and tangible patrimony (land or *rentes* or usually both of these combined in the entail). During the Bourbon Restoration an ordinance of 10 February 1824 stipulated that if the founder of the *majorat* died before the necessary entailment of the property had been completed then the hereditary transmission would be cancelled. Another ordinance of 10 October 1828 increased the bureaucratic stringency. Failure to complete the formalities of entailment within six months of the title being granted would risk its loss.[42]

In the France of the 1820s members of the *ancienne noblesse* were preoccupied about possession of the documents pertaining to titles.[43] The problem for them was that nobility of 'extraction' (dating back to 'time immemorial') did not necessarily mean there was a document in existence to prove it. Correspondence in *archives privées* reveals the frustration of those nobles whose attempts to 'prove' their status were going to succeed only if they could furnish documentation that had been destroyed or lost. One soldier in 1820 battered away trying to convince the *référendaires au Sceau* of his right to be known as a *chevalier*. Misery lay in the knowledge that he had on paper less evidence of nobility than a commoner awarded a nobiliary title by Napoleon.[44]

When David Higgs made his archival study of social mobility and the *majorats-sur-demande* there was a perplexing issue left unresolved in the mind of the historian. 'More curious is the large group of bachelors (forty-two or almost fifteen per cent of the total) who went to the trouble of setting up majorats.'[45] The answer to that particular puzzle springs out when the study of *majorats* is brought together with the study of adoption and illegitimate births.

Among the eighty-two adoption cases from Paris that Kristine Elizabeth Gager uncovered for the period 1540–1690, there was one 'outstanding case' from 1634 that 'dramatically highlights the possibility for upward social mobility through adoption'. Charles de Pelerin, who served in the court of the duchesse d'Angoulême, travelled to Paris to sign a contract by which he adopted Henry Barbier, the son of a master printer Jean Barbier and Jean's wife Jehanne. Pelerin pledged to make a will in order to transmit his property to Henry 'just as he would do for his own heir'. Gager notes that there is no record of any payment made by Charles

de Pelerin to the couple in Paris or any further information available
to explain this 'striking exception'. Pelerin's act broke with ideas about
'the centrality of the bloodline for the nobility and the general prejudice
against adoption harboured by the upper classes' in seventeenth-century
France.[46]

Adoptions in the nineteenth century

Some historians have argued that in the sixteenth century when the
renewed focus on bloodline emerged among *la noblesse d'épée* earlier
medieval conceptions of nobility, which had emphasised military prowess
and other virtous actions, were overtaken by concern for pedigree.[47]
Where we find a renewal of discourses about racial purity, but this time
combined with notions of military honour 'in the blood', is right at the
end of the nineteenth century. It is not that pedigree ever disappeared
from nobles' concerns. Rather, an accumulation of factors, including
France's defeat in the Franco-Prussian War, triggered a resurgence of
alarm in the cultural climate of the 1880s and 1890s when there were
widespread fears about depopulation and degeneracy.[48] By then, however,
the option to adopt was already embedded into nobles' family strategies.

'From the moment that a family is augmented by a new member it
reserves a place for him or her in its thought. Whether this new member
enters by birth, marriage, or adoption, the family marks this event with
a date and notes the circumstances under which it has happened.'[49]
Halbwachs's words about the entry of a 'new member' into a family have
a literal application in registration of births and court decisions about
adoption. Similarly when a person changes their name or when transmission of a nobiliary title occurs in France there is documentation that
marks the date and circumstances. The Archives du Sceau is the repository for this documentation.[50]

Table 4 contains thirty-four adoption cases among the nobility in
nineteenth-century France which show a variety of ways in which a
name and a title could be passed on. These thirty-four cases are the
total number of adoptions by nobles mentioned in the vicomte Albert
Révérend's book on titles and ennoblement in the nineteenth century; the
cases encompass all of the different 'types' of nobility known in France.[51]
In the majority of cases (around three-quarters) adoption involved
adding a new layer of relationship between adopter and adoptee on to
an existing familial relationship, continuing the principles of *parenté*
that had informed substitution. Transmission of a name and title from

Table 4 Adoptions in the nineteenth century

Name of adopter	Name of adoptee	Pre-existing kin relationship	Transmission of title (where applicable)
1. baron Louis Alexander Agis de Saint Denis	Marie-Antoine-Léon Mallard de La Varende	maternal uncle to nephew	baron Agis de Saint-Denis by ordonnance 9 July 1841, title and majorat transmission confirmed by arrêté ministériel 23 May 1851
2. baron Jacob-Derk-Burchard-Anne Van Heeckeren	Georges-Charles d'Anthès		baron van Heeckeren (Dutch title authorised in France) by letters patent 2 September 1843
3. comte Colchen	Christine Colchen	grandfather to grandson (the son of adopted daughter Christine)	baron Baudon de Mony-Colchen by letters patent 27 December 1843, then comte Baudon de Mony-Colchen by letters patent 7 May 1870 for Christine's son, Charles-Victor-Auguste Baudon de Mony
4. général comte Louis Liger-Belair	Louis-Charles Bocquillon	maternal uncle to nephew	comte Bocquillon-Ligair-Belair by letters patent 2 July 1836
5. baron Nicolas Seillière	Florentin-Ernest Bordères-Seillière		baron Seillière by letters patent 22 June 1846
6. vice-amiral comte Willaumez	Louis-Edouard Bouet		comte Bouet-Willaumez by letters patent 8 September 1845
7. général baron Christiani	Jacques-Michel-Oscar Chevreau	stepfather to stepson	baron Chevreau-Christiani by letters patent 25 June 1840

Table 4 *continued*

Name of adopter	Name of adoptee	Pre-existing kin relationship	Transmission of title (where applicable)
8. baron Anne-Elie-Pierre-Jean Commaille	five children by mademoiselle Lepez (the baron had no children by his wife Wilhelmine-Zisca-Eudoxie-Ghislaine de Brancas)		
9. comte Achille-Jean-Louis-Hippolye Tourteau de Septeuil	Achille-Armand Delaroche		comte Delaroche-Tourteau de Septeuil by letters patent 7 January 1843 and decision of the Conseil du Sceau de France 1 August 1870
10. baron Gabriel-Guillaume-Gustave Pavée de Vendeuvre	Jules-Louis-Marie-Florent-Ernest Evain	maternal uncle to nephew	baron Evain-Pavée de Vendeuvre by arrêté ministériel 16 October 1873
11. général comte Pierre-Augustin Hulin	Henri Hulin	paternal uncle to nephew	comte Hulin by letters patent 28 November 1844
12. marquis Charles-Louis Huguet de Sémonville	Louis-Désiré de Montholon	stepfather to stepson	marquis de Sémonville by letters patent 14 August 1829, title transmission confirmed by arrêté ministériel 30 July 1840
13. baron Pierre Mourier	Pierre-Léon Chameau (authorised to change surname to Mourier)	great-uncle to great-nephew	baron Mourier by letters patent 9 November 1841, title transmission confirmed by letters patent 30 April 1845
14. maréchal de camp baron Jean-Baptiste-Nicolas Nicolas	Jean-Charles-Valric Nicolas-Nicolas	paternal uncle to nephew	baron Nicolas by letters patent 10 August 1842, confirmed by arrêté ministériel 7 September 1854

15. duc Étienne-Denis Pasquier	Edme-Armand-Gaston d'Audiffret	great-uncle to great-nephew	duc Pasquier by letters patent 3 February 1845
16. lieutenant-général vicomte Pierre-Léon-François Paultre de La Motte	Pierre-Charles-Amédée Paultre de La Vernée	paternal uncle to nephew	vicomte Paultre de La Vernée de La Motte by letters patent 19 February 1845
17. marquis Louis-Hyacinthe-Henri d'Alphonse	Marie-Jean-Alfred de Serres	'uncle' to nephew (that is, nephew of the adopter's wife)	marquis d'Alphonse by letters patent 2 August 1865
18. comte Jules-Camille Bouquet d'Espagny	Jacques-Auguste-Henri de Laire-Bouquet d'Espagny	paternal uncle to nephew	comte Bouquet d'Espagny by letters patent 4 May 1870
19. Philippe de Meyronnet-Saint-Marc	Philippe-Émilien de Boyer de Fonscolombe	maternal uncle to nephew	
20. général baron Gabriel-Henry Chatry de La Fosse	Henry-Gabriel Voirel (authorised to change surname to Chatry de La Fosse)	grandfather to grandson (the son of adopted son)	baron Chatry de La Fosse by letters patent 9 June 1868, confirmed by arrêté ministériel 15 July 1892
21. marquis Jacques-Joseph-Guillaume Dalon	Henri-Joseph-Marie de Rolland	maternal uncle to nephew	marquis de Dalon by décret du Président de la République 5 November 1874
22. comte Auguste-Michel-Étienne Regnault de Saint-Jean-d'Angély	Edmond Davillier	father-in-law to son-in-law (the husband of step-daughter Flore-Angélique Mongrard)	comte Davillier-Regnault de Saint-Jean-d'Angély by decision of the Conseil du Sceau de France 1 August 1870 for Flore-Angélique Mongrard's husband, Edmond Davillier
23. lieutenant baron Marie-Henri-François Dornant	Marie-Édouard d'Ornant	paternal uncle to nephew	
24. baron Jean-Louis Dubreton	Jean-Louis-Félix Dubreton		baron Dubreton by décret imperial 21 February 1866

Table 4 *continued*

Name of adopter	Name of adoptee	Pre-existing kin relationship	Transmission of title (where applicable)
25. comte Charles-Marie-Louis de Lyonne	Charles-Albert-Félix Gigault de Crisenoy	stepfather to stepson (adoptee was son by first marriage of the comte's wife, widow of Hippolyte-Michel Gigault de Crisenoy)	comte de Lyonne by décret imperial 21 December 1861
26. Alexis-Marie-Paul de Chamborant de Perissat	Charles-Guillaume Goursaud (authorised to change surname to Goursaud de Chamborant de Perissat, then authorised to remove 'Goursaud' and change surname to baron de Chamborant de Perissat)		baron de Chamborant de Perissat by letters patent 26 June 1867
27. baron Gilbert-Joseph-Gaspard-Constant-Henri-Charles-Maxime Gruyer	Marie-Joseph-Charles-Alfred Hervé	'uncle' to nephew (that is, nephew of adopter's wife)	
28. marquis Charles-Jean-Marie-Félix de Lavalette	Samuel Welles de Lavalette	stepfather to stepson (Sammy Welles was the son of the marquis's second wife Adeline Fowle, widow of Samuel Welles)	comte Welles de Lavalette by décret impérial 23 March 1863 (title while adopter was still alive) then marquis Welles de Lavalette by décret impérial 23 June 1863
29. général marquis Alexandre-Charles de Lawoestine	Clémentine-Henriette-Auguste-Oscarine de Cetto (authorised by decree to change surname to Cetto de Lawoestine)	father-in-law to son-in-law (the husband of adopted daughter); the adopted daughter was a niece	marquis de Lawoestine by décret impérial 20 July 1859 for Clémentine's husband, Jean-Paul-Auguste de Valabrègue

30. marquis Arnail-François de Jaucourt	Louis-Charles-François Le Visse de Montigny de Jaucourt	'godfather' and father to illegitimate son	marquis Levisse de Montigny de Jaucourt by décret 27 July 1860
31. Charles-Louis Huguet, marquis de Sémonville	Louis-François-Alphone de Montholon-Sémonville, prince d'Umbriano del Precetto		marquis de Montholon-Sémonville by arrêté ministériel 28 April 1865
32. baron Henri Rottembourg	Louis-Claude-Albert-Henry Novel-Rottembourg	uncle to nephew	baron Novel-Rottembourg by letters patent 12 September 1846, confirmed by arrêté ministériel 27 May 1857
33. comte Edmond-Florimond-Louis-Hérard de Raymond	Georges-Florimond-Martin Duffour de Raymond	uncle to nephew	
34. Paul Carbonnié, marquis de Marzac	Paul-Louis Carbonnié, marquis de Marzac		

adopter to adoptee happened from uncle to nephew, from grandfather to grandson, from stepfather to stepson, and from father-in-law to son-in-law. Révérend does mention noblemen's adoption of a female (as in numbers 3 and 29 on Table 4) but within the nobility adoption of a male was of greater strategic benefit for preserving the patronym.

Illegitimacy

When the Civil Code was introduced 'the father lost his right to offer full inheritance benefits to a natural child, and even patriarchs had no right to introduce illegitimate children or concubines into the family home'.[52] Number 30 in Table 4 concerns the marquis Arnail-François de Jaucourt, adopter of Louis-Charles-François Le Visse de Montigny. A note in the Jaucourt family archive explains that Louis-Charles-François was in fact the marquis de Jaucourt's illegitimate son. Jaucourt had an affair with Charlotte Bontemps who at the time was married to the comte de la Chattre.[53] In a case such as this where illegitimacy was involved it could be in the family's interests to maintain a silence on biological origins. Adoption was a way to ensure rights to inheritance benefits were kept.

Another example of initial concealment from the public of the true paternity concerns Auguste, duc de Morny, illegitimate son of Charles de Flahaut.[54] In the summer of 1811 Hortense de Beauharnais travelled to Aix-les-Bains then to a house owned by her mother, Joséphine, at Prégny, on the lake of Geneva. There Hortense was joined by her lover Charles de Flahaut whose child Hortense was carrying. The birth took place on 15 or 16 September 1811. When the birth was registered in Paris in October, the name given to the child was Charles-Auguste-Joseph-Louis Demorny, son of Auguste-Jean-Hyacinthe Demorny (an old soldier and pensioner of Joséphine de Beauharnais). Auguste was brought up and educated by his paternal grandmother and eventually adopted by Charles de Flahaut. Auguste never took the name Flahaut; he received the ducal title by letters patent.

Emperor Napoleon III had two illegitimate sons from his liaison with Eléonore Vergeot during captivity at the Fort de Ham. The emperor later recognised those sons as his own and granted them the titles of comte de Labenne and comte d'Orx on 11 June 1870.[55] In the family archive of Lucien Bonaparte and his descendants are letters that were sent to Roland Bonaparte in the 1880s accusing Roland's father the prince Pierre Bonaparte of fathering at least one illegitimate child. It is impossible to determine the veracity of the claims that were accompanied by demands for Roland to pay money and threats of stories in the press. The name Bonaparte was widely loathed in the early Third Republic, because of France's defeat in the Franco-Prussian War, so the letters may simply be an expression of a more general animosity.[56]

Secrecy around biological origins in the aristocratic milieu was a theme developed by French author Paul Bourget in his novel *L'Émigré* published in 1907. It was a theme guaranteed to make an impression upon readers at a time when there were cultural concerns about the French 'race' and masculinity. Bourget uses illegitimate birth as a twist in a tale concerning identity, property, and bloodlines. The hero of the novel, Landri, is summoned to the home of a wealthy bourgeois man named Jaubourg, a friend of the family, who is dying. In his final moments Jaubourg reveals that Landri is in fact his own son owing to an affair that Jaubourg had with Landri's mother.[57]

> 'I am the son of Jaubourg! ...' This brutal revelation about his birth began to translate itself into a concrete reality. The social atmosphere in which he had lived for nearly thirty years gave a very particular character to what he saw. He had so often heard people in his world ... talk about 'race' and it was in his race that he felt himself suddenly attacked. This blood that ran in his veins – and he looked at his hands while trembling – was the blood of Jaubourg.[58]

Landri is determined to uphold his own honour as he reflects on his mother's extramarital affair with Jaubourg. He had grown up in the belief that his father was a nobleman, the marquis de Claviers-Grandchamp. Bourget's story provides an illustration of Robert Nye's argument that in this period in France honour for a bourgeois male was about demonstrating that he was a man; honour for an aristocratic male was considered to be 'in the blood'.[59]

Adoption and the construction of family narrative

The alternative to maintaining silence on biological origins was to establish a narrative around an adoptee. In the following case study we can see how noble families' traditions of story telling provided a way of trying to integrate an act of adoption into family identity.

On 26 December 1828 the Cour royale in Paris issued a decree authorising the prince Georges Comnène, chevalier de Saint Louis, living in Saint Germain-en-Laye, to adopt his great-nephew Adolphe-Constant de Geouffre de La Pradelle. The father of Adolphe-Constant was a Limousin nobleman, Pierre de Geouffre de La Pradelle, descended from seigneurial judges of Brive (Corrèze) who had held office over seven generations. Geouffre de La Pradelle was – and still is – a noble bloodline in which the men showed tremendous dedication to the practice of law.[60] In 1828 Pierre de Geouffre de La Pradelle was alive and consented to his son's adoption. Pierre's wife, Cécile (née Permon), had died on 10 *pluviose, an* IV, a short while after giving birth to Adolphe-Constant on 28 *nivose, an* IV (23 January 1795). Adolphe-Constant gave his own consent to become adopted when he was thirty-three years old and a captain in the Garde royale.[61]

There were both political and personal reasons for the prince Georges Comnène, at the age of seventy-four, to adopt his great-nephew from Limousin during the Bourbon Restoration. This act of adoption formed one of the last peculiar pieces fitting into a sprawling jigsaw of international relations, military interventions, and imperial dynastic ambitions that stretched over some eight hundred years. We need briefly to trace the history of the Comnène dynasty, and then the family's story telling tradition about it, to see why the adoption took place.

In the history of the house of Comnène there featured six emperors of Byzantium, commencing with Isaac I who was elected on 31 May 1057 and crowned in the church of Saint Sophia in Constantinople. John II Comnène ruled from 1118 to 1143 and he chose his younger son Manuel I, born in 1118, to succeed him. Under Manuel I's reign (1143–80) the so-called Comnenian Restoration was characterised by the emperor's ambitious foreign policy and keen interest in ecclesiastical affairs. The 'Comnenian system' established various aristocratic courts and drove a culture of patronage in support of literature and the arts.[62] Manuel I's second wife, Maria of Antioch, bore him a son, Alexius Porphyrogenitus, who married Agnès of France in 1180. The succession of Alexius Porphyrogenitus to a minority reign proved disastrous for Byzantine culture as the extended aristocratic family 'system' splintered into factions. The decline of the Byzantium empire led various members of the Comnène family to settle on lands to the east of the Black Sea. There they established the empire of Trébizonde that lasted some 250 years.[63]

The victory of Sultan Mehmed II in the 1453 siege of Constantinople led to the Ottoman conquest of the empire of Trébizonde in 1461.[64] By order of the sultan, the emperor David Comnène of Trébizonde, three of David's children (Basile, Manuel, and Georges) and David's nephew, Alexis V, were massacred on 1 November 1463. Scholarly investigation and debate have clarified certain points regarding the chronology and politics of this violent episode as well as the blood and marital relationships of those who were killed. The sparsity of original evidence and contradictory later interpretations, however, mean that some questions may never be fully answered, including about David's wife Hélène Cantacuzène, and David's niece Théodora, wife of Uzun Hasan.[65]

Ambiguities in historical accounts of fifteenth-century Trébizonde opened up space for a particular narrative about the Comnène family to be elaborated. That narrative was presented some three hundred years after the 1463 massacre to a receptive audience in the France of Louis XVI. By 1780 in Europe diplomats were preoccupied with affairs in the East because manoeuvring had begun for the Austro-Russian alliance to divide up the Ottoman Empire.[66]

According to Comnène family tradition, a certain Nicéphore Comnène – claimed to be a son of David – had managed to escape the 1463 massacre and obtain asylum in Morea (now Greece). This Nicéphore had children, and several generations on it was one of Nicéphore's descendants Démétrius Comnène who explained the family story at the French court of Louis XVI. Démétrius Comnène convinced Louis XVI and royal genealogist Chérin that he was the rightful holder of the title 'prince of Trébizonde' and managed to have this title as well as 'comte Comnène' incorporated in letters patent of 1782.[67] Démétrius then wrote a *précis* of the Comnène dynasty tracing the male lineage from David, last emperor of Trébizonde, to himself, that he had published in Amsterdam in 1784.[68] Démétrius's *précis* served as the guide for subsequent authors to recount and to defend the Comnène legend.[69]

Démétrius Comnène died without posterity in 1821. The only male Comnène left was Démétrius's younger brother, known as prince Georges Comnène. Georges was not married and never had been. By his own account, and according to descriptions of him by others, Georges suffered from ill-health. He had produced no offspring. In these circumstances, Georges Comnène adopted his great-nephew Adolphe-Constant de Geouffre de La Pradelle (son of Pierre and Cécile).[70]

In her memoirs the duchesse Laure d'Abrantès, a niece of Georges and Démétrius Comnène, complains about the way the Comnène family was described by Las Cases in the *Mémorial de Sainte-Hélène*.[71] According to the duchesse d'Abrantès her uncles had certainly not usurped a great name or fabricated noble ancestry. Rather the uncles wanted 'to extinguish a great name' that was 'no longer anything more than a source of humiliations and suffering'.[72]

Comnène family tree

Constantin Comnène
died 1772

Jean-Étienne Comnène
vicar of Bourges, died 1816

Démétrius Comnène
died 1821

Georges Comnène

Laure Comnène
married Charles Martin Permon

Albert Permon
died 1828, one daughter

Cécile Permon
married Pierre de Geouffre de La Pradelle
one son, Adolphe-Constant

Laure Permon
duchesse d'Abrantès
married général Junot duc d'Abrantès

The prince Georges Comnène, however, published his own separate account, *Sur la Grèce* (1831) that gave a contradictory view:

> Démétrius is dead. I have survived him and did not want to let the name Comnène perish. I adopted as the heir of my names, titles and rights, Adolphe-Constant de Geouffre ... I hope that the adoption, this moral grafting of families, will revive the blood of the Comnène.[73]

Georges, the last surviving male Comnène, was acutely conscious of the fact that without the adoption the patronym would be extinguished. His political motive for publishing *Sur la Grèce* in 1831 was to tell the French public of the Comnène claim to the throne of Greece owing to the position his ancestor Nicéphore established in fifteenth-century Morea.

John D. Niles writes that tradition 'is no hypostatic entity, airy and transcendent. Nor can we think of it as hard and durable, like an old chair passed down from hand to hand ... It is a volatile process.'[74] To perpetuate a narrative underpinning tradition a story teller in a family will call up the images and ideas about the past that contribute to the conditioning of other members of their family who listen to the story. But if multiple narratives emerge that compete with one another then the family tradition is at risk of breaking up. Such volatility in the process can be seen in the way prince Georges Comnène and his niece Laure published separate contradictory accounts.

Where a tradition is made up of human actions 'it is not the particular concrete actions which are transmitted'. Rather, 'the transmissible parts of them are the patterns or images of actions which they imply or the beliefs requiring, recommending, regulating, permitting, or prohibiting the re-enactment of those patterns.'[75] The impact of the Comnène family tradition ultimately lay in the way it conditioned the use of language and behaviours of three men involved in the 1828 act of adoption: prince Georges Comnène the adopter, Adolphe-Constant the adoptee, and Adolphe-Constant's father Pierre de Geouffre de La Pradelle.

When the Greeks won the war of independence against the Ottomans in 1832, Otto I of Bavaria was installed as king. French aristocratic politicians had opposed the prince Georges Comnène's claim to the Greek throne. These events were being talked about in Parisian high society because of the French aristocrats involved in the diplomacy, and because Parisian ladies had been organising charitable fundraising events to show solidarity for the Greeks.[76] King Otto I offered to prince Georges Comnène some lands in Greece as a hereditary apanage, and those lands were inherited by Adolphe-Constant after Georges's death. With a letter of recommendation from French minister Casimir Périer, Adolphe-Constant travelled with Pierre to Greece in 1834 to claim those lands. Pierre de Geouffre de La Pradelle had long argued to authorities in France that Adolphe-Constant was inheritor of the title prince Comnène because an adoptee 'has the same rights as a legitimate child'.[77]

For his part Adolphe-Constant was hesitant about travelling to Greece but felt, after signing the 1828 act to be adopted by prince Georges Comnène: 'I must submit to all of the consequences ... there will remain the feeling of an obligation fulfilled.' Adolphe-Constant was not a royalist and in the France of the July Monarchy, having no admiration for King Louis-Philippe, he felt adrift in his military career. Adolphe-Constant described himself as a 'child of Napoleon's military schools and passionate for [Napoleon's] glory, brought up in a way under the tent of one of his most audacious lieutenants'. Under a Bonapartist imperial regime, 'I would have found the destiny I wished for ... I made an error in remaining a soldier in the aftermath of Waterloo'.[78]

While in Greece Adolphe-Constant's father Pierre de Geouffre de La Pradelle suffered an attack of apoplexy and died on 13 July 1835; he was buried in Athens. Adolphe-Constant liquidated the inherited Greek properties and returned to France to pursue his military career. In December 1849 Adolphe-Constant held the rank of colonel. Louis-Napoléon Bonaparte was at that point prince-president and reviving French people's memories of the imperial legend of Napoleon I. The prince-president decided to make Adolphe-Constant a commander of the Legion of Honour. Less than two weeks after attending a reception at the invitation of Louis-Napoléon Bonaparte, Adolphe-Constant fell ill and died in hospital, aged fifty-four. He was unmarried and left no heir. The name Comnène was finally extinguished.

Adoption in the twentieth and twenty-first centuries

Between 1875 and 2006 in France there were a total of 376 French nobles who benefited from an *arrêté* issued by the Garde des Sceaux enabling a title to be held in legal validity. The numbers of investitures have been steadily falling over the decades as families die out. One authoritative list, based on the Association d'entraide de la noblesse française membership, gives 136 extinctions of bloodlines between 1933 and 2006.[79]

The law of 19 July 1923 made possible in France the adoption of minors. A further major development came in the law of 11 July 1966 that gave adopted children rights that are identical to those of biological children; Georges Pompidou advocated this reform and (like Napoleon I) was an adopter. The law of 11 July 1966 introduced to the Civil Code the terminology for the two distinct modes of adoption: *l'adoption plénière* and *l'adoption simple*.[80]

The purpose of *l'adoption plénière* is to give the adoptee the same relationship in law with the adopters that a legitimate child has with their parents. In other words this mode of adoption breaks the legal links between the adoptee and their original family. *L'adoption plénière* is regarded as irrevocable so the adoptee ceases to belong to their original family and their original filiation can no longer be established. Indeed the rupture in law is total to the point of imposing erasure (*l'oubli*) of the act of birth. The court judgement authorising the adoption is transcribed on the registers of the *état civil* in the place of the birth certificate.[81]

By contrast, the purpose of *l'adoption simple* is to retain the adopted individual's relationship in law with their original family (including rights to succession), but to add a new relationship with the adopter. There is no minimum age requirement for the adoptee. There is no requirement that the adoptee live in the home of the person adopting them. The relationship of *l'adoption simple* is manifest primarily in the fact that the adoptee adds to their own name the surname of their adopter and assumes rights to the succession.[82]

Jurisprudence shows how nobiliary law intersects with the Civil Code in cases of adoption. Napoleon I, as we have seen, had created nobiliary titles that were transmissible to 'legitimate, natural or adoptive' heirs. The Garde des Sceaux therefore issued on 12 September 2003 an *arrêté* conferring the title of duc de Reggio upon the eldest of the duc's two adopted sons (the title had originally been awarded by Napoleon I to Maréchal Oudinot in 1810). For titles of the *ancien régime*, matters are more complicated and when the 1966 law on adoption was passed there was lengthy debate on what it would mean for nobles. Legal doctrine generally allows for the transmission of an *ancien régime* title to an adopted son. The Garde des Sceaux issued an *arrêté* on 30 April 1987 so that the adopted son of the marquis de Vibraye could inherit the title.[83]

Conclusion

'In all European aristocracies ancestors, current and future members of the family are one; they exist outside the conventions of space and time. The family and its glory has to be at the centre of the thinking of every member.'[84] Emperor Napoleon I certainly understood this imperative of *la gloire* in noble culture, and by introducing nobiliary titles then the *majorat* system in 1808 he helped to smooth the emergence of a post-revolutionary social elite that he planned as a synthesis of *ancienne noblesse* and *titrés*. The 'granite mass' the emperor envisaged, however, proved over the course of the nineteenth century prone to fracture and re-fusion in manifold ways.

This chapter has shown that the innovation of adoption, debated in the Convention of 1793 and incorporated into the 1804 Civil Code at the wish of Napoleon I, has been beneficial overall for the French nobility. The law on adoption functioned for transmission of names and titles, it did promote social mobility in some cases, and it could provide a form of socially acceptable cover for the births of illegitimate children who, without the adoption, could not inherit from their father. The traces of adoption among nobility are found in legal texts, archives, and fiction of France from the nineteenth and twentieth centuries. There are gaps and silences in the historical record. We do not know, for example, whether among the bachelors or married men who adopted there were noblemen who were sexually attracted to men. Astolphe de Custine is an example of a nineteenth-century nobleman who had fathered a child by his wife, but after the wife and child died Astolphe lived openly with his male lover. There may have been cases (not just among nobility) in which a bachelor adopter did not marry but wished for a companion in life to care for him in old age, as well as an heir to inherit property.[85]

Not all cultures permit the telling and retelling of stories by outsiders. In order to protect oral traditions as part of intangible cultural heritage protocols may apply for writing because the original story teller 'owns' the story.[86] Had that been the case in the France of the 1830s the duchesse d'Abrantès and various journalists of the nineteenth century might not have been legally able to publish competing versions of the Comnène legend. Adolphe-Constant and Pierre de Geouffre de La Pradelle, two provincial noblemen from Limousin, might have been spared the fate of venturing into Greece. Conditioning in noble culture means intangible patrimony holds a privileged place in the noble psyche. The names of ancestors 'transmitted and retained are those whose memory has become the object of a cult by men who remain at least fictitiously in contact with them'.[87]

Notes

1 K. Marx, *Ébauche d'une critique de l'économie politique* cited in P. Bourdieu, *Le Sens pratique* (Paris, 1980), p. 96.

2 M. Halbwachs, *On Collective Memory (Les Cadres sociaux de la mémoire, 1925)*, ed. and translated by L. A. Coser (Chicago, 1992), pp. 123–4. In the French language the word *noble* derives from the eleventh-century Latin word *nobilis*. E. Baumgartner and P. Ménard, *Dictionnaire étymologique et historique de la langue française* (Paris, 1996), p. 526.

3 'What names, what glories and what miseries!' as one soldier put it (in reference to Ney and Murat). E. C. Macknight, *Aristocratic Families in Republican France, 1870–1940* (Manchester, 2012), p. 40.

4 Aristotle, *De la richesse, de la prière, de la noblesse, du plaisir, de l'éducation. Fragments et témoignages*, ed. P. M. Schuhl (Paris, 1968), pp. 80–133. Compare also Aristotle, *Politique*, ed. and translated by J. Aubonnet (Paris, 1971), parts 3, 4, and 5 with Aristotle, *Rhétorique*, ed. M. Dufour (Paris, 1938), parts 1 and 2. The philosopher insisted on virtue (*arété*), nobility of birth (*eugeneia*), and lineage (*genous*) but noted that nobles did not need to be rich. On ancient Greek and Roman ideas about nobility see M. McDonnell, *Roman Manliness: Virtus and the Roman Republic* (Cambridge, 2006); H.-L. Fernoux and C. Stein (eds), *Aristocratie antique: modèles et exemplarité sociale* (Dijon, 2007).

5 The UNESCO Convention for the Safeguarding of the Intangible Cultural Heritage (Paris, 2003) covers 'oral traditions and expressions, including language as a vehicle of the intangible cultural heritage'. On the importance of names within cultures and safeguarding oral traditions see, for example, D. Nettle and S. Romaine, *Vanishing Voices: The Extinction of the World's Languages* (Oxford, 2000); A. Stockdale, B. MacGregor, and G. Munro, 'Migration, Gaelic Medium Education and Language Use' Report for Ionad Nàiseanta na h-Imrich (2003); S. von Lewinski (ed.), *Indigenous Heritage and Intellectual Property: Genetic Resources, Traditional Knowledge and Folklore* (The Hague, 2004); L. Smith and A. Natsuko (eds), *Intangible Heritage* (London, 2009); Australia Council, *Protocols for Producing Indigenous Australian Writing* 2 ed. (Surry Hills, 2007); N. Ndimande-Hlongwa, 'The role of indigenous place names in preserving living heritage of the Zulu people in KwaZulu-Natal', *Proceedings of ICONN* 3 (2015), 533–9.

6 K. F. Werner, 'L'Apport de la prosopographie à l'histoire sociale des élites' in K. S. B. Keats-Rohan (ed.), *Family Trees and Roots of Politics* (Woodbridge, 1997), pp. 1–22; G. T. Beech, M. Bourin, and P. Chareille (eds), *Personal Names and Studies of Medieval Europe* (Kalamazoo, 2002).

7 A. d'Uzès, *Souvenirs de la duchesse d'Uzès née Mortemart*, Préface de son petit-fils le comte de Cossé-Brissac (Paris, 1939).

8 The first Elzéar and Delphine were canonised in 1369. The marquise Delphine

de Sabran was born in 1770 and her brother was named Elzéar. A. Muhlstein, *A Taste for Freedom, The Life of Astolphe de Custine*, translated by T. Waugh (New York, 1999), pp. 6–9, 192–3. Whilst pregnant in 1936–7, the duchesse de Sabran-Pontevès read family history: 'In drawing upon the examples there I hoped to serve better the memory of those whose tradition and name I had been called to continue.' Duchesse de Sabran-Pontevès, *Bon sang ne peut mentir* (Paris, 1987), pp. 191, 223–30, 287. See also M. R. Salzman, *The Making of a Christian Aristocracy: Social and Religious Change in the Western Roman Empire* (Cambridge, MA, 2002).

9   A. Texier, *Qu'est-ce que la noblesse?* (Paris, 1988), pp. 427–35; É. Mension-Rigau, *Aristocrates et grands bourgeois: éducation, traditions, valeurs* (Paris, 1994), pp. 103–7.

10   Halbwachs, *On Collective Memory*, pp. 72–3. Nicknames function in a similar way: see S. Hazareesingh, *The Legend of Napoleon* (London, 2005), preface.

11   C. B. Bouchard, 'The origins of the French nobility: a reassessment', *American Historical Review* 86 (1981), 501–32; S. Johns, *Noblewomen, Aristocracy and Power in the Twelfth-Century Anglo-Norman Realm* (Manchester, 2003), pp. 53–164; A. Livingstone, *Out of Love for My Kin: Aristocratic Family Life in the Lands of the Loire, 1000–1200* (Ithaca, 2010), pp. 158–65.

12   An ordinance from Henri II in 1555 required that the king's permission be sought for a change of name. J. d'Eschavannes, *Traité complet de la science du blason* (1880) (Puiseaux, 1994), p. 16.

13   Halbwachs, *On Collective Memory*, p. 180. The significance of titles varies between nobilities of different European countries. H. M. Scott (ed.), *The European Nobilities in the Seventeenth and Eighteenth Centuries* 2 vols (Harlow, 1995), vol. 1, pp. 22–4, 59–61, 65–6, 127, 191–3, 239, and vol. 2 pp. 35, 59–61, 73–4, 88–91, 150–2, 224–6, 290.

14   E. Wasson, 'European nobilities in the twentieth century', *Virtus: Journal of Nobility Studies* 22 (2015), 249; Macknight, *Aristocratic Families*, conclusion; J. Descheemaeker, *Les Titres de noblesse en France et dans les pays étrangers* 2 vols (Paris, 1958); M. L. Bush, *Rich Noble, Poor Noble* (Manchester, 1988), pp. 6, 7–29, 174; J. Dewald, *The European Nobility, 1400–1800* (Cambridge, 1996), pp. xvi, 22–7.

15   Macknight, *Aristocratic Families*, ch. 2 and on transmission in the female line pp. 15–16; Mension-Rigau, *Aristocrates*, pp. 24–5; C. Grange, *Les Gens du Bottin Mondain: y être c'est en être* (Paris, 1996), pp. 154–5, 160–1, 507; M. H. Darrow, 'French noblewomen and the new domesticity, 1750–1850', *Feminist Studies* 5 (1979), 41–65.

16   Descheemaeker, *Les Titres de noblesse*, vol. 1; S. de Dainville-Barbiche, 'Les Archives du Sceau: naturalisations, mariages, changements de nom, titres', *La Gazette des archives* 160–1 (1993), 127–51; M. Guillaume, 'Le Sceau de France, titre nobiliaire et changement de nom', Speech to the Académie des sciences morales et politiques. 3 July 2006.

17 J. Hardwick, *The Practice of Patriarchy: Gender and the Politics of Household Authority in Early Modern France* (University Park, 1998); S. Desan, *The Family on Trial in Revolutionary France* (Berkeley, 2004); S. Desan and J. Merrick (eds), *Family, Gender, and Law in Early Modern France* (University Park, 2009); J. Hardwick, *Family Business: Litigation and the Political Economies of Daily Life in Early Modern France* (Oxford, 2009); M. Gerber, *Bastards: Politics, Family, and Law in Early Modern France* (Oxford, 2012).

18 Y. Knibiehler, *Les Pères aussi ont une histoire ...* (Paris, 1987); J. Delumeau and D. Roche (eds), *Histoire des pères et de la paternité* (Paris, 1990); R. A. Nye, *Masculinity and Male Codes of Honor in Modern France* (Oxford, 1993); L. Tuttle, 'Celebrating the *père de famille*: pronatalism and fatherhood in eighteenth-century France', *Journal of Family History* 29 (2004), 366–81; C. E. Forth, *The Dreyfus Affair and the Crisis of French Manhood* (Baltimore, 2004); J. Surkis, *Sexing the Citizen: Morality and Masculinity in France, 1870–1920* (Ithaca, 2006); R. G. Fuchs, *Contested Paternity: Constructing Families in Modern France* (Baltimore, 2008); A.-M. Sohn, '*Sois un homme!*' Construction de la masculinité au XIXe siècle (Paris, 2009).

19 Hazareesingh, *The Legend*, p. 2; S. Hazareesingh, 'Memory, legend, and politics: Napoleonic patriotism in the Restoration era', *European Journal of Political Theory* 5 (2006), 71–84. See also G. Gengembre, *Napoléon: la vie, la légende* (Paris, 2001) and on myth-making, J. Tulard, *Le Mythe de Napoléon* (Paris, 1971); P.-M. Schuhl, *Le Culte des grands hommes* (Paris, 1974); N. Petiteau, *Napoléon de la mythologie à l'histoire* (Paris, 1999).

20 J.-D. Lanjuinais, *La Charte, la liste civile et les majorats, au sujet d'une proposition de récompense nationale* (Paris, 1819), p. 12; J.-M. Berton, *Des majorats et substitutions et de la pairie héréditaire* (Paris, 1831), pp. 13–15.

21 Civil Code (article 735); J. Chevallier and L. Bach, *Droit civil* (Paris, 1978), vol. 2, p. 153. For much more detail see L. Barry, *La Parenté* (Paris, 2008).

22 P. Nicole, *Substitutions et majorats* (Paris, 1861), pp. 11–14; J.-M. Berton, *Des majorats et substitutions et de la pairie héréditaire* (Paris, 1831), pp. 13–15; N. Parant, *Commentaire de la loi du 2 mai 1835 sur les majorats* (Paris, 1835); H. Boissard, *Des substitutions et des majorats* (Paris, 1858).

23 *Traité des majorats*, pp. 7–8.

24 Gerber, *Bastards*, pp. 49–71; J.-P. Labatut, *Les Noblesses européennes de la fin du XVe siècle à la fin du XVIIIe siècle* (Paris, 1978), pp. 139–49.

25 In heraldry the image of a helmet placed at the centre of the escutcheon (*écu*) signifies protection of the warrior chief's head. Normally the visor is open because the chief sees and commands. For a bastard the helmet was represented as being made of steel (inferior to silver or gold) with the visor completely closed. Eschavannes, *Traité complet*, pp. 171, 176.

26 Chevallier and Bach, *Droit civil*, vol. 2, pp. 221–7; É. Martin Saint-Léon, *Des substitutions fidéicommissaires* (Paris, 1886). Prior to 1792 substitutions were

already forbidden in Bourbonnais, Marche, Montargis, Auvergne, Nivernais, Bretagne, Normandie, and Hainaut except for duchies of the peerage.

27 W. Dworzaczek, 'La mobilité sociale de la noblesse polonaise aux XVIe–XVIIIe siècles', *Acta Poloniae Historica* 36 (1977), 147–61; R. Frost, 'The nobility in Poland-Lithuania, 1569–1795' in Scott, *The European Nobilities*, vol. 2, p. 187.

28 K. E. Gager, *Blood Ties and Fictive Ties: Adoption and Family Life in Early Modern France* (Princeton, 1996), pp. 3–4, 51–6. On adoption in ancient Rome see Barry, *La Parenté*, pp. 500–8; Y. Thomas, 'Adoption en nature', *Revue historique de droit* 6 (1988), 44.

29 L. Hunt, *The Family Romance of the French Revolution* (Berkeley, 1992), p. 151; Gager, *Blood Ties*, pp. 160–1.

30 Desan, *The Family on Trial*, pp. 214, 294, 325–6, 329; J. Boudon, 'Les Projets de code civil "de Cambacérès" et le thème de l'imitation de la nature (1793–1804)', *Droits* 39 (2004), 91–106.

31 *Discours sur l'éducation de M. le Dauphin et sur l'adoption* (1790), cited and translated by in Gager, *Blood Ties*, p. 158.

32 The French verb *'adopter'* was taken from the fourteenth-century Latin *adoptare* 'to choose'. Baumgartner and Ménard, *Dictionnaire*, p. 15.

33 Gager, *Blood Ties*, p. 162.

34 N. L. Paul, *To Follow in Their Footsteps: The Crusades and Family Memory in the High Middle Ages* (Ithaca, 2012), p. 11.

35 On silence to 'close rank' and protect the weak see E. C. Macknight, 'Honor and the military formation of French noblemen, 1870–1920', *Historical Reflections/Réflexions historiques* 35 (2009), 105. On silence to exclude see Mension-Rigau, *Aristocrates*, pp. 81–3.

36 During legislative debate on the Matteï law of 5 July 1996 the right of the adoptee to know the identities of biological parents was associated with the convention on human rights. J. Carbonnier, *Droit civil* vol. 2 *La Famille* 18 ed. (Paris, 1997), pp. 489–90, 500; M. Soulé, *Le Secret sur les origines* (Paris, 1984).

37 F. Mossiker, *Napoleon and Josephine: The Biography of a Marriage* (London, 1965), pp. 243–5; M. Garraud and R. Szramkiewicz, *La Révolution française et la famille* (Paris, 1978), pp. 101–2; V. Vanoyeke, *Les Bonaparte* (Paris, 1991), pp. 106–9; Gager, *Blood Ties*, p. 161.

38 Carbonnier, *Droit civil*, pp. 497–8; Mossiker, *Napoleon and Josephine*, pp. 290–1, 317.

39 S. Stegmann von Pritzwald and F. Pascal, *Répetoire des familles nobles de l'Empire et de la Restauration titulaires d'un majorat sur demande* (Paris, 2005); N. Petiteau, *Élites et mobilités: la noblesse d'Empire au XIXe siècle (1808–1914)* (Paris, 1997), pp. 26–60, 131–59, 252–91.

40 On debates among Spanish jurisconsults see *Traité des majorats* (Paris, 1808), pp. 5, 48, 86. In areas of France where there was Spanish influence upon cus-

tomary law the *majorat* had existed before 1808 (Franche-Comté, Roussillon, Artois, and Flanders).

41 Decree of 1 March 1808, Dépôt des Lois numéro 527, *Bulletin des Lois*, no. 186. The word *majorat* is a cognate of the Latin word *major* meaning 'greater in quality, strength or age' and comes from the idea that the eldest son must inherit the property (*natu major*). D. Spring (ed.), *European Landed Elites in the Nineteenth Century* (Baltimore, 1977), pp. 6–10; H. M. Scott (ed.), *The European Nobilities in the Seventeenth and Eighteenth Centuries* vol. 1 (Harlow, 1995), pp. 31–5; G. V. Taylor, 'Noncapitalist wealth and the origins of the French Revolution', *American Historical Review* 72 (1967), 469–96, esp. 472.

42 Texier, *Qu'est-ce que la noblesse?* pp. 420–3; D. Higgs, 'Social mobility and hereditary titles in France, 1814–1830: the majorats-sur-demande', *Histoire sociale/Social History* 14 (1981), 29–47.

43 G. Bertier de Sauvigny, *La Restauration* 2 ed. (Paris, 1963), p. 248.

44 Du Teil correspondence with the *référendaire au Sceau* in AD Haute-Loire 61J/61 Fonds Pradier d'Agrain.

45 Higgs, 'Social mobility', 35.

46 Gager, *Blood Ties*, pp. 78–9.

47 E. Schalk, *From Valor to Pedigree: Ideas of Nobility in France in the Sixteenth and Seventeenth Centuries* (Princeton, 1986); A. Jouanna, *L'Idée de race en France au XVIe siècle et au début du XVIIe siècle* (Montpellier, 1981); A. Dvyer, *Le Sang épuré: les préjugés de race chez les gentilhommes français de l'ancien régime (1560–1720)* (Brussels, 1973). For a counter-argument see M. Motley, *Becoming a French Aristocrat: The Education of the Court Nobility, 1580–1715* (Princeton, 1990).

48 Macknight, *Aristocratic Families*, pp. 44, 48, 220; Forth, *The Dreyfus Affair*, ch. 6; Surkis, *Sexing the Citizen*, pp. 73–109, 214–19.

49 Halbwachs, *On Collective Memory*, p. 70.

50 Série BB/11/13391/2—13391/10 Successions aux titres et aux majorats. Inventory and by extract only owing to the fragility of the documents.

51 Vicomte A. Révérend, *Les Familles titrées et anoblies au XIXe siècle* (Paris, 1974).

52 Desan, *The Family on Trial*, p. 296. On *recherche de paternité* (introduced 1912) see Fuchs, *Contested Paternity*, chs 3–4.

53 AN AP 86/9 Fonds de la Maison de Jaucourt.

54 Mossiker, *Napoleon and Josephine*, p. 373; R. Pflaum, *The Emperor's Talisman: The Life of the Duc de Morny* (New York, 1968), pp. 6–9.

55 Descheemaeker, *Les Titres de noblesse* vol. 1, p. 21.

56 AN AP 103/39 Fonds Lucien Bonaparte. On Lucien Bonaparte, his son Pierre Bonaparte, and Pierre's son Roland see J. Valynseele, *Le Sang des Bonaparte* (Paris, 1954), pp. 37, 41, 50, 58, 59.

57 P. Bourget, *L'Émigré* (Paris, 1907), pp. 150–2.

58 Bourget, *L'Émigré*, p. 175.

59 Bourget, *L'Émigré*, p. 206; Nye, *Masculinity*, pp. 41, 67, 217.

60 R. de La Pradelle, *Aux frontiers de l'injustice* (Paris, 1979). One of France's most eminent twentieth-century lawyers, Raymond de Geouffre de La Pradelle, defended the interests of Ethiopia against the Italian fascist government. Raymond's father was Albert de Geouffre de La Pradelle (1871–1955), chair of public law at the Faculté de Droit and founder of the Institut des Hautes Études Internationales of the University of Paris. Albert served as jurisconsult to the Ministère des Affaires Étrangères.

61 'Arrêt d'adoption enregistré à Paris, le 6 janvier 1829' AD Corrèze 54J Fonds Geouffre de La Pradelle (*fonds 'en vrac'*, not classed at time of consultation).

62 F. Chalandon, *Les Comnène: étude sur l'empire byzantin aux XIe et XIIe siècles* 3 vols (Paris, 1900–12); M. Angold, *The Byzantine Empire, 1025–1204: A Political History* 2 ed. (London, 1997); P. Magdalino, *The Empire of Manuel I Komnenos, 1143–1180* (Cambridge, 1993); P. Stephenson, *Byzantium's Balkan Frontier: A Political Study of the Northern Balkans, 900–1204* (Cambridge, 2000).

63 There were periods of rulership by Georges Comnène from 1266 to 1280, by George's brother Jean II from 1280 to 1297, and by George's half-sister Empress Théodora who contested Jean II's rule (c.1284–5). M. Kuršanskis, 'L'usurpation de Théodora Grande Comnène', *Revue des études byzantines* 33 (1975), 187–210.

64 S. Runciman, *The Fall of Constantinople: 1453* (Cambridge, 1965).

65 M. Kuršanskis, 'La descendance d'Alexis IV, empereur de Trébizonde. Contribution à la prosopographie des Grands Comnènes', *Revue des études byzantines* 37 (1979), 239–47; D. M. Nicol, *The Byzantine Family of Kantakouzenos* (Washington, 1968); A. Bryer, 'Ludovico da Bologna and the Georgian and Anatolian Embassy of 1460–1461', *Bedi Kartlisa* 19–20 (1965), 196–7.

66 G. Rudé, *Europe in the Eighteenth Century* (London, 2002), pp. 233–4.

67 Chérin's words were: 'On ne peut se refuser à croire que messieurs Comnène soient issus de David Comnène, empereur de Trébizonde', *honneurs de la cour* 1782, 1785, 1786. F. Bluche, *Les Honneurs de la cour* 2 ed. (Paris, 2000), p. 44.

68 D. Comnène, *Précis historique de la maison impériale des Comnènes* [...] *depuis David, dernier empereur de Trébisonde jusqu'à Démétrius Comnène actuellement capitaine de cavalerie en France* (Amsterdam, 1784).

69 G. Comnène, *Sur la Grèce* (Paris, 1831); Duchesse d'Abrantès, *Mémoires de madame la duchesse d'Abrantès* vol. 1 (Paris, 1830), pp. 24–30; L. de Nussac, 'La couronne des Comnène et le trône de Grèce', *L'Opinion*, 13 November 1920. Albert de Geouffre de La Pradelle contested a version, based on 'incomplete documentation', that was put forward in S. Pappas, 'Les Comnènes et le trône de Grèce' in *Messager d'Athènes* 30 January 1932. The response to Pappas's article is a typed document in the family archive AD Corrèze 54J

Fonds Geouffre de La Pradelle (*fonds 'en vrac'*, not classed at time of consultation).

70 Nussac, 'La couronne'; Abrantès, *Mémoires*, pp. 344–7, 351–2.

71 On *Mémorial de Saint Hélène* and diverse reactions to it, Hazareesingh, *The Legend*, pp. 164–71, 178, 181, 189–90, 200, 210, 220.

72 Abrantès, *Mémoires*, p. 20.

73 Comnène, *Sur la Grèce*, p. 42.

74 J. D. Niles, *Homo Narrans: The Poetics and Anthropology of Oral Literature* (Philadelphia, 1999), p. 173.

75 E. Shils, *Tradition* (Chicago, 1981), p. 12.

76 A. Martin-Fugier, *La Vie élégante ou la formation du Tout-Paris 1815–1848* (Paris, 1990), p. 160; F. Démier, *La France de la Restauration (1814–1830): l'impossible retour du passé* (Paris, 2012), pp. 769–75, 806–7.

77 2 July 1829 in AD Corrèze 54J Fonds Geouffre de La Pradelle (*fonds 'en vrac'*, not classed at time of consultation).

78 26 May 1832 in AD Corrèze 54J Fonds Geouffre de La Pradelle (*fonds 'en vrac'*, not classed at time of consultation). On the impact of Waterloo in art see D. Poulot, *Une histoire des musées de France XVIII–XXe siècle* (Paris, 2008), pp. 124–9. On military careers see R. Blaufarb, *The French Army, 1750–1820: Careers, Talent, Merit* (Manchester, 2002); N. Petiteau, *Lendemains d'Empire: les soldats de Napoléon dans la France du XIXe siècle* (Paris, 2003).

79 R. Valette, *Catalogue de la noblesse française* (Paris, 2007), p. 197; Texier, *Qu'est-ce que la noblesse?* pp. 140–1.

80 Carbonnier, *Droit civil*, pp. 479, 502–3; Texier, *Qu'est-ce que la noblesse?* pp. 420–3; M.-P. Marmier, *Sociologie du droit de l'adoption* (Paris, 1972); C. Launay, *L'Adoption, ses données médicales et psychosociales* 6 ed. (Paris, 1978); M. Soulé, *L'Adoption, données médicales, psychologiques et sociales* (Paris, 1978); M. Soulé (ed.) *Le Nouveau Roman familial* (Paris, 1984).

81 J. Chevallier and L. Bach, *Droit civil* vol. 1, 7 ed. (Paris, 1978), pp. 234–8.

82 Chevallier and Bach, *Droit civil* vol. 1, 7 ed., p. 239; Carbonnier, *Droit civil*, pp. 498, 501. The Hague Convention of 29 May 1993 established conditions for adoption where the adoptee is born abroad; France became a signatory state in 1995. J.-P. Gutton, *Histoire de l'adoption en France* (Paris, 1993); J. Rubellin-Devichi and R. Frank (eds), *L'Enfant et les Conventions internationales* (Lyon, 1996); A. Meunier, *Le Choix d'adopter* (Paris, 1997).

83 Guillaume, 'Le Sceau de France'; Texier, *Qu'est-ce que la noblesse?* pp. 403, 407–10, 420.

84 K. Urbach, 'Age of no extremes? The British aristocracy torn between the House of Lords and the Mosley movement' in K. Urbach (ed.), *European Aristocracies and the Radical Right 1918–1939* (Oxford, 2007), p. 64.

85 Muhlstein, *A Taste for Freedom*; W. A. Peniston and N. Erber (eds), *Queer Lives: Men's Autobiographies from Nineteenth-Century France* (Lincoln, NE, 2007).

86 For indigenous Australians from diverse Aboriginal and Torres Strait Islander cultures: 'The telling of stories is a right given to particular and qualified individuals. The re-telling of those stories by unqualified outsiders may be offensive to customary law beliefs.' Australia Council, *Protocols*, pp. 3, 6. For further examples see Lewinski, *Indigenous Heritage*; Smith and Natsuko, *Intangible Heritage*.

87 Halbwachs, *On Collective Memory*, p. 73.

4

Incapacity and debt

Fortuna perit, virtus et fama manent.[1]

Many questions about the nobility's economic capital have proved difficult for historians to answer for the post-revolutionary period. When David Higgs surveyed the historical literature in the 1980s it was not clear whether the maximum to minimum range of wealth found in noble families looked any different from the maximum to minimum range of wealth found in bourgeois families of the nineteenth century. It was debatable whether nobles were any less 'capitalist' or 'entrepreneurial' in their approach to business and financial investment than the bourgeoisie. Scattered evidence suggested that 'the nobility was the wealthiest section of landed society until 1848 and perhaps long after'. A more straightforward conclusion was reached on the consequences of poverty. 'In the short term aristocratic antecedents or personal loyalties might permit a noble in reduced circumstances to "tenir son rang" but it remained true that status not fertilized by cash was a perishable flower'.[2]

The kinds of questions of interest to Higgs, Daumard, Gibson, and other historians investigating the fortunes of nobility 'touch on some of the most important themes that modern historians seek to address'.[3] Prior to 1789 the laws of *dérogeance* meant that nobles risked certain penalties if they were seen to be engaging in trade. Yet management of an estate and the exploitation of resources from the land meant there were business dimensions to the aristocratic lifestyle.[4] The nobility largely recovered from the economic blows of the French Revolution and some nobles profited in material terms, especially those who managed to clear debts in the 1790s or who bought up *biens nationaux*. Unsold lands that had been confiscated were restored to *émigrés* in 1800–2 and the law of 5 December 1814 permitted the restitution of forests. Nobles' possession of landed property, in total about 10 per cent of all land, served as a basis of political power under the July Monarchy when ten of the fifteen richest men in the country were *ancien régime* nobles. Diversification in strategies for income generation can be seen in the trend for shareholding as nobles' pattern of investment shifted away from real estate and into the stock market. In 1902 noblemen made up 30 per cent of the directors of railway companies and 23 per cent of the directors of large banking and steel companies.[5]

While historians acknowledge that some of the data is patchy and difficult to interpret, there is recognition of the need to try to get behind what it is nobles say about economic capital to look at what they do. Various sources written by nobles in the nineteenth century reveal a mistrust of financiers, haughtiness toward people engaged in commerce, and a commitment to career choices among men that distinguished them from classes below. The comtesse Marie d'Armaillé, youngest daughter of the général de Ségur, recalled the attitude within her Parisian milieu during the 1850s where 'lack of fortune' and 'the need to live economically' produced behaviours that were a source of 'very justifiable pride'. Over one hundred years later nobles' responses to questions about attitudes toward money in the 1980s indicate a rejection of ostentatious signs of wealth and a preference not to converse about financial matters. There have been cases of professional success among French nobles in banking and insurance, for some reached extremely high ranks within the financial industry.[6] For a milieu that aims to be discreet about the economic capital it detains, one might anticipate silence on cases of failure.

This chapter investigates nobles' behaviour when problems arose in successions owing to a lack in human ability to manage material resources. The first problem to be explored is that of finding a solution when an heir proved incapable of exercising responsibility for property affairs owing to a long-term illness or disability. In situations of this kind refusal to address incapacity in an heir could jeopardise not only the individual's patrimony but also the maintenance of the family's economic, cultural, and social capital. The manner in which nobles sought to mitigate the effects of long-term illness or disability, both through consultation among relatives and through recourse to external professional expertise, is therefore important for understanding resilience and adaptation among nobility in challenging circumstances.

The second problem to be explored is the nature of nobles' responses when it was difficult to access liquid funds to meet the demands of creditors because of prior debt or loss of control over capital. Much of the historical scholarship on aristocratic debt in Britain and continental Europe has centred upon interpretations of the 'decline' or 'crisis' of nobilities.[7] Historians have investigated which items were sold off, and for what sums of money, when families tried to clear debt and avoid bankruptcy. Yet lists of goods and sale prices do not get us very far in understanding the emotional costs of debt and its effects on health, nor do they reveal anything about moral attitudes surrounding borrowing. My approach is to combine analysis of the causes of financial difficulties, with attention to how nobles regarded debt, what they did about it, and the implications of chronic indebtedness for succession and family dynamics in late modern France.

Each of the problems treated in this chapter was highly emotive for the nobility in the nineteenth and twentieth centuries, but we must not read back into the past the feelings and associations they generate in today's world where debt and disability are understood differently. By drawing on a variety of legal and personal documents from the modern period my aim is to illuminate the emotions and opinions expressed by family members and their advisers at that time. There are ambiguities and silences in the historical record that need to be weighed along with the words that appear on paper.

Legal protection

Since its introduction to France in 1804 the Civil Code has always included provision for the protection of vulnerable individuals' rights to property. *Tutelle* and *curatelle* are systems of representation or assistance for another person who requires help to manage his or her interests before the law. These two systems had developed during the *ancien régime* in the territories subject to written law and were adopted by the drafters of the Civil Code.[8]

Tutelle is the provision of representation; this system is based upon the principle that the person represented is not capable of expressing their personal will in a legal sense. *Tutelle* is principally designed to protect the rights of minors. It can also be used, however, in the case of someone who has attained the age of majority but whose behaviour shows a derangement of mental faculties causing persistent difficulty for them adjusting to adult responsibilities. The age of majority was set at twenty-one years until the law of 5 July 1974 amended it to eighteen years. A *tuteur*, normally a parent, undertakes to manage the property owned by a minor and to perform other legal duties on their behalf. Designation of a *tuteur* is a parental prerogative so if one parent dies then it passes to the other; the surviving parent has to name a *tuteur* in his or her will (*la tutelle testamentaire*) or by declaration to a notary. If no *tuteur* has been named, and both parents are deceased, then the Civil Code (articles 397, 402–3) stipulates that the role passes to the nearest ascendant of the person requiring representation (*la tutelle légale*).[9]

Curatelle is the provision of assistance; this system is based upon the principle that the person assisted is capable of expressing their personal will in a legal sense, but does not have sufficient intellectual clarity or firmness of mind to manage effectively his or her own interests. A *curateur* must assist the person for any act of legal consequence, for example to sign a contract of employment or to make a donation in a will. Because it may be very difficult to distinguish whether the *tutelle* or the *curatelle* is the most appropriate system to adopt for an individual, family members who have their own opinions and subjective judgements need to seek external advice. The legal consequences of choosing one system over another need to be considered carefully, and reviewed regularly, according to the degree of incapacity and its evolution. The establishment of a family council (*un conseil de famille*), required by the Civil Code, is intended to serve as a support structure for decision-making in the *tutelle* or the *curatelle*. Normally composed of four to six persons, who may be relatives, friends or neighbours of the person under *tutelle* or *curatelle*, the family council is appointed by and meets in the presence of a *juge des tutelles*.[10]

At the legal opening of a succession involving a minor or an adult under *tutelle*, the *tuteur* is able to accept the terms of the succession on their charge's behalf subject to provision of an inventory. Only with the authorisation of the *conseil de famille* can a *tuteur* accept or renounce a succession on their charge's behalf where there is no inventory. These and other provisions for managing succession in the regimes of *tutelle* or *curatelle* were incorporated into the Civil Code. In families of nobility during the nineteenth and twentieth centuries an uncle was often nominated to fulfil the role of *tuteur* if both parents had died. Uncles were regarded as appropriate figures to provide this kind of security and guardianship, just as they did within aristocratic families living near Blois and Chartres during the eleventh and twelfth centuries.[11]

The subject of an heir's incapacity for administering affairs owing to long-term illness or disability has been a rich theme for biographers and historians of royal and imperial families dating back to the Middle Ages. Royal or imperial health and even tiny physical 'flaws' that seem trifling today could have implications for rulers' public image, the stability of the realm, and international relations.[12] What happened when an heir's incapacity touched the ranks of lesser nobility confronting the challenges of landownership in the modern world?

Weakness of men's physical or mental constitution is rarely discussed in nobles' memoirs where descriptions of male ancestors focus instead on 'masculine' attributes of strength, dominance, and valour. Yet weakness in the male sex is a matter of profound importance because of men's symbolic role, with innumerable practical dimensions, *à la tête de la maison*. In addition to genetic dispositions and diseases, noblemen, like other civilians, sustained various kinds of illnesses and injuries from their engagement in warfare over the centuries. Negative repercussions for male health were understandably not something that the aristocracy, proud of its heritage as a 'warrior caste', wanted to dwell on publicly. But those repercussions, for noblemen and their relatives, are acutely apparent in documentation from *archives privées*. Let us look at two case studies.

Jean-Baptiste de Théas, comte de Thorenc, was an ambitious young officer during the Napoleonic wars. He and his sister Flore had been orphaned as children. Their elderly father François de Théas passed away in July 1794 and their mother Julie died in poverty in May 1800. So it was primarily to his maternal grandmother Émilie de Montgrand that Jean-Baptiste wrote about his military exploits in Spain (1810–13). At Carcatenxte in June 1813 Jean-Baptiste was struck by enemy fire that shattered his right tibia; instead of amputating the leg, a surgeon insisted on transport to Alcira where he removed seventeen fragments of bone and reconstructed Jean-Baptiste's leg.[13] After months of convalescence, followed by return to France in 1814, Jean-Baptiste served as officer in the Garde royale, was promoted to the rank of captain of the hussars, and finally squadron commander in 1821. But the comte displayed increasing mental instability and was forced to retire from the army by royal decision of 24 April 1822.[14] With his military career terminated, Jean-Baptiste first travelled to Italy – the country where, as a boy, he had spent the 1790s with his sister and mother – then back to France where his worsening symptoms frightened relatives and friends.

In the spring of 1823 the effects of Jean-Baptiste's mental derangement were such that his sister Flore no longer felt it was safe for him to be living in Grasse (Alpes-Maritimes) where he 'only ran about buying things everywhere ... which could ruin him'. Flore begged her husband, the comte de l'Escarène, to take urgent action to obtain a court order of protection (a restraining order) with the support of the mayor and deputy-mayor, a *curé*, sub-prefect, king's procurer, and a justice of the peace. Flore and Monsieur Fabre, 'a true friend', who was helping her to cope with the embarrassment and worry caused by Jean-Baptiste's spending sprees, were of the same opinion: 'It is absolutely necessary to save the life and a bit of the fortune of this unfortunate brother.'[15] On 12 May 1823 the Tribunal civil in Grasse granted the order of protection for the comte de Thorenc owing to 'a brain inflammation that deprives him absolutely of his moral and intellectual faculties'. Taken into permanent care at an institution for sufferers of epilepsy and nervous disorders at Saint-Rémy de Provence (Bouches-du-Rhône), the former soldier died of apoplectic seizure on 30 June 1823. The seizure was triggered by an incident in which the comte had believed himself to be in Paris and in terrifying agitation started shouting commands and ordering carriages to go and see the king.[16]

We are unlikely ever to know how many soldiers who fought in the Revolutionary and Napoleonic Wars suffered permanently from the traumas of military life.[17] The severity of the comte de Thorenc's mental illness made him completely unable to exercise responsibility over money or any other property, a disastrous position to be in as the titular *chef de famille*. His kin, Provençal *petite noblesse* of modest wealth, could plainly see the potential for ruin. When her brother died, Flore inherited what was left of his patrimony comprising a few small pieces of land (La Sabrane, Les Aspres) planted with olive trees, plus a house, furniture and library, estimated at a total worth of 9,500 francs.[18]

A second case study of an heir's incapacity is found in the Croÿ family. The origins and prestige of the Croÿ can be traced back to twelfth-century Picardy; of the multiple branches established in different European countries before the First World War only the Croÿ-Solre branch exists today.[19] On 1 August 1885, at its first meeting in Le Roeulx (Hainaut, Belgium), a *conseil de famille* convened by the local justice of the peace appointed His Serene Highness Monseigneur Rodolphe, duc de Croÿ, as *tuteur* for the *tutelle* of his nephew, prince Alfred Emmanuel de Croÿ. The order of protection for Alfred Emmanuel de Croÿ had been issued by the Tribunal de Premier Instance in Mons on 2 July 1885. He was then aged forty-three, married, with three children by his English wife, Élisabeth Mary (née Parnall). It is not clear from the archive what the precise medical reason for Alfred Emmanuel's incapacity was, but its deleterious effects meant that his parents rented a house in Bruges for Alfred Emmanuel to live in, where his sister Georgina and a valet oversaw his care, whilst Élisabeth Mary and the three children lived in Tunbridge Wells.[20] One of duc Rodolph's first tasks as *tuteur* in August 1885 was to accept on behalf of his nephew the share of inheritance that came to Alfred Emmanuel from his late father, the prince Emmanuel, who had died in January 1885.

The terms of the prince Emmanuel's will of 19 June 1881 are revealing on two matters. First, there are striking intra-familial concentrations of Croÿ property from marriages between first cousins in two successive generations. The prince Emmanuel de Croÿ (1811–85), who made this will, had married his first cousin, princesse Léopoldine de Croÿ (1821–1907). Emmanuel's father, the prince Fernand de Croÿ (1791–1865), had married his first cousin, princesse Anne-Louise de Croÿ-Solre (1789–1869). Among the properties in the succession, Emmanuel's eldest son Alfred Emmanuel inherited the estate of Sobre while the younger son Gustave inherited the château and estate of Le Roeulx in Belgium.[21] Both of these brothers died when they were aged only in their mid-forties: Alfred Emmanuel in 1888 and Gustave in 1889. Longevity improved in the next generation for Alfred Emmanuel's eldest son, prince Léopold de Croÿ (1877–1965), died in his eighties having fathered eight children by his wife and survived military service in the First and Second World Wars.

A second matter apparent in the prince Emmanuel's 1881 will is the dilemmas for a nobleman trying to apportion patrimony in the knowledge that his eldest son was not capable of assuming normal adult responsibilities. The prince Emmanuel had been paying a pension to Alfred Emmanuel, and making repayments for debts contracted by this same son, expenditure that amounted to some 603,955 francs in January 1881. By July 1885, when the order of protection was in place, there were further debts that had been incurred by Alfred Emmanuel, on top of taxes for the succession, which the *conseil de famille* decided to pay for by selling some lands in France and Belgium. All of the revenues from the estate of Sobre were to be put towards meeting the needs of Alfred Emmanuel, his wife and children.

The contrast between the amount of patrimony involved for the Théas de Thorenc family of Provençal *petite noblesse* compared with the amount involved for the Croÿ family of northern feudal-origin aristocracy reminds us of the diversity of fortunes and lifestyles long apparent within nobilities across Europe.[22] The cases are similar, however, in showing that

an heir's incapacity in the modern era required relatives to work closely
with a range of state officials and other professionals to find a solution.
The issuing of a court order of protection and subsequent setting up of a
conseil de famille and *tutelle* or *curatelle* arrangement meant that mayors,
justices of the peace, lawyers, and medics became involved in these
cases. By organising care within the family, relatives could try to protect
privacy. But the State's laws gave that care a public dimension, nonetheless. Incapacity through illness or disability could strike in any family, and
when it did so the protection of patrimony was more than ever a delicate
and challenging matter.

Finance and children's futures

In the personal correspondence of nobility from the nineteenth and
twentieth centuries parents often expressed to one another, as well as
to close friends and relatives, their hopes and concerns about how their
children would establish themselves as autonomous adults. Financial
independence was not the only measure of autonomy, for other measures
included emancipation from parental control and age of majority.[23] In
law, however, the arrangements for dowries, donations, *majorats*, and
pensions all created connections between the criteria for 'adulthood' and
assessments of economic capital in nobles' possession. Nobles' ambitions
for their offspring went hand in hand with doubts, self-questioning, and
reflections of various kinds upon their own youth. Letters reveal parents
worrying about future security of income for their children, frustration
over the undetermined career path of a son, and disappointment with the
marriage suitors of a daughter. Of course there were statements of bright
optimism too. Mothers and fathers liked to voice opinions but were not
objective commentators on their progeny.[24]

Anxious laments from parents about their children's future had a lot
to do with how successive changes of political regime in France impacted
the nobility's capital investments, sources of revenue, and access to credit.
Experience of events over which nobles had no control and only limited
capacity for insuring against losses heightened their sensitivity to risks
and uncertainties. Revolutionary turmoil in 1789, 1830, and 1848 created
a legacy of fear and resentment of popular violence. Nobles and their
agents expressed the same fear for property in the context of 1814–15 and
in the Paris Commune of 1870–1.[25]

The outcomes of treaty negotiations did sometimes prove unfavourable to those nobles to whom sovereigns had previously granted rights

to property as a donation in gratitude for service. Owners were not compensated for loss of holdings in areas subject to territorial redivision or when holdings attracted higher taxes and charges because of change to another nation's jurisdiction. Napoleon I's reputation for munificence in granting lands to his princes, ducs, and other nobiliary title-holders evolved into a legacy of expensive legal work for those families trying to establish ownership rights in territories no longer under French control. Jean Tulard estimated that prestigious beneficiaries among the *noblesse d'Empire*, men such as Ney, Masséna, Davout,and Caulaincourt, suffered losses in the order of 40 per cent on average for the period 1808–13. The problems were aggravated for less wealthy *titrés* who did not have the means to employ intendants abroad to look after their interests.[26]

Another area where the experiences of one generation could leave problems in the wake for the next generation is charitable commitments. Historians have identified nineteenth-century proselytising messages directed at nobility to 'return to the land' in order to fulfil moral obligations to the Church and people in the countryside. One of the influential lobby groups was the Oeuvre des campagnes, founded in the 1850s by the *curé* Jean-Marie Vandel and a Legitimist aristocrat, the comtesse de La Rochejaquelain. Across the nineteenth century nobles were active in charitable patronage.[27] Their patterns of donating, and networking with priests, monks, and nuns resemble patterns established by nobles of the Middle Ages and early modern period. Maintaining traditions of charity work in support of the Catholic Church, however, meant that during the early Third Republic nobles came into conflict with successive governments, especially over privately founded schools. The small buildings in which these schools operated, mostly houses of rural villages and towns that were bought and converted by noble owners, were in no way a lucrative investment. Their upkeep required expenditure and nobles could be taken to court for breaking republican laws by continuing to use the building as a school for Catholic-based education.[28]

For those nobles who were especially pious their observation of materialistic extravagance within the aristocratic milieu resulted in self-reflection and moralising to others. The baronne Mathilde de Mackau visited and provided charitable aid to victims of poverty and illness in Parisian suburbs and near the Mackau estate of Vimer in Normandy. Mathilde was a wealthy woman (her dowry was just over three million francs) and she saw the privileged position afforded by her birth as a means to serve others. She was repelled by ostentatious displays of fortune like that found in one grandly furnished *hôtel particulier*:

My austere taste is revolted by this gilding ... this money stuck to the walls
without profit for thought, intelligence, or heart ... How selfish is the person
who shuts himself in these tombs of marble and gold and for whom the
world finishes at the sumptuous grille of his rich prison! And humanity that
works, that suffers, that weeps, that struggles, what does it count for in his
life!![29]

Access to credit and mutual aid

As among the bourgeoisie, when nobles took out a loan it was not necessarily a sign of financial distress. Access to credit was needed for nobles to
develop their estates and many were genuinely interested in agricultural
innovation and improvement.[30] There was strategic use of personal networks for securing loans of money. Figeac analysed 201 loans that nobles
registered with five different notaries in Gironde between 1801 and 1830.
Fifty-three of those loans were from noble to noble, in other words between
acquaintances, friends, or relatives.[31] Borrowing and lending money in
this way was a form of mutual aid that we shall see again in Chapter 8. It
meant that within the nobility an individual's ability to recover from dips
in economic capital was never disassociated from their detainment of
social capital. Nobles of small or middling-sized fortunes also took salaried
positions to supplement landed revenue; they looked for positions that
matched the ethos of 'service'. The army, magistrature, and diplomacy were
favoured career paths and remained so for noblemen across the nineteenth
century and into the twentieth. Noble used their personal networks to help
obtain positions, either for themselves or for relatives and friends, and the
nepotism worked for them up until the Third Republic.[32]

Connections between nobility and financial service to the State stretch
back into the early modern period; there were international connections
in the world of *la haute banque* before the installation of Meyer Anselm
Rothschild's five sons in European cities of the 1820s. From the 1840s
there was steady growth in the numbers of banks and mutuals in France
for which nobles became clients. The nobility also held non-executive
positions on the governing boards of banks and were involved in founding them.[33] The marquis Alexandre de Ploeuc (1815–88) provides an
example; he was among the founders of the Banque Ottomane and of
the Union Générale as well as holding executive responsibility for the
Banque de France during the Paris Commune. In 1882 when the Banque
de l'Union Financière folded Jean de Montebello was among the clients
who lost a part of their capital. Two years later the Union Générale went

into receivership. The marquis Charles-Marie-Christian de Biencourt was one of the directors of the bank and had to pay 1.1 million francs when it came under judicial administration. In 1899, when the Biencourt family sold the château d'Azay-le-Rideau, it was said their fortune had been 'ruined' because of the consequences of the banking disaster fifteen years earlier.[34]

Correspondence between family members for the first half of the nineteenth century shows how nobles broached fiscal matters with one another, and described difficulties, as well as the steps they took to try to mitigate risk. It also contains the advice that nobles received from relatives and close friends on ways of anticipating or countering problems. When grappling with short-term dips in liquidity, or threats to economic capital tied up in investments, nobles alerted and reached out for support to extended kin. In the same way that cousins, uncles, and aunts were involved in decisions for long-term management of patrimony, there was an impulse to keep in touch with collateral branches and friends of the family about immediate crises affecting solvency.

Louis Charles Théodat de Taillevis de Perrigny descended from Navarrese nobility who had bought real estate in the Vendômois during the sixteenth century. His ancestor Raphaël de Taillevis had served as doctor to Antoine de Bourbon and Jeanne d'Albret from 1542 and was ennobled by Henri II. During the French Revolution the sequestration of colonial properties owned by the Taillevis family in Saint Domingue diminished Louis Charles's capital and revenue. A naval officer during the period of Napoleon's military command, he entered politics after the fall of the Empire, serving as president of the electoral college of Romarantin in 1815 then as mayor of Fontaines-en-Solange in 1820.

Following marriage to his second wife, Marie-Louise Charlotte Devezeaux de Rancougne, Louis Charles established a home with her on the estate of La Ravinière (Loir-et-Cher). It was the entailment of this property to the benefit of his eldest son Théodat that Louis Charles began to consider in late February 1808, when Napoleon I was on the point of introducing the *majorat* legislation to France. Théodat was still a minor so, as father and *tuteur* for his son, Louis Charles had to gather paperwork and prepare the dossier. In a letter to his friend Monsieur Caron who had helped him in his plans, Louis Charles wrote on the subject of Théodat's future:

Thank you for the opening you have provided me for my son. I wanted to rouse myself to action on his behalf because I love him and I no longer have ambition for myself but do have ambition for Théodat. He is the empress's cousin ... He is a good and pretty child, full of spirit and of a strong aptitude for everything.[35]

Napoleon I authorised the creation of the *majorat* for Théodat de Taillevis de Perrigny, requested by Louis Charles, on 1 April 1809. The act containing the emperor's decision outlines the property to be entailed, which was broadly similar in composition with that of other *majorats*.[36] It also provides an interesting comment on the nature of a father–son relationship, as it was understood in the Napoleonic era. Charles is described as having completed 'all of the duties imposed by his double role as father and *tuteur*'. 'He wishes today to give to his son a new proof of his tenderness in fulfilling the formalities prescribed by legislation for the establishment of a *majorat* with the title of baron.'[37] Louis Charles Théodat de Taillevis de Perrigny, whose own material circumstances had been affected by loss of colonial property, was successful in his efforts to use the legal route of the *majorat* to secure future income for his son.

For Alexandre Chaudruc de Crazannes the First Empire had brought career opportunities and fulfilment. Born in 1782, he completed his education in Sorèzes and took up his first professional post as secretary to his uncle Balguerie, prefect of Gers. In 1809 he was appointed general secretary of the department of Loiret and after four years in this post was made a baron of the Empire on 25 February 1813.[38] When Louis XVIII was installed as king in March 1814 Alexandre Chaudrac de Crazannes initially supported the Bourbon regime, which meant that the change of political leadership did not upset his career; by July of that year he was appointed *maître des requêtes* to the Conseil d'État. One relative wrote to counsel Alexandre on financial matters: 'The essential point, my friend, is to be in command of one's expenses, not be commanded by them.'[39]

It was not long before Alexandre was punished for political vacillation. In March 1815 he welcomed Napoleon's return from the isle of Elba and displayed Bonapartist rather than royalist sympathies during the Hundred Days. As a result, after the defeat at Waterloo in June 1815, Alexandre was cast into disgrace by supporters of the Bourbons and removed from office. An old friend général Lafont learned about this ride on the wheel of political fortune from the newspaper *Les Gazettes*. Lafont wrote to Alexandre on 29 July 1815 to offer commiserations and sage suggestions:

If, by dividing up [the estate of] Crazannes, you are able to get two-thirds of what it might be worth I advise you to do it. You will be better off for ridding yourself of a bad property, laden with taxes and ruinous in maintenance costs for immense buildings of no use.[40]

Liquidating goods was a strategy used commonly by nobles with a calculated intent to raise cash and then reinvest at a later point in time. There are plenty of examples from the French Revolution and through the nineteenth and twentieth centuries where furniture, art and book collections were sold quickly, usually at auction as discussed in Chapter 8. Parcels of land were put on the market or traded between relatives; landed estates and urban properties could be whittled down if not sold in their entirety.[41]

During the Bourbon Restoration and into the early 1830s the comte de Bouillé travelled regularly between France and England. He wrote a series of pessimistic letters to his cousin, the marquis Charles François Guillaume de Chanaleilles, about the implications of revolutionary scenes in Paris. Whilst staying in the capital on 8 September 1830 Bouillé was preoccupied by his daughter Louise's health and by preparations for departure to England to rejoin his wife.

> After the liquidation [of our Parisian property] there remains for us only five to six thousand francs in *rentes* because I no longer count on anything from our colonial revenues … I still have lots to do here. I sold some goods at a terrible price, my horses went for a passable sum but there remain carriages, furniture [and] my poor apartment … I never had a great deal of personal ambition so I resign myself easily to this great reversal of fortune in so far as it concerns me … but it is the future of my poor children, it is their ruin, that brings distress to my heart.[42]

Chanaleilles sent a prompt and sensitive reply from his 'feudal towers' in the department of Ardèche for which Bouillé wrote to thank him on 29 September. 'I cannot tell you, my dear Chanaleilles, how touched I was by your kind letter; I shed tears over it and shall not forget these expressions of your attachment for me and for my children. Yes, certainly I will count on you.'[43]

Five months later Bouillé and his wife were back in Paris mourning the death of their daughter Louise. On 27 February 1831 he wrote to his cousin:

> Again I would like to vegetate in shelter from revolutionary storms. But it is my poor [son] Gaston who worries me. To be at his age without career, without fortune, without future is to be really unlucky. If I bring him back with me [to England] what will he do in a foreign country? His existence will be miserable and filled with regrets because he loves his own

country and finds it better than anywhere else. On the other hand if he stays here and I go it means we shall be separated for Lord knows how long.[44]

Distraught, and hesitant about the best course of action for his nuclear family, Bouillé was reliant on his cousin Chanaleilles's kindness and promises of aid. 'I will be able to rest with my trust placed in you.'[45]

The examples above, concerning the Taillevis de Perrigny, Chaudrac de Crazannes, and Bouillé families, shed light on the private side of nobles' existence during the nineteenth century. The confidences about financial matters shared with friends and relatives in correspondence were not necessarily those that nobles considered suitable to write about in memoirs destined for publication. Nor did the most frank reflections enter into the dossiers that nobles, with the help of accountants and lawyers, submitted to state authorities on tax, succession, and insurance. It is not that the nobility wanted confidentiality any more than persons of other classes in society involved in making declarations on fortune. But the motivations for seeking tax reductions or government assistance to preserve aristocratic property mean that almost anything that nobles put before the State on fiscal issues has to be treated with caution.[46]

An understanding of this private side of nobles' existence comple-ments the interpretations made of nobles' public attitudes and political behaviours toward revolutionary social change. It has been argued that the 1830s and 1840s marked an 'internal emigration' or retreat from politics by those Legitimist nobles who had developed distaste for public affairs and sought a life of quiet routine on their landed estates.[47] Bouillé's letter to Chanaleilles of 22 March 1832 distils the sentiment of longing for evasion: 'In a century of vissitudes such as this one nothing seems better to me than to live tranquilly at one's home and especially in a good château if one owns it. This would have been my life's dream and it evapo-rates like all my illusions of happiness.'[48]

Debt and its emotional costs

In the archives of French nobility references to debt and loans are ubiqui-tous and found across many different kinds of documents. Yet although debt was a longstanding cultural norm, at least for this class in society, it could still provoke an occasional burst of amazement or supercili-ous remark from one member of kin to another. In the autumn of 1790 Jeanne-Camille de Miramon, comtesse de Saint-Paul du Chayla, received a letter from her sister-in-law the marquise de Miramon (née Bardonin de Sansac):

> Your brother is no longer here, my dear sister. I wanted to have news of you and your daughter [so] I opened your letter, in accordance with an understanding between your brother and me, hoping that you would not find it disagreeable that I should do so. I am in the greatest astonishment at what you say about your affairs. You benefit from 40,000 *livres* worth of rents. You spend extremely little. How have you found it necessary to borrow so much? I know nothing of your affairs, no doubt. I know only what the public can say about it. One thinks with good reason that you have a lot of money locked away.[49]

In France women did not have the right to open a bank account in their own name until 1881 because politicians, on the left and the right, feared the 'threat' of women's financial independence would undermine the husband's authority. Noblewomen, who were accustomed to some control over financial capital, did sometimes argue with their husband over the household budget or blame him when expenditure got out of hand.

The archives of the Albertas family from Provence contain documentation of how marital relations were affected by different attitudes to money and also how relatives of the married couple were kept informed about the evolution of financial affairs. The marquis Félix d'Albertas (1789–1872) married Flavie Caussiny de Valbelle. This couple's eldest son, Arthur, married an Italian noblewoman Angéline Tornielli di Borgolavezzaro. At the time Arthur and Angéline became engaged in December 1846, one of the Albertas's agents, Tissot, was with them in Novare, Italy. Tissot was writing letters back to Arthur's father, the marquis Félix d'Albertas, which contain his impressions of the fiancée and her Italian relatives, as well as updates on Arthur's financial debts and repayments.

On 23 December 1846 Tissot's report was wholly positive about Mademoiselle Tornielli, to whom he attributed 'reflection, foresight, order, moderation, a rare discernment in everything, a balanced temper'; these were 'qualities in which Arthur is little endowed'. Six months later Tissot was in despair about the behaviour he was observing between Arthur and his now wife. On 2 June 1847 he alluded to marital arguments and described how 'the language Arthur uses most of the time when speaking to Madame la comtesse is far from appropriate'.[50] On 30 June 1847 Tissot wrote:

> There is no longer any peace between them … Monsieur your son is often at fault, insisting too violently of Madame his wife that she either give up or

do some trifling domestic or social activity ... She has a strongly ordered approach to her spending ... I should inform you that *the subject of money* has often led to petty quarrels between them ... One day Madame was in a bad temper and severely hurt Monsieur Arthur's feelings. Neither one of them dares speak to the other about money since their arrival here last Saturday.[51]

By 1900 in France some 1.5 million women had a bank account and 93 per cent of women's accounts had been opened without the husband's permission.[52] Noblewomen's high level of involvement in property matters, however, means that their own views are very apparent in the archives on the subjects of borrowing and lending money far earlier than this.

For the duchesse d'Abrantès pride was no stumbling block to her pleading for loans from friends and relations after her husband's suicide in 1813. To her devoted brother-in-law, Pierre de Geouffre de La Pradelle, she wrote of facing penury: 'the need I have for money is not this time for jewels, bonnets and gowns, but for bread, meat, wine, wood, the means for myself, my children, and my uncles to subsist'.[53] Pierre was very accustomed to the duchesse's urgent requests for loans and his replies were tactful but firm:

> Your situation, my dear sister, distresses me greatly. I did not believe you to be on a bed of roses, but I did not suppose that the bundle of thorns on which you sat was so prickly ... You see, dear, it is utterly impossible for me to help you. If I did not go into these details [his own list of expenses], which I can prove with papers in hand, one would not have missed the opportunity to say, I could [lend money] and did not want to![54]

The lightness of tone in these exchanges should not disguise the seriously entrenched nature of some nobles' debts and the enormous sums involved. Statistical study of successions shows that those individuals with the largest amounts of patrimony experienced proportionally greater losses than those with more modest amounts especially during the 1920s and 1930s. The direction in which nobles chose to invest played a determining role, for not all nobles directed their money toward the same goals. For example debt appeared only in less than 4 per cent of Parisian nobles' successions declared in 1911; many of these 'Parisians' held on to inherited properties but instead of buying more land were investing in the stock market.[55] By contrast, nobles who did not have a residence in Paris were more inclined to build up their land holdings so loans were taken out both as mortgages and for agricultural improvement.

When rents and land prices fell by one-third between 1880 and 1912 these 'non-Parisians' could find themselves in negative equity and were more likely to struggle with loan repayments. At least one nobleman is known to have served time in prison for bankruptcy.[56] Permanent anxiety about debt amounted to a virtual prison for others.

The prince Gaston de Béarn died in Pau on 18 June 1893, leaving behind six children from his marriage to Cécile (née de Talleyrand-Périgord); she had died on 11 December 1890. In his will, Gaston named his younger brother, the comte Jean de Béarn, as *tuteur* for the orphaned children. Jean, who was a father himself, had an affectionate regard for his nephews and nieces. On 3 May 1895 he described to the eldest nephew, Henri, the imminent change to their relationship before the law.

> You reach the age of majority [twenty-one years] tomorrow, which means that from tomorrow I shall cease to be your *tuteur* and you become master of your life, your conduct, and your interests. Fate has deemed that in your youth you must assume the role of junior head of the family, and in the coming few days you will probably feel more than ever the absence of your father and mother. You are entering into adult life amid difficult circumstances, during the liquidation of the very weighty affairs of your parents' succession, with the obligation to cut a suitable figure in society, to tighten the familial bonds that have been weakened by events, to take part in many business matters that up until now have escaped your worry … Grave concerns and a heavy responsibility await you on the threshold of your majority.[57]

It was indeed a complicated situation for which Henri had to take charge as young *chef de famille*. The overall debt featured in the successions of the prince and princesse de Béarn mostly related to mortgages on various châteaux and landed estates distributed across northern, western, and south-western France that Gaston and Cécile had separately inherited from their respective ascendants.[58] These mortgages tallied together required interest payments amounting to 40,000 francs each year. There were also fees (*le droit de mutation*) running to hundreds of thousands of francs owed to the Treasury. Some five million francs of the debt comprised small sums owed to 140 individual creditors (tradesmen, doctors, dentists, lawyers, notaries, vendors of food and other produce) in Paris, Pau, and Arcachon. The family's annual income was no more than 200,000 francs. Liquidation was the only way to bring the level of debt down. Otherwise each heir accepting a share of inheritance (which in law necessarily came with a proportionate share in the debt) would experience ongoing financial difficulties.[59]

Gaston and Cécile had married in 1873. It was a passionate love match. Cécile meant 'everything' to her husband; she was his soul mate, the 'excellent mother' of his children. After Cécile's death Gaston grimly stated 'our reunion alone will satisfy me'.[60] The couple's marriage contract of 5 May 1873 was based on *la communauté réduite aux acquêts* so provided for joint ownership limited to goods acquired after the couple wed. In 1885 the prince and princesse had conceived a plan for working together to eradicate the debt from previous successions so as not to pass that burden on to their six children. The final years of life for these two nobles, marred by stress and near continual illness for each of them, were wholly focused on the execution of their plan with the professional assistance of their lawyer Duquaire.

A first step was to apply for a *séparation de biens* to end the contract of *communauté* which was approved by the Tribunal Civil de la Seine on 7 December 1885. Cécile was a devout Catholic and agreed to this legalistic alteration to her marriage with the greatest reluctance. Over the next five years, she and Gaston kept steadfastly to their joint commitment and by selling various properties managed to reduce the mortgage debt of eight million francs to just under two million francs by 11 December 1890, the date on which the princesse died.

The emotional toll of trying to clear the debt is vividly conveyed in correspondence between the prince and princesse through the late 1880s when Gaston was required to travel regularly to Paris for meetings with relatives, lawyers, and agents. From the opposite end of the country in Pau, Cécile mulled incessantly over the slow progress on liquidating assets and prayed that God would bless and aid them in their efforts. For this deeply loving couple physical separation from one another was experienced as a form of suffering and sacrifice. Letters from Cécile in March 1887 convey her sense of the couple's plan being akin to a religious mission:

> Should the good Lord wish us to complete the sale of the *hôtel* [in Paris] and of La Roche [La Rochebeaucourt, Dordogne] then we would be completely at ease. Once the task is accomplished, we will no longer be apart from one another. That is my sole desire and my single ambition; I hope it will happen. The sale of Chassy [Nièvre] is a great step forward, I am sure that it disconcerted many people.[61]

> When we finish we will have only Sermois [Nièvre], here [a villa in Pau], Arcachon [Gironde] and Carrières ... we will be able to attend to [these properties] very easily whilst being completely free in our movements. Eight days ago we were together at Lourdes, *mon cher petit*, I have kept such

a good memory of it and hope that God willing we shall soon return there to thank Him.[62]

I received three letters from you this morning so none are missing ... I ask God to give us peace at last, to make you finish quickly so that you will be able to return here.[63]

Cécile died before she and Gaston achieved their aim. A month after her death, a *conseil de famille* was convened by a justice of the peace in January 1891 to address matters pertaining to the inheritance rights of the six children who were all minors.

Recently widowed, the prince Gaston was doing his best to assist the *conseil de famille* when he was dealt a further blow by the death of his mother, Marguerite (née de Choiseul-Praslin). The opening of her complex succession propelled Gaston and his three younger siblings into a distressing tussle. Gaston tried to explain the situation to his eldest child Henri:

I have terrible troubles for my mother's succession. Your aunt Blanche, your uncle Jean, and I are perfectly united and in agreement, but your uncle Arsieu is causing difficulties. It is absolutely necessary that you six [Gaston's children] stay united ... Unity is in all our interests, because every divided house shall perish. Remember this, my dear Henri, that being the eldest it will be up to you to make concessions in order to maintain unity [with your siblings].[64]

A year later, exhausted and ill, Gaston told Henri:

You must not imagine that one can finish important business in a few days. Everything is long and difficult. Unanticipated obstacles appear that it is necessary to overcome. There are delays of all kinds. It is only through patience and perseverance that one succeeds. I hope that at the end of the week we will be able to sign [the concluding documents for] the partition of my mother's succession.[65]

For Gaston the desire to avoid the sibling disagreement exploding into a court case, with the likelihood of publicly shameful consequences, was about protecting the honour of the Béarn family. But even as he sought to negotiate with relatives, and to be accommodating of competing claims and interests contrary to his own, Gaston was not about to be trodden down. He wrote to Henri: 'I am not enjoying it I assure you, but they [lawyers acting for relatives in dispute] wanted to make me lose my position and as a result your own ... I defend myself with fierce determination.'[66]

Conclusion

Incapacity and debt were issues of longstanding significance to the nobility in France and the legal processes for managing their implications in the nineteenth and twentieth centuries had their origins in models from written law under the *ancien régime*. Documentation of the *tutelle* and *curatelle* systems operating prior to 1789 sheds light on family dynamics and understandings of adulthood for the Middle Ages and early modern period. Where documentation survives of *tutelle* or *curatelle* regimes after 1804 we can see continuities for example in the naming of an uncle to fulfil the role of *tuteur*. In the requests that nobles made to their relatives for loans of money, and in their attempts to deal with the consequences of severe indebtedness, we find reliance on collateral branches and wide kin networks to support nuclear bonds of care and responsibility. Nobles were in frequent communication with one another, and with a range of non-noble professionals such as medics and judges, to take decisions and to observe legal and administrative instructions.

Class-based dispositions shaped the nobility's reactions to incapacity and debt and this can be seen in various ways from the tone and content of extant letters. Some of the problems nobles encountered were specifically connected with nobiliary status, for example in the difficulties created for Napoleon's *noblesse d'Empire* when property received in a donation was no longer under French control. Other types of problems, for example those that resulted from the poor management of banks and businesses, brought losses for nobles just as for other citizens. Nobles' descriptions of making economies or liquidating holdings are often couched in terms of despair and despondency. Gloomy reflections on the decay of a family fortune, however, were part and parcel of the nobility's inclination for nostalgic visions of the past.

Such sentiments also need to be read with a perspective on the relative nature of the financial difficulties encountered by nobility compared with the difficulties facing people of lower classes. Grinding poverty, poor nutrition, unsanitary living conditions, and injury and ill health from excessive hours of work in factories and fields were not part of nobles' lives.[67] This minority group retained its disproportionate representation among the wealthy elite through the nineteenth century. The concept of *noblesse oblige* combined with religious piety to inform nobles' charitable actions in assistance to the urban and rural poor. Catholic faith also features in the emotional confidences of some nobles about their own financial situations. Riches were flaunted in certain quarters, by nobles and by wealthy bourgeois. Expressions of deep unease about luxury emerge in aristocratic writings because of the stark disparities in fortune that characterised their society.

Notes

1 G. Comnène, *Sur la Grèce* (Paris, 1831), p. 41.

2 D. Higgs, 'Social mobility and hereditary titles in France, 1814–1830: the majorats-sur-demande', *Histoire sociale/Social History* 14 (1981), 29–47, esp. 45–6; D. Higgs, *Nobles in Nineteenth-Century France: The Practice of Inegalitarianism* (Baltimore, 1987), pp. 102–29.

3 E. Wasson, *Aristocracy and the Modern World* (New York, 2006), p. 109.

4 H. M. Scott (ed.), *The European Nobilities in the Seventeenth and Eighteenth Centuries* vol. 1 (Harlow, 1995), pp. 18, 118, 150–1, 156–7; G. V. Taylor, 'Noncapitalist wealth and the origins of the French Revolution', *American Historical Review* 72 (1967), 469–96.

5 A. Daumard, 'Richesse de la noblesse' in F. Braudel and E. Labrousse (eds), *Histoire economique et sociale de la France* (Paris, 1976), vol. 3, pp. 933–7; A. Daumard, *Les Fortunes françaises au XIXe siècle* (Paris, 1973), pp. 3–40, 257–67; A. Daumard, 'Wealth and affluence in France since the beginning of the nineteenth century' in W. D. Rubenstein (ed.), *Wealth and the Wealthy in the Modern World* (New York, 1980), pp. 90–121; R. Gibson, 'The French nobility in the nineteenth century – particularly in the Dordogne' in J. Howorth and P. G. Cerny (eds), *Elites in France: Origins, Reproduction and Power* (London, 1981), pp. 7–11; R. Gibson, 'The Périgord: landownership, power and illusion' in R. Gibson and M. Blinkhorn (eds), *Landownership and Power in Modern Europe* (London, 1991), pp. 79–98; D. Sutherland, *France 1789–1815: Revolution and Counterrevolution* (London, 1985), pp. 384–9; C. Charle, 'Noblesse et élites en France au début du XXe siècle' in *Les Noblesses européennes au XIXe siècle* (Rome, 1988), pp. 407–33; J.-M. Wiscart, *La Noblesse de la Somme au XIXe siècle* (Amiens, 1994), pp. 148–51.

6 M. d'Armaillé, *Quand on savait vivre heureux (1830–1860)*, translated in Higgs, *Nobles*, pp. 212–13, and compare pp. 120–2; É. Mension-Rigau, *Aristocrates et grands bourgeois: éducation, traditions, valeurs* (Paris, 1994), ch. 7.

7 C. Jago, 'The "crisis of the aristocracy" in seventeenth-century Castile', *Past and Present* 84 (1979), 60–90; D. Cannadine, *The Decline and Fall of the British Aristocracy* (London, 1992); D. Cannadine, *Aspects of Aristocracy: Grandeur and Decline in Modern Britain* (New Haven and London, 1994); J. Habbakuk, *Marriage, Debt and the Estates System: English Landownership* (Oxford, 1994); P. G. M. Dickson and J. V. Beckett, 'The finances of the dukes of Chandos: aristocratic inheritance, marriage, and debt in eighteenth-century England', *Huntington Library Quarterly* 64 (2001), 309–55.

8 J. Chevallier and L. Bach, *Droit civil* vol. 1, 7 ed. (Paris, 1978), pp. 96–105, 106–11.

9 Chevallier and Bach, *Droit civil* vol. 1, 7 ed., pp. 96–102, 109–10.

10 Chevallier and Bach, *Droit civil* vol. 1, 7 ed., pp. 110–11.

11 On the role of uncles see A. Livingstone, *Out of Love for My Kin: Aristocratic Family Life in the Lands of the Loire, 1000–1200* (Ithaca, 2010), pp. 37–8, 93–4, 218.

12 On Charlemagne and his eldest son Pippin 'the Hunchback' see J. L. Nelson, 'Charlemagne: pater optimus?' in P. Godman, J. Jarnut, and P. Johanek (eds), *Am Vorabend der Kaiserkrönung: das Epos 'Karolus Magnus et Leo papa' und der Papstbesuch in Paderborn 799* (Berlin, 2002), pp. 271–83. On Louis XIV see S. Perez, *La Santé de Louis XIV: une biohistoire du Roi-Soleil* (Seyssel, 2007). Prince Ferdinand 'Nando' Hohenzollern-Sigmaringen (later King of Romania) was born with protruding ears that his family tried to correct by instructing the nurse to pin them back with bandages; the remedy failed. H. Pakula, *The Last Romantic: A Biography of Queen Marie of Roumania* (London, 1995), pp. 40, 54.

13 AD Alpes-Maritimes 25 J/264 Archives du château de Mouans-Sartoux.

14 AD Alpes-Maritimes 25 J/262–66 Archives du château de Mouans-Sartoux.

15 10 March 1823 in AD Alpes-Maritimes 25 J/269 Archives du château de Mouans-Sartoux.

16 AD Alpes-Maritimes 25 J/270 Archives du château de Mouans-Sartoux.

17 On military careers see I. Woloch, *The French Veteran from the Revolution to the Restoration* (Chapel Hill, 1979); J.-P. Bertaud, 'Napoleon's officers', *Past and Present* 112 (1986), 91–111; J. R. Elting, *Swords around a Throne: Napoleon's Grande Armée* (New York, 1988); R. Blaufarb, *The French Army, 1750–1820: Careers, Talent, Merit* (Manchester, 2002); N. Petiteau, *Lendemains d'Empire: les soldats de Napoléon dans la France du XIXe siècle* (Paris, 2003). On soldiers' trauma from shell shock in the First World War see R. A. Nye, *Masculinity and Male Codes of Honor in Modern France* (Oxford, 1993), pp. 216–28.

18 AD Alpes-Maritimes 25 J/271-2 Archives du château de Mouans-Sartoux.

19 In 1913 the family had branches in Belgium, France, and Prussia. Rodolphe, duc de Croÿ, became hereditary member of the Chambre des seigneurs of Prussia in 1854. The *Almanach de Gotha* contains historical details of the house of Croÿ.

20 'Tutelle' (1885) and 'Dépenses faites pour l'entretien de S.A.S. le prince Alfred Emmanuel de Croÿ' in AD Nord 26J (E2508)/5 Papiers de la famille de Croÿ.

21 Le Roeulx was the seat for one of Hainaut's peerages in the eleventh century; the estate and château have been in the hands of the Croÿ since 1429 when Jacqueline of Bavaria ceded the property to Anthony de Croÿ. When the Croÿ-Roeulx branch expired in 1767 the châteaux du Roeulx passed with the ducal title to the Croÿ-Solre branch.

22 M. L. Bush, *Rich Noble, Poor Noble* (Manchester, 1988), pp. 6, 7-29, 174;

J. Dewald, *The European Nobility, 1400–1800* (Cambridge, 1996), pp. xvi, 22–7; Scott, *The European Nobilities*; Wasson, *Aristocracy*, ch. 3.

23 Chevallier and Bach, *Droit civil*, vol. 1, pp. 104–5. The law of 20 September 1792 fixed the age of matrimonial majority at 21 years for both sexes; until they had reached that age men and women had to have parental consent. The Code Civil set the minimum age for marriage at 15 years for a woman and 18 years for a man (with parental consent required). On 5 July 1974 the age of civil and matrimonial majority was set at 18 years for both sexes.

24 E. C. Macknight, *Aristocratic Families in Republican France, 1870–1940* (Manchester, 2012), chs 6 and 7.

25 S. Hazareesingh, *The Legend of Napoleon* (London, 2005), p. 72; P. Mansel, *Paris between Empires 1814–1852* (London, 2001), pp. 10–37, 170–4, 383–422; F. Démier, *La France de la Restauration (1814–1830): l'impossible retour du passé* (Paris, 2012), ch. 17; Macknight, *Aristocratic Families*, pp. 132–3.

26 J. Tulard, *Napoléon et la noblesse d'Empire* (Paris, 1979), pp. 113–17.

27 É. Mension-Rigau, *Le Donjon et le clocher* (Paris, 2003), pp. 35–7; Higgs, *Nobles*, pp. 151–2, 207; J. Nagle, *Luxe et charité, le faubourg Saint-Germain et l'argent* (Paris, 1994); E. C. Macknight, 'Faiths, fortunes, and feminine duty: charity in Parisian high society, 1880–1914', *Journal of Ecclesiastical History* 58 (2007), 482–506; M. Figeac, *Destins de la noblesse bordelaise (1770–1830)* 2 vols (Bordeaux, 1996), vol. 2, pp. 746–65.

28 E. C. Macknight, 'The Catholic nobility's commitment to *écoles libres* in France, 1850–1905', *Historical Reflections/Réflexions historiques*, forthcoming.

29 May 1866 in 'Comment elle a aimé les petits selon le monde', AP 156 (I)/ 314 Fonds Mackau. N. Petiteau, *Élites et mobilités: la noblesse d'Empire au XIXe siècle (1808–1914)* (Paris, 1997), p. 349.

30 G. Postel-Vinay, 'Les Domaines nobles et le recours au crédit' in *Les Noblesses européennes*, p. 203; F. Lalliard, 'Propriété aristocratique et innovation agronomique au XIXe siècle', *Histoire et Sociétés Rurales* 13 (2000), 67–92; D. Picco, 'Les Femmes et la terre dans les élites françaises (XVII–XVIII siècles)' in C. Le Mao and C. Marache (eds), *Les Élites et la terre du XVIe siècle aux années 1930* (Paris, 2010), pp. 223–32.

31 Figeac, *Destins* vol. 2, pp. 626–7.

32 C.-I. Brelot, *La Noblesse réinventée: les nobles de Franche-Comté de 1814 à 1870* 2 vols (Paris, 1992), vol. 1, p. 367; C. Charle, *Les Hauts fonctionnaires en France au XIXe siècle* (Paris, 1980), pp. 12, 34–9, 121; Mension-Rigau, *Aristocrates*, pp. 405–7, 458–60.

33 F. Braudel, *L'Identité de la France* vol. 2 *Les Hommes et les choses* (Paris, 1990), pp. 441–71; On nineteenth-century banking see B. Gille, *La Banque et le crédit en France de 1815 à 1848* (Paris, 1959); J. Bouvier, *Le Krach de l'Union générale: 1878–1885* (Paris, 1960); A. Plessis, *La Banque de France et ses deux*

cents actionnaires sous le Second Empire (Geneva, 1982); Higgs, *Nobles*, pp. 107–8, 120–2, 126–7.

34 AN AP 272/14–25 Fonds Ploeuc (esp. 272/19 on the Banque de France); AD Indre-et-Loire 152J/153 Fonds de Biencourt; Duchesse de Sabran-Pontevès, *Bon sang ne peut mentir* (Paris, 1987), p. 127.

35 17 February 1808 in AD Loir-et-Cher 97J/13 Fonds Taillevis et familles alliées.

36 Tulard, *Napoléon et la noblesse d'Empire*, pp. 9–11; N. Petiteau, *Élites et mobilités: la noblesse d'Empire au XIXe siècle (1808–1914)* (Paris, 1997), pp. 52–7.

37 AD Loir-et-Cher 97J/13 Fonds Taillevis et familles alliées.

38 Alexandre's father Jacques Chaudruc de Crazannes had also been ennobled by office as *président trésorier* in La Rochelle.

39 Undated (1814) in AD Charente-Maritime 177J/3 Fonds Chaudruc de Crazannes.

40 29 July 1815 in AD Charente-Maritime 177J/5 Fonds Chaudruc de Crazannes.

41 Figeac, *Destins*, vol. 1, pp. 52–118, and vol. 2, ch. 2; Higgs, *Nobles*, pp. 53–7; Wiscart, *La Noblesse*, pp. 141–4.

42 8 September 1830 in AD Ardèche 39J/332 Chartrier de Chambonas.

43 29 September 1830 in AD Ardèche 39J/332 Chartrier de Chambonas.

44 27 February 1831 in AD Ardèche 39J/332 Chartrier de Chambonas.

45 27 February 1831 in AD Ardèche 39J/332 Chartrier de Chambonas.

46 On tax avoidance in France see M. Lévy-Leboyer, M. Lescure, and A. Plessis (eds), *L'Impôt en France aux XIXe et XXe siècles* (Paris, 2006); pp. 84–5; Daumard, *Les Fortunes*, pp. 34–9.

47 See for example, A.-J. Tudesq, *Les Grands Notables en France (1840–1849): étude historique d'une psychologie sociale* 2 vols (Paris, 1964); R. Price, 'Legitimist opposition to the Revolution of 1830 in the French provinces', *Historical Journal* 17 (1974), 755–78; D. Pinkney, *The Revolution of 1830* (Princeton, 1972); J. M. Merriman (ed.), *1830 in France* (New York, 1975); A. Jardin and A.-J. Tudesq, *Restoration and Reaction, 1815–1848*, translated by E. Forster (Cambridge, 1983), ch. 5; Mansel, *Paris*, ch. 9; Démier, *La France*, epilogue.

48 22 March 1832 in AD Ardèche 39J/332 Chartrier de Chambonas.

49 October 1790 in AD Haute-Loire 23J–24J/193 Archives Langlade du Chayla et Familles Apparentées.

50 23 December 1846 and 2 June 1847 in AD Bouches-du-Rhône 31E/8037 Archives de la famille d'Albertas.

51 30 June 1847 in AD Bouches-du-Rhône 31E/8037 Archives de la famille d'Albertas.

52 V. Antomarchi, *Politique et famille sous la IIIe République 1870–1914* (Paris, 2000), pp. 18–22.

53 12 June [year illegible] in AD Corrèze 54J Fonds Geouffre de La Pradelle (*fonds 'en vrac'*, not classed at time of consultation).

54 14 August 1833 in AD Corrèze 54J Fonds Geouffre de La Pradelle (*fonds 'en vrac'*, not classed at time of consultation).

55 Daumard, *Les Fortunes françaises*, pp. 115–77, 264–7; A. Daumard, 'Noblesses parisiennes et civilisation bourgeoise au XIXe siècle' in C.-I. Brelot (ed.), *Noblesses et villes (1780–1950)* (Tours, 1995), p. 113.

56 Wiscart, *La Noblesse*, pp. 141–5.

57 3 May 1895 in AD Charente J1093 Fonds Galard, Brassac, Béarn, Chalais.

58 The couple's property holdings were situated in multiple departments, chiefly Nièvre, Loire-Inférieure, Charente, Charente-Maritime, Dordogne, Tarn, and Basses-Pyrénées.

59 'Consultation pour les mineurs de Béarn: délibération du conseil de famille du 2 mars 1894' and 'Relevé des dettes chinographiques réclamés depuis le décès du prince de Béarn' in AD Charente J1077 Fonds Galard, Brassac, Béarn, Chalais; *Tribunal Civil de la Seine Audience du samedi 22 juin 1895. Plaidorie de Me Derch*; *Tribunal Civil de la Seine Audience du samedi 25 avril 1896. Plaidorie de Me Labori* in AD Charente J1250 Fonds Galard, Brassac, Béarn, Chalais.

60 12 February 1891 and 10 October 1891 in AD Charente J1092 Fonds Galard, Brassac, Béarn, Chalais.

61 11 March 1887 in AD Charente J1080 Fonds Galard, Brassac, Béarn, Chalais.

62 13 March 1887 in AD Charente J1080 Fonds Galard, Brassac, Béarn, Chalais.

63 29 March 1887 in AD Charente J1080 Fonds Galard, Brassac, Béarn, Chalais.

64 10 March 1891 in AD Charente J1092 Fonds Galard, Brassac, Béarn, Chalais.

65 21 March 1892 in AD Charente J1092 Fonds Galard, Brassac, Béarn, Chalais.

66 5 October 1891 in AD Charente J1092 Fonds Galard, Brassac, Béarn, Chalais.

67 See for example M. Perrot, 'The three ages of industrial discipline in nineteenth-century France' in J. M. Merriman (ed.), *Consciousness and Class Experience in Nineteenth-Century Europe* (New York, 1979), pp. 149–68; L. Strumingher, *Women and the Making of the Working Class: Lyon 1830–1870* (St Albans, 1979); J. Donzelot, *The Policing of Families*, translated by Robert Hurley (New York, 1979); W. H. Sewell, *Work and Revolution in France: The Language of Labor from the Old Regime to 1848* (Cambridge, 1980); R. G. Fuchs, *Abandoned Children: Foundlings and Child Welfare in Nineteenth-Century France* (Albany, 1984); G. Noiriel, *Workers in French Society in the Nineteenth and Twentieth Centuries*, translated by H. McPhail (London, 1990); A. Corbin, *Women for Hire: Prostitution and Sexuality in France after 1850*, translated by A. Sheridan (Cambridge, MA, 1990); R. G. Fuchs, *Poor and Pregnant in Paris* (New Brunswick, NJ, 1992).

5

Landed estates in operation

The servants are quite unlucky to be obliged to serve us, to carry out our wishes for the whole day and never their own, to be exposed to our whims, our moods and our fantasies without ever being free to complain about it.[1]

During the nineteenth and early twentieth centuries landownership remained the core of aristocratic identity and the primary source of income for the French nobility. Yet these continuities operated within a markedly different context from the *ancien régime* in which nobles' privileged hold on land had originated and developed over time.[2] Wealthy commoners, who for centuries had purchased land to achieve the semblance of nobility, but who had lacked the feudal privileges of the Second Estate, were now able to compete more readily for status and social authority through possession of property – not only land, but also manufacturing and commercial real estate as France slowly became a more urban, industrialised nation. Prior to the French Revolution nobles had owned about 25 per cent of France's territory. By the 1830s these landowners still held around 10 per cent of the land, but the size of estates had diminished. Most French nobles owned tiny amounts of land in comparison with the vast aristocratic estates maintained in some other parts of continental Europe and in Britain well into the twentieth century.[3]

The transformations wrought by the French Revolution meant that throughout the nineteenth and twentieth centuries there was no French equivalent of the 'landed interest' represented by the English peerage, Scottish nobles, or Prussian Junkers, for example. In historical scholarship the economics of elite landowning in modern France remained for a long time 'an almost virgin field'. As Theodore Zeldin observed, 'historians have been interested far more in the history of peasant owner- ship'.[4] In 1789 about one-third of the total land was owned by the peas- antry and this proportion increased over the next hundred years. By the 1880s close to half of agricultural land in France consisted of small and medium-sized properties comprising less than twenty hectares. Research on peasant experiences is thus crucial for rural history and it is this that scholars such as Georges Lefebvre, Emmanuel Le Roy Ladurie, and others placed at the very heart of French history.[5] Historians' reticence on the subject of aristocratic landowners can also be explained by the growth of interest in urban history where new approaches have developed around questions of gender, religion, and race. Important for this scholarship, and more broadly for modern history, has been historians' concern to explain the rise of the bourgeoisie.[6]

In France a historian seeking to answer questions on nobles' landown- ership must take into account the juridical distinction between public and private archives because this has a bearing on the types and organi- sation of information available for research.[7] *Archives publiques* contain information on what the authorities representing the State recorded about landownership in the population as a whole. By contrast, in nobles' *archives privées* the context for producing documents about landowner- ship was the daily management of the family's estate.[8]

Access to *archives privées* really matters in France for any researcher wanting to understand the interdependency of male and female roles and the gendered dimensions of ownership, management, and labour on nobles' estates. This is because, whilst the involvement of women is very apparent across all kinds of documents in *archives privées*, either there is no mention of women in documents like the electoral rolls in *archives publiques*, or else the experiences of women are almost always conveyed through the writings of men. *Archives privées* are also very rich for addressing the personal interactions of people from different class back- grounds. This includes peasant women whose experiences are among the hardest to find written evidence for and to interpret from *archives publiques* owing to low rates of literacy. Letters addressed to nobles by the first generations of rural working-class women to benefit from free and compulsory state schooling, introduced by the Ferry laws of 1880–82, provide precious access to such women's concerns.

In French rural history because the focus of most researchers' interest has lain with the peasantry – hence the academic field of 'peasant studies' – nobles tend to appear as rather peripheral figures in the literature on rural communities (only partly explained by aristocratic absenteeism).[9] A dominant theme in this literature is that of conflict over vested interests. Any exercise of private proprietorial rights that interfered with common use rights, like the ability to collect firewood or enable animals to graze, exacerbated the precariousness of peasant livelihoods. Tensions between peasants and lords that could simmer for years produced sporadic violence and occasionally erupted into outright rebellion. In the most extreme of cases, aristocratic disdain for peasant circumstances and dogmatic defence of private property rights in the face of peasant opposition resulted in the brutal murders of noblemen in 1830.[10]

There is every reason for historians to study conflict. *Archives privées* contain myriad examples of the contest for power: between family members, between landowners and tenants, between villagers and mayors, between clergy and parishioners, and others. Yet these archives also document the day-to-day exercise of power. Historians investigating landowners' routine exercise of power have described their task as 'reversing the perspective' because scholarly attention is so often directed toward non-routine instances where that power was contested.[11] The continuities behind noble landowners' exercise of power also involved people's vested interests and the desire to protect those interests by 'keeping the peace'.[12] For the wealthy, safety and prosperity were at stake; for the poor, the continuities were rooted in economic dependency. In the documentation about daily routine on a noble estate lie some of the explanations for why, after short outbreaks of violence, the aristocratic lifestyle was restored and maintained, and why after such episodes, in the vast majority of cases, nobles did not fundamentally alter their residency patterns, household structures, systems of estate management, or charitable practices.

Ownership

Nobles' culture of ownership was a familial one. Relatives had to work together to find solutions to problems of property, and the 'education' of offspring was designed to inculcate dispositions that would protect the collective interest or *l'esprit de famille*. Nobles learnt the responsibilities of estate ownership from their parents and other senior relatives. These women and men were accustomed to daily interaction with domestic servants of both sexes and with outdoor labourers. Working-class culture was not 'foreign' to nobles. They did not participate in it (except indirectly in childhood when some learnt to speak *patois* from their nurse) but they were conditioned to know how to respond to it, and were educated by senior relatives in the capacity to give orders to working-class women and men.[13]

In the French language the noun *la gestion* to denote administration or management became increasingly used in the France of the 1940s and the advent of 'management studies' as an academic discipline in France dates from the 1960s.[14] Yet the verb *gérer* (from the Latin *gerere*), and other cognate terms for the exercise of authority and control, appear from the fifteenth century in nobles' writings about property.[15] It is instructive therefore to begin by looking at how such terms were applied in historical documents of the nineteenth and twentieth centuries and what the duties of aristocratic estate ownership involved.

On the morning of 16 January 1836, in the office of the royal notary of Toulouse, Charles Louis de Tournier-Vaillac obtained a document that gave power of attorney to his eldest son Eugène to manage, govern, and administer (*régir, gouverner, et administrer*) properties owned by Charles Louis in the departments of Haute-Garonne and Lot. The Tournier-Vaillacs were robe nobility whose investments included landholdings and urban property in Toulouse. Charles Louis de Tournier-Vaillac lived in a townhouse at 3 rue de la Magdelaine, and his son Eugène was a magistrate in the same city. Under the terms of the 1836 power of attorney Eugène was given legal mandate:

> To appoint and establish all the stewards, sharecroppers, *maîtres-valets*, private forest or field wardens; to give them notice in order to employ new ones; to lease for farming [*affermer*] in total or in part the said properties according to the prices, clauses, and conditions that he will decide; to settle all of the accounts relating either to the administration in which he will engage by virtue of this mandate or to the preceding administration. To sell all of the commodities and products of any kind from these properties; to demand the payment of sums that will or may fall due [including] farm rents ... To keep watch over the upkeep of these properties; to raise issues if there is cause; to agree to the placement and identification of boundary markers; to ascertain any encroachment and if there is need to pursue redress ... To issue summons and to appear before all judges and tribunals; to undertake preliminaries toward conciliation if necessary; to bring and defend all suits ... To sign all public or private deeds, and generally to undertake for the maintenance and administration of the said properties all that circumstances shall require.[16]

We can see from this 1836 document that the power of attorney invested in Eugène encompassed a great range of activities and functions involving authority and control. He had responsibility for people, responsibility for goods, and responsibility for maintaining profitable connections between people and goods. All of these responsibilities involved paperwork of various kinds (accounts, letters, deeds) as well as human interaction with professionals in different sectors from forestry to law. Eugène was obliged to give his father Charles Louis information on real estate income and expenses accompanied by all receipts. Everything was noted down to the last centime, from the payment of tax to the purchase of a ladder.[17]

Around one hundred years later, in the north of France, the Montlaur family adopted a similar arrangement when an estate was left undivided to the heirs in a succession. In 1946 the estate of La Thibaudière, comprising a château and land situated in the department of Maine-et-Loire, was inherited by three adult siblings: Marie-Antoinette de Montlaur, the marquis Humbert de Montlaur, and the comte Guy de Montlaur. After dividing among themselves the furnishings of the château, so that each one received a share, the siblings agreed that the comte Guy de Montlaur should have the option of buying the real estate shares of his sister and brother in order to become sole owner of La Thibaudière. The property first had to be valued by an expert appointed by mutual agreement (it was valued at 2 million francs), and the possibility of buying his siblings' real estate shares was made available to the comte Guy de Montlaur for a period of three years to allow him time to raise sufficient funds.

In order that the estate was looked after in the meantime, the three siblings signed an agreement in which the comte Guy de Montlaur was 'designated as Administrator of the property [and] to this effect all powers are accorded to him to occupy and live in the château; to engage or give notice to farmers, sharecroppers, and domestic staff; to establish and conclude all leases and arrangements; to deal with the public authorities'. In signing this agreement with his siblings Guy committed himself 'to maintain the property in its current state'. He was allowed to keep any profit from the exploitation of land at La Thibaudière on the condition that his brother and sister receive payments in cash and in kind made annually. Humbert and Marie-Antoinette were each to receive from Guy: the cash value of 1,000 kilograms of beef; the cash value of twenty-six quintals of wheat; thirty steres of wood; and six chickens, four dozen eggs, six pounds of butter, and one fat duck.[18]

The comte Guy de Montlaur made notes on the labour involved for exploitation of the land and estimates of what he could expect in the way of annual returns and expenses. The principal people whose livelihoods were linked with the estate, but who were not part of the Montlaur family, were a man named Alexandre Allard employed as caretaker, plus Allard's wife, son, and daughter. Guy noted that the Allard family was to continue to live in a house on the estate and to work the garden. They were free to make use of the horse and two cows already there as well as the poultry and rabbits. Allard was to send twenty kilograms of vegetables each week to the Parisian residence of the marquis Humbert de Montlaur at 25 rue de Lübeck, 16th arrondissement, and to sell eighty kilograms of vegetables each week in Angers; any surplus vegetables Allard was able to keep for his own family's consumption. By deducting the wages paid to Allard (7,000 francs per month), the wages paid to Allard's son (4,500 francs per month), and the social insurance, Guy estimated that the sale of vegetables from the garden would bring in a net profit of 61,600 francs per year.[19]

A second group of people involved on the estate of La Thibaudière is referred to in Guy's notes as the *basse-cour* household. The term *basse-cour* dates back at least as far as the fourteenth century and refers to an outdoor space within a château's grounds that typically contained elements such as barns, stables, cowhouses, dovecotes, washhouses, wine-presses, bakeries, and kitchens. This 'lower court' where various tasks were carried out by servants and labourers was separated from the spaces occupied by nobles; for example, to reach the château from the *basse-cour* might involve crossing a drawbridge or climbing a hill.[20] Since the individuals in the *basse-cour* household are not named in Guy's notes it is impossible to tell the male–female ratio, but it is clear that these were people employed to work the fields and look after the horses, cows, and chickens. For centuries women had featured among the servants and labourers of the *basse-cour*, and their participation in farm work continued to be essential in 1946 owing to the male death and injury tolls of two world wars.[21]

Guy estimated the annual returns he could expect from sales of potatoes, milk, eggs, hay, wheat and oats. All of this produce together was calculated to bring in 223,000 francs gross per year.[22] By deducting from this sum the wages paid to the *basse-cour* household, and the social insurance, Guy estimated a net profit of 78,100 francs per year.[23] A further source of income at La Thibaudière consisted of rents paid by individuals for the right to hunt on parts of the estate. In 1946 Guy expected 100,000 francs per annum from hunting leases that would more than cover the annual payment of 80,000 francs in land tax (*crédit foncier*) for the property. The estate's location in the department of Maine-et-Loire meant it was accessible within a few hours by car or by train for elite Parisians wanting to form a hunting party for the weekend.[24]

From the examples above concerning the Montlaur and Tournier-Veillac families there are two key points to note. First, the duties of landownership for nobles rested on a working knowledge of the fiscal dimensions of estate administration; it would be erroneous to imagine aristocratic ignorance of economic capital. On the contrary, nobles were versed in notions of credit and debt because their lifestyle hinged upon extracting rents, obtaining loans, and spending. The business of exploiting a landed estate required knowledge of how to read and query accounts, which noblewomen as well as noblemen did. Second, if we were to depict this culture of noble ownership in diagram form, then the noble family 'circle' would be surrounded by and interlock with other 'circles' representing non-noble families. Labour on an estate typically involved the efforts of a husband, wife, and children, even if it was only the husband in the non-noble family who received a wage. This participation of family members in labour on noble estates is a long-term continuity that was still evident in France after the Second World War. It is a continuity that has been accompanied by gradual adjustments in gendered roles and expectations within rural working-class families through periods of social upheaval and change.[25]

Archival records indicate that in aristocratic marriages it was the husband who mostly made decisions about the exploitation of an estate for income. Yet the nature of the marriage contract (*la communauté* or *le régime dotal*) determined whether the husband or the wife, or both parties acting together, held ultimate legal powers over property that was inherited by one of them or jointly purchased by the couple. Evidence of noblewomen's decision-making tends to appear most in the context of widowhood or a husband's prolonged absence from an estate, a subject we shall return to later in this chapter.

The 1830s and 1840s saw a rise in the numbers of agricultural improvement societies at departmental level and *comice agricoles* at canton level, which were often dominated by Legitimist landowners.[26] During this period Auguste de Bonald was developing exploitation of fruit among other crops for harvest on the estate of Vielvayssac (Aveyron). As in early modern times, beside a château or *maison de maître*, there was an enclosed field where a gardener tended fruit trees, flowers and *herbes potagères*.[27] In correspondence about a nobleman's enquiries on the strengths and weaknesses of different species, and tips for planting and cultivation, we can see again the patterns of the noble family 'circle' interconnecting with non-noble family 'circles'.

On 30 March 1834 a man with the wonderfully apt name of Bonnaterre wrote from a plant nursery at Saint Geniez d'Olt (Aveyron). He was giving advice on varieties of apple because Bonald was interested in cider production. Bonnaterre also sent cuttings for graft, some of which he had received from the manager of the plant nursery of Luxembourg and were varieties unfamiliar to him. Exchange of information on American techniques and species was part of wider cross-cultural networking about agriculture in which nobles were heavily involved.[28]

1. *Bédan* – I don't know the fruit
2. *Blanc doux* – small white apple, red skin … the tree is sturdy and produces a lot of fruit
3. *Gros doux* – beautiful yellow apple … very productive, one of the best I have
4. *Amer doux* – medium sized apple, very sweet … it is a sturdier tree
5. *Peau de vache* – medium sized dark red apple and mediocre by comparison …
6. *Harrison* – apple from America. This variety is reputed to make the best cider whether in America or in Normandy. It is a very good eating apple (*pomme à couteau*)
7. *Summer pippin* – apple tree from America. It is a summer *reinette*
8. *Monstron pippin* – another apple tree from America, these last two varieties were sent to me as good eating apples and are the largest American apples. I have not yet seen the fruit.[29]

One of Auguste de Bonald's in-laws living in Vigan sent information on how best to plant mulberry trees, and seeds for them, which was also an opportunity to give news of mutual acquaintances and of brothers and sisters. Eugène Séguret had gone to some trouble to complete this commission for Auguste and finally obtained the seeds from Aix-en-Provence 'because we do not cultivate mulberry in this *pays*'. Advice had come from Sarrasin who was the gardener of a cousin, and from another acquaintance. Sarrasin belonged to a generation of French people given names drawn from nature.[30] Gardeners like him were involved in mulberry cultivation on nobles' estates in other parts of the country. On the comte de Francheville's estate of Truscat in Morbihan mulberry was grown along with apricots, peaches, *reine claude* plums, and pears during the 1840s. Seeds could be obtained from nurseries in Loire and Ardèche and the comte de Francheville was sharing his findings on mulberry and silkworms with the Société d'agriculture in Brest.[31]

These kinds of interactions, for arboriculture, horticulture, and animal husbandry continued in much the same way as they had in previous centuries. Correspondence and conversations refreshed longstanding relations and generated new links between people living in urban and rural areas. Experimental innovations as well as traditional *savoir-faire* were percolating all of the time through early modern France.[32] The nineteenth century witnessed ongoing filtration of ideas and techniques through society, not always in a 'top-down, urban to rural' way but sometimes because a person from a village, who was learning from others, shared information with a noble who asked.

Management

The French noun *la régie*, like *la gestion*, has been used since the fifteenth century to denote management, but it was not until the eighteenth century that the verb *régir* (from the Latin *regere*) became commonly applied to the activity of managing an agricultural estate. *Le régisseur*, one of the French terms for steward (the other commonly used term is *l'intendant*), dates from the eighteenth century.[33] The daily routine and economic productivity of an aristocratic estate hinged upon this key relationship between landowner and manager that functioned to relieve, but not to remove, some of the burden of administration from the owner. An aristocratic head of the household employed a *régisseur* to manage the estate, and the *régisseur* co-ordinated many of the tasks necessary to generate income for his employer. Some of those tasks were delegated by the *régisseur* to servants and outdoor labourers, whilst others he undertook himself like the collection of rents.

The relationship between landowner and *régisseur* was the cornerstone of a management system used across estates of all sizes. Among the wealthiest families of the aristocracy owning multiple estates there were more plentiful sources of income and expenditure requiring oversight. If the family's landholdings were geographically dispersed across different regions of France, or located in different countries, several *régisseurs* were employed with each one taking charge of a separate estate. For the majority of noble families, however, whose sole estate was made up of parcels of land spread across several communes in the same department, daily operational responsibilities of management could be entrusted to a single *régisseur*.

Nobles' employment of *régisseurs* did not end with the outbreak of the First World War, although the military mobilisation of men employed in this position meant it was disrupted. The *archives privées* of nobility deposed in state repositories tend to have more evidence of *régisseur* activities from the pre-1914 period; collections (*fonds*) in which documentation extends further into the twentieth century will also contain *régisseur* correspondence and accounts.[34] For the estate of Issarts at Rognonas (Bouches-du-Rhône), for example, the *régisseur* Berlhe reported to the baronne Benoist d'Azy and the vicomte Benoist d'Azy between 1939 and 1953.[35]

Close reading of correspondence between a noble and a *régisseur* is needed to interpret the dynamics particular to each relationship. Of course this is not possible in every case because while some archival *fonds* contain extensive sets of letters exchanged between the two parties, other *fonds* contain only one side of a correspondence or just a few letters. Drawing on a wide range of *fonds* in which such correspondence survives is thus the only way to assess the patterns of language in these social relationships, the typical concerns and issues discussed, and the behaviours that were common or unusual. The need for a *régisseur* to write letters rather than to speak with his employer is indicative of nobles' periods of absence from an estate; yet 'absence' could have different meanings depending on the circumstances of the landowner. An aristocratic diplomat serving abroad might visit his provincial estate only once a year for a summer holiday. A noblewoman might reside year-round in her château but receive her *régisseur's* letters about another property less than a hundred kilometres away. By studying the correspondence of nobles and *régisseurs* together with other documents in the same *fonds* a noble's near-permanent absenteeism can normally be distinguished from a noble who is temporarily absent but in fact lives most of the time in close proximity.

A letter from the *régisseur* to the marquis de Biron written on 29 August 1838 provides an illustration of the theme of absence entering into correspondence. In the first half of the nineteenth century the principal items of real estate owned by the Gontaut-Biron family comprised the estate and château de Biron (Dordogne); lands in the northern departments of Marne, Nièvre, Oise, and Seine-et-Marne; some forest in the department of Loiret; and three *hôtels particuliers* in Paris. This geographic dispersion of property meant the family employed several *régisseurs* so that each one was responsible for the land in a separate department.[36] The marquis de Biron was a French peer, so he participated in the customs of *le Tout-Paris* by spending the winter 'Season' in the capital then moving to the countryside during the summer for socialising *en villégiature*. As the owner, but infrequent resident, of the château de Biron the marquis had to exchange letters with his *régisseur* in the department of Dordogne in order to keep up with ongoing property concerns for the Biron estate that were reported to him by post.

We expected you in this month of August, Monsieur le marquis, as you had given us hope. Unfortunately our wait was in vain because, apart from the pleasure that your presence would have brought us, we must presume that the waters of Vichy will not have done the good [as a cure for your health] that you anticipated ... Since reading the letter that you kindly wrote to me from Vichy, I have been continually in search of information for the most suitable and economical way to repair the flagstone and gallery of the chapter house ... I have fixed upon a new discovery; that is to say, to use Fumel's Roman cement. And to give you an indication, Monsieur le marquis, I enclose a brochure on the cement ... The wheat harvest this year is 95 hectolitres, while last year it was 73 hectolitres. The maize this year is at 138 sous, last year it was 191 sous ... Our pigs sold well.[37]

The central themes of this 1838 letter, a mixture of maintenance issues as well as reports on income and expenditure, represent the standard content in *régisseurs'* letters across dozens of different *fonds*. How frequently and in what level of detail such property matters were reported give clues about the regularity of face-to-face contact that the *régisseur* had with his employer. By comparing sets of correspondences we may note, for example, a contrast between the lifestyle of the marquis de Biron, characterised by high levels of absenteeism from his provincial landholdings, and the lifestyle of a less wealthy nobleman, François de Boisbaudran, who did not own any Parisian property and lived year-round in the south-west at the end of the nineteenth century. Letters of a *régisseur* to François de Boisbaudran show that this *régisseur* had more regular opportunities to speak with his employer: 'I shall not write on the subject of the large quince trees that would take too long ... I would rather wait until you are here to explain things.'[38]

Among the crucial variables in estate management were the extent to which the *régisseur* was known and trusted by local people and was implicated through his own family's circumstances in the life of the surrounding area (*le pays*). The need to liaise with people engaged in all kinds of artisanal trades, services, and agricultural work meant the *régisseur* developed experience and insights that could be useful to a noble landowner – provided of course that the landowner had faith in the *régisseur's* advice. Contact with people in the community also meant the *régisseur* was able to negotiate opportunities for them, and make recommendations to his employer that altered or established new relationships between the noble family and non-noble families. In a *régisseur's* letter from 1911, for example:

One might give [Darnat] accommodation in the *maison de la tuilerie*, with the garden included, at minimum rent. He could bring some poultry. Darnat could leave half the potatoes to seed and thus feed a pig for its lard. His wife could be given a few days' work in the hunting reserve or at the château if needed ... By hiring a strong labourer (300 francs wage) Darnat could cultivate the estate but he would need this labourer for five years before his children would be strong enough to perform all the agricultural work.[39]

Letters provide illustrations of the way estate management should be understood not simply as a relationship between two individuals, but rather in terms of a relationship between the noble family and the *régisseur's* family. The giving of gifts on a reciprocal basis was a mark of the ties between these two groups. Bourdieu draws attention to such behaviour and its effects where he described: 'the *institutionally organized and guaranteed misrecognition* which is the basis of gift exchange and, perhaps, of all the symbolic labour intended to transmute, by the sincere fiction of a disinterested exchange, the inevitable and inevitably interested relations imposed by kinship, neighbourhood or work, into elective relations of reciprocity'.[40] Gift exchange promotes continuity of interpersonal relations by binding the receiver to the giver with a sense of gratitude. In order for the gift exchange to be successful there must be a 'collectively maintained and approved self-deception' so that each agent refuses to recognise the truth of the exchange as part of a system governed by laws of interested calculation.[41]

In correspondence between *régisseurs* and nobles the subject of gifts is often linked to women's participation in the relationship. On 16 April 1898 the *régisseur* to François de Boisbaudran wrote: 'Last Saturday I posted a package to you containing two chickens and fifteen eggs. I had the eggs wrapped up by my wife who says she took every precaution to ensure they would not break. I hope that they arrived safely?' On 8 January 1899: 'Yesterday I took to the station a package containing a hare that it is my pleasure to give to Madame de Boisbaudran ... The weather has been very fine here. We are planting some oaks along the empty borders and working on the harvest of the chestnuts.' Letters also acknowledge counter-gifts of a non-material form, such as favours, from the noble family to the *régisseur's* family, again referencing women's participation in the exchange. Writing to his employer on 21 March 1911, for example, a *régisseur* concluded: 'My wife and I thank you for the permission to keep a goat ... We hope that you and Madame are in very good health.'[42]

That the effort of perpetuating relations of reciprocity was a collective undertaking in which both sexes participated is amply illustrated in the extensive archives of the Lévis Mirepoix family about the estate of Léran in the department of Ariège. Documentation from this archive allows the analysis of gift and counter-gift to be taken a step further by considering how people outside the relationship perceived it. During the early nineteenth century three men successively occupied the post of *régisseur* at Léran: Vincent Laffitte from 1810 to May 1834, Léopold Bauzil from 1834 to September 1846, and Jacques Pascal Casse from September 1846. Each of these men regularly corresponded with their employer Athanase-Gustave de Lévis, duc de Mirepoix, who was married to Charlotte Adélaïde de Montmorency-Laval.[43]

Casse, like his predecessors in the role of *régisseur*, repeatedly mentions various members of his own family as well as members of the Lévis Mirepoix family involved in patterns of gift exchange. From Léran on 21 January 1847 Casse wrote to the duc: 'I am touched by and very grateful for the kind assistance you are giving for advancing [my son-in-law] Monsieur Ferru's career [as a school principal] … like us, he will be happy to learn that you are taking care of his destiny.'[44] The duc's 'kind assistance' to Casse's relative required a counter-gift that was deferred in time and different.[45] A few months later, on 10 April 1847, the *régisseur* wrote:

> My son has been busy making many copies of your farm leases and some other documents … I will put all of these papers together in the same envelope and send them straight away to you in Paris. I also thought to bring you enjoyment, Monsieur le duc, by sending the two crates on consignment. The first contains two pots of *confits* prepared by my wife … the second contains fifty bottles of the best *blanquette* from Limoux, which I hope you find delicious. I will keep the rest [of this wine] here at the château de Léran in anticipation of your visit to Ariège with your ladies and gentlemen next summer.[46]

The lapse of time that separated gift and counter-gift encouraged 'the deliberate oversight' or misrecognition by the agents about the nature of such exchanges. Between noble and *régisseur* there was created a bond of obligation more complex, and familial because of the spouses and relatives involved, than the type of connection normally associated with the terms employer and employee. Each act of giving perpetuated an unconscious duty to give in return; the receiver of the gift was left to choose the timing of future interaction essential to build a stable relationship based on gratitude and indebtedness. 'To abolish the interval is also to abolish strategy.'[47]

Yet the misrecognition that allowed for 'fake circulation of fake coin' between the noble family and the *régisseur's* family came with risks for both parties.[48] A change in external circumstances, such as a particularly bad harvest or a new law, could expose the strategy as exceptionally fragile. Perceptions of the 'employer–employee' relationship among people outside of that relationship mattered because in those perceptions 'the inevitable and inevitably interested relations' remained.

A landowner bore the risk that the *régisseur* might not put the noble family's interests first. In 1821 a lawyer acting for the Lévis Mirepoix family, assisted by the municipal tax collector, identified errors in the *régisseur* Laffitte's accounts that amounted to a loss of 29,000 francs incurred by the duc. The nobleman was reluctant to terminate Laffitte's administration of the estate of Léran and continued to employ the *régisseur*. In 1834, however, external circumstances had become marked by bitter tensions between peasants and landowners over forests, the so-called War of the Demoiselles.[49] Suspicions arose over Laffitte's interpretation of forest leases and the duc accused the *régisseur* of giving away piles of wood to farmers and millers rather than charging money for the wood. The duc demanded that 'a lucrative use be established for my profit'.[50] Laffitte resigned from the post of *régisseur* but because he did not give his employer the outstanding accounts Athanase-Gustave de Lévis pursued litigation.

A *régisseur* bore the risk that by doing his job effectively he would attract resentment and hatred among rural working-class people. Letters written in the 1850s by an anonymous 'very humble and respectful servant' to the duc and duchesse de Lévis Mirepoix warned them about the 'vile', 'incapable' Casse, who was characterised as 'a miserable hypocrite' and 'a thief'. Casse and Casse's son were accused of 'revolting conduct', of enriching themselves and lording it over 'the poor ruined farmers', rather than the duc who was raising the farm rents and pressing his *régisseur* to send money. The Lévis Mirepoix were urged by someone of poor handwriting and poor spelling to sack these 'two employees who are known good-for-nothings' before they compromised the ducal family's interests, dignity, and 'illustrious name'.[51]

Labour

It is precisely on this topic of the nature of the labour relations, the daily rapport, which continued to connect nobles with their agents and with rural working-class people through the final decades of the Third

Republic and into the Fourth Republic that there is still scarce knowledge among modern historians. Michelle Perrot remarked in 1979 that surprisingly little historical research had been done to answer the question 'how did French workers view their bosses?'[52] Although there is now a rich literature on experiences of blue-collar and white-collar workers across many industries, labour historians for a long time ignored the agricultural sector.[53] Agriculture remained central to the political and economic interests of nobles and, because the employment of labour was essential to the running of nobles' estates, this was a sector in which noblewomen and noblemen formed a category of 'bosses' through the nineteenth century and into the twentieth. Trade unions began to form in France after the law of 21 March 1884 but fifty years later many rural people did not belong to a union; in 1937 the Fédération de l'Agriculture, constituted by rural unions, had only 7 or 8 per cent of all agricultural workers in its membership.[54] The roles of women in the day-to-day operations of noble estates, and long-term continuities such as the participation of working-class family members in labour, can only really be comprehended through *archives privées*.

In 1914, the vast majority of the men employed as servants or seasonal outdoor labourers on an estate left to serve in the army, unless they were too old or unfit to enlist. Perhaps the most significant of these departures, for its effect on the overall running of an estate, was that of the *régisseur*. Correspondence in the *archives privées* shows that typically it was the *régisseur's* wife who took on some of her husband's responsibilities, including reports to the estate owner.

The widowed marquise de Marcieu (née Isabelle de Chanaleilles) spent most of the First World War in the château de Crépol (Drôme). She was in her eighties and lived there with the second of her three sons, the comte Humbert de Marcieu, and his wife Pauline de Beauffort; this couple had three grown-up children. For news regarding another estate, Chambonas in the Ardèche, which the marquise had inherited from her Chanaleilles ancestors, she relied on the letters of Maria Gaillard, wife of the *régisseur*. Maria regularly sent provisions from Chambonas to the marquise, including chickens, vegetables, and fruit: 'Today I posted by express mail a parcel of English cherries. There have been very few this year.' She also reported on crops and farm animals: 'There is a lot of hay this year. Madame la marquise asks me whether her cow still has milk. About three or four litres per day, [from which is made] a pound of butter per week that I sell every Saturday. [The cow] is doing very well. I think she has a calf but it is difficult to be sure just yet.'[55] Maria often mentioned her husband's news, for he sent her letters from the front, and Gaillard also wrote directly to the marquise de Marcieu. In October 1915 he reported on an injury received when a bullet hit his left ankle: 'I was evacuated to the hospital in Nevers where we [soldiers] are very well looked after.' In July 1917 Gaillard was granted three weeks' leave for agricultural work and returned to Chambonas to help Maria. He told the marquise: 'I am very happy to be with my wife and children who are in good health. I am tackling the most urgent work, firstly the garden, some clearing in the park, and a bit of forage ... the most I am able to do to bring comfort to my wife.'[56]

Maria Gaillard's letters to the marquise de Marcieu, always polite and respectful in tone, reflect the women's very different social backgrounds and also the age gap. These letters would not have been written were it not for the fact of Gaillard's employment at Chambonas, which continued after the end of the war; it was the economics of his wage earning on which the connection between his wife Maria and the marquise rested.

The comtesse de Fontaines (née Jacqueline Maillard de la Gournerie) was also widowed before the war; her husband, Pierre-Henri-Léon de Fontaines, died on 4 August 1912 at the age of forty-three. After her husband's death the comtesse de Fontaines had sole responsibility for the family property, the château de Marillet near Faymoreau (Vendée). She received letters from rural working-class women and men about a range of matters, from baptisms to fallen trees and crop fertiliser. It is difficult to determine from surviving correspondence how regularly the comtesse met in person with the farmers on her land.[57]

One regular correspondent in 1922–3 was Henriette Baty, housekeeper at Marillet, who wrote on behalf of herself and her husband Louis. When the comtesse de Fontaines was absent from Marillet staying at another château in Calvados, Henriette sent updates about the farm animals ('The sheep must be shorn tomorrow and it's about time since the poor beasts must be very hot!') and garden produce ('There are fine potatoes, even the little ones that Madame finds so pretty'). Henriette planted out the quantities of petunias, cineraria, fuchsia, dahlias and geraniums that the comtesse paid to have transported to the Vendée by rail. Henriette's letters mix personal news with employment matters. On 15 December 1923, she explained that her duties at Marillet might be affected owing to her mother's declining health: 'The housework will be done on Saturday for your arrival and if I cannot be there then Esther will come soon.'[58]

Through the interwar decades and after the Second World War rural working-class men and women wrote letters to nobles to negotiate about the pay and conditions in various service roles. As in the late nineteenth century, agreements were often made between a worker and an employer that did not reflect collective bargaining processes involving trade unions. On 9 January 1923 Marie Gillier who was employed as a cook by the comtesse de Fontaines wrote: 'Maids are hard to find and very expensive [at] 100 francs [in wages] per month ... or more when employed on farms. For a cook one must pay 150 francs [in wages] per month.'[59] Among the conditions of employment typically discussed in letters were whether the servant would be provided with a livery to wear, whether the livery and other work clothing worn by the servant would be laundered in the noble household, and whether wine would be included with the meals that servants ate together. There were also enquiries about the provision of accommodation on the noble estate. On 7 December 1948 Joseph Cladreuil wrote to the marquis de Montlaur to express interest in the post of gardener at La Thibaudière: 'If possible, I would prefer to be housed and fed [on the property]!'[60] To receive board, laundry and meals on properties of varying sizes had not fallen out of custom in rural areas by the middle of the twentieth century.[61] For nobles, in addition to the cost of wages, there was the cost of insurance to bear. In 1941 the company Eagle Star charged one employer a premium of 632.20 francs per year for insurance against accidents at work among domestic staff plus a premium of 259.55 per year for insurance against fire in the château.[62]

To find a service position working-class men and women responded to advertisements placed in local newspapers. Conversations with relatives, friends, and previous employers were another source of information about possible job openings on noble estates. On 4 March 1940 Albert Desforges wrote:

I have the honour of offering you our services for the work advertised in Depêche du Centre. I am fifty years old. My wife is forty-four years old. We have a little daughter aged four and a son aged ten. We have always been employed in châteaux and always in this region. For four years we were in the home of Mademoiselle de Croÿ, château de Monteaux [then] for six years in the home of Monsieur le marquis de Terrière le Voyer. It was thanks to his intermediary that we returned here where we have been for four years. Not having told my employer of my intention to leave him, and wishing to separate on good terms, I ask that if you and I come to an arrangement between ourselves you will allow me the necessary delay [before taking up the new post]. We wish to leave because my wife is not employed. I have my driving licence. Since we have always worked in the homes of people who are friends with one another I have no certificate of employment.[63]

Although word-of-mouth recommendations could help working-class people to obtain positions, where problems arose with one employer there was the risk for the employee that information would be passed on through oral communication and correspondence between nobles. Decisions about hiring staff were influenced by written references from past employers ('She is very good tempered and obliging', 'I part with her with much regret').[64] Nobles also wrote to one another about impressions of potential hires ('The husband is a blond thirty-three-year-old from Alsace … the wife seems intelligent, lively and capable').[65]

Michelle Perrot has observed for late nineteenth-century France that, although hostility dominated when workers expressed themselves on the subject of their bosses, 'one cannot rule out other types of rapport, of representations, of language'.[66] Expressions of deference toward nobles are common in correspondence, like that of gardener Jean Garrigue. He closed his letters to the marquise Tredecini de Saint-Sévérin by sending his profound respects to her whole family as a devoted servant who was 'always very loyal to the house'.[67] For Garrigue, like for many other working-class men and women on noble estates, deferential language and behaviour made 'practical sense' as a way to cultivate a stable relationship with an employer.[68]

Conclusion

This chapter has investigated the core characteristics of ownership, management, and labour on landed estates that underpinned nobles' aim of maintaining patrimony in modern France. Letters, legal paper-work, receipts, and account books are rich sources of evidence for the social relationships arising out of nobles' landownership. The abundant documentation has much to tell us about aspects of daily life in the countryside and about issues widely affecting rural communities. Nobles, their agents, and household staff have for too long been relegated to the fringes of French rural history for the post-1789 period. By contrast, the past lives of such people are central to the historical investigation of landed estates that is flourishing in Britain, Ireland, Scandinavia, the Netherlands, Germany and other countries of continental Europe.[69] Empirical research is essential to build knowledge of how events and eco-nomic pressures impacted relations between owner, manager, and labour in separate countries; only then does it become possible to proceed with comparative studies.[70]

Far more durable in France than is often supposed, the tripartite structure of ownership, management, and labour analysed in this chapter survived through the nineteenth century and beyond the Second World War. That is not to say there was no change at all in the nature of relationships among landowners, *régisseurs*, and workers. But some of the substantial developments that affected those relationships, for example the spread of trade unionism in rural areas or the evolution in gendered roles and expectations within rural working-class families, occurred very gradually. The documented examples presented here provide equally important evidence of long-term continuities in rural household economies and employment conditions for staff on nobles' estates.

The goal in researching the social relationships of nobles arising from their landownership is to better understand the human dispositions that result from conditioning, which are reinforced by institutions and in symbolic practices, and which lead to continuities in power relations over periods of time. This approach is not intended to downplay the episodes of conflict that are a dominant theme in the literature of 'peasant studies'. It is designed instead to balance attention to contestation with attention to ritual acceptance of a 'world of tradition experienced as a "natural world" and taken for granted'.[71] We have seen examples of such ritual acceptance in the way noblewomen and noblemen ensured that the administrative responsibilities of estate ownership were fulfilled in each generation; in the way *régisseurs* and estate owners cultivated complex bonds between their respective families in gift exchange; and in the way labour on noble estates was carried out with the participation of husbands, wives, and children following patterns that lasted for many centuries.

Notes

1 Comtesse d'Armaillé, 'Livre des conseils à sa fille' in AD Maine-et-Loire 17J/1 Fonds de la famille d'Armaillé.

2 G. Duby, *Qu'est-ce que la société féodale?* (Paris, 2002), pp. 67–107, 208–28, 280–313; J. B. Henneman, 'Nobility, privilege and fiscal politics in late medieval France', *French Historical Studies* 13 (1983), 1–17. On early modern developments see the discussion of dues and terriers in W. Doyle, 'Was there an aristocratic reaction in pre-revolutionary France?' *Past and Present* 57 (1972), 97–122.

3 W. H. Sewell Jr, 'Property, labor and the emergence of socialism in France, 1789–1848' in J. M. Merriman (ed.), *Consciousness and Class Experience in Nineteenth-Century Europe* (New York, 1979), p. 51; R. Gibson and M. Blinkhorn (eds), *Landownership and Power in Modern Europe* (London,

1991); D. Spring (ed.), *European Landed Elites in the Nineteenth Century* (Baltimore, 1977); E. Wasson, *Aristocracy and the Modern World* (New York, 2006).

4 T. Zeldin, 'France' in Spring (ed.), *European Landed Elites*, pp. 129, 138. For comparisons see F. L. Carsten, *A History of the Prussian Junkers* (Aldershot, 1989), chs 8–10; M. Beard, *English Landed Society in the Twentieth Century* (London, 1989); D. Lieven, *The Aristocracy in Europe, 1815–1914* (London, 1992), chs 2–3; K. Brown, *Noble Society in Scotland: Wealth, Family and Culture, from Reformation to Revolution* (Edinburgh, 2000); S. Becker, *Nobility and Privilege in Late Imperial Russia* (Dekalb, 1985); A. L. Cardoza, *Aristocrats in Bourgeois Italy: The Piedemontese Nobility, 1861–1930* (Cambridge, 1997); J. Cruz, *Gentlemen, Bourgeois and Revolutionaries: Political Change and Cultural Persistence among the Spanish Dominant Groups 1750–1850* (Cambridge, 1996).

5 G. Lefebvre, *Les Paysans du Nord pendant la Révolution française* (Paris, 1924); E. Le Roy Ladurie, *Les Paysans de Languedoc* 2 vols (Paris, 1966); F. Braudel and E. Labrousse (eds), *Histoire économique et sociale de la France* 4 vols (Paris, 1970–82); G. Duby and A. Wallon (eds), *Histoire de la France rurale* 4 vols (Paris, 1975–77). For later approaches by Anglophone scholars see, for example, L. L. Frader, *Peasants and Protest: Agricultural Workers, Politics, and Unions in the Aude, 1850–1914* (Los Angeles, 1991); R. A. Jonas, *Industry and Politics in Rural France: Peasants of the Isère, 1870–1914* (Ithaca, 1994). On the evolution of rural studies see S. C. Rogers, 'Natural histories: the rise and fall of French rural studies', *French Historical Studies* 19 (1995), 381–97.

6 See for example G. Duby (ed.), *Histoire de la France urbaine* vols 3–4 (Paris, 1981–83); D. Garrioch, *The Formation of the Parisian Bourgeoisie 1690–1830* (Cambridge, 1996); C. E. Harrison, *The Bourgeois Citizen in Nineteenth-Century France: Gender, Sociability, and the Uses of Emulation* (Oxford, 1999); A. Daumard, *Les Bourgeois et la bourgeoisie en France* (Paris, 1987); A. Martin-Fugier, *La Bourgeoise: la femme au temps de Paul Bourget* (Paris, 1983). From the 1980s the shift of away from rural studies towards urban studies was also evident in anthropology and sociology. See Rogers, 'Natural histories', esp. 385, 388.

7 *Code du patrimoine*, livre II, art. 211–4 and 5. For discussion see J. Favier (ed.), *La Pratique archivistique française* (Paris, 2008), pp. 70–9.

8 To preserve as much information as possible about that context an archivist will order documents within a collection in such a way as to show changes in ownership and management over time, and to distinguish different items of real estate.

9 The *Journal of Peasant Studies* founded in 1973 became the *Journal of Agrarian Change* in 2001. On developments in the field see H. Bernstein and T. J. Byres, 'From peasant studies to agrarian change', *Journal of Agrarian Change* 1 (2001), 1–56; Rogers, 'Natural histories', 381–97.

10 G. Duby and A. Wallon (eds), *Histoire de la France rurale* vol. 3 *Apogée et crise de la civilisation paysanne de 1789 à 1914* by M. Agulhon, G. Désert, and R. Specklin (Paris, 1976), pp. 136–7; D. Hunt, 'Peasant movements and communal property during the French Revolution', *Theory and Society* 17 (1988), 255–83; P. McPhee, *Revolution and Environment in Southern France: Peasants, Lords, and Murder in the Corbières 1780–1830* (Oxford, 1999), ch. 8. For another differently motivated murder of a nobleman see A. Corbin, *Le Village des cannibales* (Paris, 1990).

11 Gibson and Blinkhorn, *Landownership and Power*, p. 2.

12 The dominant classes 'have an interest in defending the integrity of doxa'. P. Bourdieu, *Outline of a Theory of Practice*, translated by R. Nice (Cambridge, 1977), p. 169.

13 E. C. Macknight, 'A "theatre of rule"? Domestic service in aristocratic households under the Third Republic', *French History* 22 (2008), 316–36. On nurses and nobles' language learning see E. C. Macknight, *Aristocratic Families in Republican France, 1870–1940* (Manchester, 2012), chs 6 and 7.

14 J. Clarke, *France in the Age of Organization: Factory, Home and Nation from the 1920s to Vichy* (New York, 2011), pp. 24–6, 167.

15 E. Baumgartner and P. Ménard, *Dictionnaire étymologique et historique de la langue française* (Paris, 1996), p. 357.

16 'Copie de la procuration, cahier 1836' in AD Tarn-et-Garonne 43J Fonds Granié (*fonds 'en vrac'* not classed at time of consultation).

17 'Cahier 1836' in AD Tarn-et-Garonne 43J Fonds Granié (*fonds 'en vrac'* not classed at time of consultation).

18 'Convention' in AD Maine-et-Loire 249J/5 Fonds de la famille Montlaur.

19 Typed undated notes and 'Conventions avec Allard et sa femme 26 July 1946' in AD Maine-et-Loire 249J/5 Fonds de la famille Montlaur.

20 For photographs and drawings see M. Girouard, *Life in the French Country House* (London, 2000), pp. 265–79.

21 G. Duby and A. Wallon (eds), *Histoire de la France rurale* vol. 4 *La Fin de la France paysanne depuis 1914* by M. Gervais, M. Jollivet, and Y. Tavernier (Paris, 1977), chs 2 and 4.

22 Potatoes (65,000 francs from planting the front field; 52,000 francs from planting the orchard fields), hay (26,000 francs), milk and eggs (60,000 francs), and wheat and oats (20,000 francs). Wages paid to the *basse-cour* household (11,500 francs per month).

23 Typed undated notes in AD Maine-et-Loire 249J/5 Fonds de la famille Montlaur. See also the 'Estimation du cheptel' in the same archival box that lists the farm animals at La Thibaudière in January 1948.

24 On hunting parties see E. C. Macknight, 'Le Sport et les divertissements du Tout-Paris 1880–1914', DEA *mémoire*, Université de Versailles Saint-Quentin-en-Yvelines, 2004.

25 Duby and Wallon, *Histoire de la France rurale* vol. 4, chs 6–9.

26 Duby and Wallon, *Histoire de la France rurale* vol. 3, pp. 105, 116–18. On earlier agricultural initiatives and comparisons see É. Justin, *Les Sociétés royales d'agriculture au XIIIe siècle (1757–1793)* (Saint-Lô, 1935); J.-M. Moriceau, *L'Élevage sous l'Ancien Régime (XVIe–XVIIIe siècles)* (Condé-sur-Noireau, 1999); J.-M. Moriceau, R. Bourrigaud, C. Marache, F. Ploux, and J. Vigreux (eds), *Les Campagnes dans les evolutions sociales et politiques en Europe* (Lassay-les-Châteaux, 2005).

27 G. Duby and A. Wallon (eds), *Histoire de la France rurale* vol. 2 *L'Âge classique des paysans de 1340 à 1789* by H. Neveux, J. Jacquart, and E. Le Roy Ladurie (Paris, 1977), p. 254.

28 D. J. Brandenburg, 'A French aristocrat looks at American farming: La Rochefoucauld-Liancourt's voyages dans les États-Unis', *Agricultural History* 32 (1958), 155–65; G. Pacini, 'A culture of trees: the politics of pruning and felling in late eighteenth-century France', *Eighteenth-Century Studies* 41 (2007), 1–15.

29 30 March 1834 in AD Aveyron 71J/23 Fonds de Bonald de Vielvayssac.

30 2 May 1823 in AD Aveyron 71J/24 Fonds de Bonald de Vielvayssac. Buckwheat (*le sarrasin*) came from Holland and was grown in Brittany from the fifteenth century. F. Braudel, *L'Identité de la France* vol. 2 *Les Hommes et les choses* (Paris, 1990), pp. 56, 72.

31 'Prix-courant des mûriers pour l'automne 1841 et le printemps de 1842' and letters 19 May 1840, 23 April 1844, 16 August 1845 in AD Morbihan 93J/321 Archives du château de Truscat. On arboriculture at Truscat see 93J/323 Archives du château de Truscat.

32 On innovations, Braudel, *L'Identité* vol. 2, pp. 326–36. On older *savoir-faire* and resistance to new techniques, pp. 72–5, 100–4. See also R. Forster, 'Obstacles to agricultural growth in eighteenth-century France', *American Historical Review* 75 (1970), 1600–15; F. Lalliard, 'Propriété aristocratique et innovation agronomique au XIXe siècle', *Histoire et Sociétés Rurales* 13 (2000), 67–92; D. Danthieux, 'Métayage et grande propriété foncière dans le département de la Haute-Vienne: entre utopie sociale et innovation agricole (fin 19e–début 20e siècle)', *Ruralia* 14 (2004), 75–94.

33 Baumgartner and Ménard, *Dictionnaire*, p. 674.

34 Most nobles' estate records from the 1960s onward tend to be held privately, not deposed in the State's archives.

35 AD Bouches-du-Rhône 140J Fonds Foresta.

36 Seigneurie de Biron in AD Dordogne 13 J/5–10 Fonds Gontaut-Biron. On the land in the Marne and *régisseur* accounts 13J/11–13. On the land in the Nièvre and *régisseur* accounts 13J/14–18. On the land in the Oise and *régisseur* accounts 13J/19–20. On the land in the Seine-et-Marne and *régisseur* accounts 13J/21–22. On the Parisian properties 13J/23–27. On the forest in the Loiret 13J/28.

37 29 August 1838 in AD Dordogne 13 J/7 Fonds Gontaut-Biron.

38 16 April 1898 in AD Charente 4J/22 Fonds Lecoq de Boisbaudran.

39 21 March 1911 in AD Charente 4J/22 Fonds Lecoq de Boisbaudran.

40 Bourdieu, *Outline*, p. 171; P. Bourdieu, *Le Sens pratique* (Paris, 1980), p. 191.

41 Bourdieu, *Outline*, pp. 4–9, 172–3.

42 16 April 1898, 8 January 1899, 21 March 1911 in AD Charente 4J/22 Fonds Lecoq de Boisbaudran.

43 Copies of the letters written by Athanase-Gustave de Lévis, by his son Guy de Lévis, and by Guy's son, Adrien de Lévis, are preserved in the archive.

44 21 January 1847 in AD Ariège 46J/390 Archives Lévis Mirepoix.

45 Bourdieu, *Outline*, p. 5.

46 10 April 1847 in AD Ariège 46J/390 Archives Lévis Mirepoix.

47 Bourdieu, *Outline*, p. 6.

48 Bourdieu, *Outline*, p. 6.

49 T. L. Whited, *Forests and Peasant Politics in Modern France* (New Haven, 2000).

50 21 March 1834 and 29 April 1834 in AD Ariège 46J/391 Archives Lévis Mirepoix.

51 12 August 1853 and undated letters in AD Ariège 46J/391 Archives Lévis Mirepoix.

52 M. Perrot, 'Le Regard de l'Autre: les patrons français vus par les ouvriers (1880–1914)' in M. Lévy-Leboyer (ed.), *Le Patronat de la seconde industriali-sation* (Paris, 1979), pp. 293–306. See also M. Perrot, 'The three ages of indus-trial discipline in nineteenth-century France' in Merriman, *Consciousness*, pp. 149–68.

53 Duby and Wallon, *Histoire de la France rurale* vol. 4, p. 438.

54 Duby and Wallon, *Histoire de la France rurale* vol. 4, pp. 320–3, 428–45.

55 20 May 1914 and 11 May 1916 in AD Ardèche 39J/314 Chartrier de Chambonas.

56 4 October 1915 and 11 July 1917 in AD Ardèche 39J/314 Chartrier de Chambonas.

57 AD Loire-Atlantique 58J/5 Archives de la famille de Fontaines.

58 6 May 1923, 19 March 1923, 12 June 1922, 15 December 1923 in AD Loire-Atlantique 58J/5 Archives de la famille de Fontaines.

59 9 January 1923 in AD Loire-Atlantique 58J/5 Archives de la famille de Fontaines.

60 7 December 1948 in AD Maine-et-Loire 249J/5 Fonds de la famille Montlaur.

61 Duby and Wallon, *Histoire de la France rurale* vol. 4, pp. 289–94, 439.

62 9 May 1941 in AD Loir-et-Cher 111J/23 Fonds de la famille Gilbert-Beauregard.

63 4 March 1940 in AD Loir-et-Cher 111J/23 Fonds de la famille Gilbert-Beauregard.

64 References for Maud Harris, August 1912, in AD Meurthe-et-Moselle 52J/66 Fonds de la famille Metz-Noblat.

65 11 November 1910 in AD Loir-et-Cher 111J/23 Fonds de la famille Gilbert-Beauregard.

66 Perrot, 'Le Regard de l'Autre', pp. 293–306.

67 20 February 1906 in AD Savoie 46F/4 Fonds Tredecini de Saint-Séverin.

68 Repetition of deferential language and behaviour over many years in service compounded the individual's adherence to *doxa*; that is, submission to a set of arbitrary values and discourses that seem true and necessary. Bourdieu, *Outline*, p. 164.

69 M. Malatesta, 'The landed aristocracy during the nineteenth and early twentieth centuries' in H. Kaelble (ed.), *The European Way: European Societies in the Nineteenth and Twentieth Centuries* (New York and Oxford, 2004), pp. 44–61; E. Conze and M. Wienfort (eds), *Adel und Moderne. Deutschland im europäischen Vergleich im 19. und 20. Jahrhundert* (Cologne, 2004); E. A. C. Smeets, 'Landscape and Society in Twente & Utrecht: A Geography of Dutch Country Estates, circa 1800–1950' (PhD thesis, University of Leeds, 2005); A. Snellman, 'Suomen aateli: yhteiskunnan huipulta uusiin rooleihin 1809–1939' [The Finnish Nobility: From the Top of the Society to New Roles 1809–1939] (PhD thesis, University of Helsinki, 2014); Y. Kuiper, N. Bijleveld, and J. Dronkers (eds), *Nobilities in Europe in the Twentieth Century: Reconversion Strategies, Memory Culture and Elite Formation* (Leuven, 2015); J. Erichsen and M. Venborg Pedersen (eds), *The Danish Country House* (Aarhus, 2015); P. McCarthy, *Life in the Country House in Georgian Ireland* (New Haven and London, 2016).

70 'The Land Agent in transnational context: an interdisciplinary conference' supported by the Centre for the Study of Historic Irish Houses and Estates, the Institute for the Study of Welsh Estates, and Centre for Scotland's Land Futures, University of Dundee 2015; C. Reilly *The Irish Land Agent: The Case of King's County* (Dublin, 2014).

71 Bourdieu, *Outline*, p. 164.

6

Residences and gardens

> I write these lines in the presence of the ancestors whose medallions you
> sent me to put with those we already owned. I was able to form a small
> gallery of twenty portraits in miniature.[1]

In 1880 César de Moré, comte de Pontgibaud wrote to his cousin Eulalie
de Moré de Charaix to make a joyful announcement. Eulalie was the most
senior surviving representative of the elder branch of the Moré family
who owned the château and estate of Cheminades in the department of
Lozère. César wanted Eulalie to know that his son was to marry Pauline
Roussy de Sales, the great-grandniece of Saint François de Sales of Savoy.
Since the bride's maternal grandparents lived in Auvergne, the comte de
Pontgibaud hoped that Pauline and his son would visit the region after
the wedding. He wished to receive the couple at his home, the château
de Pontgibaud in Puy-de-Dôme, and accompany them for sightseeing in
Lozère. It would be an ideal opportunity to introduce Pauline to cousin
Eulalie and to show her the town of Mende and the lands surrounding
the villages of Cheminades and Serverette. These lands had been owned
by the Moré since the twelfth century and were 'the cradle of the family'.[2]
Eulalie was a single woman in her sixties who had never married and
had no children of her own. Her two elder siblings, Charles and Virginie,
had already passed away; neither of them left issue because of their vows
of celibacy as a priest and a nun. The youngest sibling Hortense also had
no children. In reply to her cousin, Eulalie mentioned that she had been
contemplating whether the estate of Cheminades might in due course
have to be put up for sale.[3] The news came as a 'wrench to the heartstrings'

for César because of 'the precious memories of childhood' he associated with this property where the cousins had spent time together. César requested that certain family heirlooms be transported from the château de Cheminades to his home, the château de Pontgibaud. With Eulalie's co-operation he obtained medallion cases containing little pictures of their ancestors, a large portrait of his great-grandfather 'who held the name César like me', some items from the family chapel, various parchments, and the trumpet that had once belonged to Eulalie's brother, the abbé Charles de Moré de Charaix, vicar of Mende. Thanking his cousin for the additions to his collection of family heirlooms – 'I was able to form a small gallery of twenty portraits in miniature' – César invited Eulalie to visit the château de Pontgibaud where he felt 'the presence of [our] ancestors'.[4]

This late nineteenth-century correspondence between the comte de Pontgibaud and Eulalie de Moré de Charaix provides an illustration of the way property ownership and class created for nobles a particular relationship with space, artefacts, and the passage of time. 'When a noble looks at the portraits of his ancestors in a gallery of his castle or looks at the walls and towers built by them, he strongly feels that what he is today depends on events and persons of which these are only vestiges.'[5] For Halbwachs, reflecting upon the society of France in the Middle Ages, ownership of an estate by nobility was more than just 'an external link between wealth so acquired and the person in possession of it'. What mattered were the 'links of friendship, mutual services, testimony, esteem and consideration' that united families of different social ranks in a community, 'the remembrance of which is transmitted from generation to generation'.[6]

Bourdieu's concept of misrecognition, intrinsic to the gift exchange occurring on nobles' estates, connects with a phenomenon that Halbwachs discussed whereby a 'zone of personal relations' becomes 'naturalised' in a geographic territory. Within the zone of personal relations associations between place and persons build up to create a durable connection in people's minds. Once the arbitrariness of those associations no longer enters conscious thought, in groups brought together by kinship, neighbourhood or work, group members are more likely to misrecognise the interests that lie behind reciprocal giving. In Halbwachs's description of French rural society under feudalism, people associated nobility with features in a geographic territory because of the naturalised zone of personal relations inherent to frameworks of collective memory.

Behind the fields, forests, and fertile lands the personal face of the lord is perceived. The voice of the laborers answering the question of to whom these lands belong with 'This belongs to the Marquis of Carabas' is the voice of the land itself. Such an assemblage of lands, forests, hills, and prairies has a personal physiognomy arising from the fact that it reflects the figure and history of the noble family that hunts its forests, walks through its lands, builds castles on its hills, supervises its roads – the noble family that brought together its lands acquired through conquest, royal gift, inheritance or alliance. Things would be quite different and would not inspire the same feelings or memories if other persons or another family were in command instead of the present owners.[7]

Nineteenth-century French novelists explored in fiction and memoir a cultural fascination for perceptions of living space that are similar to Halbwachs's notion of a 'personal physiognomy' for lands in nobles' possession. In authors' creative imagination rooms and their contents are personified and take on the characteristics of their inhabitants. For example, in *La Curée* (1871) Émile Zola described the home of sixty-year-old Monsieur Béraud de Châtel, 'the last of an ancient bourgeois family'. The solemn orderliness of the domestic interior, with aged household objects 'of an unyielding hard-wearing comfort', are imbued with a sense of the owner's sad, calm propriety. In *Le Serviteur* (1918) Henri Bachelin described the home in which he grew up in a village of Morvan where his father was a day labourer and church sexton. The lamplit room where, in the evening, young Henri's father read about the lives of the saints was a warm and secure haven, like the paternal embrace. Bachelin addresses his father in the book: 'Comfortably seated in my chair, I basked in the sensation of your strength.'[8]

Such cultural fascination for the relationship between people's social background and habitat is of course neither typically French nor restricted to the nineteenth century. The ways in which a person's selection of household items and organisation of living space are informed by class and gender has been a topic of academic inquiry for diverse settings.[9] In the historiography of modern France studies have addressed how evolving notions of 'privacy' and knowledge about hygiene shaped practices within households.[10] For the urban bourgeoisie much has been written on the economics of property investment and employment of servants, as well as on bourgeois 'taste' in furnishing and decoration of interiors.[11] Historians have also examined the variety of working-class domestic cultures found on farms, in towns and in cities. The rise of café sociability, the introduction of paid holidays, and the affordability of cars and household appliances are just a few of the factors that impacted home environments.[12]

Pierre Bourdieu and Monique de Saint Martin analysed domestic spaces using the concepts of capital and habitus, and their respective works continue to stimulate sociological and anthropological investigations of elites.[13] Drawing on theoretical insights from these scholars, and from Halbwachs, this chapter pursues in sequence two approaches to the history of French nobles' residences and gardens. Here the focus is on the long nineteenth century; discussion of the world wars and post-1940s will follow in Chapters 7 and 8.

The first approach is to explore the 'internal' or subjective perspectives of noble family members who inhabited châteaux, villas, and *hôtels particuliers*, and who had historical links to other residences of these kinds because their ancestors had owned them. Nobles' discourses about their home environments, in personal correspondence and autobiographical writings, contributed to the elaboration of collective memory. By sharing plans and ideas for current property, and by reflecting upon former homes, nobles were solidifying associations between place and persons in their own minds, and in the minds of other people.[14]

Châteaux began to appear in the French landscape during the ninth and tenth centuries as a means of defence and demonstration of status for their owners. Many of the ancient ones have been of strategic importance in military campaigns and battles of the Middle Ages and early modern era.[15] Less often written about by historians are the hundreds of châteaux constructed after the French Revolution. Architectural specialists observe that the interest of these buildings has not been well recognised because the Gothic features found on many of them were judged to be aesthetically hideous by commentators in the twentieth century. Nineteenth-century châteaux have suffered from shifting tastes that have led the architecture of the eighteenth century to be deemed superior.[16]

My purpose is to analyse not architectural merits or styles, but rather nobles' sentiments about their homes; therefore the evidence primarily consists of written accounts that nobles left about their dwellings. Artistic views of châteaux and fortress ruins in the landscape are common in paintings, drawings and lithographs from the late eighteenth and nineteenth centuries. Lithography, invented in 1796, was used in the series *Voyages pittoresques et romantiques dans l'ancienne France*, a publishing project of baron Taylor and Charles Nodier. These illustrated volumes and other artwork are not discussed in any detail because they are problematic for interpreting what it was like to live inside a building.[17] Before photography started to be used for private and commercial purposes pictorial evidence of the interiors of French châteaux was rarely produced.

There was not the tradition in France of making sketches and watercolours of aristocratic domestic interiors that existed in England prior to the 1850s.[18]

The second approach in the chapter is to consider nobles' residences and gardens from an 'external' angle, drawing on evidence left by non-noble professionals who had contact with nobility. Upkeep of residences required nobles to be constantly interacting with *régisseurs*, servants, and labourers, as well as with architects, horticulturalists, designers and artisans. Whether a coastal manor, a riverside château, or an alpine villa, these properties and their dependencies regularly needed repair and beautification. Owners dictated when modern conveniences like electric lighting and plumbing were introduced to their homes, how furnishing and art should be selected and arranged, and what kinds of features would characterise the exterior, such as arboreta, fountains, and garden beds. Plans, receipts, advertisements, and correspondence offer information about French nobles' choices in fashioning domestic and outdoor spaces, as well as the opinions of professionals and services of hired labour.

Prior to the First World War the real estate of nobles was 'private property' and, with few exceptions, not open for visiting by the general public. The term 'private' in this context refers to legal ownership but needs to be qualified on two grounds with regard to property use. First, nobles' residences and gardens were venues for sociability. Guests were invited into the home following an exchange of cards. For occasions such as balls, hunting parties, and afternoon teas, the various spaces of the property such as the hall, salons and dining room were used in public displays of status, even when entertaining 'privately'.[19] Second, there was projection of aristocratic residences and gardens to readers through the nineteenth century. Authors of the French canon such as Chateaubriand, Balzac, Sand, Bourget, and Proust as well as lesser-known writers featured châteaux in their novels, memoirs, plays, and poetry. Landed estates in private ownership were described by French and foreign travellers, many of whom also visited museums and galleries in Paris.[20] Major newspapers and the provincial press carried reports of weddings and other social events at châteaux. Illustrated journals such as *La Vie à la campagne* and *Fermes et châteaux* contained property sales advertisements, as well as articles about agriculture, animal husbandry, and horticulture.

Bringing the two approaches together in this chapter allows for 'internal' and 'external' perspectives to be compared. During the nineteenth century nobles' privately owned real estate gradually came to be thought of, and assessed by others, in terms of historic monuments.[21] The French word *monument* comes from the Latin *monumentum* and the first use of the expression '*monument historique*' in France appears to date from 1790 in Aubin-Louis Millin's prospectus, *Antiquités nationales*.[22] Nineteenth-century development of the protection of historic monuments was happening not only in France but also in Britain and other countries of Europe. Records of French nobles' contact with architects and conservators employed by the State show that the opinions of heritage experts start to have impact on nobles' decision-making in France through the century. But such communication was slow to develop and owners of private property held autonomy. After the 1887 law on historic monuments was passed few owners initiated a response to the requirements of the new legislation. Some went so far as to block State intervention, for there were 110 properties delisted from the historic monuments register before 1900.[23]

Planting the seeds of family memory

In the nineteenth century rich nobles owned several estates including at least one with a château while nobles who were less well off possessed one estate with a large residence that was not impressive enough to call a château, so known as a *maison de maître, gentilhommière*, or, in the southwest, a *castel*.[24] We have seen in Chapter 5 how patterns of residency varied; provincial nobles lived year-round in the countryside but aristocrats with Parisian property tended to spend less time on landed estates.

Châteaux were sites of ancestral commemoration for nobles. Nicholas Paul writes of the Middle Ages that noble families 'inhabited a landscape that was thick with ancestral memories of all kinds. Each new generation … was raised to believe that its worth (*probitas*) depended largely on its ability to maintain and preserve the best of what its ancestors had accomplished and acquired.'[25] Historians, conservators, and archaeologists are able to use medieval artefacts and sites 'to reconstruct the material framework undergirding much of the commemorative discourse.'[26] Buildings found near the château often included a private family chapel and tomb. Nobles made the château a symbol of their family's anchoring in the land and in the past.

Where archival or published records exist in which different noble relatives wrote about the same family home, then a comparison of such sources can provide a window on to 'the plurality of ideas that individuals might have about their kin and ancestors'.[27] In 1880 César de Moré, comte de Pontgibaud had fond memories of the château de Cheminades that he visited as a child but was not where he lived as an adult. On receiving the family heirlooms from cousin Eulalie, César put the large portrait of his great-grandfather in a magnificent frame to hang in the salon of the château de Pontgibaud. He also commissioned reproductions of that same portrait that he distributed to his descendants 'so that it may have a place of honour in all the manors of the family'.[28]

Eulalie on the other hand had her own memories of the château de Cheminades that feature in handwritten notes about the life of her brother, the abbé Charles de Moré de Charaix, vicar of Mende. Part family memoir and part obituary of the abbé Charles, the notes recount the experiences of the four children (Charles, Virginie, Eulalie and Hortense) born to Vincent-Antoine de Moré de Charaix (1766–1847) and his wife Louise Sophie Renée de Molette de Morangiès. The château de Cheminades is associated with family gatherings (as it was for Eulalie's cousin). Instead of the great-grandfather César featured in the large portrait, the notes accord 'place of honour' to the abbé Charles.[29]

Correspondence between children and parents provides insight to how the associations between family members and landed estates were communicated within the nuclear relationship. From the age at which a child was learning to write, the child's mother normally became a favoured correspondent. It was common to spend stretches of time apart because youngsters could be left in the care of servants and governesses when parents were travelling for business or to visit friends. On reaching adolescence many noble girls were educated by nuns in convent schools, while noble boys were sent to colleges run by priests and monks.

Marie-Jeanne Léontine de Nettancourt Vaubecourt was aged fifteen when she was enrolled as a boarder in the Parisian convent school of Sainte Clotilde. Her mother Marie-Josephine (née d'Oryot d'Apremont) lived on the estate of Thillombois near Saint Mihiel (Meuse) where she was busy attending to property matters following the death of her husband, the comte de Nettancourt. From Sainte Clotilde convent on 28 December 1848 the school pupil sent greetings to her mother for the approaching New Year. 'It is 6 o'clock in the evening and I am still seated in my chair in front of the blackboard of my airy classroom.' Marie-Jeanne's thoughts circled around the estate of Thillombois and she asked the comtesse to bring her the treats carrying a familiar taste of the *pays* on her next visit. Like Proust's Narrator with the madeleine, Marie-Jeanne wanted to savour 'the fine sugared almonds [*dragées*] of Verdun, especially aniseed ones, and a box of red and white sweets from Bar-le-Duc'.[30]

Ten years later when Marie-Jeanne had left the convent school, and was a married woman, her letters to her mother who still lived at Thillombois continue to evoke memories of activities they had shared on that estate together. On 23 October 1858 Marie-Jeanne recounted to her 'dear mama' that she had given orders that day to a gardener for the planting of 'a small clump of green trees designed to surround and give shade to an outdoor bench'. Planning this spot, 'brought back to me the times I helped you at your plantations ... everything takes me back to these joys of my childhood'.[31]

Parents' letters to children also describe activities on estates and reminisce about time spent together. During the 1880s Henri de Béarn, the eldest of six children, attended the École de l'Immaculée-Conception in Toulouse. Henri's mother, the princesse Cécile de Béarn, wrote to him from various properties to which she and her husband Gaston regularly travelled from their principal residence in Pau. In 1888–91 the princesse Cécile was developing an estate named Eslayon by the river Gave (Pyrénées-Atlantiques). The château de Eslayon, with chapel, glasshouse, barns, farmhouse and *basse-cour*, sat on sixty hectares of land; this estate together with five other estates nearby, all owned by the Béarn family, made up 204 hectares in total. Celebrating the Spring in April 1888 Cécile wrote to Henri: 'Right near the bridge we found magnificent buttercups, as beautiful as those you picked along the road ... I was really sorry you were not there to pick me a lovely bouquet. With Blanche and Bernard [two of Henri's siblings] we went to Eslayon the other day where there were periwinkles, orchids, etc. They filled a basket full of them.' 'We ate the first strawberries from the *potager*.'[32]

Interactions with rural working-class families were essential, such as during an excursion originally made with the intention 'to buy two cows for Eslayon in order to have butter and milk'. 'We could not reach agreement with their owner who was asking too high a price.' Instead, the outcome of the trip was to hire 'a couple and their fifteen-year-old son [who] will be responsible for looking after the livestock'. Cécile's children and their governess were tasked with commissions. 'Blanche [one of Henri's sisters] has taken over from you at the sewing machine. We have nearly finished all the curtains for the salon.' 'I am waiting on chickens and a rooster that Mademoiselle Grandjux went to choose for me at the Jardin d'Acclimation, and the copper-coloured turkey cocks of the Nivernais to replace all those that died from disease this past winter.'[33]

In February 1890 when there was a profusion of violets in the garden and the anemones were also starting to bloom, Cécile outlined to Henri the plans for future planting at Eslayon. 'We will plant an avenue of walnut trees that will begin from the farm courtyard and continue in a straight line ... to a bridge across the small arm of the river Gave.'[34] To take forward such projects required many short trips each month to Eslayon – some for just forty-eight hours at a time – where instructions could be given to gardeners and farm labourers and the rate of progress assessed. This planning and execution was going on simultaneously with Cécile's projects in the garden at the Béarn family's villa in Pau. For example, at the villa, 'I brought back from Toulouse some beautiful honeysuckle and we planted three clutches of it in front of the salon between the palms and the rose bushes.'[35]

The details in the princesse Cécile's letters point to the way in which this noblewoman was exercising authority in the design of living spaces, both indoors and outdoors. Noblewomen in early modern France had similarly enjoyed wide creative freedoms to develop their estates and model farms.[36] In Britain and Ireland too elite women invested in creating the interiors and gardens that were settings for a country-house lifestyle.[37] When the weather was fine, gardens and parklands of a château were used for leisure pursuits and entertaining; walks and games, fishing, butterfly hunts and pony rides occupied children. As mistress of the home, a noblewoman made decisions either independently or in consultation with her husband and the *régisseur*. The flowers, herbs, or summer berries she desired to grow in her *jardin d'agrément* or *potager* could be picked by her children or staff to feature in the vases and *corbeilles* that appeared on the dining room tables of aristocratic households.[38]

The meaning of garden spaces to noblewomen in the nineteenth century was not the same as the meaning attached to the gardens of royal residences in seventeenth-century France. Scholars have argued that under the *ancien régime*, especially in the France of Louis XIV, 'nature was mobilized' and 'transformed into a diplomatic vehicle, through which the natural wealth and political power of France could be made manifest'.[39] Such interpretations, specific to the French State of the early modern period, are not transferable to private gardens of the nineteenth century. We will return to the subject of garden design from 'external' perspectives, but the 'internal' familial experience was primarily about pleasure and repose. For the baronne Mathilde de Mackau the estate of Vimer in Normandy was where she found 'restfulness, the freedom from all the current events of Paris ... I think of our tranquil paths that will be covered in grass and flowers in a few weeks.'[40]

Gardens just as much as interior spaces evoked memories. The prince

Gaston de Béarn's memories of his wife Cécile were principally connected with a chalet in Périgord owned by her family, the Talleyrand-Périgord. This was for sentimental reasons because the couple's courtship had taken place there in 1872 and they continued to make periodic visits to ensure its maintenance. After Cécile's death in 1890 Gaston wrote to his son Henri about this chalet. His recollections are not drawn from one specific point in time but rather represent a synthesis of many memories across the nineteen years of marriage.

> I spent such wonderful times with your dear mother in this chalet in which each corner contains memories for me ... In the dining room, to give me pleasure, she put a patterned wallpaper of *fleur de lys*, and several times a year she used to make with her own hands the sandwiches filled with foie gras from her *basse-cour* ... In the stables she went to give bread, carrots, or corn to the horses, then grains, mincemeat, and leftover salad to her poultry each day.[41]

As a widower Gaston found comfort in continuing the projects at Eslayon that his wife had not been able to complete before she died. He explained to Henri:

> I am very pleased that the avenue of walnut trees shall be planted because it is one of the things your dear and incomparable mother envisaged for Eslayon. She would have been happy to go there to see her avenue that in a few years' time will rustle with nuts and offer shade ... This autumn I will try to develop the orchard that she planned. She had even made the list of all the species that she wished to have growing in it and attributed a place to each tree. I shall do everything exactly in the manner she had desired and thought out.[42]

The prince de Béarn's letters would have brought to his son Henri, upon reading them, mental images of Henri's mother that were not precisely the same images that existed in the mind of the letter-writer. The prince de Béarn alone could remember the Cécile he developed intimacy with before their children were born. Henri had other memories particular to his experience as a son. Gaston Bachelard reminds us from his findings in phenomenology that each person has 'an oneiric house, a house of dream-memory, that is lost in the shadow of a beyond of a real past'. When the subconscious is prompted, the 'house of memories becomes psychologically complex'. To 'write a room' or to 'read a room' sets up an implicit link between author and reader, but each individual has their own house of dream-memory that does the 'speaking'. The author in the act of writing, like the reader in the act of reading, is soon 'listening to the recollections of a father or a grandmother, of a mother or a servant, of "the old faithful servant," in short of the human being who dominates the corner of his most cherished memories'.[43]

Intermediaries and ancestral property

What were nobles' attitudes and behaviours in relation to the potential for repurchase of property previously owned by their ancestors but no longer in the family's posession? To answer this question we will look first at two cases involving *immeubles*, and both cases relate to the 1870s and 1880s when land prices were beginning to fall as a result of the spread of phylloxera and agricultural crisis. One might anticipate that in such an economic context selling prices would be cheaper to begin with and lowered if needed for a quick sale. A complicating factor in the case of nobles presenting themselves as potential buyers lay in the conditioning that meant estates were sites of family memories. To be sure, this did not apply to every parcel of land nobles might purchase. But land located in a former *seigneurie* – especially where the *nom de terre* matched, or had been appended to, the noble patronym – was perceived in a special way (a zone of personal relations naturalised in a geographic territory).[44] Bourdieu explained how the concern for 'symbolic patrimony' could lead a person into conduct that was financially ruinous. 'A piece of land takes on a symbolic value disproportionate with its strictly technical and economic qualities' and to buy it back 'becomes an affair of honour'. The role of an intermediary may influence what happens because not only can the seller demand 'an exorbitant price' but also any 'third party' (middleman) is in a position to make a profit.[45]

The Estienne de Saint-Jean de Prunières family, ennobled by office in 1572, had been *seigneurs* of Saint-Jean, La Salle, and Prunières among other seigneurial lands in Provence and Dauphiné. In 1872 the vicomte Ludovic d'Estienne de Saint-Jean and his wife Marie Charlotte (née de Tourtoulon de La Salle) lived in a townhouse in Aix-en-Provence. Ludovic became aware that the owners of the château de Grand Saint-Jean proposed to sell this property. He made contact with the couple, Monsieur and Madame Double, and asked to be allowed to see the interior of their château, not initially as a prospective buyer but because of his family's name and historical connection with the land of Saint-Jean. The visit of the vicomte and vicomtesse d'Estienne de Saint-Jean to the château is recounted in a letter of recrimination written by Ludovic to Madame Berthe Double on 15 February 1873. There had been a conversation between Ludovic and the Double couple about portraits, papers, and books that Ludovic strongly wished to buy in the belief that these items had originally belonged to his ancestors. The sellers proposed a sale price for the château inclusive of its contents, the vicomte accepted at 100,000 francs, so the deal was concluded with the help of a notary for the formalities. On taking possession of the château de Grand Saint-Jean, however, the vicomte and vicomtesse realised there were no portraits inside. 'I only bought Saint-Jean for the *souvenirs de famille*,' pleaded Ludovic in vain. 'I paid more than was necessary ... I paid very dearly for those items that Saint-Jean contained and I received them in a very diminished state.'[46] Unfortunately for the nobleman there was nothing to be done on the basis of the sale contract.

The second case has some similarity because of the symbolic patrimony being offered at 'an exorbitant price' but the outcome was different. In 1877 the marquis Ripert d'Alauzier was on diplomatic posting abroad when he received a letter from a group of Catholic women in the town of Seyne (Alpes de Haute Provence). The women had formed a charity association to raise funds for construction of a small chapel as a local Sacred Heart monument overlooking the valley. Seyne was also the name of the canton in which were located ruins of the château de Monclar, a former property of the house of Ripert. Although the marquis Ripert d'Alauzier had been born in the canton he had, as an adult, established residence in another part of Alpes de Haute Provence. The Catholic women wrote about their project of the Sacred Heart chapel: 'Your fellow countrymen (*compatriots*) would be happy and proud to have a stone placed by your noble hand on this dear monument and to inscribe your name among those of its donors.'[47] The marquis arranged an international payment order for fifty francs to reach the treasurer of the charitable association. 'I do not forget the ties of family and the memories that attach me to the canton of Seyne. I am very happy to see that others consider me always as being one of its children.'[48]

A decade later, in the summer of 1889, when diplomatic work had taken him to Havana, the marquis Ripert d'Alauzier received another letter concerning the canton of Seyne. This time he was being contacted about an opportunity to buy back the land on which the ruins of the château de Monclar stood. The farmer who owned the land was interested in buying other land and needed to raise capital to do so. The marquis wrote to an acquaintance, Maxime Michel, in the department's prefecture Digne-les-Bains asking him to establish the actual market value of the land and see what negotiations might be done. 'I could not be more flattered by the trust you show in me,' Maxime Michel assured the marquis.[49]

Maxime Michel visited Seyne two months later in September 1889. The property in question, he wrote, was not worth more than 2,000 francs but the farmer was asking for 4,000 from the marquis Ripert d'Alauzier, as the price 'to own the land, the ruins that are the cradle of your family'. Maxime Michel had also met with some local inhabitants who had heard rumours of the potential sale. 'They hope that as the owner at Monclar you will come and spend some time among them each year and that you will rebuild the former château.'[50]

The marquis Ripert d'Alauzier thanked Maxime Michel for his prudence in not discussing the price further before checking back with him: 'I am not surprised given the personal interest that the land holds for me and nothing would seem more natural than to pay an additional 15 to 20 per cent for it … but 100 per cent more (and, with the charges, 110 or 115 per cent) seems a bit much.' There was no intention of rebuilding the château but negotiations for buying the land might be done at a later date if the owner would consent to 'a very considerable reduction' in price. The marquis Ripert d'Alauzier was not prepared 'to throw money out of the window' but on the subject of the 'old stones of Monclar' he admitted feeling a sentimental attachment because of 'inherited friendships'.[51]

When seen together, the two sets of letters indicate the shifting dynamic of relations between Ripert d'Alauzier and the rural community. In the 1877 communication between the marquis and the Catholic women of Seyne there had been a modest gift that was given to promote 'continuity of interpersonal relations by binding the receiver to the giver with a sense of gratitude'.[52] The marquis had made his donation for the Sacred Heart monument and the Catholic women thanked him: 'Distance and absence cannot weaken a noble heart's attachment to place of birth [*le pays natal*].'[53] By contrast, in the 1889 communication between the marquis and the farmer via the intermediary of Maxime Michel, 'laws of interested calculation' interfered with the maintenance of self-deception. The marquis Ripert d'Alauzier had been born in the canton of Seyne but he had long since moved away and, as a diplomat, he had to meet the costs associated with his professional career and residency outside of France. Even though 'the truth' was apparent to the marquis Ripert d'Alauzier, conditioning still disposed him to think 'nothing would seem more natural than to pay an additional 15 to 20 per cent' for a patch of land on a hill thousands of miles from his diplomatic post in Havana.

It is quite possible, although not stated by Maxime Michel, that 'laws of interested calculation' guided his action as intermediary. He mentions in his September 1889 letter to the marquis Ripert d'Alauzier that a reason for the two months' delay in making the trip to Seyne was that he had been busy with elections in the department's prefecture Digne-les-Bains.[54] Too obvious a connection with the noble house of Ripert d'Alauzier on a matter of landownership might not have served Michel's political interests as an electoral candidate in 1889.

The nostalgic feelings expressed in the marquis Ripert d'Alauzier's letters can help us to understand the appeal to nobles of landscape painting that captured what Diderot referred to as '*les belles ruines*'. Depictions of feudal towers perched on hills overlooking rural landscapes fitted into the 'historic' genre of art that was popular among well-to-do collectors, exhibited at the Paris Salon, and also purchased by the State.[55] It was far more convenient for a French diplomat to buy a painting at auction, which he could transport, rather than to invest in land he would rarely be able to visit.

Living with inherited items?

Studying nobles' correspondence with intermediaries is needed not just for interpreting particular cases but also for developing broader perspectives on class and taste. The existence of so many wills, and the battles between siblings that arose in successions, means we can be certain nobles did very much want to have inherited items in their homes, especially family portraits. But there is a certain amount of information historians cannot obtain from a will alone. Unless there is correspondence, it may not be clear from an archive whether an heir renounced their share to avoid paying inheritance tax or taking on debt.

Questionnaire responses suggested that nobles in the 1980s felt a mix of pride and frustration over 'sacrifices' to keep inherited items in the family. There was also a tendency to distinguish their own families' practices in furnishing and decoration from practices they associated with the bourgeoisie. To browse (*chiner*) for second-hand goods at a *brocante* was looked down upon as 'bourgeois'.[56] There is a bit of myth-making going on in such responses because archival records from the nineteenth century provide plenty of evidence that nobles bought what they liked if they could afford it, including from shops selling antiques. We will also see in Chapter 8 that twentieth-century nobles parted with precious inherited items through auction houses. Nevertheless, in nobles' efforts to govern markers of 'legitimate taste' as opposed to 'middle-brow taste' the habitus did regulate attitudes and behaviours in furnishing and decorating.[57] We have seen that it made nobles susceptible to pursue symbolically valuable items 'at all costs'. Purchases were also about personal interests and emerging trends.

Billiards became very popular among nobles in the nineteenth century, so it would not do to invite guests to the château if the game was not available for them to play.[58] Athanase-Gustave de Lévis Mirepoix gave instructions to his *régisseur* Bauzil on 15 May 1836:

> Among the cases there is one that contains a billiards table. Please unwrap it and set it up in the large room that is between the *salon de compagnie* and the *salon à manger*. You will find in the case all the billiards accessories … plus a large green cloth destined to cover the table with a tool to fit it properly. A specialist tradesman will be needed for the task.[59]

This installation of the billiards table at the château de Léran (Ariège) involved the essential input of the *régisseur* for practical arrangements. Sometimes nobles went further with requests to a trusted agent to do the selection of items on their behalf. Of course, if the noble did not think the selection fitted 'aristocratic' taste the item could be returned, but involving bourgeois agents in purchasing means nobles' self-conscious distancing from 'bourgeois' practices was partly an act of performance.

Marguerite de Choiseul-Praslin was busy with interior decoration at the château de La Rochebeaucourt in August 1844. A card from Pillot Jeune Antiquités in Bordeaux which sold *objets d'art* such as paintings, sculpture, Sèvres porcelain, and bronzes suggests some purchases came from there. Pillot Jeune also offered taxidermist and art restoration services. Marguerite wrote to her *régisseur* Monsieur Doré in Paris thanking him for the cases of crystalware, cloth and clocks he had sent to her, 'all in perfect taste', and requested another batch of items including some small daguerrotypes and muslin for curtains. Marguerite told Doré that she was anticipating a visit from her husband, the comte: 'I hope the thermal waters of Bagnères will have dispatched his nasty rheumatism.'[60] Monsieur Doré continued to complete lots of 'little commissions' for Marguerite over the years. In October 1851 she asked him for tulips bulbs from Guinot (île de la Cité) as well as silk and purple satin to be sent from Paris to Angoulême railway station for collection. Doré's help was solicited for obtaining a sculpted wooden lamp and music stand, as well as toys for her children 'which they really need'. To keep them occupied until toys arrived the children were embroidering flowers on a tablecloth.[61]

Correspondence about regular purchasing means that when looking at a will, or other documentation about the dividing up of *meubles*, it should not be assumed all the items had been carefully conserved in the family over many generations. In the division of *meubles* from the château de la Thibaudière three heirs each received a share of paintings, silverware, furniture and porcelain. The silverware clearly was particular to this family, the Montlaur, and in all probability had been given as wedding presents. It was traditional among nobility for the bride's family coat of arms to be engraved on the silverware with the groom's family coat of arms. So, in the dividing up, one heir received the *cafetière* Réclesne Brachet, and another received a dish for vegetables and large round plate Montlaur Réclesne – the patronyms were those of the marriage couple. Lots of other items in this division of *meubles* may have been purchases. There is a mix of furniture styles from different periods, which was typical in nobles' residences: a clock in the style of Louis XVI, a rosewood table in the style of Louis XV, a chair in the style of Louis XIII, and an Empire commode. Porcelain was a mixture of Japanese, Italian and Russian.[62]

Unlike bourgeois family homes, where there was more likely to be consistency in furniture style, nobles' residences were filled with items of different styles. The marking of 'legitimate taste' involved discernment of the special quality of a single item rather than aiming for homogeneity. Not everything was necessarily antique, for nobles who preferred a modern aesthetic could buy or commission Art Nouveau furniture that featured at the 1900 Paris Exposition and was sold at Galérie Bing.[63]

The bequest of an entire library to an heir, rather than splitting a collection of books, was not uncommon in noble families. An inventory of the library had to be prepared as part of the inventory process for the whole estate always done at the legal opening of a succession. In the Sarcus family an inventory of the library at the château de Saint-Léger was prepared in 1876. This château with the library and other *meubles* passed into the hands of Marie Augustin René de Sarcus and Louise Mélanie Marie de Rioult de Neuville who wed in 1877.[64] Michel Figeac's research on the libraries of nobility in Gironde and other histories of personal libraries in France is made possible because of records in public and private archives that extend from the early modern period into the twentieth century. By contrast next to nothing is known about the libraries of the nobility in Germany in the nineteenth and twentieth centuries.[65]

Books and papers, like portraits, were symbolically valuable to nobles but they were commercially of interest to dealers. During the early 1880s Louis de L'Escale received letters from Frédéric Brossu who lived in Levallois-Perret. Brossu had in his possession a handwritten genealogy of the L'Escale family prepared by Antoine Louis Etienne de L'Escale, *seigneur* of Bois-Hébert (Normandy) in 1786. By giving sufficiently clear information about provenance Brossu was able to convince Louis de L'Escale that this was an authentic document, but he was reluctant to lend it. Brossu kept feeding L'Escale little snippets of information about the genealogy and other items like books and silverware that he might be prepared to sell. He was a dealer aiming to get a response to messages by invoking 'precious objects of the family'. A note in the archive states that Brossu died in 1884 or 1885, that the silverware was sold and that the genealogy 'so much desired by me' went missing when Brossu's widow moved house.[66]

Renovations, or the act of destroying to create

Histories of châteaux in particular departments or regions of France show there were a lot of new constructions during the nineteeth century. One study of the Sologne estimated that from a total of 560 châteaux two-thirds were rebuilt or reconstructed between 1800 and 1914. Nineteenth-century building projects are linked with the subject of demolition, of whole structures or parts of them. It was the tearing down or changes made in old buildings, including churches, which inspired Victor Hugo's call for a halt in his article 'Guerre aux démolisseurs' published in *Revue des deux mondes* in 1829.[67]

The Bourbon Restoration and early July Monarchy saw private repurchasing and restoration of *hôtels particuliers* in Paris, and nobles were involved in setting the tone of sociability in prestigious *quartiers*.[68] The historiography on urban housing has concentrated a good deal on Paris for the later regimes of the Second Empire and Third Republic; population growth also affected housing in centres like Lille, Bordeaux, Toulouse, Lyon, and Marseille.[69]

All of the rebuilding, and also demolition, was providing vital business for skilled artisans, manufacturing suppliers, postal workers, and outdoor manual labourers in urban and rural areas.[70] Records of nobles' renovation projects for their residences are therefore pertinent to larger questions often asked in social and economic history. In archival documentation we can see how employment of labour was remunerated, where materials were sourced, and the kinds of interactions generated between rural and urban communities. Of course some elements of history may not be observable or only glimpsed in the archive, such as the nature of human interactions happening at the micro-level within supply chains, between bosses and customers, between shopfloor supervisors and workers from small towns and villages. As John Merriman writes: 'We should not exaggerate the antagonism between town and country even before the Third Republic at the expense of understanding some essential relationships between them.' In the 'complex, subtle and intense' relations between town and country 'workers had many ties to the countryside, the *pays natal* for many of them'.[71]

In the spring of 1829 Auguste de Bonald was making arrangements to renovate the wing of his residence, the château de Vielvayssac (Aveyron). He commissioned the architect Bertrand to design, as part of this wing, a gallery featuring stone pillars and exposed timber beams surmounted by a slate roof. Perhaps it was Auguste de Bonald who made the little pencil sketch showing a rather romantic scene that the drawer imagined would take place in this gallery: a man wearing a top hat and long-tailed suit presents a rose to a lady in elegant dress and feathered hat.[72]

On 17 May 1829 François Gaffard, a local carpenter, was hired to undertake all of the necessary labour under the architect Bertrand's supervision. A team of a dozen men first had to dismantle the old timberwork from the wing of the château taking care to salvage any beams and rafters that might be used in the planned renovations. The timber planks to be purchased locally were specified in the contract to be the 'very beautiful' oak or chestnut that was sold in Rodez, and the owner Auguste de Bonald wished to make the selection himself of the exposed beams for the gallery.[73]

Regular maintenance work needed on properties in rural areas mean that nobles and *régisseurs* typically had well-established relations with particular artisans. One of the men in the team for the 1829 restoration was Joseph Ladet who was frequently tasked with carpentry repairs at Auguste de Bonald's properties in Rodez and Vielvayssac. Between June 1828 and January 1831 Ladet was employed for various odd jobs: 'to repair the stable', 'to make the door for the plant nursery', 'to repair the door to the cellar', 'to make the chapel door, fit the lock, and make the door frame for the little bedroom'. The charge for Ladet's labour was calculated at 2.25 francs per day but this did not mean Ladet was paid in cash. A summary of charges for materials and labour, and payment terms, compiled in January 1831 records Ladet receiving six setiers of rye and twelve setiers of wheat.[74]

As in early modern France, innovative features found their way into the residences of nobility as architects and suppliers based in urban centres also helped bring these to the attention of nobles.[75] The château de

Saint-Thomas lay on a seventy-six-hectare estate encompassing private chapel, parkland, fields and vineyards, and five sharecropping lots in the commune of Saint-Étienne-de-Montluc (Loire-Atlantique). In February 1826, an architect in Nantes, who was supervising work at the château de Saint-Thomas wrote to the comte Louis-Marie de Chevigné asking to be put in touch with the comte's plumber ('*votre plombier*') regarding installation of the 'English watercloset' (*la garde robe à l'Anglaise*). At 100 francs it was not an inexpensive addition to the property. The architect pressed: 'I always believed it to be your intention to install English latrines because they are the best to have in a home.'[76] It is not clear in the archive whether the comte Louis-Marie de Chevigné or his *régisseur* already knew exactly who to contact for plumbing. Chevigné was mayor of the commune Saint-Étienne-de-Montluc and extremely well connected with Legitimist nobles living in Nantes and the surrounding countryside. He would have had ample opportunity to remark to other nobles on the advantages or disadvantages of *la garde robe à l'Anglaise*.[77]

Further improvements to this same property were completed by the next generation. Louis-Marie's son, the comte Olivier de Chevigné, secretary to the comte de Chambord, married Marie-Thérèse-Eugénie Baudelet de Livois in 1864. After she died in 1878, the comte Olivier de Chevigné made a second marriage to Anna Stevens in 1882. This couple's Parisian home was at 17 rue de la Boëtie. From 1895 the comte and comtesse de Chevigné undertook very extensive renovation (and destruction for creation) at the château de Saint-Thomas. A quote given at the start of the project amounted to 25,050 francs. The work included: blocking up doorways, creating new chimneys, replacing worn parquet floors with new parquet, demolishing servants' staircases, building a large central staircase, piercing ceilings and floors to install a goods-lift (*le monte-charges*) from the cellar to the mansards, painting interior walls, inserting bay windows and cleaning brickwork. Gold and blue *fleur de lys* tiles were laid as a finishing touch.

Receipts and quotes show a mix of Parisian, regional, and local suppliers and artisans. A new heating system was purchased at a cost of 2,600 francs from Michel Perret (7 place d'Iéna, Paris) gold medallist at the 1878 Exposition Universelle. Croué et Fils in Tours supplied 333 metres of pink silk (792 francs). Duru in Paris was the source of furniture and tapestries. Ecomard in Nantes supplied locks (3,450 francs). Lannezval in Nantes handled all of the electrical work and installation of a telephone (692.75 francs). A local artisan Leray, from the commune of Saint-Étienne-de-Montluc, did the carpentry.[78]

Heritage legislation and 'living nobly'

The period 1842 to 1875 witnessed the first phase of classing historic monuments. In keeping with his earlier campaign against *démolisseurs*, Victor Hugo was in favour of putting in place a system of control by specialised services. The first law on historic monuments in France was adopted on 30 March 1887. This law contained the core prescriptions that have continued to inform subsequent legislation to safeguard monuments and objects deemed to have artistic or historical interest. From 1892 the Commission des monuments historiques oversaw the appointment of chief architects who were selected via national competition for technical competencies and devotion to preservation.[79]

Before any work could be undertaken on a building registered as a historic monument, a report had to be prepared. The report contained a technical analysis, a survey and assessment of existing conditions, and a description of the proposed restoration.[80] Under article 4 of the 1887 law, no building registered as a historic monument, nor any part of a registered building, could be destroyed. Any kind of restoration work, repair, or modification to a building required prior consent from the minister for Beaux-Arts. Ministerial authorisation was thus a requirement for a very comprehensive range of potential changes to a registered property. Authorisation was needed for large-scale exterior and interior work (such as roof tiling, the replacement of doors or window panes, or plumbing) down to small 'fixes' like mending of chipped plaster.

The prefect of Loir-et-Cher first contacted the baron de Fougères about the new law concerning historic monuments on 29 March 1888. He explained the circumstances in which a private owner could submit a claim for reimbursement of repair and restoration expenses. The baron wrote the following day to the minister for Beaux-Arts citing articles 3 and 7 of the new law to explain his refusal to give consent to the registration of his property, the château de Fougères. The matter lay dormant for the next two and half decades.

In 1912 the prefect of Loir-et-Cher tried another approach. He wrote to the mayor of the commune Fougères-sur-Bièvre: 'The Commission des monuments historiques has brought to the attention of the minister for Beaux-Arts the interest that the château de Fougères-sur-Bièvre represents ... In keeping with article 3 of the law of 30 March 1887 for the conservation of monuments and objects holding historical or artistic interest, I request that you contact the owner of the building with a view to obtaining his consent to the planned registration and let me know when possible the result of this action.'[81] This time the administration's efforts were successful. The Commission issued its report on 26 July and the baron de Fougères formally agreed to the proposal for registration of his château on 5 September 1912. There are a number of contextual factors that may explain the baron's change of heart on registration of his property.

The decade before 1914 saw some new serial publications become available in France that resembled the journal *Country Life* in England.[82] Through the articles published in *La Vie à la campagne* and *Fermes et châteaux* nobles were able to exercise considerable control in bringing to the public's attention their private investment in property. The nobility's capacity to show off grand homes was helped by the fact that journalists were tapping into a voyeuristic appetite for the signs of aristocratic distinction. Like the early nineteenth-century declarations made for the *majorats-sur-demande* the articles on residences in *La Vie à la campagne* magnify the capital of the owners. They functioned like *majorat* declarations to showcase 'the importance of the estate symbolism, with its obligatory signs of seigneurial dominion: château, parklands, the *allée* leading to the *grande cour*, all structures in stone sufficiently weathered to suggest ancestral possession and dignity'.[83]

In each issue of *La Vie à la campagne* there was a feature article on one grand residence or garden. The journal appeared fortnightly from 1 October 1906. To see what proportion of these feature articles were for properties owned by nobles the following samples were taken: set A issues 1 to 6 (1 October 1906 to 15 December 1906); set B issues 19 to 42 (1 July 1907 to 15 June 1908); and set C issues 55 to 62 (1 January 1909 to 15 April 1909). In set A nobles owned four out of six properties. In set B nobles owned fourteen out of twenty-four properties (including one held by an English lord and another by a Russian duke). In set C nobles owned three out of eight properties.

Readers of the journal were introduced to noble families such as the Balleroy whose members in the late eighteenth century had been 'victims of the Terror' and whose 'traditions have been loyally followed' down the generations. 'The marquis de Balleroy, like his ancestors, passionately loves the old estate he has inherited.' The château de Balleroy near Caen (Calvados) had been rendered more comfortable with heating but care had been taken to conserve 'the ancient decoration, so harmonious and rich'. At the manoir de Keraval near Quimper it was the coats of arms that impressed the visitor, including those of the marquis de Coëtloquen, governor of Dinan and Saint-Malo. Contemplating Vitry-la-Ville near

Châlons-sur-Marne, the reader was invited to reflect upon 'the religious respect of our old French families for ancestral patrimony'.[84]

Among the gardens that featured in *La Vie à la campagne* were: the *jardin à l'anglaise* at Ermenonville (Oise) owned by prince and princesse Constantin Radziwill, the gardens at the villa Valetta near Cannes owned by grand-duc Michel of Russia, and the *jardin à la française* at the villa Vigier near Nice owned by the vicomte Vigier. There was also a visit to the château de Malmaison (Seine), owned by the State, to gaze upon the gardens through which Joséphine de Beauharnais had wandered with Empeor Napoleon I.[85]

In discussing the gardens in its feature articles *La Vie à la campagne* provided snapshots into the long history of international exchanges that had characterised garden design in France. A 'garden' had been defined in *Littré* as a space normally enclosed and planted with useful or decorative vegetation. But gardens were also about pleasure and expected to express 'an art of living' and 'a moving spectacle'; they were in early modern France the expression of 'the supreme refinement of kings'.[86] The reign of Louis XIV had been 'the climax of baroque and formal theatrical gardens'. Following the death of Louis XIV's gardener André Le Nôtre 'geometry, perspectives and vanishing points of the formal seventeenth-century landscape were gradually abandoned in favor of real objects, irregular shapes, contrast and unexpected vistas'. Eighteenth-century gardens, dubbed picturesque, were 'all about surprises'.[87]

During the 1730s and 1740s Turkish features were introduced in the gardens at Lunéville, residence of Stanislas Leszczynski. Cross-channel influences were also important, as ideas for gardens went from France to Britain and vice-versa. Sir Thomas Hanmer spent a good deal of time in France during the seventeenth century and he described the fashions he observed in French gardens in his manuscript the *Garden Book*, later published by his descendant John Lord Hanmer in 1876. The arboretum became fashionable in Britain during the 1830s to complement the country house and English designers of arboreta drew inspiration from tree plantings beside châteaux in France. In the other direction, English influence can be seen in the creation of a *jardin à l'anglaise* at the hôtel de Brancas. Salomon de Caus (1576–1626), a specialist of the *trompe-l'œil* garden, had been largely responsible for the spread of Florentine motifs and concepts throughout Europe. The garden of the duc de Richelieu's château at Rueil featured Florentine touches and was the work of Jean Lemaire.[88]

La Vie à la campagne also carried propery sales advertisements. Across the nineteenth century 'there was a brisk demand for property carrying a ready-made aroma of *bon ton*'.[89] One of the properties that changed hands in 1906 was the château de Villandry in the Loire valley, purchased for 120,000 francs by the Spanish physiologist Joachim Carvallo. With his wealthy American wife, Ann Coleman, Carvallo devoted energy to returning the château and its gardens to glory. Carvallo's ownership of Villandry was the genesis for forming the association La Demeure historique and its journal of the same name of which Carvallo served as editor.[90] La Demeure historique, as we shall see in the next two chapters, was to become a critical lobby group in which nobles have been actively involved throughout the twentieth century and into the 2000s.

In addition to reading about historic homes, travelling to see them was becoming easier for the wealthy. The rise of the automobile had an impact on people's sense of outdoor space as well as their understanding of time.[91] As Proust remarks in connection with driving, 'Distances are only the relation of space to time and vary with it. We express the difficulty that we have in getting to a place in a system of miles or kilometres which becomes false as soon as that difficulty decreases.'[92] Around 1900 motoring became a weekly hobby for nobles as well as a source of adventure, discovery and international exchange. In 1897 the duchesse d'Uzès hired a private instructor and became the first French woman to receive her driver's licence. She then founded and served as president of the Automobile club féminin de France that organised annual driving rallies, including one to Rome. In the spring of 1905 the princesse Marthe Bibesco, her husband Georges, and five others made a driving tour through Persia in two chauffeur-driven Mercedes and a Fiat.[93]

The Touring Club de France was launched following a trip by driving elites to London in 1890. By 1906 the club had 100,000 members. It organised trips to picturesque locations and historic sites; the preservationist interests of members resulted in efforts to protect churches, backing the campaign of the nationalist intellectual Maurice Barrès.[94] In September 1913 the prince and princesse Murat and their children made a fortnight-long journey to Evian-les-Bains because the princesse was a member of the Touring Club de France. The family, as well as the princesse's *femme de chambre*, prince's *valet de chambre* and the chauffeur stayed at Le Royal, *un hôtel de grand luxe*, located in a large park with views of the lake. Expenses included hotel rooms (2,206.35 francs in total), golf and bridge (36 francs), and tips (40 francs). Monthly wages for the mechanics were between 250 and 300 francs. By 1913 the Murat family had already completed automobile trips to Sweden, Norway, and

Denmark (1908), Deauville, Vittel, and Aix-les-Bains (1910), Montcalm, Compiègne, Brussels, and Vittel (1911), and Brussels and Luxembourg (1912). Such travel was part of an expansion in mass leisure and consumption, linked to the automobile, which benefited the bourgeoisie as well as the elite: by 1911 in France there were 64,000 registered vehicles and a ready market for Michelin guides.[95]

Conclusion

Historians have characterised the three decades prior to 1914 as the 'triumph of the republic' and argued that the increased social, political, and economic power of the bourgeoisie was evident culturally, for example in what Leora Auslander calls 'a bourgeois stylistic regime' in furnishing. Under the *ancien régime*, new styles had been identified with kings and some items were so expensive that only the court aristocracy could afford them. The bourgeoisie is considered to have driven consumer demand in late nineteenth-century France for 'historicist pastiche' furniture, signalling through home furnishing that it was 'the dominant social group' in the Third Republic regime.[96]

This chapter has presented a counter-argument to the kinds of connections scholars of modern France have drawn between representations of home, class and nation. Instead of 'taste and power' resting with the bourgeoisie, nobles were maintaining social and cultural authority as private owners of residences and gardens that were admired by non-nobles and elevated to the position of 'national' heritage. The State wanted to be able to control what happened to such residences and the development of measures to protect historic monuments set off 'symbolic struggles' with private owners. Nobles wanted to keep control because their conception of the tangible patrimony in question was fundamentally tied to their families' intangible patrimony. In circumstances of 'struggle', nobles did not always gain the upper hand. Contact between the marquis Ripert d'Alauzier and the community of Seyne in the 1870s and 1880s shows how differences in the collective memories of families and social classes in the nineteenth century were implicated in understandings of nobles' ancestral estates.

In making their residences and gardens into sites of commemoration for ancestors French nobles were behaving like nobles in other parts of Europe. They put every effort into reinforcing associations with the past, using the home both for transmission of familial identity and as a symbol of their families' importance on a grand stage of nation and the European continent. That is not to say that, in privileging memories of the past, nineteenth-century nobles were uninterested in innovation and experimentation on landed estates. We have seen that like their early modern predecessors they were introducing new features, designs and techniques, some of which were imported from abroad. Nobles' experiences of living in châteaux of France through the nineteenth century point to the challenges and contradictions of 'modernity', as people's perceptions of what was modern evolved over the *longue durée*.[97]

Notes

1 Undated letter (1880) in AD Lozère 4J/56 Fonds Molette de Morangiès et Moré de Charaix.

2 The Moré family originated from Gévaudan and branches were named after seigneuries: Moré de Charaix, Moré de Préviala, Moré de la Salle and Moré de Pontgibaud. *Nobiliaire d'Auvergne* vol. 4 (Clermont-Ferrand, 1851).

3 A letter of 2 July 1868 addressed to Eulalie enquires about the rumour that the Moré sisters might sell Cheminades. AD Lozère 4J/44 Fonds Molette de Morangiès et Moré de Charaix.

4 Undated letter (1880) in AD Lozère 4J/56 Fonds Molette de Morangiès et Moré de Charaix.

5 M. Halbwachs, *On Collective Memory* (*Les Cadres sociaux de la mémoire*, 1925), ed. and translated by L. A. Coser (Chicago, 1992), p. 129.

6 Halbwachs, *On Collective Memory*, pp. 122–3.

7 Halbwachs, *On Collective Memory*, p. 123.

8 É. Zola, *La Curée* (1871–2); H. Bachelin, *Le Serviteur* (1918).

9 C. Knevitt, *Shelter: Human Habitats from around the World* (San Francisco, 1996); A. Ludtke (ed.), *The History of Everyday Life: Reconstructing Historical Experiences and Ways of Life*, translated by W. Templer (Princeton, 1995); V. de Grazia and E. Furlough (eds), *The Sex of Things: Gender and Consumption in Historical Perspective* (Berkeley, 1996); B. Fowkes Tobin and M. Daly Goggin (eds), *Material Women: Consuming Desires and Collecting Practices 1750–1950* (Farnham, 2009).

10 B. G. Smith, *Ladies of the Leisure Class: The Bourgeoises of the Nord in the Nineteenth Century* (Princeton, 1981); A. Corbin, *The Foul and the Fragrant: Odor and the French Social Imagination* (Cambridge, MA, 1986); M. Perrot (ed.), *A History of Private Life* vol. 4, translated by A. Goldhammer (Cambridge, MA, 1990); A. Corbin, *Time, Desire, and Horror*, translated by J. Birrell (Cambridge, 1995); A.-M. Sohn, *Chrysalides: femmes dans la vie privée (XIXe–XXe siècles)* 2 vols (Paris, 1996); M. L. Stewart, *For Health and Beauty: Physical Culture for Frenchwomen, 1880s–1930s* (Baltimore, 2002).

11 A. Daumard, *Maisons de Paris et propriétaires parisiens au XIXe siècle*

1809–1880 (Toulouse, 1965); A. Martin-Fugier, *La Place des bonnes: la domes-
ticité féminine à Paris en 1900* (Paris, 1979); R. G. Saisselin, *The Bourgeois and
the Bibelot* (New Brunswick, 1984); D. Berthelot, *La Bourgeoisie dans tous
ses états: le roman familial de la Belle Époque* (Paris, 1987); A. Daumard, *Les
Bourgeois et la bourgeoisie en France* (Paris, 1987); W. Walton, *France at the
Crystal Palace: Bourgeois Taste and Artisan Manufacture in the Nineteenth
Century* (Berkeley, 1992), L. Auslander, *Taste and Power: Furnishing Modern
France* (Berkeley, 1996), pp. 220–4, 261–305; P. Nord, 'Republican politics
and the bourgeois interior in mid-nineteenth century France' in S. Nash (ed.),
Home and its Dislocations in Nineteenth Century France (Albany, 1993), pp.
193–214.

12 G. Duby and A. Wallon (eds), *Histoire de la France rurale* vol. 4 *La Fin de
la France paysanne depuis 1914* by M. Gervais, M. Jollivet, and Y. Tavernier
(Paris, 1977); M. Segalen, *Love and Power in the Peasant Family: Rural
France in the Nineteenth Century*, translated by S. Matthews (Oxford, 1983);
J. Shaffer, *Family and Farm: Agrarian Change and Household Organization
in the Loire Valley, 1500-1900* (Albany, 1982); S. C. Rogers, *Shaping Modern
Times in Rural France* (Princeton, 1991); S. Haine, *The World of the Paris Café:
Sociability among the French Working Class, 1789-1914* (Baltimore, 1996);
K. Silver, 'The peasants of Paris: Limousin migrant masons in the nineteenth
century', *French History* 28 (2014), 498–519.

13 P. Bourdieu, *Distinction: A Social Critique of the Judgement of Taste*, translated
by R. Nice (London, 2000); M. de Saint Martin, *L'Espace de la noblesse* (Paris,
1993). See also M. Pinçon and M. Pinçon-Charlot, *Dans les beaux quartiers*
(Paris, 1989); M. Pinçon and M. Pinçon-Charlot, *Les Ghettos du gotha: au
coeur de la grande bourgeoisie* (Paris, 2007); Y. Kuiper, N. Bijleveld, and
J. Dronkers (eds), *Nobilities in Europe in the Twentieth Century: Reconversion
Strategies, Memory Culture and Elite Formation* (Leuven, 2015).

14 Halbwachs, *On Collective Memory*, p. 59.

15 J. Mesqui, *Châteaux et enceintes de la France médiévale: de la défense à la rési-
dence* 2 vols (Paris, 1993); A. Debord, *Aristocratie et pouvoir: le rôle du château
dans la France médiévale* (Paris, 2000); R. Le Jan, 'Continuity and change in
the tenth-century nobility' in A. J. Duggan (ed.), *Nobles and Nobility in
Medieval Europe: Concepts, Origins, Transformations* (Woodbridge, 2000), pp.
53–68; J. R. Ruff, *Violence in Early Modern Europe 1500-1800* (Cambridge,
2001), pp. 44–72; B. Sandberg, *Warrior Pursuits: Noble Culture and Civil
Conflict in Early Modern France* (Baltimore, 2010); M. Costambeys, M. Innes,
and S. MacLean, *The Carolingian World* (Cambridge, 2011), pp. 285–95,
379–427.

16 M. Girouard, *Life in the French Country House* (London, 2000), ch. 8; J.-M.
Pérouse de Montclos, *Histoire de l'architecture française: de la Renaissance
à la Révolution* (Paris, 1989). There is a large literature on the Gothic
revival in architecture, literature, and art. On architecture see for example

F. Bercé, *Eugène Viollet-le-Duc* (Paris, 2013); M. Bressiani, *Architecture and the Historical Imagination: Eugène-Emmanuel Viollet-le-Duc 1814–1879* (London and New York, 2014).

17 D. Jarrasse, *La Peinture française au XVIIIe siècle* (Paris, 1998), pp. 148–58; J. Zutter, 'The rise of modern landscape painting in France' in M. Hilaire, J. Zutter, and O. Zeder (eds), *French Paintings from the Musée Fabre, Montpellier* (Canberra, 2003), pp. 141–62. C. Nodier and baron I. J. S. Taylor, *Voyages pittoresques et romantiques dans l'ancienne France* 23 volumes (Paris, 1820–63) discussed in F. Choay, *L'Allégorie du patrimoine* 4 ed. (Paris, 2007), pp. 93, 99; D. Poulot, *Patrimoine et musées: l'institution de la culture* (Paris, 2003), p. 120.

18 Girouard, *Life*, p. 304.

19 A. Martin-Fugier, *La Vie élégante ou la formation du Tout-Paris 1815–1848* (Paris, 1990); E. C. Macknight, 'Cake and conversation: the women's *jour* in Parisian High Society, 1880–1914', *French History* 19 (2005), 342–63; A. Bravard, *Le Grand Monde parisien 1900–1939: la persistance du modèle aristocratique* (Rennes, 2013).

20 R. B. Bernard, *A Tour Through Some Parts of France* […] *During the Summer and Autumn of 1814* (London, 1815); W. D. Fellowes, *Paris During the Interesting Month of July 1815. A Series of Letters Addressed to a Friend in London* (London, 1815); F. Hall, *Travels in France in 1818* (London, 1819); W. E. Frye, *After Waterloo, Reminiscences of European Travel 1815–1819 by Major W. E. Frye*, ed. Salomon Reinach (London, 1908); S. Bellanger, *La Touraine ancienne et moderne* (Paris, 1845); G. Touchard-Lafosse, *La Loire historique, pittoresque et biographique de la source de ce fleuve à son embouchure dans l'océan* (Tours, 1851); abbé C. Chevalier, *Promenades pittoresques en Touraine: histoire, legends, monuments, paysages* (Tours, 1869).

21 A. Riegl, *Le Culte moderne des monuments: son essence et sa genèse* (Paris, 1984); Choay, *L'Allégorie*, ch. 4; P. Verdier, *Le Service des Monuments historiques, son histoire, son organisation, administration, législation* (Paris, 1936); J.-P. Bady, *Les Monuments historiques en France* (Paris, 1985); P. Preschez, *Cours de droit: législation et monuments historiques* (Paris, 1994); R. Recht (ed.), *Victor Hugo et le débat patrimonial* (Paris, 2003).

22 Choay, *L'Allégorie*, p. 14; J.-P. Babelon and A. Chastel, *La Notion de patrimoine* (Paris, 1994), p. 71.

23 P. Mandler, *The Fall and Rise of the Stately Home* (New Haven, 1997), pp. 160, 169, 172, 187–91, 238–40, 266, 270–4, 282; E. Karlsgodt, *Defending National Treasures: French Art under Vichy* (Stanford, 2011), pp. 103–13; A. Swenson, *The Rise of Heritage: Preserving the Past in France, Germany, and Britain 1789–1914* (Cambridge, 2015), pp. 314–16, 321–3.

24 D. Higgs, *Nobles in Nineteenth-Century France: The Practice of Inegalitarianism* (Baltimore, 1987), pp. 35, 41–8; N. Petiteau, *Élites et mobilités: la noblesse d'Empire au XIXe siècle (1808–1914)* (Paris, 1997), pp. 392–7.

25 N. L. Paul, *To Follow in Their Footsteps: The Crusades and Family Memory in the High Middle Ages* (Ithaca, 2012), p. 201.
26 Paul, *To Follow*, pp. 95–7; M. Figeac, *Châteaux et vie quotidienne de la noblesse: de la Renaissance à la douceur des Lumières* (Paris, 2006), pp. 54–8.
27 Paul, *To Follow*, p. 10.
28 Undated letter in AD Lozère 4J/56 Fonds Molette de Morangiès et Moré de Charaix.
29 AD Lozère 4J/58 Fonds Molette de Morangiès et Moré de Charaix.
30 28 December 1848 in AD Meuse 39J/50 Archives de la famille Nettancourt.
31 23 October 1858 in AD Meuse 39J/50 Archives de la famille Nettancourt.
32 23 April 1888 and 29 April 1888 in AD Charente J 1093 Fonds Galard, Brassac, Béarn, Chalais. On Eslayon estate AD Charente J 1210 Fonds Galard, Brassac, Béarn, Chalais.
33 25 November 1888, 12 March 1889, 18 May 1889 in AD Charente J 1093 Fonds Galard, Brassac, Béarn, Chalais.
34 20 February 1890 in AD Charente J 1093 Fonds Galard, Brassac, Béarn, Chalais.
35 12 March 1889 in AD Charente J 1093 Fonds Galard, Brassac, Béarn, Chalais.
36 D. Picco, 'Les Femmes et la terre dans les élites françaises (XVII–XVIII siècles)' in C. Le Mao and C. Marache (eds), *Les Élites et la terre du XVIe siècle aux années 1930* (Paris, 2010), pp. 223–32.
37 T. Lummis and J. Marsh, *The Woman's Domain: Women and the English Country House* (London, 1990); S. Bell, 'Women create gardens in male landscapes: a revisionist approach to eighteenth-century English garden history', *Feminist Studies* 16 (1990), 471–91; D. Arnold, *The Georgian Country House: Architecture, Landscape and Society* (Stroud, 1998), pp. 79–99; M. Laird, *The Flowering of the Landscape Garden: English Pleasure Grounds 1720–1800* (Philadelphia, 1999); R. Baird, *Mistress of the House: Great Ladies and Grand Houses 1670–1830* (London, 2003); J. Martin, *Wives and Daughters: Women and Children in the Georgian Country House* (London, 2004); J. Munroe, *Making Gardens of their Own: Advice for Women, 1500–1750* (Aldershot, 2007); P. Horn, *Ladies of the Manor: How Wives & Daughters Really Lived in Country House Society over a Century Ago* (Stroud, 2012); S. Bending, *Green Retreats: Women, Gardens and Eighteenth-Century Culture* (Cambridge, 2013).
38 E. C. Macknight, 'Dining in aristocratic households of nineteenth-century France: a study of female authority', *Virtus: Journal of Nobility Studies* 23 (2016), 105–23.
39 C. Mukerji, 'The political mobilization of nature in seventeenth-century French formal gardens', *Theory and Society* 23 (1994), 651–77; E. Hyde, *Cultivated Power: Flowers, Culture and Politics in the Reign of Louis XIV* (Philadelphia, 2006); J. Guillaume, 'Château, jardin et paysage en France du XVe au XVIIe siècle', *Revue de l'Art* 124 (1999), 13–32; J. Guillaume, 'Le

jardin mis en ordre: jardin et château en France du XVe au XVIIe siècle' in *Architecture, jardin, paysage. L'environnement du château et de la villa à la Renaissance* (Paris, 1999), pp. 103–36. For a *longue durée* approach see M. Mosser and G. Teyssot (eds), *Histoire des jardins de la Renaissance à nos jours* (Paris, 2002).

40 'Comment elle a aimé Vimer et la nature', AN AP 156 (I)/314 Fonds Mackau. Vimer (*vent de mer*) was the residence of baron Armand de Mackau's aunt, the comtesse de Saint-Alphonse. On Mathilde's love of this place see notebook 14, AN AP 156 (I)/315 Fonds Mackau and her published novel *Ce que disent les champs* (Tours, 1873).

41 10 October 1891 in AD Charente J 1092 Fonds Galard, Brassac, Béarn, Chalais.

42 7 April 1892 in AD Charente J 1092 Fonds Galard, Brassac, Béarn, Chalais.

43 G. Bachelard, *The Poetics of Space*, translated by M. Jolas (Boston, 1994), p. 14. Halbwachs used the case of dreaming to explore the relationship of individual memory to collective memory. Halbwachs, *On Collective Memory*, pp. 49–50.

44 T. Barthelemy, 'Patronymic names and noms de terre in the French nobility in the eighteenth and the nineteenth centuries', *History of the Family* 5 (2000), 181–97.

45 P. Bourdieu, *Le Sens pratique* (Paris, 1980), pp. 205–6.

46 15 February 1873 in AD Bouches-du-Rhône 3E 241 Famille Estienne de Saint-Jean. The vicomtesse (1855–1933) kept a journal that is in the *fonds*.

47 5 May 1877 in AD Vaucluse 43J/228 Fonds Ripert d'Alauzier. The women's initiative in Seyne was part of a wider Catholic movement. R. Jonas, *France and the Cult of the Sacred Heart: An Epic Tale for Modern Times* (Ewing, 2000).

48 7 June 1877 in AD Vaucluse 43J/228 Fonds Ripert d'Alauzier.

49 29 June 1889 in AD Vaucluse 43J/228 Fonds Ripert d'Alauzier.

50 6 September 1889 in AD Vaucluse 43J/228 Fonds Ripert d'Alauzier.

51 30 September 1889 in AD Vaucluse 43J/228 Fonds Ripert d'Alauzier.

52 P. Bourdieu, *Outline of a Theory of Practice*, translated by R. Nice (Cambridge, 1977), pp. 4–9, 172–3.

53 14 June 1877 in AD Vaucluse 43J/228 Fonds Ripert d'Alauzier.

54 6 September 1889 in AD Vaucluse 43J/228 Fonds Ripert d'Alauzier.

55 D. Poulot, *Une histoire des musées de France XVIIIe-XXe siècles* (Paris, 2008), ch. 9; Hilaire et al., *French Paintings*, pp. 141–62.

56 É. Mension-Rigau, *Aristocrates et grands bourgeois: éducation, traditions, valeurs* (Paris, 1994), pp. 107–17, 366–7, 383–6, 395–6; J.-B. Naudin and C. de Nicolay-Mazery, *Visite privée: hôtels particuliers de Paris* (Paris, 1999), pp. 57, 63, 117, 136–7, 140, 154, 192; M. Gaillard, *Les belles heures de Champs Elysées* (Amiens, 1990).

57 Bourdieu, *Distinction*, p. 16; E. C. Macknight, 'A touch of distinction: furnishing French aristocratic homes in the nineteenth and twentieth centuries' in

B. Fowkes Tobin and M. Daly Goggin (eds), *Material Women: Consuming Desires and Collecting Practices 1750–1950* (Farnham, 2009), pp. 75–91.

58 Girouard, *Life*, pp. 187, 255, 303, 308, 311, 325.

59 15 May 1836 in AD Ariège 46J/391 Archives Lévis Mirepoix.

60 17 August 1844 in AD Seine-Maritime 7J/93 Fonds du château de Clères. Marguerite de Choiseul-Praslin was married to the comte de Béarn but she normally signed with her natal patronym 'Choiseul-Praslin, comtesse de Béarn'.

61 12 October 1851 in AD Seine-Maritime 7J/93 Fonds du château de Clères.

62 Typed lists of items (1940s) in AD Maine-et-Loire 249J/5 Fonds de la famille Montlaur. On French furniture styles see Stéphane Faniel, *Le XIXe siècle français* (Paris, 1957), pp. 35–69, 195–222. On tapestries, ceramics, and bronzes, pp. 71–97, 119–93.

63 *The Musée d'Orsay, Paris*, translated by J. Brenton (Paris, 1986), pp. 169–81; *1900* exhibition catalogue (Paris, 2000), pp. 92–5, 110–29, 159–63, 184–5, 190, 234–7, 279; *Le Décor de la vie de 1900 à 1925* exhibition catalogue (Paris, 1937), pp. 1–55, 74–94; N. J. Troy, *Modernism and the Decorative Arts in France: Art Nouveau to Le Corbusier* (New Haven, 1991), pp. 7–51; *Japonisme et Mode* exhibition catalogue (Paris, 1996).

64 Catalogue de la bibliothèque (1876) in AD Seine-Maritime 116J/100 Chartrier de Maulévrier.

65 C. Jolly (ed.), *Histoire des bibliothèques françaises* vol. 2 *Les Bibliothèques sous l'Ancien régime, 1530–1789* (Paris, 1988); M. Figeac, *Destins de la noblesse bordelaise (1770–1830)* 2 vols (Bordeaux, 1996), vol. 1, pp. 256–71. On reading, M. Lyons, *Le Triomphe du livre: une histoire sociologique de la lecture dans la France du XIXe siècle* (Paris, 1987). On publishing, R. Chartier and D. Roche, *Histoire de l'édition française* (Paris, 1984). On German nobility, Christof Dipper, 'Les Noblesses allemandes depuis la chute de la monarchie état des recherches actuelles' in D. Lancien and M. de Saint Martin (eds), *Anciennes et nouvelles aristocraties de 1800 à nos jours* (Paris, 2007), p. 58.

66 2 July 1880, 22 July 1880, 25 September 1881, 10 July 1882, note about Brossu's death and correspondence with the widow in AD Meuse 29J Collection de L'Escale (*fonds 'en vrac'*, not classed at time of consultation).

67 M. Bedon, *Le Château au XIXe siècle en Vendée* (Fontenay-le-Comte, 1971); B. Toulier, *Châteaux en Sologne* (Paris, 1992); P. Grandcoing, *Les Demeures de la distinction: châteaux et châtelains au XIXe siècle en Haute-Vienne* (Limoges, 1999); J. Vassort, *Les Châteaux de la Loire au fil des siècles: art, politique et société* (Paris, 2012). V. Hugo, 'Guerre aux démolisseurs' was written in 1825 : see Choay, *L'Allégorie*, pp. 107–11, 225.

68 P. Mansel, *Paris between Empires 1814–1852* (London, 2001), pp. 209–10; A. Martin-Fugier, *La Vie élégante ou la formation du Tout-Paris 1815–1848* (Paris, 1990).

69 D. Pinkney, *Napoleon III and the Rebuilding of Paris* (Princeton, 1958);

Daumard, *Maisons de Paris*; A.-L. Shapiro, *Housing the Poor of Paris, 1850–1902* (Madison, 1985); Perrot, *A History of Private Life*; D. P. Jordan, 'Haussmann and Haussmanisation: the legacy for Paris', *French Historical Studies* 27 (2004), 87–113. On regional cities, J. M. Merriman (ed.), *Consciousness and Class Experience in Nineteenth-Century Europe* (New York, 1979), chs 4–6; J. M. Merriman (ed.), *French Cities in the Nineteenth Century* (London, 1982); W. H. Sewell, *Structure and Mobility: The Men and Women of Marseille, 1820–1870* (Cambridge, 1985); J. M. Merriman, *The Margins of City Life: Explorations on the French Urban Frontier, 1815–1851* (Oxford, 1991).

70 G. Crossick and H.-G. Haupt (eds), *Shopkeepers and Master-Artisans in Nineteenth-Century Europe* (London, 1984), pp. 3–34; G. Duby and A. Wallon (eds), *Histoire de la France rurale* vol. 3 *Apogée et crise de la civilisation paysanne de 1789 à 1914* by M. Agulhon, G. Désert, and R. Specklin (Paris, 1976), pp. 68–74; P. Kriedte, H. Medick, and J. Schlumbohm, *Industrialization before Industrialization* (Cambridge, 1981), ch. 2; W. Reddy, *The Rise of Market Culture: The Textile Trade and French Society, 1750–1900* (Cambridge, 1984).

71 J. Merriman, 'Incident at the statue of the Virgin Mary: the conflict of old and new in nineteenth-century Limoges' in Merriman, *Consciousness*, p. 135. Essays in Merriman's volume contribute in key ways to the debates on E. Weber, *Peasants into Frenchmen: The Modernization of Rural France 1870–1914* (London, 1976). On migration and the 'mental universe' of rural people see L. Page Moch, *Paths to the City: Regional Migration in Nineteenth-Century France* (Beverley Hills, 1983) and on earlier centuries, G. Duby and A. Wallon (eds), *Histoire de la France rurale* vol. 2 *L'Âge classique des paysans de 1340 à 1789* by H. Neveux, J. Jacquart, and E. Le Roy Ladurie (Paris, 1977), pp. 89–92, 290–9.

72 AD Aveyron 71J/25 Fonds de Bonald de Vielvayssac. On galleries see J. Guillaume, 'La Galerie dans le château français: place et fonction', *Revue de l'Art* 102 (1993), 32–42.

73 17 May 1829 in AD Aveyron 71J/25 Fonds de Bonald de Vielvayssac.

74 État des journées Joseph Ladet' in AD Aveyron 71J/25 Fonds de Bonald de Vielvayssac. On the early modern period see Duby and Wallon, *Histoire de la France rurale* vol. 2, pp. 254–5, 286–90.

75 Figeac, *Châteaux*, chs 1, 3, 7, 8.

76 3 February and 8 February 1826 in AD Loire-Atlantique 190J/111 Fonds Chevigné.

77 On the Quiberon monument see AD Loire-Atlantique 190J/42 Fonds Chevigné and 190J/43 for Chevigné's professional and administrative career including as mayor of the commune. Girouard gives an introduction to 'plumbing – or the lack of it', with photographs, and notes the need for further research on water supply. Girouard, *Life*, pp. 219–37.

78 AD Loire-Atlantique 190J/111 Fonds Chevigné.

79 Choay *L'Allégorie*, ch. 4; Verdier, *Le Service*; Bady, *Les Monuments historiques*.

80 J. Francou, 'Historic structure reports in France: a history of guidelines and a case study', *APT Bulletin* 28 (1997), 23–8.

81 24 August 1912 and see also 29 March 1888 and 9 July 1888 in AD Loir-et-Cher 83J/127 Fonds de Bizemont-Lambot de Fougères.

82 Mandler, *The Fall*, pp. 148–50, 183, 214, 230, 241, 243, 246, 255, 273–4, 287–9, 291, 293–8, 300.

83 D. Higgs, 'Social mobility and hereditary titles in France, 1814–1830: the majorats-sur-demande', *Histoire sociale/Social History* 14 (1981), 40. The journal *Fermes et châteaux* is discussed in Girouard, *Life*, ch. 8.

84 *La Vie à la campagne* 15 July 1907, no. 20; 1 March 1909, no. 59; 1 November 1906, no. 3.

85 *La Vie à la campagne* 15 August, 1907, no. 22; 1 January 1908, no. 31; 15 February 1909, no. 58. On Malmaison and gardens of *la noblesse d'Empire* see *La Vie à la campagne* 15 November 1907, no. 28; J. Tulard, *Napoléon et la noblesse d'Empire* (Paris, 1979), p. 139; M.-B. d'Arneville, *Parcs et jardins sous le Premier Empire: reflets d'une société* (Paris, 1981).

86 R. Pechère, 'Les Jardins historiques, leur restauration, leur intérêt pour les jardins contemporains', *APT Bulletin* 15 (1983), 15–21.

87 F. Clarke d'Hardemare, 'The follies of a king-duke', *Garden History* 37 (2009), 56–67. On eighteenth-century ideas of nature and of gardening see A. Bagermann and R. Dekker, *Child of the Enlightenment: Revolutionary Europe Reflected in a Boyhood Diary*, translated by D. Webb (Leiden, 2009).

88 R. Duthie, 'The planting plans of some seventeenth-century flower gardens', *Garden History* 18 (1990), 77–102; B. Elliott, 'From the arboretum to the woodland garden', *Garden History* 25 (2007), 71–83; P. Elliott, C. Watkins, and S. Daniels, '"Combining science with recreation and pleasure": cultural geographies of nineteenth-century arboretums', *Garden History* 35 (2007), 6–27; R. Perry, 'François-Joseph Belanger's bath-house at the hotel de Brancas', *Architectural History* 44 (2001), 377–85; L. Morgan, 'The early modern "trompe-l'oeil" garden', *Garden History* 33 (2005), 286–93.

89 Higgs, 'Social mobility', 40.

90 Vassort, *Les Châteaux de la Loire*, pp. 302, 324–5.

91 A. Buisseret, 'Les femmes et l'automobile à la Belle Époque', *Le Mouvement Social* 192 (2000), 41–64; A. Corbin (ed.), *L'Avènement des loisirs 1850–1960* (Paris, 1995); D. Crouch (ed.), *Leisure/Tourism Geographies: Practices and Geographical Knowledge* (London, 1999), chs 3, 5, 14, 17–19; C. McConnell, *The Record-Setting Trips: By Auto from Coast to Coast 1909–1916* (Stanford, 2003).

92 M. Proust, *In Search of Lost Time*, translated by C. K. Scott Moncrieff and T. Kilmartin, revised by D. J. Enright 6 vols (London, 1993), vol. 4, p. 457. On Proust's doomed relationship with the driver Agostinelli see J.-Y. Tadié, *Marcel Proust: A Biography*, translated by E. Cameron (New York, 2000), pp. 495, 585–90, 598–9, 605–6, 615–19.

93 A. d'Uzès, *Souvenirs de la duchesse d'Uzès née Mortemart* Préface de son petit-fils le comte de Cossé-Brissac (Paris, 1939), pp. xxvi–xxvii. M. Bibesco, *Au bal avec Marcel Proust* (Paris, 1939), pp. 24–30, 36–8; C. Sutherland, *Enchantress: Marthe Bibesco and Her World* (New York, 1996), chs 3 and 4; R. Lacey, *Aristocrats* (London, 1983), pp. 149–52.

94 M. Barrès, *La Grande Pitié des églises de France* (Paris, 1912). On the Touring Club of France and English equivalents see Swenson, *The Rise of Heritage*, pp. 135, 139.

95 13 August 1913 and dossiers 1908–1913 in AN AP 31/99 Fonds Murat. For wage records AN AP 31/292 Fonds Murat. S. L. Harp, *Marketing Michelin: Advertising and Cultural Identity in Twentieth-Century France* (Baltimore, 2001); G. Vigarello, 'Le temps du sport' in Corbin, *L'Avènement des loisirs*, pp. 193–221.

96 Auslander, *Taste and Power*, pp. 255–6.

97 H. L. Agnew, 'Noble nation and modern nation: the Czech case', *Austrian History Year Book* 23 (1992), 50–71; G. Aliberti, 'Elites e modello nobiliare nel secolo XIX', *Storia Contemporanea* 26 (1995), 211–26; H. W. Whelan, *Adapting to Modernity: Family, Caste and Capitalism among the Baltic German Nobility* (Cologne, 1999); W. D. Godsey, 'Nobility and modernity', *German History* 20 (2002), 504–21; G. B. Clemens, 'Ancestors, castles, tradition: the German and Italian nobility and the discovery of the Middle Ages in the nineteenth century', *Journal of Modern Italian Studies* 8 (2003), 1–15; E. Glassheim, *Noble Nationalists: The Transformation of the Bohemian Aristocracy* (Cambridge, MA, and London, 2005); M. Wienfort, *Adel in der Moderne* (Göttingen, 2006); L. Jakubowska, *Patrons of History: Nobility, Capital and Political Transitions in Poland* (Farnham, 2012).

7

Holding the fort in the world wars

Each generation is only the temporary guardian of a patrimony. Managing this precious and glorious heritage, it has the responsibility to transmit it to descendants.[1]

The château du Coudray-Montpensier stands on top of a gently sloping hill in the commune of Seuilly about twelve kilometres from the town of Chinon (Indre-et-Loire). Records of the *seigneurs* of Coudray tell us that the nobleman Guillaume de Montsoreau founded the Abbaye de Seuilly in 1090. The construction of the château, known as a 'fine and beautiful fortress', dates from the twelfth century with some later architectural embellishment in the thirteenth and fourteenth centuries. It was here, in March 1429 during the Hundred Years War, that Joan of Arc lodged overnight with her two travelling companions, Jean de Metz and Bertrand de Poulengy. On the following day, 8 March, the comte de Vendôme rode out to the château du Coudray-Montpensier to meet Joan and accompany her to Chinon where the king was staying. When Joan of Arc identified Charles VII amidst a crowd of courtiers she told him that the king should be blessed in Reims and the English army forced to retreat from France.[2]

Five centuries later, the French military was fighting a very different style of war. In November 1916, it was the sub-prefect of Indre-et-Loire who drove out to the château du Coudray-Montpensier because of a letter sent by the château's inhabitant. The comtesse de Chauvelin had written to the prefect in Tours on 10 August 1916:

I would like a group of prisoners as soon as possible to cut up some fallen trees and to work the fields. There are about ten hectares to sow etc. and since I have not been able to procure anyone to do the work my farm animals, sheep, horses etc. are dying of hunger ... I had two Belgians to help last year. Now I would have work for ten men for at least two months. I also have a farm leased out ... the woman living there alone with four children does not think to cultivate the land.[3]

Owing to the stationery's header, 'Le Coudray-Montpensier, Chinon (Indre-et-Loire)', the sub-prefect first made enquiries in the town. He reported:

I went to the Gendarmerie, then to the Commissariat, and finally to the Mairie where, after searching through all the records, I was told that this person did not exist in Chinon. The secretary of the Mairie, catching sight of a local shop owner, asked him if he had not encountered this person among his acquaintances. The shop owner responded that indeed he knew her ... Mlle de Chauvelin, divorced, comtesse de Durfort, château du Coudray ... I went to this address where I was received by an elderly maid who said that Madame could not be seen. After I insisted on the purpose of my visit the maid went to tell Madame de Chauvelin that I was asking to speak with her about the prisoners' labour that she had requested. The maid came back and said 'Madame no longer wants the labour; she asked for it for the month of October [but] now it is too late.'[4]

Three weeks later, in December, a second letter arrived at the prefect's office, this time addressed to the sub-prefect who had come out to the château.

My fields are all uncultivated so I could not take twenty men during the shortest days of the year only to cut the wood ... If it should be possible in March to send me ten men for the work proposed then I would be happy to take them. I have also enquired about the charges and conditions for them required by the military government ... Please accept my apology for the delay in sending this letter. When you called to see me I was already very unwell owing to my heart problem.[5]

From this small handful of documents about life in a rural community in 1916, a range of questions might be asked about the place of the nobility in the society of early twentieth-century France. To what extent did the world wars change the nature of class relations on and around landed estates? How were gender relations and gender roles in nobles' households affected by the absence and return of men? Were nobles able to afford to repair the damage to property resulting from military operations or wartime neglect?

The great unsettling of social structures and the economy that marked the early decades of the twentieth century has been widely researched and debated; very few histories of France for this period, however, touch on these types of questions. In 1987 David Higgs reflected on the difficulty of making nobles a subject for academic research. 'The historian is too often assumed to side with the people he is studying. More than one French historian has been frightened off the subject.'[6] In 2007 Hagen Schulze observed: 'Although the British aristocracy still exerts influence on the British "sites of memory" and cleverly reinvented itself as national guardians of British heritage, its twentieth-century political legacy is less well known. The question of what happened to other European aristocracies after the Great War is even more obscure.'[7]

This chapter builds upon Stephan Malinowski's essay about the politics of the aristocracy in twentieth-century France, as well as engaging with the work of scholars investigating nobilities in other European countries.[8] While the aim in such research must be 'to use political, economic, and social history in combination', as well as to integrate cultural approaches, a challenge for historians lies in the limitations of archival material. Karina Urbach realised in her exhaustive work on the British and German aristocracies that even when permission for access is granted: 'private collections often turn out to have been sanitized. Descendants have understandably developed a selective memory – connections with authoritarian regimes or radical right-wing groups were not seen as laudable after 1945 and were thereafter erased from the family archives.'[9] French historians have used public and private archives in the study of right-wing groups but even some authoritative works have 'never heard of the aristocracy' or turn up 'no more than a few scattered facts'.[10]

My objective is to study the interactions between nobles and other citizens in French society because 'politics' was not confined to parliament but broadly manifest in class and gender relations. In the two decades prior to the First World War, Socialists were increasingly elected to run municipalities, there was new legislation regulating factory work hours, and growth in the number of *bourses du travail*. The Confédération générale du travail (CGT) was founded and there were major strikes in the coal-mining and wine-growing industries.[11] When the order for war mobilisation came in August 1914, it produced a shortage of men to perform jobs in many sectors and this in turn expanded the range of employment available to working-class and middle-class women.[12] Wartime experiences made necessary and commonplace some forms of independence for the female sex that had been controversial in the late nineteenth century, like driving a car. Yet the demographic impact of 1914–18 also produced a context in which traditional gender roles were heavily promoted. French feminists' campaigns to secure more fundamental rights for women stalled or suffered major setbacks.[13] France entered the 1920s with a fragile economy, a conservative government, and a massive imbalance in the sex ratio of its population. Confrontations between the Right and the Left escalated into strikes and street protests during the 1930s. As international tensions peaked, war was declared and France fell to the Germans in 1940.[14]

The subject of life at the château may seem incongruous with these more familiar topics associated with French experiences of 'modernity' between the turn of the century and the Liberation.[15] Yet, as the encounter between the perplexed sub-prefect and the elderly maid suggests, beneath a patina of 'old worldliness', developments in rural communities during these decades were affecting the daily life of château inhabitants. To examine their world is to look from a different angle on the history of early twentieth-century France.

Gender and generations

Nobles featured in this chapter may be divided broadly into three generations. The first generation comprised those who were over the age of fifty, many of them grandparents, in 1914–18. The second generation were younger adults, many of them parents, in 1914–18. The third generation born after 1900 were adults in 1939–44. Members of each generation understood themselves to be temporary custodians of patrimony and they all felt the weight of responsibility for transmission of patrimony to descendants. In managing this 'precious and glorious heritage', twentieth-century nobles had to make choices and adapt their strategies owing to factors beyond their control.

Following the lead of Pierre Bourdieu and Monique de Saint Martin, scholars from a range of disciplines investigate conversions and reconversions of capital (economic, social, cultural and symbolic) among European nobilities.[16] 'Conversion' and 'reconversion' both involve interaction between forms of capital but were originally conceived as separate theoretical concepts. Reconversion was explained by Bourdieu as 'a *restructuring* of the system of investment strategies' that arises out of 'the relationship between a person's patrimony (in terms of both amount and structure) and the system of instruments of reproduction'. An individual will try 'to maintain their position in the social space … at the cost of *reconverting* the forms of capital they hold into forms that are more profitable or more legitimate'. Conversion of capital will cause temporary destabilising effects upon identity as an individual crosses between social trajectories; it may be subjectively experienced as a 'change in taste or vocation'.[17]

Saint Martin has sought to address some confusion between conversion and reconversion. In 2011 she proposed that 'the concept of reconversion should only be used in situations where there is a complete break with the former inheritance'.[18] Saint Martin expands her explanation by comparing human experiences in different historical contexts. Her research with Sofia Tchouikina on Russian nobles after 1917 was clearly about reconversions. For these nobles 'the idea of the future as the continuity of the past had to be abandoned'. There was a 'complete break' as all kinds of inherited property and former resources were discredited and no longer accessible to them under the Soviet regime.[19] By contrast, Saint Martin argues, various businessmen in twentieth-century France did not complete reconversions but rather converted capital when needed in order to perpetuate a dominant position.[20]

I will adopt the term conversion because, as we have seen in preceding chapters, nobles in France were continuously using strategies to hold on to familiar resources such as landed estates, titles, traditions of sociability and education, military and diplomatic roles, and ecclesiastical contacts. Their conception of family was similar to a chain in which each generation linked to the next and each served as the temporary guardian of patrimony. It was this understanding of a moral obligation to perpetuate traditions across generations that guided nobles in formulating plans for the future.

Researchers disagree about whether nobles living year-round in a department of France occupied a more or less powerful position compared with the nobles who could afford to rent or own property in Paris. In one interpretation there was a deepening gulf during the interwar decades. 'Culturally and economically the provincial nobility have lost out to this urban-oriented aristocracy. This is why the provincials seek compensation by nurturing symbolic capital, that is the preservation of ancestral homes, degrees of noble lineage and religious traditions.'[21] A competing interpretation emerges from research on Brittany. Levels of political support for aristocratic landowners varied between departments of this region. In David Bensoussan's argument Breton nobles in the 1920s and 1930s occupied a position of cultural dominance based on a rural lifestyle and ownership of a château that contributed to their prestige and influence.[22] Relevant to this debate is Claude-Isabelle Brelot's point that a change in family fortunes can be difficult for historians to assess when viewed within the parameters of a single generation. A move up or down the social ladder happens over two or three generations as grandparents and parents transmit a familial culture to children and the family integrates diverse outside influences.[23]

The context of the world wars is particularly rich for the study of noble family traditions and gender because of the ways in which military heritage interacted with cultural and social expectations. Among nobility 'decisions and actions took place in the context of powerful discourses and an elaborate cultural system that at least conditioned their creative acts to make them much more predictable'.[24] Since the Middle Ages noblewomen have played essential roles in managing estates when male members of the family were away fighting wars: 'whilst some military engagements might last only a matter of weeks, others could last months, and, with the advent of the Crusades, even years. Such absences posed a challenge to aristocratic families'.[25] The twentieth-century equivalent of the 'crusader's wife', then, had no shortage of historical role models.

Ancestral example was a more fraught issue for noblemen. Military careers still lay at the heart of the educational system, values and aspirations of male nobles in France, as in other European countries.[26] But in France army life and masculinity had been heavily scrutinised owing to the twin dramas of the nation's defeat in the Franco-Prussian War of 1870–1 followed by the Dreyfus Affair of 1894–1906.[27] The French government's undercover investigation of Catholic army officers in the so-called *affaire des fiches* and efforts to restrict the types of careers available to noblemen made it harder for males to fulfil the gendered ideal of 'manly action', inculcated from youth through sports such as fencing, hunting, and shooting.[28] Government efforts to modify military service legislation had exposed division between those who advocated equality in the military system and those who held tenaciously to the spirit of privilege operating in the barracks. In the 1870s noblemen made up around 8 per cent of the officers in the French army. William Serman and Antoine Prost document examples of hostility from regular soldiers toward career officers and the various ways in which class differences were manifest.[29]

Up until 1944 officers in the French army did not have the right to vote. Only officers who had resigned or retired were able to stand as candidates for election.[30] These limitations on political participation may have affected nobles' responses to groups and leagues, including those on the extreme right such as Action française, the Croix-de-feu, and Parti social français.[31] At a time when parties of the right and centre were opposed to women's suffrage, the Croix-de-feu attracted some hundred thousand female members and the Parti social français perhaps four hundred thousand female members. Kevin Passmore argues that these hierarchically structured organisations with anti-feminist discourses seemed to afford the women who joined them 'room to maneuver' and political agency when they were unable to vote.[32]

A concentration of nobles in Action française and Croix-de-feu does not mean that the concept of aristocratic racial supremacy was a 'guiding principle' for the extreme right in France in the way that it was Germany.[33] Nobles adopted diverse stances towards the models of fascism in Italy, Spain and Germany, not least because of the international familial networks to which nobles belonged.[34] In France some nobles' initial interest in Action française turned to rejection of it after the pope condemned Action française in 1926. Some nobles modified their right-wing activities, for example by shifting allegiance from Action française to the Parti social français or to Le Faisceau. Some supported Dorgères's Défense paysanne and stood for election but were defeated.[35] Others always despised the extreme right and fascist models, were attracted instead by humanist intellectual currents, and joined the Resistance.[36] In France, as in other countries of continental Europe and Britain, the nobility's conservationist impulses and concern for position and property inspired a broad spectrum of actions and contrasting political choices during and beyond the First and Second World Wars.

Traditions of Catholic faith and military careers

France's 'Sacred Union' established at the outset of the First World War was designed to bring divergent forces in politics together by setting aside the bitter clerical versus anti-clerical disputes that had peaked with the 1901 Law on Associations and 1905 Separation of Church and State. Within the wartime context, Catholic teaching about the sanctity of the marriage bond did not prevent soldiers' recourse to prostitution during the war, although religious faith was profoundly important to some military men.[37] Religion also shaped the responses of some women and men to the death of a child or to widowhood. In Malinowski's view the social Catholic movement that had developed in late nineteenth-century France meant that 'the aristocratic attempt to reach out politically and build bridges to the lower classes was expressed in the language not of pre-fascism but of Catholic conservatism. The moderating influence of this exercise, which lasted over several generations, was still noticeable within the French aristocracy of the interwar years.'[38]

There are examples that support this thesis in memoirs and archives about the first generation, that is, those adults, many of whom were grandparents, in 1914–18. In the Vogüé family, Louise de Vogüé was strongly influenced in her pedagogical ideas by the works of père Laberthonnière and had a 'personal, profound, and discreet faith' that she endeavoured to pass on to her children and grandchildren. Her husband Louis de Vogüé was a follower of the social Catholic movement and belonged to a group of friends inspired by the Catholic reformers Lacordaire, Ozanam, de Montalembert, and de Mun.[39]

Similarly, correspondence between the marquise de Marcieu and the *régisseur's* wife Maria Gaillard points to a bond between the two women that stemmed from Catholic faith and attachment to the rituals of the Church. 'I gave news of Madame la marquise to Monsieur le curé [who is] very busy these days with the religious festivals and preparing children for the Solemn Communion that will take place on the Sunday after Easter.'[40] The marquise de Marcieu was a regular benefactor to the Church, receiving numerous thankyou letters through the 1910s and 1920s from the archbishop of Sens, the bishop of Viviers, and the bishop of Valence. Her strong piety is evident in the account of her husband's death in 1888, and she must have appreciated Maria's concern to raise the three Gaillard children in the Christian faith.[41] The women's shared identity as Catholic mothers is evoked most strongly in 1917, when the marquise's twenty-year-old grandson, Paul, a brigadier pilot, died from injuries received in a flying accident. Maria wrote: 'I ask God and our Holy Mother to bless his poor relatives and console them in their great grief, granting them resignation and courage.'[42]

The archives of two aristocratic families from Brittany provide insight into the experiences of being a devout Catholic widower and single mother responsible for a landed estate in the 1910s and 1920s. In these records we can see noblewomen of the second generation, those adults who were parents in 1914–18, grappling with decisions over patrimony and how 'to change so as to conserve.'[43]

Yvan-Francisque-Marie Dondel, comte de Kergonano, died on 9 March 1911 nine months after suffering a stroke in Vannes. His wife the comtesse Dondel de Kergonano (née Carheil de la Guichardaye) and their only child Alain continued to live at the château de Kergonano during the First World War. In May 1915, when Alain was preparing for his First Communion, his mother copied out for him some recollections she had written down a few days after her husband's death about the comte de Kergonano's sources of spiritual support. 'Keep them and from time to time reread these lines that will remind you of the examples you have received and help you to imitate the Christian who was your father.'[44]

The comte had been decorated with the medal of Tonkin for military bravery; his ancestor Jean-Jacques-Hyacinthe Dondel had participated in the Quiberon expedition of 1795. In 1919 it was for her adolescent son's benefit that the comtesse contemplated a visit to the battlefields of northern France and asked a male cousin for his advice on the idea. This trip had to be postponed because of the expense it would entail at a time when the comtesse de Kergonano was taking steps to cut living costs, whilst needing to fund Alain's private tuition in English, French, piano, drawing, maths, and accounting. The comtesse moved to an apartment in Nantes, took in sewing orders for 'Aide aux veuves de la guerre' and sold the château de Kergonano. Her cousin wrote on 18 September 1919 offering congratulations on the sale price of 215,000 francs. 'Such a result must alleviate, to a certain extent, the bitterness of giving up this property that you loved and which meant so much to you and Alain.'[45]

The comtesse de Fontaines (née Jacqueline Maillard de la Gournerie) was in a similar position of making decisions to adjust investment strategies to meet the needs of her children and herself as a single parent. Numerous prayer cards strongly suggest that Jacqueline was a devout practising Catholic. Her principal home, the château de Marillet near Faymoreau (Vendée), lay in a region renowned for its commitment to the Church.[46] A central preoccupation for the comtesse de Fontaines lay in the education and activities of her two sons, Eugène and Pierre. Jacqueline's own father, Jules-Marie-Humbert Maillard, comte de la Gournerie, had risen to the rank of captain in the cavalry and also served as mayor of Saint-Herblain (Loire-Atlantique). This classic combination of military service, landownership, and political representation was very typical for noblemen of the nineteenth century, but for the grandsons of those men the combination looked less secure as a career path.

There were noblemen among the deputies elected to the 'Blue Sky' chamber after the Treaty of Versailles but aristocratic numbers remained greater in the army and diplomatic service. To succeed in a diplomatic career required 'the construction of a reputation, specialised competencies, a network of relationships, investments and sacrifices'.[47] Nobles had a head start for some of the essentials such as languages because they grew up in a deeply literate environment where international mobility was considered normal. The evolution in France with regard to noblemen's representation in politics and diplomacy is comparable with that in Italy. There had been large numbers of nobles in the Italian government up until 1876 (43 per cent) then a dramatic decline. In the Italian diplomatic corps 43.2 per cent were noble between 1861 and 1915.[48]

The letters of Eugène de Fontaines to his mother during the 1920s provide insight into the difficulties and frustrations for the younger generation in trying to model themselves on military heroes and the 'man of action'.[49] On 22 March 1923 Eugène announced to his mother that he now held the rank of brigadier, although his excitement was tempered by the realisation that in joining the 33rd artillery regiment he would be accommodated with more senior officers ('who will obviously always be in the room to see if it is tidy').[50] Within three months, the young soldier's enthusiasm for his military duties had been snuffed out by boring routine. From the Modern Hotel opposite Poitiers railway station, he wrote: 'Here I am, completely fed up with my new life ... we have nothing or next to nothing to do.'[51]

Eugène's brother, Pierre, was also endeavouring to embody 'masculine' honour and action. In the Paris of the 1920s he had taken up the traditionally aristocratic sport of fencing and was formally introduced into the elegant Cercle de l'Épée by one of his mother's relatives, 'uncle' Tinguy du Pouët. But neither this pastime nor his competing in equestrian events, nor day trips to watch the horse races at Auteuil, entirely relieved a gnawing anxiety over his studies at the Institut National Agronomique. After examinations, he reported glumly:

> The results are out and, as I suspected, I failed ... My intention therefore, if you have no objection, is to pursue Law and Political Science in order to go into the embassies or the consulates ... Perhaps at the same time I will complete a degree in History or Literature ... All these studies are much more to my taste and I ask myself why I did not think of this earlier.[52]

Probably to reassure and convince his mother, Pierre emphasised that 'uncle' Tinguy du Pouët was sympathetic and supportive of his plans to change direction. 'He advised me to take the finance stream at the Sciences Po [which] leads to the Cour des comptes, the Banque de France or, if I wished, the Inspection des finances.'[53]

For noblemen in the 1920s pursuing studies in agronomy the challenges to 'living nobly' on the land seemed greater than ever. There were fewer men to work as labourers, and many of those who did return from the battlefields had been severely maimed or sustained other health problems.[54] Some areas in the north, notably Lorraine, had been completely devastated. Rural communities and local economies were slowly rebuilt with mutuals and co-operatives formed to help this process.[55] Hervé Budes de Guébriant, who had studied at the Institut National Agronomique, expressed landowner pride but also a hint of the social responsibility incumbent on noblemen: 'All my interests are in the land; I have extensive properties. The relations between the tenants who work my land and me are quite familial.'[56]

Conversions of capital to cross into a different social trajectory were not necessarily successful and they involved discomfort. At the Sciences Po, Pierre de Fontaines found there were 'few people I know'; most of his classmates came from bourgeois families. The young nobleman was trying to access a career in finance administration, which was still very unusual for someone of his background, but he was not mixing socially in the bourgeois circles that might have helped him to make professional contacts. The milieu Pierre frequented outside of his studies was decidedly aristocratic and Catholic. He looked for accommodation near the Institut Catholique, including the option of board with the abbé de Lavaleth where two other young noblemen, Jacques de Maupeou and Jacques de la Selle, were staying whilst they completed studies in 'Agro' at the Lycée Henri IV. Much of Pierre's socialising took place in the company of other Breton nobles. In writing to his mother he was very dismissive of any young female presented to him if he did not recognise their family name; only nobles counted for him as potential candidates for marriage.

A quick way to build economic capital was to marry a wealthy heiress but there were social pressures from within the noble milieu that could discourage males from taking that route. Leandro Losada writes: 'Exogamic tendencies could have been crucial for the survival of an elite, but they could have also influenced – or even caused – its downfall. Endogamy, for its part, tends to be functional to a consolidated group, but it can also trigger its decline if it results in a group excessively closed to outsiders.'[57] For France statistical analysis of couples named in high-society annuals shows a slight decrease in the rate of endogamy among nobles. For marriages contracted in the period 1850–1918 the rate of noble endogamy is calculated at 0.86, dropping to 0.75 for marriages contracted in the period 1919–45.[58] Sex and order of birth within the family influenced nobles' decisions to marry within or outside their own milieu; overall, the nobility remained 'a strongly endogamous group'.[59]

Pierre de Fontaine's political views are not explicitly stated in letters to his mother, but he mentions social activities that generally conform

to the conservative tendencies of his milieu. In 1923 he went along to
the annual '*grande séance*' of the Action française, an occasion he found
disappointing: 'I had to stand up for two hours listening to nothing very
interesting.' Other nobles were drawn to the extreme right agenda, they
knew Charles Maurras personally, and were 'very passionate' about the
Action française.[60]

Sales and transformations of châteaux

From the 1910s into the second half of the twentieth century, nobles
received numerous typed letters and circulars from estate agents offering their services to help sell a property. That this type of mail was kept
rather than thrown away in the twentieth century suggests that more
nobles were facing up to the possibility or the reality of needing to sell,
like the comtesse Dondel de Kergonano in 1918. Estate agents' letters and
circulars are a mine of historical information on how elites were responding to the evolving economic and political climate. This evidence needs
to be treated with caution (agents were salesmen trying to attract clients
and make a commission) but it does provide insight into early twentieth-
century mentalities about property.

Claudius Gaime of Régie Centrale d'Immeubles in Aix-les-Bains
(Savoie) wrote to the marquise Trédecini de Saint-Séverin (née Jeanne
Françoise Marie de Roussy de Sales) in July 1916:

> Further to our conversation the other day, I am writing to tell you that as
> long as the law on war benefits is not voted upon, the industrialists – who
> are currently building large fortunes – will not buy, out of fear of [the gov-
> ernment] putting up the taxation rate ... But once the tax rate is fixed, and
> cannot be set any higher, they will buy at that moment ... We have at Aix[-
> les-Bains] numerous clients and rich families. Business seems to be picking
> up. I have very good families as tenants, including madame la duchesse de
> Vendôme, monsieur le duc, and all their family (sister and brother-in-law
> of the King of Belgium) whom I have installed at the Hôtel de La Bauche
> having not found a sufficiently large château either in the vicinity of Aix-les-
> Bains or near Chambéry.[61]

The marquise Tredicini de Saint Séverin was a widow with two adult
sons and younger children, all from her marriage to the marquis Henri
Tredicini de Saint Séverin. He had died in 1906, aged forty-eight. In her
own name and the names of her children the marquise gave legal mandate
to Gaime to find buyers for two family properties: the estate of Candie at
Chambéry-le-Vieux (Savoie) and the Villa Saint Séverin, avenue Godillet

in Hyères (Var). The mandate was not exclusive to Gaime (the marquise reserved the right to approach potential buyers herself) but in the event that Gaime did secure a buyer then he had the right to a 5 per cent commission on the sale price. The mandate document also stipulated that Gaime should apply discretion in negotiating with potential buyers. The marquise evidently did not want to attract local attention to her family's circumstances and wished 'that no announcement of the property being for sale be made public in the region'.[62]

Gaime provided updates to the marquise of the people with whom he had discussed the properties. These were industrialists like Messieurs Chiron, 'very nice people and who can pay in cash'.[63] The château de Candie with its park and garden, a twenty-five-hectare farm with buildings, and approximately ten hectares of woods were sold on 8 May 1918 to the industrialist Gaston Vasseur from Epierre (Savoie) for 150,000 francs. Gaime had found this buyer and was paid the 5 per cent commission. The new owner of Candie was in touch with the marquise two months after the sale to ask for a special receipt, wary of future claims by the State 'that still remain possible for anything that pertains to the domain of religion'.[64] The marquise graciously acquiesced, sending a special receipt for the walnut pew in the church of Chambéry-le-Vieux.

Examples of nobles liquidating landed property in France during the 1910s and 1920s fit with patterns historians observe in other countries. In northern Italy some large estates were being sold off. In England many landowners divested 'medium-sized chunks to their former tenants' and sold outlying properties so the main estate became smaller and more geographically concentrated; others sold everything and left the land.[65] Part of the dilemma for the English aristocracy was uncertainty over what to do with a big house, and in France too there were similar problems concerning châteaux.

Aware of some inadequacies in the law of 1887 for the protection of historic monuments the State took action in preparing a more ambitious text for the law of 31 December 1913. The new law allowed the State to class a building or item, such as a piece of furniture, as a historic monument without the owner's consent. Private owners had to notify the State of any planned renovations or modifications. Sanctions for non-compliance were introduced. In addition to the pre-existing primary register (*les monuments classés*) a new secondary register (*l'inventaire supplémentaire*) was proposed in 1913, then formalised in a law of 23 July 1927. In theory, international agreements also meant historic monuments would be spared from damage. The Hague Conventions of 1899 and 1907 were of little effect, however, in the prevention of aerial bombing during the First World War.[66]

In 1915, when the baron de Fougères was serving as mayor of the commune of Fougères-sur-Bièvre, he wrote to the under-secretary for the Beaux-Arts with a proposal to use some of the soil that filled the ancient moats of his property, the château de Fougères, to construct a path to the new railway station. The motives cited for this project were: a reduction in the expense to the commune for constructing the path; the historical and archaeological interest that would arise from clearing out the moats to show the outline of the old dungeon; and the creation of a job for the workers who had not been called to serve in the army because of their age. The under-secretary informed the prefect of Loir-et-Cher that he was pleased to give consent to the baron's proposal, on condition that the State would not bear any expense for the work, and he reminded the prefect of article 28 of the law of 31 December 1913 concerning any objects that might be discovered as a result of clearing out the moats. The chief architect of the Monuments historiques for the department of Loir-et-Cher, Monsieur Grenouillot, was charged with supervising the project.[67]

Grenouillot was diligent and knowledgeable, but his job was not an easy one because it involved an element of 'policing' the conservation of privately owned properties and also persuading owners to part with their money. In July 1919 Grenouillot informed the baron de Fougères that the minister had decided the State's financial contribution to the upkeep of classified buildings would depend on the sum that owners contributed themselves. The following year Grenouillot was obliged to follow-up on an auction sale he had read about in the local paper involving materials from the demolition of a building adjacent to the south-east wing of the château de Fougères. The architect already knew about the demolition, but he was concerned to find out whether the baron had thought to put a clause in the auction notice to safeguard any items of artistic, historic, or archaeological interest. If one found 'fragments of sculpture, old coins, or other items, as already seen elsewhere, it would be regrettable if they did not remain your property. The stones could be used in possible restoration work.'[68]

Indeed restoration work was in the baron's mind and he was granted ministerial authorisation, with approval for the quote at 6,491 francs, in November 1920. Grenouillot was to take care of the contracting and administrative formalities which he envisaged doing over the winter when rain and snow would impede repairs on the château's roof; the work could then commence in the spring.[69] Grenouillot, however, did not anticipate the problems of liaising with the local roofer and others who infuriated him with the delays in submitting their invoices. Over the two years it took to wind up the paperwork his exasperation about tradesmen was palpable.[70]

More serious problems were to come. On 30 September 1924 the chief architect confessed that the situation regarding the château de Fougères was awkward and he was 'very embarrassed' about it. He had given instructions to the builder to block up a damaged bay window on the ground floor using stones that remained from some old walls. But the baron de Fougères had decided to reduce his annual financial contribution for repairs from 300 francs to 150 francs, and Grenouillot was only authorised by the minister to contribute an equal sum from his own budget.[71] The chief architect was also anxious that all of his instructions for the repairs be strictly adhered to in order 'to avoid remarks from the Administration when the inspector general [of the Monuments historiques] makes his visit'. He felt perplexed:

> The repairs must be done according to the instructions of the Monuments historiques in order not to take away the character of the classed buildings … I neither can nor want to give responsibility for the work to just any little old mason … Could one get through the winter in the current state??? In blocking up [the bay window] with planks and straw?[72]

By mid-December, no solution had been found and the architect resorted to stronger language, putting pressure on the baron to raise the amount of his private financial contribution as owner from 150 francs to 300 francs:

> I expect that with revenues probably being reduced and costs going up, you wish to limit some of these expenses. But what is 150 francs for the conservation of this old gem? … [The current damage] will be its ruin, for sure. What a responsibility! Would it truly be impossible to find an additional 150 francs to ensure the conservation of this château that every person having some artistic sensibility (archaeologists, historians, artists) finds so fascinating???[73]

The architect suggested raising the amounts that the baron charged for rent. Different sections of the château were already leased out to half a dozen tenants, who each rented between two and five rooms plus in some cases a section of the garden and cellar. Rents increased by 100 per cent or more in 1925. This gave the baron a rental income for the château of 1,510 francs.

Thus, even in a short period from 1912 to 1925, the registering of the château de Fougères as a historic monument can be seen to have had wide-ranging implications. It affected the local economy of the commune, particularly through employment; it generated the administrative processes that brought the mayor, prefect, owner, and chief architect into communication with one another; it led to the doubling of tenants' rent at the château; and it legally prevented the owner from undertaking repairs that might have compromised the character of the building.

Legislation and private owners' associations

Lessons learned from the damage to historic structures in 1914–18, and the delays in repair that meant many were still in ruin in 1939, paved the way to more legislation under the Vichy regime. Louis Hautecoeur and his successor Georges Hilaire oversaw the designation of 565 buildings as historic landmarks and 914 structures listed on the secondary register between July 1940 and March 1945. The law of 25 February 1943 gave a central role to the architects of the Bâtiments de France and also extended protection of registered buildings to a five-hundred-metre radius around the site.[74]

It was during the Second World War that owners of châteaux began to develop stronger ties with the State for the protection of patrimony. Aristocratic leaders of heritage and art associations belonged to some of France's oldest lineages whose names evoked the country's monarchical past. La Sauvegarde de l'art français is dedicated to the restoration of pre-1800 religious and sacred structures. It was founded in 1921 by the duc de Trévise and the marquise de Maillé and had its headquarters at 12 avenue du Maine (15th arrondissement, Paris). In the 1940s, the duc de Noailles was president of La Demeure historique (the founder Carvallo had died in 1936); its headquarters were at 12 rue d'Anjou (8th arrondissement). La Demeure historique and La Sauvegarde de l'art français, together with the Touring Club de France, co-operated through a special joint committee set up in December 1942.

In a letter to members, the associations' presidents reported on the new joint committee and the decision to conduct a survey among owners. The survey results were intended to inform suggestions to public authorities on 'the protection of our patrimony of art and history, and especially the châteaux and historic homes that are witnesses to this history, centres of tourism interest, and the finery of our country'.

We believe that the present generation must be in a position to maintain the legacy of the past. All of our efforts are directed towards that goal. Should the owner of an old home no longer be able to maintain it or to live there, it would be possible for us to intercede with the relevant public services on an official basis, since we are in constant liaison with them, and to examine the possibility that the property be taken on, through an acquisition or a lease arrangement, as an official or private foundation (training school, study or recreation centre, retirement home, holiday camp etc.).[75]

By March 1943, as a result of the lobbying of La Demeure historique, an inter-ministerial commission was set up to address the full scope of issues from tax and succession to financial aid for large repairs and fire prevention. The commission's chair, Deroy, from the Ministry of Finance, opened the first meeting with a clear statement that the ministry was opposed to the State's purchase of châteaux and sought an alternative solution to their conservation and upkeep. To this end, Certaux, head of the Service de la coordination des administrations financières, was delegated to investigate private owners' tax and succession issues. Savin from the Cour des comptes and Lichtenberger from the Commissariat au tourisme were delegated to investigate the issue of State monetary aid for repairs and maintenance. Rousselet from the Cour d'appel in Paris was delegated to investigate civil law issues surrounding succession. In his capacity as president of La Demeure historique the duc de Noailles expressed confidence that the results would be a triumph for the association's mission: 'To keep the family in the ancestral home'.[76]

The annual membership fee for La Demeure historique was 500 francs and the association drew upon information provided by its members to establish an inventory of privately owned châteaux, old homes, and abbeys whose owners had not yet joined the association. In 1943 La Demeure historique worked 'closely with public authorities in order to ward off the requisitioning of châteaux and excessive tree felling'. Participation in the inter-ministerial commission gave La Demeure historique a voice heard by those involved in legislative debates pertaining to inheritance tax, rental value, doubling of tax on land not used for productive purposes (*les terrains d'agrément*), income tax, and the personnel needed for upkeep of a historic château. The association sought 'a reasonable legislation taking into account [owners'] expenses and sacrifices'.[77]

Peter Mandler observes for England: 'Because aristocratic wealth and confidence revived in the 1950s and 1960s it has been easy to overlook the very low ebb of the 1940s.' In place of owners' belief in sacrifices to ensure continuity, he argues 'whether willingly or grudgingly, hardly any owner in that decade believed that there was a future in country-house life'.[78] Assessing the situation in France is made more complex because of the German occupation and history of French collaboration. There were nobles with close familial and professional links to politicians and senior administrators in the Vichy regime. The comte René de Chambrun married Josée Laval in 1935 so became Pierre Laval's son-in-law. As an international lawyer, and director of his family's company Baccarat crystal, Chambrun had ambassadors, army generals, and deputies among his friends and acquaintances. Henri du Moulin de Labarthète from a Gascon noble family managed the colonial banking interests of the Nervo Group was a chief member of Pétain's cabinet.[79] Noblemen Jean de Castellane and Charles-Louis de Beauveau-Craon were among the twenty-five Germans and twenty-five French participants in the 'Table Ronde' banquets of 1942 where financial and business interests were discussed.[80]

In the nineteenth century there had similarly been 'complicated international families' whose members possessed foreign investments, corporate financial management skills, and fluency in several languages. During the Vichy regime collaboration to make profit could involve using such elite networks as social capital. Urbach calls attention to the ways in which 'hybrid' aristocrats moved with practised ease between cultures in ways that made them ideal 'go betweens'. But, as she also argues, those international aristocratic family connections were worrying to the Nazis.[81]

Assumptions should never be made about the politics of nobles just by looking at a patronym. Within some families there were sharp divisions, and relatives could be radically opposed to one another in terms of political allegiances. In the Chambrun family the marquis Pierre de Chambrun, cousin of René, was senator for Lozère and refused to support Pétain in July 1940. A nephew, Gilbert de Chambrun, joined the Resistance, serving as colonel in the Forces françaises de l'intérieur.[82] The comte Guy Courtin de Neufbourg held profound Legitimist convictions but did not support extreme-right groups or the Vichy regime. He entered the Resistance in November 1940 at the encouragement of his Polish cousins and was arrested by the Gestapo in 1943.[83]

Within châteaux' walls

Only a small proportion of those nobles who were adults in 1939–44 were old enough to have had personal memories of the Franco-Prussian War.

Yet family stories meant nobles knew something of what their grandparents had experienced during that conflict and many also had in their possession letters from 1870–1 and 1914–18.

The château and estate of Versigny have been in the Kersaint's family ownership since the mid-nineteenth century. Général de Vallière sent a letter to the comte and comtesse de Kersaint in December 1917 thanking the family for hospitality at the château. 'I hold fast to the memory of your fine welcome and of the kindness you have shown my soldiers.'[84] During the last stages of the First World War Versigny became a base for général Mangin where the planning was done for the second battle of the Marne.

During the Second World War, the estate of Versigny was an important hub for the Resistance in the Oise and Seine-et-Marne departments. Secret agent Marcel Fox created the Publican network of Resistance on 14 April 1943 that was one of the networks subordinate to the larger Buckmaster network named after British colonel Maurice Buckmaster of the Secret Intelligence Service. The comte Jacques de Kersaint was leader of Publican until his arrest on 2 November 1943. The German Luftwaffe requisitioned the château de Versigny to lodge pilots and technicians working on an airfield a few kilometres to the south of the estate.[85] In 1944 the SS sacked the estate in reprisal for Kersaint's leadership role in the Publican nework. In August 1944 Versigny was liberated with the arrival of the American troops then a French regiment occupied the château. When the comte Jacques de Kersaint returned from deportation in May 1945 his family took temporary accommodation in a farmhouse. Jacques, his son, and his grandson successively completed works to repair the damage to the château.[86]

Malinowski asks questions about 'whether and to what extent aristocratic châteaux were used as conspiratorial meeting places, and whether and to what extent aristocratic networks were used to build the resistance movement'.[87] Challenges to futher research in this area, and on châteaux used in collaboration purposes, arise out of multiple successive uses to which property was put during the 1940s. The forteresse d'Opme (Puy-de-Dôme) was the home of the future maréchal de Lattre de Tassigny and he created in the village of Opme a military training institute. The château de Chazeron also in Puy-de-Dôme served as a prison in 1940 for Léon Blum, Edouard Daladier, Paul Reynaud and général Gamelin prior to trial at Riom. Mandler's observation about England is applicable to France as well: 'The collateral damage inflicted by wartime requisitioning was far greater than any direct hits by enemy action.'[88]

The château de Villeouët, in the commune of Chailles (Loir-et-Cher) was occupied by German troops on six successive occasions between June and September 1940. On the third occasion 150 men stayed in the château from 29 June to 13 July; on the fifth occasion four telephone operators installed themselves in the owners' personal apartments from 6 August to 16 August. Numerous objects were removed; although investigation led to some being recovered, among the items not returned were the greater part of a set of Cardeilhac silverware (originally 418 pieces valued at 1.5 million francs, 110 pieces were found hidden under a pile of logs) and archives relating to Russian bonds estimated to be worth 12 million francs. From November 1940 to November 1942, with the help of a translator paid to read and write letters in German, the owners tried to obtain information on the whereabouts of these items especially archives that had been stored in trunks in the tower-room.[89] In April 1944 an indemnity payment for war damages was received from the treasury of the German Reich amounting to 500,000 francs (25,000 RM). The actual sum required for repairs and replacements based on the architects' inventory totalled over 3 million francs, excluding the loss of the archives.[90]

By government decree of 6 April 1944, published in *the Journal officiel* on 26 April, vacant or insufficiently occupied properties were to be made available for the housing of evacuees, refugees and other victims or disaster who lacked independent means to find accommodation. Prefects held authority for requisitioning where needed. For France, as for the Netherlands, the history of the confiscation and restitution of nobles' estates is 'very complex'.[91]

Force of traditions

Halbwachs wrote about 'displacement', when objects and places are removed or destroyed, and the way in which collective memory can survive displacement through active resistance. When a home is demolished for example, it 'inevitably affects the habit of a few people, perplexing and troubling them'. A former inhabitant 'who has many remembrances fastened to these images now obliterated forever feels a whole part of himself dying with these things'. A group, however, 'resists with all the force of its traditions, which have effect'.[92]

Postwar sensitivies within families, as well as conservationist and religious traditions, are illustrated in the correspondence of the Quatrebarbes family and Lambot de Fougères family who were related by marriage. In the spring of 1946 Sister Marie-Magdeleine de Quatrebarbes, at her convent in Versailles, was contemplating what to do about the château de Boissay (Loir-et-Cher). Her grandparents had owned the château and the estate passed into her ownership following the death of her brother Foulques III in 1945. On 6 April 1946 Sister Marie-Magdeleine informed her aunt Henriette de Fougères that she had not yet made up her mind on the future of Boissay, 'this property that contained so many dear memories'. 'My desire is to keep as closely as possible to the intentions and concern of my grandparents and brother in envisaging the good of the country ... I would like for it to be sold to a religious order as it would be a precious resource for the orders.'[93]

The eldest surviving male relative of Sister Marie-Magdeleine was her uncle, Henri de Quatrebarbes, and it was to Henri that she decided to leave the family papers and portraits. A complicating factor was that her aunt Henriette de Fougères had managed to save those items from being damaged during the war by removing them from Boissay and taking them to her own home at Fougères, where they still were. Sister Marie-Magdeleine informed her aunt in 1946 that most of the Boissay estate would stay in the family, but the hunting ground would be sold off in order to give money to benefit Catholic schools.[94] Henriette wrote to Henri de Quatrebarbes, providing a list of the portraits and claiming she had verbal approval from Marie-Magdeleine to retain a couple of them at Fougères because 'they were our ancestors too':

> Let us talk about Boissay ... This home that is the cradle of the family shall be saved. To think that it might have fallen into undesirable hands was a worry ... The papers that your father had classed so neatly were gathered up, but had been scattered about and are doubtless incomplete ... As for the furniture, alas it has gone from Boissay. Marie-Magdeleine seemed obliged to sell it in order to pay the tax on the inheritance.[95]

In the decision-making on property, liquidating what was less essential (furniture and hunting ground) was done as a way to preserve items more critical to the framework for collective memory. Portraits and archives especially were key to those images and sets of relationships that enabled family members to locate themselves in a kinship structure and to perpetuate a common identity.

Conclusion

The two world wars hold a special place in the traditions of commemoration among people and in the historical literature of 'les lieux de mémoire' in France.[96] Through the interwar decades and beyond French

individuals' memories of 1914–18 were continuously elaborated in relation to group memories, within families, and within social classes.[97] For
nobles, as for people of other social backgrounds, the turbulent politics
and volatile economy of the 1920s and 1930s contributed to shape choices
and actions during the Vichy regime.

Scholarship on nobles' lives and politics in the Europe of the twentieth
century is a field that Ellis Wasson argues must begin to be represented
in textbooks.[98] Research has been done on Russian, Romanian, and
Czechoslovakian nobles following the revolution of 1917 and collapse
of the Habsburg monarchy in 1918. There have been studies of Italian
and Spanish nobles' responses to fascism. 'Strategic uses' of memory are
evident among German nobles in the wake of the Second World War. In
Poland, the Netherlands, and Scandinavia, nobles are seen harnessing the
uses of memory in self-representation as 'patrons of history' and 'guardians of heritage'.[99]

French nobles, interacting with other citizens, were adapting in efforts
'to change so as to conserve'. Ancestral military traditions and Catholic
faith were transmitted in stories and behaviours. These intangibles were
kept, even as some families relinquished elements of tangible patrimony.
Not all nobles shared to the same degree the resilience or agility to
achieve successful conversions of capital. The micro-struggles involved
for widows selling estates, and sons trying to make an endogamous
marriage and launch a career, were in some families leading inexorably
toward *déclassement*. Others pulled up the drawbridge to a 'fine and beautiful fortress' to guard social, cultural, economic, and symbolic capital
that would serve them later in the century. In the 1940s management and
communication within and between French noble families on the subject
of patrimony was on the cusp of a further far-reaching transformation.

Notes

1 G. de Vassal, *Maison de Vassal 987–1987: mémoire du millénaire* (Paris, 1987),
   preface.
2 I. Cloulas, *La Vie quotidienne dans les châteaux de la Loire au temps de la
   Renaissance* (Paris, 1983), p. 15. Clippings about the château in AD Indre-et-
   Loire 11J/2 Chartrier de Coudray-Montpensier.
3 10 August 1916 in AD Indre-et-Loire 11J/2 Chartrier de Coudray-
   Montpensier.
4 Typed report 17 November 1916 in AD Indre-et-Loire 11J/2 Chartrier de
   Coudray-Montpensier.

5 8 December 1916 in AD Indre-et-Loire 11J/2 Chartrier de Coudray-
   Montpensier.
6 D. Higgs, *Nobles in Nineteenth-Century France: The Practice of Inegalitarianism*
   (Baltimore, 1987), p. xv.
7 H. Schulze, 'Forward' in K. Urbach (ed.), *European Aristocracies and the
   Radical Right 1918-1939* (Oxford, 2007), pp. v–vi.
8 S. Malinowski, 'A counter-revolution *d'outre-tombe*: notes on the French
   aristocracy and the extreme right during the Third Republic and the Vichy
   Regime' in Urbach, *European Aristocracies*, ch. 1. Malinowski has written
   an important book on nobles in Germany: S. Malinowski, *Vom König zum
   Führer. Sozialer Niedergang und politische Radikalisierung im deutschen Adel
   zwischen Kaiserreich und NS-Staat* (Berlin, 2003).
9 K. Urbach, 'Age of no extremes? The British aristocracy torn between the
   House of Lords and the Mosley movement' in Urbach, *European Aristocracies*,
   pp. 53–4. In Germany wills are not available. K. Urbach, 'Introduction' in
   Urbach, *European Aristocracies*, p. 12; K. Urbach, *Go Betweens for Hitler*
   (Oxford, 2015), pp. 14, 358–60.
10 Malinowski is commenting on J.-F. Sirinelli (ed.), *Dictionnaire historique de la
   vie politique française au XXe siècle* (Paris, 1995), and J.-F. Sirinelli (ed.), *Les
   Droites en France de la Révolution à nos jours* (Paris, 1992). Malinowski, 'A
   counter-revolution', p. 16.
11 P. Hilden, *Working Women and Socialist Politics in France, 1880-1914: A
   Regional Study* (Oxford, 1986); T. Judt, *Socialism in Provence, 1871-1914:
   A Study in the Origins of the Modern French Left* (Cambridge, 1979); L. L.
   Frader, *Peasants and Protest: Agricultural Workers, Politics, and Unions in the
   Aude, 1850-1914* (Los Angeles, 1991).
12 G. Perreux, *La Vie quotidienne des civils en France pendant la Grande Guerre*
   (Paris, 1966); P. Fridenson (ed.), *1914-1918: l'autre front* (Paris, 1978); J.-J.
   Becker, *The Great War and the French People*, translated by A. Pomerans
   (Oxford, 1985); F. Thébaud, *La Femme au temps de la guerre de 14* (Paris,
   1986); M. Darrow, *French Women and the First World War* (New York, 2000);
   R. J. Young, *Under Siege: Portraits of Civilian Life in France during World War
   I* (New York, 2000); S. Audoin-Rouzeau and A. Becker, *14-18: retrouver la
   guerre* (Paris, 2000); L. V. Smith, S. Audoin-Rouzeau, and A. Becker, *France
   and the Great War, 1914-1918* (Cambridge, 2003).
13 S. C. Hause with A. R. Kenney, *Women's Suffrage and Social Politics in the
   French Third Republic* (Princeton, 1984); M. L. Roberts, *Civilisation without
   Sexes: Reconstructing Gender in Postwar France, 1917-27* (Chicago, 1994);
   L. L. Downs, *Manufacturing Inequality: Gender Division in the French and
   British Metalworking industries 1914-1939* (Ithaca, 1995); S. Reynolds, *France
   between the Wars: Gender and Politics* (London, 1996).
14 L. Boswell, *Rural Communism in France 1920-1939* (Ithaca, 1998);
   N. Ingram, *The Politics of Dissent: Pacifism in France 1919-1939* (Oxford,

1991); J. Wardhaugh, *In Pursuit of the People: Political Culture in France, 1934–1939* (Basingstoke, 2008).

15   AHR Roundtable, 'Historians and the question of "modernity"', *American Historical Review* 116 (2011), 631–7; C. Gluck, 'The end of elsewhere: writing modernity now', *American Historical Review* 116 (2011), 676–87; C. E. Forth and E. Accampo (eds), *Confronting Modernity in Fin-de-Siècle France: Bodies, Minds, and Gender* (London, 2009).

16   P. Bourdieu, L. Boltanski, and M. de Saint Martin, 'Les Stratégies de reconversion', *Social Science Information* 12 (1973), 61–113; M. de Saint Martin, 'Towards a dynamic approach to reconversions', *Social Science Information* 50 (2011), 429–41; D. Lancien and M. de Saint Martin (eds), *Anciennes et nouvelles aristocraties de 1800 à nos jours* (Paris, 2007); Y. Kuiper, N. Bijleveld, and J. Dronkers (eds), *Nobilities in Europe in the Twentieth Century: Reconversion Strategies, Memory Culture and Elite Formation* (Leuven, 2015).

17   P. Bourdieu, *The State Nobility*, translated by L. C. Clough (Stanford, 1996), p. 277 (original italics). Compare with discussion of conversion on pp. 106–10, 184–5.

18   Saint Martin, 'Towards a dynamic approach', 436.

19   Saint Martin, 'Towards a dynamic approach', 437. M. de Saint Martin and S. Tchouikina, 'La Noblesse russe à l'épreuve de la Révolution d'Octobre: représentations et reconversions', *Vingtième siècle* 99 (2008), 105–28. In 1912 it is estimated that there were 1,900,000 nobles in Russia. M. Gorboff, *La Russie fantôme: l'émigration russe de 1920 à 1950* (Lausanne, 1995), p. 33.

20   Saint Martin, 'Towards a dynamic approach', 431.

21   Y. Kuiper commenting on M. de Saint Martin, *L'Espace de la noblesse* (Paris, 1993) in *Nobilities in Europe*, p. 8.

22   D. Bensoussan, *Combats pour une Bretagne catholique et rurale: les droites bretonnes dans l'entre-deux-guerres* (Paris, 2006), p. 193. Bensoussan builds upon S. Berger, *Peasants against Politics: Rural Organization in Brittany, 1911–1967* (Cambridge, MA, 1972).

23   C.-I. Brelot, 'La Terre, facteur de déclassement des élites? (1860–1939)' in C. Le Mao and C. Marache (eds), *Les Élites et la terre du XVIe siècle aux années 1930* (Paris, 2010), pp. 301–11.

24   N. L. Paul, *To Follow in Their Footsteps: The Crusades and Family Memory in the High Middle Ages* (Ithaca, 2012), p. 201.

25   A. Livingstone, *Out of Love for My Kin: Aristocratic Family Life in the Lands of the Loire, 1000–1200* (Ithaca, 2010), pp. 171–2; J. Brundage, 'The crusader's wife: a canonistic quandary', *Studia Gratiana* 12 (1967), 425–41; J. Brundage, 'The crusader's wife revisited', *Studia Gratiana* 14 (1967), 241–51.

26   W. Serman, *Les Origines des officiers français 1848–1870* (Paris, 1979); G. E. Rothenberg, 'Nobility and military careers: the Habsburg officer corps,

1740–1914', *Military Affairs* 40 (1976), 182–6; G. M. Hamburg, 'Portrait of an elite: Russian marshals of the nobility, 1861–1917', *Slavic Review* 40 (1981), 585–602.

27 P. Gerbod, 'L'Éthique héroique en France 1870–1914', *Revue historique* 268 (1983), 409–12; C. E. Forth, *The Dreyfus Affair and the Crisis of French Manhood* (Baltimore, 2004), p. 13.

28 M. Larkin, *Religion, Politics, and Preferment in France since 1890: La Belle Époque and Its Legacy* (Cambridge, 1995), pp. 7–8, 35, 39–52, 79–81.

29 E. Dennery, 'Democracy and the French army', *Military Affairs* 5 (1941), 233–40; A. F. Kovacs, 'French military legislation in the Third Republic 1871–1940', *Military Affairs* 13 (1949), 1–13; A. Prost, *In the Wake of War: Les Anciens Combattants and French Society 1914–1939*, translated by H. McPhail (Oxford, 1992), pp. 54–5; Serman, *Les Origines*, pp. 305–6, 349.

30 M. Dogan, 'Les Officiers dans la carrière politique (du Maréchal MacMahon au Général de Gaulle)', *Revue française de sociologie* 2 (1961), 88–99.

31 Mension-Rigau, *Aristocrates*, pp. 471–3; C. de Bartillat, *Histoire de la noblesse française* vol. 2 *Les Nobles du Second Empire à la fin du XXe siècle* (Paris, 1991), pp. 427–30; K. Passmore, 'Planting the tricolor in the citadels of Communism: women's social action in the Croix-de-feu and the Parti social français', *Journal of Modern History* 71 (1999), 814–51; C. Campbell, 'Women and gender in the Croix-de-feu and the Parti social français: creating a nationalist youth culture, 1927–1939', *Proceedings of the Western Society for French History* 36 (2008), 249–64; C. Campbell, *Political Belief in France, 1927–1945: Gender, Empire, and Fascism in the Croix de feu and Parti social français* (Baton Rouge, 2015).

32 Passmore, 'Planting the tricolor', 814–51.

33 Malinowski, 'A counter-revolution', pp. 22–3, 26–7.

34 Urbach, *Go Betweens*, pp. 66–7; A. L. Cardoza, *Agrarian Elites and Italian Fascism* (Princeton, 1982); A. L. Cardoza 'The long goodbye: the landed aristocracy in north-western Italy, 1880–1930', *European History Quarterly* 23 (1993), 323–58; S. Baranowski, 'Conservative elite Anti-semitism from the Weimar Republic to the Third Reich', *German Studies Review* 19 (1996), 525–37; G. C. Jocteau, 'I nobili del fascismo', *Studi storici* 3 (2004), 691–723; A. Bullón de Mendoza, 'Aristócratas muertos en la Guerra Civil Española', *Aportes* 44 (2000), 77–106; Malinowski, *Vom König zum Führer*; M. Malatesta, 'Les Élites foncières italiennes de l'unification au fascism. Un aperçu' in Le Mao and Marache, *Les Élites et la terre*, pp. 70–6.

35 B. Goyet, *Charles Maurras* (Paris, 2000), pp. 361–78; W. Z. Silverman, *The Notorious Life of Gyp: Right-wing Anarchist in Fin-de-Siècle France* (Oxford, 1995), pp. 210–13; E. Weber, *Action Française: Royalism and Reaction in Twentieth-Century France* (Stanford, 1962); Bensoussan, *Combats*, pp. 410–20, 421–69, 503, and ch. 16; Berger, *Peasants Against Politics*, ch. 5, and on corporatism and responses to Dorgères, pp. 129–39.

36 E. d'Astier de la Vigerie, *Sept fois sept jours* (Paris, 1961); B. Comte, *Une utopie combattante: l'école des cadres d'Uriage, 1940–1942* (Paris, 1991); B. Destremau, *Jean de Lattre de Tassigny* (Paris, 1999); C. Levisse-Touzé, *Philippe Leclerc de Hautecloque (1902–1947): La Légende d'un héros* (Paris, 2002); A. Lacroix-Riz, *Les Élites françaises entre 1940 et 1944* (Paris, 2016), pp. 126, 264–5, 274, 282, 320, 359, 362, 369.

37 A. Becker, *La Guerre et la foi* (Paris, 1994); Neil M. Hayman, *World War I* (Westport, 1997), p. 181; M. K. Rhoades, 'Renegotiating French masculinity: medicine and venereal disease during the Great War' *French Historical Studies* 29 (2006), 293–327.

38 Malinowski, 'A counter-revolution', p. 20. B. F. Martin, *Count Albert de Mun* (Chapel Hill, 1978); Berger, *Peasants against Politics*, pp. 42–54, 65–71.

39 M. de Vogüé, *La Fontaine du cerf. Histoire de Louis et Louise, marquis et marquise de Vogüé 1868–1958* (Poitiers, 1983), pp. 19, 24, 82–4.

40 20 April 1916 in AD Ardèche 39J/314 Chartrier de Chambonas.

41 AD Ardèche 39J/266 Chartrier de Chambonas.

42 22 June 1917 in AD Ardèche 39J/314 Chartrier de Chambonas. On 'courage' in this context see R. A. Nye, *Masculinity and Male Codes of Honor in Modern France* (Oxford, 1993), conclusion. On mothers, S. R. Grayzel, *Women's Identities at War: Gender, Motherhood and Politics in Britain and France during the First World War* (Chapel Hill, 1999).

43 Bourdieu cited in Saint Martin, 'Towards a dynamic approach', 430.

44 AD Morbihan 50J/10 Chartrier de Kergonano.

45 18 September 1919 and bill for Alain's private lessons in AD Morbihan 50J/10 Chartrier de Kergonano.

46 'L'Eglise vivante et parlante' in AD Loire-Atlantique 58J/7 Archives de la famille de Fontaines.

47 M. Loriol, 'La Carrière des diplomates français: entre parcours individuel et structuration collective', *SociologieS: Théories et recherches* (2009), 2; Dogan, 'Les Officiers dans la carrière politique', 88–99.

48 S. Romano, 'La nobiltà, lo Stato e le relazioni internazionali' in *Les Noblesses européennes au XIXe siècle* (Rome, 1988), p. 536; A. M. Banti, 'Note sulle nobiltà nell'Italia dell'Ottocento', *Meridiana. Rivista di storia e scienze sociali* 19 (1994), 13–27.

49 Gerbod, 'L'Éthique héroïque'; Forth, *The Dreyfus Affair*, p. 13.

50 22 March 1923 and 10 May 1923 in AD Loire-Atlantique 58J/4 Archives de la famille de Fontaines.

51 22 June 1923 in AD Loire-Atlantique 58J/4 Archives de la famille de Fontaines.

52 Tuesday [undated, 1923] in AD Loire-Atlantique 58J/3 Archives de la famille de Fontaines.

53 23 June 1923 in AD Loire-Atlantique 58J/3 Archives de la famille de Fontaines.

54 G. Duby and A. Wallon (eds), *Histoire de la France rurale* vol. 4 *La Fin de la France paysanne depuis 1914* by M. Gervais, M. Jollivet, and Y. Tavernier (Paris, 1977), chs 2 and 4; T. Kemp, *The French Economy 1913–1939: The History of a Decline* (New York, 1972); J. Horne, *Labour at War: France and Britain, 1914–1918* (Oxford, 1991).

55 H. D. Clout, 'The revival of rural Lorraine after the Great War', *Geografiska Annaler* 75B (1993), 73–91; A. Becker (ed.), *Journaux des combattants et civils de la France du nord* (Villeneuve-d'Ascq, 1998); H. McPhail, *The Long Silence: Civilian Life under the German Occupation of Northern France, 1914–1918* (London, 1999).

56 Berger, *Peasants against Politics*, pp. 64–5.

57 L. Losada, 'Marriage market, social status, and cultural patterns: the case of traditional Argentine families between 1900 and 1940', *Journal of Family History* 37 (2012), 364–80, esp. 316.

58 The method comes from R. Boudon, *Mathematical Structures of Social Mobility* (Amsterdam, 1973), pp. 22–6. The results cited are based on data derived from the *Bottin mondain*. C. Grange, *Les Gens du Bottin mondain: y être, c'est en être* (Paris, 1996), p. 104. See also C. Grange, 'Fusion des élites aristocratiques et bourgeoises à la belle époque: les mariages à Paris et en Provence' in C.-I. Brelot (ed.), *Noblesses et villes (1780–1950)* (Tours, 1995), pp. 247–59.

59 M. de Saint Martin, 'Les Stratégies matrimoniales de l'aristocratie', *Actes de la recherche en sciences sociales* 59 (1985), 74–77; C. Charle, 'Noblesse et élites en France au début du XXe siècle' in *Les Noblesses européennes au XIXe siècle* (Rome, 1988), pp. 407–33, esp. 421.

60 30 April 1923, 22 June 1923, Friday [undated, 1923] in AD Loire-Atlantique 58J/3 Archives de la famille de Fontaines; Mension-Rigau, *Aristocrates*, p. 471.

61 23 July 1916 in AD Savoie 46 F/2 Fonds Tredicini de Saint-Séverin.

62 1 September 1917 in AD Savoie 46 F/2 Fonds Tredicini de Saint-Séverin.

63 20 January 1918 in AD Savoie 46 F/2 Fonds Tredicini de Saint-Séverin.

64 29 July 1918 and Act of sale 8 May 1918 in AD Savoie 46 F/2 Fonds Tredicini de Saint-Séverin.

65 Cardoza, 'The long goodbye', 348; P. Mandler, *The Fall and Rise of the Stately Home* (New Haven, 1997), pp. 228, 246. On landed estates in Britain during wartime see C. Seebohm, *The Country House: A Wartime History, 1939–45* (London, 1989); G. Gliddon, *The Aristocracy and the Great War* (Norwich, 2002); J. M. Robinson, *Requisitioned: The British Country House in the Second World War* (London, 2014); A. Tinniswood, *The Long Weekend: Life in the English Country House between the Wars* (London, 2016).

66 L. Kennett, *The First Air War, 1914–1918* (New York, 1991); S. R. Grayzel, '"The souls of soldiers": civilians under fire in First World War France', *Journal of Modern History* 78 (2006), 588–622.

67 20 March 1915 in AD Loir-et-Cher 83J/127 Fonds de Bizemont-Lambot de Fougères.

68 22 May 1920 in AD Loir-et-Cher 83J/127 Fonds de Bizemont-Lambot de Fougères.

69 25 November 1920 in AD Loir-et-Cher 83J/127 Fonds de Bizemont-Lambot de Fougères.

70 18 January 1920 and 12 February 1922 in AD Loir-et-Cher 83J/127 Fonds de Bizemont-Lambot de Fougères.

71 30 September 1924 in AD Loir-et-Cher 83J/127 Fonds de Bizemont-Lambot de Fougères.

72 27 October 1924 in AD Loir-et-Cher 83J/127 Fonds de Bizemont-Lambot de Fougères.

73 12 December 1924 in AD Loir-et-Cher 83J/127 Fonds de Bizemont-Lambot de Fougères.

74 E. Karlsgodt, *Defending National Treasures: French Art under Vichy* (Stanford, 2011), pp. 103–13; E. Polack and P. Dagen, *Les Carnets de Rose Valland: le pillage des collections privées d'oeuvres d'art en France durant la Seconde Guerre mondiale* (Dijon, 2011).

75 10 December 1942 in AD Loir-et-Cher 111J/13 Fonds de la famille Gilbert-Beauregard (my italics).

76 14 April 1943 and letter from the Ministry of Finance 22 March 1943 in AD Loir-et-Cher 111J/13 Fonds de la famille Gilbert-Beauregard.

77 24 December 1943 in AD Loir-et-Cher 111J/13 Fonds de la famille Gilbert-Beauregard.

78 Mandler, *The Fall and Rise*, pp. 316–17.

79 Y. Pourcher, *Pierre Laval vue par sa fille, d'après ses carnets intimes* (Paris, 2002); Lacroix-Riz, *Les Elites*, pp. 19–20, 29–31, 45, 50–1, 53, 55, 65, 75–6, 164, 181, 185, 187, 196, 202, 207, 221–2, 237, 259–60, 269–71, 275, 291, 315, 377, 392.

80 Lacroix-Riz, *Les Elites*, pp. 149, 159, 164, 377; H. R. Lottman, *The Purge* (New York, 1986), p. 217; R. O. Paxton, *Vichy France: Old Guard and New Order, 1940–1944* (New York, 1972), pp. 330–52.

81 Higgs, *Nobles*, pp. 31, 125–8; Urbach, *Go Betweens*, introduction and pp. 66–7.

82 Malinowski, 'A counter-revolution', p. 32; G. de Chambrun, *Journal d'un militaire d'occasion* (Montpellier, 2000).

83 M. Luirard, *Le Forez et la révolution nationale* (Saint-Etienne, 1972), pp. 103, 106–7, 109–13; M. Luirard, *La Région stéphanoise dans la guerre et dans la paix (1936–51)* (Saint-Etienne, 1981), pp. 467–79.

84 31 December 1917 in AN AP 22/2 Papiers des familles de Kersaint et de Coëtnempren.

85 On fears of bombing, M. Bloch, *Strange Defeat, A Statement of Evidence Written in 1940*, translated by G. Hopkins (New York, 1968), pp. 128–9.

86 AN AP 22/2 Papiers des familles de Kersaint et de Coëtnempren.
87 Malinowski, 'A counter-revolution', p. 30.
88 Mandler, *The Fall and Rise*, p. 314; J. Damase and J. Raflin, *Des Châteaux en Auvergne* (Clermont-Ferrand, 2011), pp. 70, 78.
89 Réginy Kuhn was paid one franc per line for his translations. 21 September 1940 and 23 September 1940 plus copy of Louis Lieker's deposition, and officer's letter about the military tribunal in AD Loir-et-Cher 111J/14 Fonds de la famille Gilbert-Beauregard.
90 15 February 1943 and 15 April 1944 in AD Loir-et-Cher 111J/14 Fonds de la famille Gilbert-Beauregard.
91 'Le Relogement des Sinistrés évacués, expulsés et réfugiés' [unidentified newsletter] 26 April 1944 in AD Loir-et-Cher 111J/13 Fonds de la famille Gilbert-Beauregard. Y. Kuiper, 'Memory, residence and profession: aspects of the process of reconversion of a Dutch noble family in the twentieth century' in *Nobilities in Europe*, p. 138.
92 M. Halbwachs, *The Collective Memory* (*La Mémoire collective*, 1950), translated by F. J. Didder Jr and V. Yazdi Ditter (New York, 1980), pp. 134–5.
93 6 April 1946 in AD Loir-et-Cher 83J/112 Fonds de Bizemont-Lambot de Fougères. On the Quatrebarbes family see L. Wylie (ed.), *Chanzeaux: A Village in Anjou* (Cambridge, MA, 1966), ch. 2. The Catholic Church benefited from Pétain's decree law of 15 February 1941 to recuperate 22 million francs' worth of property it had given up in 1906 after the Separation of Church and State. M. Larkin, *Church and State after the Dreyfus Affair* (London, 1974), pp. 222–3.
94 7 August and 20 August 1946 in AD Loir-et-Cher 83J/112 Fonds de Bizemont-Lambot de Fougères.
95 23 August 1946 in AD Loir-et-Cher 83J/112 Fonds de Bizemont-Lambot de Fougères.
96 'Pierre Nora's celebrated work on *lieux de mémoire* does not remember the aristocracy.' Malinowski, 'A counter-revolution', p. 16. While there is no dedicated entry on nobles, châteaux are the subject of J.-P. Babelon's essay about the Loire valley in volume 3. P. Nora (ed.), *Les Lieux de mémoire* 7 vols (Paris, 1984–92). Parisian scorn towards provincial nobility is discussed in A. Corbin, 'Paris-Province' in P. Nora (ed.), *Realms of Memory: Rethinking the French Past*, English ed. L. D. Kritzman, translated by A. Goldhammer, 3 vols (New York, 1996–98), vol. 1, ch. 2.
97 G. Mosse, *Fallen Soldiers: Reshaping the Memory of the World Wars* (Oxford, 1990); A. Becker, *Les Monuments aux morts: Mémoire de la Grande Guerre* (Paris, 1990); J. Winter, *Sites of Memory, Sites of Mourning* (Cambridge, 1995); A. Becker, *Oubliés de la guerre: Humanitaire et culture de guerre* (Paris, 1998); D. J. Sherman, *The Construction of Memory in Interwar France* (Chicago, 1999).
98 E. Wasson, 'European nobilities in the twentieth century', *Virtus: Journal*

of Nobility Studies 22 (2015), 250. Pioneering works were H.-U. Wehler (ed.), *Europäischer Adel 1750–1950* (Göttingen, 1991), and D. Lieven, *The Aristocracy in Europe, 1815–1914* (London, 1992).

99 M. Funck and S. Malinowski, 'Masters of memory: the strategic use of auto-biographical memory by the German nobility' in A. Confino and P. Fritzsche (eds), *The Work of Memory: New Directions in the Study of German Society and Culture* (Chicago, 2004); L. Jakubowska, 'Memory-making among the gentry in Poland' in F. Cappelletto (ed.), *Memory and World War II: Ethnographic Approach* (Oxford, 2005), ch. 7; E. Glassheim. *Noble Nationalists: The Transformation of the Bohemian Aristocracy* (Cambridge, MA, 2005); J. Dumanowski and M. Figeac (eds), *Noblesse française et noblesse polonaise: mémoire, identité, culture XVI–XXe siècles* (Pessac, 2006), pp. 613–18; D. Smith, *Former People: The Final Days of the Russian Aristocracy* (New York, 2012); L. Jakubowska, *Patrons of History: Nobility, Capital and Political Transitions in Poland* (Farnham, 2012); Y. Kuiper, N. Bijleveld, and J. Dronkers (eds), *Nobilities in Europe in the Twentieth Century: Reconversion Strategies, Memory Culture and Elite Formation* (Leuven, 2015).

8

Initiatives for preservation and tourism

True grandeur is free, sweet, familiar, popular; it allows one to touch and to handle; it loses nothing by being seen close up.[1]

On 25 May 1946 the Association d'entraide de la noblesse française (ANF) approved by vote at its annual general meeting an application for membership from the comte Joseph de Montgrand. Prior to the meeting, the Montgrand dossier had been scrutinised by the association's *commission des preuves* that comprised experts on nobiliary law, genealogy and documentary 'proof' of nobility. This committee undertook the same rigorous procedure of assessment for all applications to the ANF in order to certify noble status and filiation according to very strict rules of transmission.[2] The Montgrand family originated from the Vivarais where one of the earliest known ancestors, Guillaume de Montgrand, lived in 1275. During the seventeenth century Claude de Montgrand (1616–1706) was ennobled by office; he served the king as *conseiller-secrétaire* and resided in the family's *hôtel particulier* in the town of Villeneuve-de-Berg (Ardèche). In 1946 the ANF reported the successful outcome of the comte Joseph de Montgrand's application in a letter sent from its headquarters at 9 rue Richepance in Paris's 8th arrondissement to the comte's address in Marseille. Montgrand was invited to subscribe to publications such as the *Receuil des Personnes ayant fait leurs preuves de Noblesse devant les Assemblées de l'ANF*. He was able to exercise the duties of being a member including to vote upon the adhesion of other candidates applying for ANF membership.[3]

The objectives of the ANF's *commission des preuves* present some intriguing similarities with rulings and investigations on noble status more often associated with kings of France during the early modern era. Verification of documents to establish filiation was the type of work that occupied Chérin as *le généalogiste des ordres du roi* during the eighteenth century; assessment of *preuves* enabled delicate discrimination to be made between those nobles who were eligible for participation in *les honneurs de la cour* and those who were not. The ANF procedures also recall a past in which *la grande recherche* on French nobility was launched in 1666, and Charles René d'Hozier led the compilation of armorial bearings in the realm following Louis XIV's edict in 1696. Two and a half centuries later, in the France of the Fourth Republic, a committee devoting time and expertise to matters of genealogy and nobiliary law presents an unusual image. The civic association's criteria for membership seem at odds with the profile of a nation better known since the 1880s for its republican, rather than heraldic and courtly, symbols.[4]

The contexts were very different, of course. In international politics France's position by the middle of the twentieth century in no way resembled what it had been in the seventeenth century. The 'crucial year' of 1946 was marked by the failure of negotiations between French officials and Ho Chi Minh that resulted in war between France and Indochina. In May the following year France accepted its first loan of US$250 million via the Marshall Plan, despite American opposition to Communism creating tensions for the French government over the Parti communiste français. As the Cold War commenced, France was a nation grappling with decolonisation and a tangle of legacies resulting from the Vichy regime and its demise. Industrial unrest peaked in the 1947 wave of strikes.[5] Conservative views on gender continued to inform pronatalist policy-making. In a speech made in 1945 Charles de Gaulle called for 'twelve million bouncing babies in ten years'. State incentives such as family allowances, tax relief, housing allowances, cheaper transport and cinema tickets were to encourage young couples to have plenty of children.[6]

The interests of ANF members in upholding Catholic values and perpetuating the noble 'race' were in alignment with government policies to lift the birth rate.[7] The 1946 Constitution stated that women's first duty lay in motherhood: 'The Nation guarantees woman the exercise of her functions as female citizen and worker in conditions that allow her to fulfil her role as mother and her social mission.' Large families were more common in the ANF milieu than in France's population as a whole. Among 'practising' Catholic nobles married between 1900 and 1929 the average birth rate was 4.4 children and the noble average was 3.2 children.[8] In the house of Montgrand, for example, Charles de Montgrand (1825–1912) fathered nine children by his wife Berthe. This couple's son Joseph (1872–1958) who joined the ANF in 1946 fathered five children by his wife Madeleine. In 1941 Madeleine received a bronze medal of the French family and certificate signed by the Chief of State Maréchal Pétain.[9]

Bearing in mind the contrast between the political context of the Fourth Republic and that of Louis XIV's reign, let us probe beneath the first impression of similarities between the work of the ANF's *commission des preuves* and early modern investigation into 'proof' of French nobility. Coats of arms provide a point of entry because, in the same way as a patronym, arms function as a mark of identity.[10]

The famous edict promulgated by Louis XIV in November 1696 was not intended to limit the bearing of arms to a particular social category; communities and individuals from a range of social backgrounds were able to possess armorial bearings. Whilst promoted as a way to remedy abuses of heraldic code, and the problem of usurpations of nobles' patronyms and arms, the real purpose behind the edict was a fiscal one. Registration of arms in the *Armorial général de France* was subject to payment at a rate of twenty *livres* for an individual. This was one of a number of strategies for helping bring money to the State following a depletion of its finances resulting from the wars of the League of Augsburg. Various armorial bearings were created and carefully registered in the *Armorial général de France* without the owners of those arms ever using them. There were some imaginative, if slightly ridiculous, inventions. For an apothecary of Brittany, for example: '*d'azur à la seringue d'argent accompagnée de trois pots de chambre de même*'. For André Le Nôtre, architect of the gardens of Versailles: '*d'azur à trois limaços d'or couronnés d'une feuille de chou du même*'.[11]

Usurpation of noble patronyms and arms continued through the eighteenth century, resulting in a series of royal edicts in 1713, 1723, 1725, 1730, and 1771 to try to stamp out the problem. It was also a nineteenth-century phenomenon against which nobles frequently protested but over which they had no control. As the duchesse d'Abrantès complained in her memoirs: 'the usurpation of a great name, a false pretention to noble ancestry is completely despicable'. Although usurpation was forbidden by article 259 of the Penal Code, punishment was hardly ever brought. There was no effective way to stop the widespread practice of persons changing their name to give it an aristocratic appearance. By the 1900s perhaps half a million bourgeois were falsely presenting themselves as noble.[12]

Usurpations during the interwar years were a primary reason behind nobles' decision to take collective action. 'We feared the disappearance of the nobility, its dilution into a titled bourgeoisie,' recalled the comte Jean de Bodinat.[13] A general assembly held in Paris on 13 March 1932 brought together one hundred nobles and resulted in the formal establishment of the ANF. Members of a provisional committee issued an inaugural statement in the bulletin for 1933 where the association was defined as a 'work of justice' (oeuvre de justice) and a 'social work'.

> We wish the confusion to cease between the true and the false. Without any vanity, we consider it unjust that families who over many centuries have consecrated their activity, their fortune, and often their blood for the greatest glory of France should be supplanted by newcomers today ... more than ever names and titles are pillaged ... never have the genealogical dispensaries been more numerous ... in fifty years it will perhaps be very difficult to distinguish a family of old French stock (une famille de vieille souche française) ... from a dubious family who will have been able to appropriate with impunity a false genealogy and a false civil status.[14]

In their analysis of the ANF's creation, Éric Mension-Rigau and Bruno Dumons emphasise the interwar worries about usurpations, and certainly the 1920s and 1930s did see usurpation linked with other problems of concern to nobles such as attempted extortion.[15] A far more insidious danger within the French society of this period, however, was the mounting hostility towards anyone perceived to be 'foreign' – and there were some very experienced noble instigators of such hostility.[16] As its 'social work' the ANF's objectives included mutual finance to assist nobles in debt or unable to make payments of one sort or another, thus putting into effect the 'd'entraide' in the association's name. Charity fêtes were held to raise funds and dozens of noble families received support via a dedicated ANF budget.

Dumons has explained elsewhere that the association's establishment in 1932 can also be interpreted as the outcome of networking among Legitimist noblemen, particularly in the Lyonnais, during preceding decades. From the 1860s noblemen with specialist or amateur interests in genealogy and heraldry were producing regional nobiliary guides promoted by monarchist circles. In 1885 the vicomte Oscar de Poli founded the Conseil héraldique de France. These initiatives were precursors to the ANF and underpinned by a web of personal connections. Poli's grandson was the comte Guy Courtin de Neufbourg, one of the key organisers on the ANF's provisional committee.[17]

My reading of the inaugural statement from the 1933 bulletin places ANF concerns about usurpation and efforts at mutual assistance into a *longue durée* perspective. That does not mean losing sight of the climate of the 1930s in which people from a range of class backgrounds expressed xenophobia and anti-Semitism in diverse public settings. The language of the ANF statement is important, both for what is said and for what is left unsaid.[18] 'In fifty years it will perhaps be very difficult to distinguish a family of old French stock ... from a dubious family who will have been able to appropriate with impunity a false genealogy and a false civil status.' Looking back into the past, however, the multiplicity of routes into the Second Order and different notions about 'authenticity' and 'quality' of nobility had been exercising writers in the sixteenth and seventeenth centuries. Nobles were known for being suspicious about each other's bloodlines and 'true' pedigree.[19] Mutual assistance (*d'entraide*) among nobility in circumstances of financial difficulty was also not new. We have seen examples in Chapter 4 where nobles reached out to extended kin for support, including loans of money, in the eighteenth and nineteenth centuries. Over the *longue durée*, in all parts of Europe, there have been nobles in debt and comparatively poor nobles.[20]

In the ANF's 1933 bulletin there is an interesting choice of words about the intangible patrimony represented by nobles' patronyms and titles: 'Let us try hard to save what remains of this ancestral patrimony for the greater good of France and of all civilisation.'[21] Captured in this sentence is an ambiguous blending of the two meanings that came to be embedded in the French term *le patrimoine* during the twentieth century. On the one hand 'this ancestral patrimony' expresses the meaning of a legal individual's property as defined in the Civil Code. It was this first meaning that mattered to the ANF with regard to interwar usurpations, hence the idea of a 'work of justice'. The phrase 'for the greater good of France and of all civilisation', however, points in the direction of the second meaning – that is, as a way of conceiving cultural or natural assets preserved through collective custodianship for all humanity.[22]

André Desvallées has traced the route by which the latter meaning for *le patrimoine* entered French government circles. The word had been used by a Greek official in talking about cultural property at a 1931 conference of the Office international des musées in Athens. During the early 1950s, Frenchman Robert Brichet participated in international networks and was president of the French delegation to The Hague where the Convention for the Protection of Cultural Property in the Event of Armed Conflict (1954) was formulated. Brichet and others began incorporating the term in their discussions and parliamentary paperwork back in France. In a speech to the Assemblée nationale in November 1959 the Minister for Culture André Malraux mostly used the term *les monuments historiques* but closed with a reference to *le patrimoine*.[23]

Recognition of the additional meaning as cultural and natural assets grew slowly among the French public, in so far as one can tell from surveys that were done. In 1978, after the ministries of culture and environment were separated, Jean-Philippe Lecat, who was in charge of culture, created a Direction du patrimoine. It was agreed with President Valéry Giscard d'Estaing that, with a boost in funding for culture, 1980 would be France's Année du patrimoine. There was tremendous excitement and a flurry of local community-organised initiatives during this year of heritage, especially outside Paris in the departments. The French public across the whole country embraced the idea with an enthusiasm that far exceeded government expectations.[24]

It seems very likely that the wording about *le patrimoine* in the ANF's 1933 bulletin reflects early awareness among nobility of the way cultural property was being talked about at the 1931 conference of the Office international des musées in Athens. A major outcome of that international conference, relayed by the press, was the Athens charter concerning restoration of historic monuments. Significant to nobles in many countries was the recommendation from delegates at Athens that private owner occupancy of monuments be maintained, a view entirely in keeping with the mission of La Demeure historique for example.[25] There were other points of overlap between matters discussed at the Athens conference, such as archaeological excavation, and the expertise of ANF organisers. The comte Guy Courtin de Neufbourg was an erudite medievalist, member of 'La Diana' learned society for archaeology and history, and married to Riga Thérèse Zamoyski, from the great Polish noble family.[26] He and other nobles involved in setting up the ANF had intellectual and professional interests in preserving charters and artefacts, knowledge of Latin and Greek, and plenty of international connections. Courtin de Neufbourg did a lot of the ANF's administrative work, but his commitment to his landed estate in the department of Loire meant the duc Antoine de Lévis Mirepoix, an author, journalist and later on a member of the Académie française, was elected ANF president in 1934. All of these elements of economic, cultural, social and symbolic capital evident within ANF circles are relevant when we turn to consider, in a broader frame of analysis, how nobles were positioned to exercise influence in heritage matters during the twentieth century.

Le patrimoine as cultural field

This chapter responds to an observation made by Stephan Malinowski that 'the lingering significance of the aristocracy in the twentieth century must always be examined at two levels. First, the genuine elite positions and the areas of influence retained by the aristocracy must be examined. And secondly, attention must be paid to the aristocratic dreams and neo-aristocratic conceptions of other groups, especially those of the educated middle classes who would dearly have loved to been "aristocrats" themselves, and who thus increased the significance of the aristocracy.'[27]

My argument here is that the twentieth century saw the full realisation of a process that commenced during the nineteenth century whereby the cultural field of *le patrimoine* (in the sense of 'national' heritage) intersected with other cultural fields, notably travel and tourism but also, for example, gastronomy. Although that process of transformation was not restricted to France, the focus on France and roles played by nobility provides some containing boundaries for the analysis. Chapter 6 looked at one stage of this intersection of fields around 1900 as elites took up the automobile and made trips for leisure to see châteaux, churches, and picturesque natural sites. As heritage became more closely associated with tourism, 'heteronomous forces' – those associated with economics, market, and commoditisation – were exerting impact.[28] Pierre Nora writes about the end of the 1970s when the government announced the year of heritage: *le patrimoine* 'connoted anything that made people feel that they had roots in a particular place and links to society as a whole … With the 1981 presidential elections looming just ahead the past had become ripe for consumption and profit.'[29]

Crucially, there were still 'autonomous forces' operating – principles and values derived from the field itself – which meant *le patrimoine* continued to be preserved and studied for its own sake, by noble families, by learned societies, and by thousands of civic associations running on volunteers' efforts. During the twentieth century, in France and elsewhere, monuments, sites, and objects became subjects of preservation *for* tourism. Equally, monuments, sites, and objects became subjects of preservation *against* tourism (limiting human access where too many visitors would risk damage). UNESCO has contributed at the global level to the rules, institutions, and practices within the field.[30] In France a large number of bodies perform different functions from policy-making and publicity to conservation and research.[31]

For nobles, managing and communicating in the cultural field has involved navigation of the commercial opportunities, also attractive to the State, while keeping in sight the intrinsic 'value' of those elements of *le patrimoine* closely associated with nobility. Precisely because nobles belonged to a network of families, all participating in similar forms of sociability, the communication often took place with one another. As Karina Urbach observes for twentieth-century Britain and Germany: 'Aristocrats preferred talking to aristocrats, and access to each other was easily gained, even if there was no family connection.'[32] But nobles in France have also interacted with government ministers, presidents of the Republic, corporate banks, and private enterprises. They have fostered and led a spectrum of initiatives, as individuals and collectively as families and civic groups. 'Education', in the broadest sense of that word, has underpinned successes and failures. The owner-administrator techniques of running landed estates, and the continuous embedding of family memory, mattered for the habitus.[33]

Some historians of French patrimony in the twentieth century have followed an argument advanced by Louis Réau that stresses widespread destruction in the decades after the Second World War. Michel Fleury and Guy-Michel Leproux characterise the 1940s to the 1970s as 'one of the most striking periods of French vandalism.'[34] Other historians such as Françoise Choay have been attentive to the political purposes of rhetoric about the destruction–creation binary operating in different historical environments. This binary appeared in the French Revolution, and during nineteenth-century debates it gained additional nuances. The comte de Montalembert's *Du vandalisme et du catholicisme dans l'art* (1839) for example distinguished 'destroyers' and 'restorers' as separate kinds of vandals.[35] This chapter presents examples of situations in the twentieth century where nobles sought to counteract what they perceived as 'vandalism'; in other situations nobles have engaged in destruction, and the reasons for that will be considered too.

Private collecting and donations to public institutions

Let us look first at some of the commercial aspects of the arts world. In the twentieth century, as in the nineteenth, commissions from nobles helped artists to further their careers as well as to drive the market for new aesthetic tastes forward. Natalie Adamson, in her article on Odilon Redon's commissioned decorative screens, identifies this process as the production of Bourdieu's 'circles of belief'. Upper-class patrons 'consecrated' the value of works within the market by buying and exhibiting them in their homes. When guests were invited to admire the work at special inauguration parties there were opportunities for the artist to obtain further commissions.[36] Edouard Vuillard's patrons included the princes Emmanuel and Antoine Bibesco. When patrons moved home they tended to ask the artist to reinstall panels so relations continued over a long period of time.[37] Parisian dealers like Georges Petit, Paul Durand-Ruel, Siegfried Bing, and the Bernheim brothers put nobles in touch with artists. At dealers' galleries nobles could purchase works direct or make arrangements for a commission; most auctions took place at the Hôtel Druout.[38]

Titled Jews such as members of the Rothschild, the Cahen d'Anvers, and the Camondo families counted amongst the most formidable collectors and committed music lovers, and some wrote drama and musical works of their own. In the first decade of the twentieth century 'cultural aspirations' may have underpinned assimilation of wealthy Jewish families into Parisian high society, as Lynn Garafola has argued.[39] We need to consider, however, not only anti-Semitism but also additional complexities facing Jews and nobles from diverse non-French backgrounds.

Shortly before he died in 1911, the comte Isaac de Camondo was offered in a unanimous decision the presidency of the Société des Amis du Louvre. Isaac declined, despite his longstanding dedication to the gallery and numerous valuable bequests. Five years earlier, on 14 December 1906, the French government had decreed that it would neither create new titles nor authorise the bearing of foreign titles, and Isaac had preferred to retain his title rather than be naturalised. Asked by a friend to explain his decision on the matter of the presidency, Isaac wrote in terms of contradiction:

> The President of the Société des Amis du Louvre takes part as of right in the Conseil des musées nationaux. However, since I am a foreigner, I cannot, it appears, be a member of the said council. I do not want to diminish the function of the president of the Amis du Louvre … I am, I agree, not French in the legal sense of the word … But can I act better as a Frenchman than give all my collections (all of them) to France for the Louvre?[40]

For all nobles the matter of regularising noble status in the France of the Third Republic was becoming a bureaucratic burden as successive governments tightened legislation; a *titre étranger* only added to the difficulty. In 1909 the Minister for Foreign Affairs Stephen Pichon sent a circular to the diplomatic corps specifying that nobles were allowed to include their nobiliary title in their signature on diplomatic documents only if they had personally obtained the formal *arrêté d'investiture*. This ministerial circular caused consternation among those engaged in *la belle carrière*. Among the forty titled nobles affected by Pichon's missive, only seven had the obligatory *arrêté*.[41]

Government policies and actions in the decade before the First World War contributed to the way in which nobles drew a distinction between 'France', which they felt proud to serve, and the 'Republic', which many of them associated with anticlericalism, rising taxation, and property confiscations. This tension raises a question about the willingness of private collectors to engage with state cultural institutions. The comte Isaac de Camondo made his generous bequest to the Louvre because he felt (but was not in legal terms) 'a Frenchman' and was donating 'to France'. Was this a model that other nobles chose to follow?

Dominique Poulot observes that the particularity of museum development in France stems from the French Revolution. 'The specificity of the French museum, in relation to [museums of] other European countries, comes from its revolutionary origins. Its construction rests on the confiscations of property from clergy then from *émigrés*, on the nationalisation of the former royal collections and on military conquests.'[42] Emperor Napoleon I appointed the artist Gros to play a role in the French army's raiding of Italian art, much of which ended up in the Musée Napoléon and other public institutions. Although the emperor later criticised nobles such as Soult, whom he called 'the greatest pillager among them', Napoleon himself did not put a stop to looting of art by soldiers and generals.[43]

The 'great enterprise of collecting the world' certainly held appeal for French nobles, as it did for French bourgeois elites like Émile Guimet.[44] When treasures were brought back from travels and military campaigns it was nobles' habit, right through the nineteenth and twentieth centuries, to keep them in their own homes, as people from other social classes did for items they collected.[45] The comte Henri de Vibraye recalled the collecting done by his ancestor the duc de Blacas, Louis XVIII's ambassador, in the kingdom of Naples during the Bourbon Restoration. Among the precious items in the duc's *hôtel particulier* were Greek vases, sculptures, cameos, and intaglios. Following the death of the duc de Blacas, most of the collection was sold at auction and some pieces from it were bought by the British Museum. The Ministry of the Beaux-Arts had offered sums far lower than those put forward from the other side of the Channel.[46]

Armand-Marie-Antoine de Biencourt (1802–62) had a military career and in the role of aide de camp to maréchal de Bourmont participated in the taking of Algiers in 1830. In that same year he left the army so that he did not have to serve Louis-Philippe under the July Monarchy. In 1824 the marquis de Biencourt had married Anne de Montmorency and it was largely thanks to his wife's immense fortune that a passion for beautiful objects embellished the Biencourt home at the château d'Azay-le-Rideau. The ancestors of Armand-Marie-Antoine had also been collectors but not on such a lavish scale. Rather than give extraordinary collections to a state institution, the Biencourts made their own château into a museum that was much admired by Balzac.[47]

Scattered records exist of nobles donating individual pieces, or more rarely a whole collection, to galleries and museums. Alphonse de Rothschild is one example of a nobleman who established a habit of donating art to museums. Another example is Fréderic-François-Arnail-Pierre de Jaucourt who travelled through Burma and Tibet; the director of the Musée Guimet wrote to express his thanks to Jaucourt for a donation made to the museum in 1911. But auction catalogues and succession documents indicate that donations to public institutions, when they happened, usually represented a minuscule fraction of what had been assembled and kept in private residences. The fashion for having a space known as 'the hall', begun by the Rothschilds at the château de Ferrières in the 1850s, was still evident in other châteaux during the early twentieth century such as at Rochefort-en-Yvelines and Le Claireau. Photographs of halls show high-ceilinged rooms filled with paintings, tapestries, and objets d'art.[48]

Nobles' attitudes on the development of France's colonial empire matter for the study of collecting and donating, for in the past private residences, like museums, have functioned as 'showcases of global imperialism'. In France a rethinking of museum exhibits and representations of empire began among curators and scholars in the 1950s and 1960s in the light of decolonisation; cultural impacts started to be analysed through postcolonial readings.[49]

Particularly after the First World War nobles expressed pride in French colonialism, although it is not clear whether the bravery of troupes indigènes in 1914–18 was a factor in their thinking. One respondent to Mension-Rigau's questionnaire about upper-class life in the 1980s described their image of France as: 'a great people rich from their colonial empire, with the idea that French civilisation was spread into the world for the good of populations'. Another respondent drew attention to the participation of family members in empire-building: 'France conducted an inspiring civilising work. It founded new countries, protected populations while respecting their culture. We had conquered an empire and we were proud of it, all the more so as representatives of our family had contributed to its creation or participated in its maintenance.' Future empirical research may shed new light on French nobles' experiences in France's overseas territories, as well as on their attitudes toward the decolonising process in the twentieth century. Karina Urbach argues that 'because the British aristocracy had always worked at many levels as local, national and imperial elite, the Empire was a safe haven in a crisis. It enabled the aristocracy to create a flourishing parallel universe.'[50]

Nobles' correspondence from the twentieth century reveals there were worries over inheritance tax (introduced 1901) and the costs of insurance for keeping valuable art in the home. Some individuals asked relatives to take paintings off their hands or suggested sharing the bill for insurance. Various records of insurance payments show owners in the 1930s to 1950s taking out cover for châteaux, furniture, farm buildings, orangeries, chapels, hangars, and other estate buildings. Fire remained a constant risk. In 1932 when fire broke out in the château de La Mothe-Chandeniers all of the furniture and art collection belonging to baron Edgard Lejeune was destroyed. Financial considerations relating to *meubles* were just one element of the larger picture of income, expenditure, and taxation relating to the *immeubles* in nobles' possession.[51]

Valorising châteaux

In Michel de Saint-Pierre's novel *Les Aristocrates*, published in 1954 and then adapted to film, the fictional character at the centre of the novel is Jean de Rémicourt-Porringes, marquis de Maubrun (a retired captain of cavalry, descended from Arthus de Rémicourt who was on crusade with Saint Louis in 1248). There is a chapter/scene in which the widowed marquis is lying in bed mulling over his estates. He mentally 'visits' them in turn and tallies up amounts of money owed, amounts of money received, and amounts that might be anticipated on bills for repair. Compared with his neighbour, the farmer Thibaut, who had just bought a new German tractor and who in Maubrun's eyes was amassing 'a small fortune', the nobleman's lot did not look superior.[52] How on earth, Maubrun asks himself, would it be possible to continue maintaining 'the sacred château de Maubrun, this great carcass of stone with roofs held up by the forests of enormous beams'? The Germans during the Occupation 'had quite simply opened a cavity in the Brunehaut Tower roof to install a submachine gun'. No payment for war damages was forthcoming while 'taxes never ceased to go up in line with the extravagant silliness of the political regime'.[53] The novel is a gentle send-up of the nobility and it captures in a humorous way – except for the fact that submachine guns *were* present – the French version of a real dilemma Peter Mandler studied for England and its country-houses. After the Second World War: 'Owners were either not able to live in their houses or unwilling to pay the price, and the public was certainly unwilling to pay that price for them.'[54]

Some estate agents in France could be very persistent in approaching owners, sending repeat letters even after receiving responses that stated no interest in selling. After the Second World War, enquiries about the estate of Villelouët (Loir-et-Cher) were made by the agencies: Bernard Guilpin (18 December 1945 and 27 January 1950); Raymond Vauchand (26 June 1950); Société Réjan (15 December 1948); Modern Agence L. Duchêne (14 December 1948); J. C. Jammes (6 April 1946); Wanecq Taisant et Guillemot (12 May 1944 and 30 March 1949); and J.–M. A. Fourreau (18 March 1949, 9 April 1949, 16 January 1950 and 9 August 1950). The agents were sometimes enquiring on behalf of companies or associations seeking properties suitable for founding retirement homes or children's *colonies de vacances*. Most enquiries, however, related to wealthy investors seeking grand residences to further enhance their property portfolio. According to France Domaines Transactions Immobilières: 'We are looking for a hunting estate for one of our Egyptian clients, currently resident in France. This client wishes to acquire a beautiful property with every desirable comfort ... Please would you be so kind as to send us a photograph or postcard of your home.'[55]

In 1948 the comte Guy de Montlaur was liaising with Lepage Pépinières in Angers for work on the gardens and park of La Thibaudière. A reduction of costs was on Montlaur's mind as he took a red pencil to the quote provided by Lepage and circled errors in the mathematical calculations, recalculating the sums for labour and plants to a total of 123,100 francs. The guard employed at the property would do some of the digging of holes for the cedars, pines, and maples. By purchasing fewer trees than initially asked for, Montlaur requested the bill be brought down to a total of 100,000 francs.[56]

La Demeure historique's priorities from the end of the Second World War were to prepare for peacetime representation of the association among organisations in the French departments, especially the regional committees for tourism that were commencing inventory work on châteaux. Members of La Demeure historique were encouraged to call a meeting in their own department to appoint or confirm in post the president of the departmental section of the association. The duc de Luynes was the association's president at national level, running affairs from the La Demeure historique office address at 146 avenue de Champs-Elysées. Nobles played lead roles at departmental level too: for example the comte de Vibraye was president for Loir-et-Cher.[57]

Jean-Pierre Rioux's account of the immense damage done to the nation's infrastructure during the Second World War provides a sense of scale to the challenge of encouraging tourism. The Fourth Republic saw a lengthy process of repair and reconstruction from the mid-1940s into the 1950s. Physical signs of the bombing, shelling, and gunfire had affected seventy-four out of ninety departments with perhaps one-quarter of all buildings ruined. Many roads, docks, and over half of the country's rail-track were not fit for use. There were initial shortages of electricity and coal.[58]

Some châteaux never recovered from war damage. In the department of Manche the marquise Gabrielle de Marescot (née d'Auxais) had under-taken restoration of the château de Chastel between 1905 and 1912. During the Second World War the furniture from Chastel was placed in a neigh-bouring farm where it was destroyed in the battles for Liberation between 20 June and 26 July 1944. Nothing remained of the château's roof and the interiors were judged to be irreparable after the war. Also in Manche the château de Theré suffered major damage during the bombing campaign. The interior was pillaged between 1945 and 1954 then the château was abandoned until bought by the Conseil général and torn down.[59]

A change in ownership of a château after the Second World War did not necessarily lead to an immediate change in its use. In the department of Haute-Loire the château du Cluzel had been transformed into a *colonie de vacances* from 1942, first under lease from the private owner Monsieur Vassal then under lease from the ministries of air and army. In 1950 the comte Antoine de Bouillé bought the château du Cluzel, which had in the past been a property of his family. The *colonie de vacances* continued to occupy the château until 1958 when the lease ran out; the château then became a private residence for the Bouillé family.[60]

The duc de Luynes wrote a letter to members of La Demeure histo-rique to inform them of the association's success in securing a measure for income tax relief in article 15 of the law of 14 August 1954. Owners were eligible to benefit from income tax relief by furnishing receipts for costs of upkeep on property in the primary or secondary register of the historic monuments. Through the reduction of income tax, the State would reimburse owners for between 40 and 50 per cent of the cost of maintenance and repairs.[61] According to Marcel Schneider, author of *Être châtelain aujourd'hui* (1977), the rupture of aristocratic families with château life occurred around 1950, although owners continued to use their properties to stage balls and receptions. Historians writing in the 1990s suggest that the 1980s witnessed a revival of interest in châteaux and the land among the nobility.[62]

Changes in the way people spent recreation time were taking place after the Second World War. There were longer holidays; the average annual holiday increased from three weeks in 1956 to four weeks in 1969. The family motorcar was an emblem of the new prosperity. In 1939 there were around half a million cars in the Paris region alone. In 1949, 1.25 million private vehicles were registered nationally and, by 1959, more than five million. Car manufacturers targeted a new mass market with the Renault 4CV, launched in 1947, hailed as the first truly affordable mass-market French large car. Since the 1920s train travellers had seen the posters designed by Constant Duval for the Paris-Orléans rail company that encouraged people to visit the châteaux of the Loire valley. Hachette's *Guides bleus* were sold in railway stations. A *Guide illustré* featuring the tourist route for visiting châteaux such as Blois, Chambord, Amboise, and Chenonceau was in its eighth edition by 1924. The Fourth Republic saw new publicity and activities develop. A *son et lumière* was created for the château de Chambord in 1952. Sound and light shows as well as performances by actors in historical costume quickly took off at other châteaux through the 1950s and 1960s. By the 2000s Chenonceau, the most visited château of the Loire valley, welcomed 900,000 visitors annually; Chambord welcomed 700,000; Blois, Amboise, Cheverny, Villandry, and Azay-le-Rideau each welcomed more than 300,000 visitors.[63]

Associations proliferate and agriculture continues

During the Fifth Republic an array of new associations in the arts and heritage sector joined the well-established ones like La Demeure historique and La Sauvegarde de l'art français. Vieilles maisons françaises was created in 1958 by Anne de La Rochefoucauld, marquise de Amodio. By the early 1970s there were twelve thousand owners involved in Vieilles maisons françaises, which had departmental committees and received government subsidies. SOS Paris was set up in 1973 by two noblewomen, Marthe de Rohan Chabot and Marie de La Martinière, to protect the urban architectural heritage of the French capital. Among its first members was Jean de Harcourt, who explained his motivation for joining: 'I saw so many horrors being made on the architectural front that I decided to get involved.'[64] La Société pour la protection des paysages et de l'esthétique de la France (SPPEPF) lobbies for the protection of aesthetic beauty of sites. Le Comité Vendôme concerns itself with the Place Vendôme, the site of jewellery boutiques patronised by the international super-elite. The Association pour le rayonnement de l'Opéra de Paris promotes musical culture at the Palais Garnier and Opéra Bastille. La Maison de la chasse et de la nature serves as both a museum and a club for meetings of hunters in the heart of the Marais. Some of the associations named have exclusively Parisian centres of interest, but La Demeure historique and Vieilles maisons françaises operate through decentralised structures. Thousands more associations and learned societies spread across the French departments create vibrant programmes of activity in their geographic locations.

The 1950s to 1970s were significant decades in scholarly research on France's rural past, with the interactions between historians taking very different approaches to the discipline of history.[65] Outside the academic world, but also contributing to public knowledge about French rural history, were nobles who participated in the learned societies. In the nineteenth century, while these societies were mostly made up of bourgeois men, there had been noblemen involved. Arcisse de Caumont (1801–73) for example established the Société des antiquaries de Normandie in 1823 and the Société française d'archaéologie in 1834, and organised conferences to bring together researchers. In the twentieth century, the vicomte Frotier de La Messelière (1876–1965) travelled by bicycle for his research on historic monuments and the genealogies and arms of noble families of Brittany. He wrote and illustrated numerous books and articles, gave public talks, and at the end of his life donated his papers to the Archives départementales in the Côtes-d'Armor.[66]

Frotier de La Messelière, like Courtin de Neufbourg and many other nobles of the same generation, witnessed and participated as a landowner in the changes in agriculture that were happening in parallel with rural depopulation. The census figures show a 30 per cent decline in the agricultural workforce between 1946 and 1954. Before the Second World War 17.5 per cent of the population worked in agriculture. Only 12.1 per cent did in 1954 and then only 8.4 per cent in 1962. Women especially were leaving rural areas in order to gain paid employment in cities and towns. While women still comprised 44 per cent of the agricultural workforce after the Second World War, the proportion of women dropped to 33 per cent in 1962.[67]

Data on the professional activities of nobles from the ANF reveals where agriculture stood in relation to other sectors. In 1963 members of the ANF were invited to complete a questionnaire. Texier gives the following breakdown of results on occupation by sector: industry (26 per cent), agriculture (22 per cent), army (18 per cent), banking (8 per cent), other (26 per cent). Since not all nobles belong to the ANF, and not all members completed the 1963 questionnaire, one cannot extrapolate the results from this non-random sample to the population of male and female nobility as a whole. In 1982 further research was undertaken within the ANF on nobles' professional activities. Agriculture (inclusive of forestry) was top of the list: 145 respondents involved. The army was second: 141 respondents involved. Then banking came a distant third place: 69 respondents involved. Cultural activities (broadly defined as work in libraries, museums, archives, journalism etc.) were the professional area of 36 repondents.[68]

Disposal and acts of resistance

As country houses in England were sold after the Second World War landowners started 'decanting their collections of manuscripts into the county record offices that were springing up around the country'.[69] To what extent was deposition of papers in state repositories happening in France?

Correspondence arising from the geneaological and family history research undertaken by nobles in the late nineteenth and twentieth centuries reveals frequent contact between relatives and requests for information. It is very unusual to find evidence of nobles deliberately destroying parts of their family archive. Patchiness in records and breaking up of *fonds* can happen for many different reasons as we saw in Chapter 1. Yet Urbach's remarks about the sanitising of British and German aristocratic family archives undoubtedly have some resonance for archives in France.[70] Halbwachs wrote about 'disposal' and 'acts of resistance' in relation to social frameworks of collective memory. In the examples below we can see that both of those concepts have application in the actions of noble relatives. There was a push–pull dynamic within families as some members took a great deal of interest in conservation while others ignored the matter.

On 11 December 1930 Madame Faurie de Vassal replied to a cousin who had written to ask her some questions about the Vassal de la Tourette branch for some family history research. She admitted in her response:

At the time of our departure from Seilhac I destroyed a lot of family papers
that were an encumbrance and I kept only those that especially concerned
the La Tourette-Mazières branch and the Nozac-Largraulière branch. I
regret having burned the others that would perhaps have been of interest
to you. I have two or three parchments that are impossible to read ... if you
should like to see them ... then my son who is studying pharmacy in Paris
could bring them to you.[71]

Arrangements were made between the two cousins for the papers to be
delivered by Madame Faurie de Vassal's son, which provided an occasion
'to renew familial ties'.

Accidental damage through forgetfulness or limited awareness of
what conservation entails was far more common in the archivist Jean
Lartigaut's view. 'The negligence and sometimes the silliness of owners,
voracious rodents, loose pipes and gutters in houses that are rarely occupied have been and are still the most obvious causes for the demise of
seigneurial or family archives.' The only intelligent solution for protection
of *fonds* was 'to accept the hospitality offered by the State in the Archives
départementales'.[72]

An archival circular of 15 April 1944 created the J series for *archives
privées* deposed in the Archives départementales to group together *fonds*
that have entered by way of gifts, purchase, or deposition by contract.
In 1974 the Archives nationales had 338 *fonds privés* already classed or
in the process of having inventories prepared. Between three and seven
contracts for deposition were signed annually and dozens more bequests
and purchases were made. For archivists arranging purchases of archives,
even before the advent of the Internet, there was the problem of competition with antiquarian dealers. Jean Sablou characterised the negotiations
between archivist and owner for a bequest as often lengthy and delicate.
Rare periods of residency in a country home complicated the task of
arranging to meet and assess the material condition of documents, or to
undertake microfilming. Reaching a decision on what to do with family
papers could take a very long time in families when many heirs had to be
consulted and disagreements arose. A decree of 17 June 1938 concerning
archives opened the possibility of classing being done by having the *fonds*
placed on the secondary register of historic monuments. The Société des
amis des archives was established in 1939. A decade later another committee was set up by decree of 14 February 1949 to bring together archivists, historians, and owners for mutual action to persuade more owners
to deposit collections in state repositories.[73]

Museum curators sometimes made enquiries or issued requests for temporary loans of documents. The comte de Francqueville d'Abancourt replied to a letter from Madame Ducourtial, conservator at the Musée national de la Légion d'honneur, in October 1970. She was helping to curate an exhibition, 'The Cult of Saint Louis in the Seventeenth Century' and hoped that documents might be available concerning Théodat de Taillevis de Perrigny, chevalier de Saint Louis, who had his left arm cut off in combat against Admiral Hood in 1795. The comte de Francqueville d'Abancourt obligingly sent a long list of documents in his possession that he was willing to lend for the exhibition and that had been left to him by his uncle who had no son of his own. Clearly eager to help, the comte had also telephoned a cousin in Paris, who recommended that the curator get in touch with an aunt about some inherited portraits of Perrigny ancestors. Madame Claude Ducourtial followed up the various suggestions, which led into contact with the Bibliothèque nationale.[74]

International networks and intangibles

Let us now set such exchanges into a wider context of networking between nobles in France and in other European countries. There were two crosscutting phenomena in the period from the late 1940s to the 1970s that shaped nobles' receptiveness toward the practice of co-operation or d'entraide among nobilities.

The first phenomenon concerns the international political environment in which governments around the world were moving to change national legislation on the bearing of titles and legal status of nobility. Some countries had started earlier, including France where changes punctuated the nineteenth century. The trend of abolishing titles and privileges is clear from the following examples. In West Germany article 109 of the Weimar constitution of 1919 allowed for the existence of nobiliary titles as part of the name, but no new titles were to be conferred in future and old titles no longer carried privileges. In Austria the law of 3 April 1919 abolished nobility, as well as secular knightly orders and certain ranks and titles. In Denmark the constitution of 5 June 1953 confirmed the provision from 1849 abolishing all privileges attached to titles of nobility, and confimed abolition of fiefs and majorats. In Greece article 3 of the constitution of 1 January 1952 prohibited nobiliary titles. In Hungary a law of 14 January 1947 forbade use of titles and emblems of nobility. In Italy article 4 of the constitution of 27 December 1947 stated titles of nobility were no longer recognised and titles ceased to be conferred after 1946. In Romania article 10 of the constitution of 1923 stated titles and privileges were abolished.[75]

With governments pushing in the direction of egalitarian democracy, by getting rid of nobility with its culture of social distinctions and hierarchical ranking, nobles increasingly co-operated among themselves. Contacts between nobilities in different countries were helped along by a series of youth congresses beginning with a two-day event held in Paris in 1957. Participating associations were the ANF, the Vereinigung der Deutschen Aldersverbände, the Club Saint Jean from Austria, the Association de la noblesse du royaume de Belgique (ANRB), and the Unione della Nobiltà Italiana. The success of the 1957 Paris meeting of young nobles from different European countries led to a second congress held in Munich in 1958, a third in Brussels in 1959, and a fourth in Vienna in 1960. The Commission d'information et de liaison des associations de noblesse d'Europe (CILANE) was established, with French used as the official language and the office headquarters in Paris. Countries with associations of nobility represented in CILANE are Germany, Belgium, Spain, France, Italy, Portugal, Switzerland, and Russia.[76]

Against this backdrop of energetic promotion by nobles investing time and resources in the future of European nobilities, the French government recognised the ANF as being of public utility on 29 July 1967. The duc Antoine de Lévis Mirepoix, ANF president and also a member of the Académie française, obtained authorisation from President Charles de Gaulle to bear the Spanish title of duc de San Fernando Luis in 1961. Membership applications to the ANF rose as the association continued its various activities, from holding an annual Catholic Mass to less formal get-togethers organised in decentralised fashion. The ANF's strength derived from the provincial nobility's socialising and strong defence of the Catholic Church. 'Provinces' mattered in this milieu, not departments, because of the way most nobles drew their familial identity from the pre-1789 past.[77]

The second cross-cutting phenomenon of the twentieth century was the commercial use of aristocratic-sounding names and titles in French brands. In effect the issue of usurpations that had so troubled the ANF founders in the 1930s assumed radically expanded dimensions because of global marketing. Not only were there still people changing their names to make them sound aristocratic but also products were being commercialised with labels and advertising to give those products an aristocratic 'appearance'. While the older generation within the French bourgeoisie were more likely to be able to afford goods with higher price tags, the generation of younger adults, better educated and with a wider range of professional careers open to them, were also immersed in this consumerist environment.

Les trente glorieuses have been characterised as years of affluence for workers. Many French people welcomed the Marshall Plan and the benefits it brought. The 1940s to the 1970s saw an average 6 per cent increase in people's real incomes but there remained large disparities in wealth. It was an age of consumer aspiration, although the purchasing of new goods and take-up of new habits was not evenly spread across society. The higher incomes and increased spending power of people in postwar France were created by economic growth and rising productivity. Between 1945 and 1975 the economy grew on average by 5 per cent per annum. By 1947 industrial production in France had climbed back to prewar levels.

One of the reasons for the growth was the active role of the State in industry, overseeing the nationalisation of public utilities and enterprises including the Électricité de France, Gaz de France, Air France, Banque de France and Renault. A second key reason behind economic growth was the Taxe à la valeur ajoutée (TVA) or Value-Added Tax (so called because 'value-added' refers to the difference between the price charged to purchaser and the value of the inputs). The TVA was introduced by statute of 10 April 1954. The French version had three special features: exports were exempted from TVA, making French products more competitive; TVA was levied at different rates ranging from 5 to 33 per cent depending on the product; and the higher rates on French luxury goods meant that those who could afford such products were charged high tax rates for them.[78]

In his book *La France noble* (1974) François de Negroni devotes a chapter to the 'National Aristocratic Universe' as it appeared by the end of *les trente glorieuses*. Initially the author points out the ways in which fictive ennoblement applied in the French naming of breeds for horses, dogs, and cats. 'Exemplary totemic animals of French society' were selected for their race. The patronyms and elaborate genealogies attributed to breeds made for the creation of 'refined social strata'. Among the canine breeds were: Prince Rodes, Diane de Retz, Comtesse de Loir, and Duc de Normandie. Pet keeping for twentieth-century owners served as a way to 'hold a bit of the aristocratic manna'. Kathleen Kete explored exactly that phenomenon operating in the nineteenth century. The lineages claimed for dogs in the 1800s led back to royal and aristocratic hounds, part of 'an impulse to recapture the past'.[79]

Negroni moves on to the application of patronyms and titles to food and drink in the 1970s, commencing with the luxury goods on the market where they serve like a guarantee 'to perpetuate a long tradition of taste'.[80] His list (complemented by black and white photographs of the products sold in shops) includes: 'Marquise de Sévigny chocolates, Comtesse du Barry foie gras, Charles de Cazenove champagne, Prince de Bourbon-Parme champagne, Marquis de Montesquiou armagnac, Prince Hubert de Polignac cognac …'. In the academic literature about gastronomy, and food studies more generally, there is debate about the persistence of aristocratic influences and the rise of a 'bourgeois' dining culture during the nineteenth century. Although products must be distinguished from dining practices, the selection of products for purchase is always revealing about the 'taste' and class of consumers; the success of marketing is still more revealing about consumer desires and aspirations.[81]

Furnishings and other household effects are next in Negroni's list: 'Ravinet d'Enfert silverware, Robert de Calatchi tapestries, Jean de Bonnot rare books, Marquis de Miromesnil antiquities, Anne de Ganay ceremonial linen'. Particularly important, Negroni points out, are the beauty products and clothes that function as intermediaries between the individual and his or her social image.[82]

Cultural historians have studied writers' discourses on the crime of 'artful dissimulation' in late eighteenth-century France or, to use Mirabeau's phrase, showing the 'mask of virtue not its face' of which the queen was accused. During the revolutionary era popular literature, much of it pornographic, depicted reviled aristocrats and the royal couple as grimacing monsters, and publishers put out dozens of books on reading character through physiognomy. Dissimulation was judged to be a peculiarly aristocratic and feminine form of behaviour. It relied 'above all on appearances, that is, the disciplined and self-conscious use of the body as a mask [to conceal true emotions]'.[83] The meaning of dissimulation was very close to that of distinction, literally the act of separating or the condition of things that are separate. Distinction 'is the result of a subtle balance between what a woman allows to be glimpsed of herself and what she keeps concealed'.[84] Michèle Lamont's sociological studies among the French and American upper-middle class of the late twentieth century demonstrate that the judgements that a person makes about the appearance and behaviour of another human being enable them to decide whether or not they fall within their own 'symbolic boundaries'. Symbolic boundaries divide the individuals or groups that a person will include in their sociability from those who they will exclude.[85]

Among the upmarket beauty products and clothing brands on the French market in the 1970s, Negroni cites: 'Princesse d'Albret perfumes, Belle de Rauch perfume, Jean d'Athène perfume, Line d'Artois lipstick, Diane d'Arçay makeup, Jeanine de Ré makeup, Charles of the Ritz facecream, Monsieur de Givenchy eau de toilette, Gérard d'Agay shampoo, Gentilhomme de Weil aftershave, Chevalier d'Orsay aftershave, Jean d'Estrées moisturiser ... Pierre d'Alby haute couture, Chantal de Kemoularia haute couture, Eliane d'Hérel prêt à porter'. Even fairly mundane items for household consumption did not escape the aristocratic references in marketing, such as in: 'Duc d'Armor sardines, Baron de l'Herme sparkling wine, d'Aucy vegetables, Comtes de Provence bouillabaisse, Jacques de Toy cider'. The overall impact, Negroni concludes, is that the promotional patronym and title acts as 'a signature, a stamp, a brand, and through its commercial success, propagates and introduces into all homes the aristocratic aura'. In exactly the same decade as Negroni was writing, Pierre Bourdieu made the social-science case for the bourgeoisie's enduring fascination for France's *ancienne noblesse*.[86]

On one level the ANF may have taken comfort in the fact that: 'No noble title suffices in and of itself to confer nobility in societies that claim to reject nobility'.[87] For some individuals, however, the commercialising of aristocratic 'intangible cultural heritage' was a nuisance that touched them at a personal level. So they challenged it. In 1936 the case of 'Orsay versus the Société des Parfums d'Orsay' was heard in court. The perfume company was using the name, title, and arms of 'comtesse d'Orsay'. Because the female accusant was married, and held the patronym 'd'Orsay' and corresponding title by virtue of marriage to her husband, the court decided not to uphold her claim against the perfume company for usurpation. The comtesse d'Orsay had rights only as a user (*usage viager*) not as an owner of the patronym and title.[88]

On another level, it suited the nobility perfectly well to have the commercial branding on luxury products because it enhanced the connotations of sophistication and prestige attached to nobility. By the 1970s the cultural field of *le patrimoine* was intersecting with the cultural field of travel and tourism, with the cultural field of gastronomy, and with the cultural field of French fashion and design. There were no new creations of nobility so noble status verified by the Garde des Sceaux according to the Fifth Republic's procedures was rare and only going up in 'value'.

From the 1980s into the 2000s

Heritage and arts associations in which nobles have been heavily involved were acting separately but for similar ends until the 1980s when they began to join forces. Mitterrand's election campaign in 1981 had borrowed a 1936 slogan 'make the rich pay'. Letters started to be written collectively by the associations to ministers or to the president of France. During the presidential elections of 2002 contact was made with Jacques Chirac and the G8 du Patrimoine was established to unify the associations. The presidents of the G8 du Patrimoine member associations began to meet once a month at the Maisons Paysannes de France in the 9th arrondissement of Paris.[89]

Family networks have remained very much in evidence in these heritage associations, just as they were in the nineteenth-century charity organisations through which nobles supported the work of the Catholic Church. In 2007 three of the principal office-holders in La Demeure historique were noblemen: the comte Jean de Lambertye (president); the comte Denis de Kergorlay (vice-president); and the comte Étienne de Bryas (treasurer). The president and past president of La Sauvegarde de l'art français were both noblemen: the vicomte Olivier de Rohan and his cousin Edouard de Cossé Brissac. One of SOS Paris's founders, Marthe de Rohan Chabot, is a relative of the vicomte Olivier de Rohan. Louis de Rohan, another cousin, is vice-president of the Club de la chasse et de la nature.

One effect of the family network can be seen at the auction houses of Christie's France and Sotheby's. In their analysis of the 'dispersion and recomposition of patrimonies' Michel Pinçon and Monique Pinçon-Charlot show that carefully engineered sales of collections mean items change hands but seller and buyer are more than likely to know one another, through membership of the ANF for example. The motives for selling range from a desire to begin a fresh collection through to obligation to sell to pay inheritance tax. It helps that the auctioneer understands this world, as Christiane de Nicolay-Mazery certainly does or her cousin Raymond de Nicolay. Board members of auction houses in 2007 included the comte Hugues de Pechpeyrou Comminges de Guitaut and Éric de Rothschild.[90]

A second effect of the family network is the informal sharing of information about neighbourhoods. Pinçon and Pinçon-Charlot point out the different ways in which private property owners protect their own interests. In 2004 the creation of a *parc naturel régional* in the Vallée de Chevreuse made objective sense to protect the forests. Those same forests are a treasured resource for enthusiasts of hunting who live in the châteaux within the borders of the *parc naturel régional*. A 'green space' (buffer zone) affords protection for historic monuments from pollution in the air. Owners of châteaux with an ecological mindset have nonetheless shown unwillingness to accept installation of wind turbines that would ruin the landscape. Denis de Kergolay, owner-resident of the château de Canisy (Manche) set on parkland of thirty hectares, characterised his personal attitude to the opening of his property to the public as conforming to a long family tradition. 'As the owner of a historic monument, I am happy to share it.' Difficulties arose, however, when Kergolay also served as mayor of the village of Canisy. A fight with the community started over the *plan local d'urbanisme* that would create an industrial and commercial zone on the border of the château parkland.[91]

In 2010 the total number of historic monuments protected under the law of 1913 and Code du patrimoine was 43,180. Of that total number, 49.5 per cent were in private ownership and nearly all the rest (43 per cent) owned by communes. From the annual total funding for protected monuments (€1.12 billion) the State contributed €560 million and the private sector €220 million. A special tax regime applies in relation to buildings on the primary or secondary register of historic monuments. Income tax deductions to compensate owners for the costs of maintaining and guarding the property, and for insurance, are more generous than they were in 1954. Costs are deductible from income tax at a rate of 100 per cent of the costs if the property is open to public, otherwise at the rate of 50 per cent. The criterion of being 'open to the public' requires that the property be accessible for tour by visitors on at least fifty days per year. Dominique de la Fourchadière, an insurance specialist for Verspieren, explains: 'Previously owners had the possibility of financing the needs of the property thanks to income from hunting and fishing leases, agricultural and forested lands. Today these activities no longer bring in much money and the owners, who may be longstanding or recent *châtelains*, are obliged to envisage other sources of revenue and to apply for grants.'[92]

For restoration work the Direction régionale des affaires culturelles (DRAC) under the auspices of the Ministry of Culture and Communication pays for a preliminary study and provides grant funding varying from 30 per cent to 50 per cent of the cost of works for a structure on the primary register of historic monuments, and from 15 per cent to 30 per cent of the costs of work for a structure on the secondary register.

The regional or departmental council may be approached for a contribution to the overall grant funding.

According to the president of La Fondation pour les monuments historiques, Benoît Bassi: 'The State is not a bad partner but we cannot ask everything from it, which is the reason we raise funds from donors to help owners pursue their projects.' La Fondation pour les monuments historiques administers a cluster of prizes bearing the names of the sponsors including Sotheby's, Villandry, François Sommer, and the French Heritage Society. A high proportion of prizes awarded annually are for châteaux projects. In 2015 restoration work for nine historic monuments (including gardens) was funded through these prizes to a total value of €100,250. The French Heritage Society prizes were for the château de La Grange (Moselle), château de Commarque (Dordogne), château de Laxion (Dordogne), château de Tholet (Aveyron), and La Chipaudière (Ille-et-Vilaine). The Sommer prize for hunting and nature went to the château de Daubeuf (Seine-et-Marne) and château de Larnagol (Lot). The Villandry prize went to the château de Daubeuf (Seine-Maritime). Finally, the *prix du jeune repreneur* was awarded to Ghislain de Castelbajac, owner of the château de Caumont (Gers).[93]

Managing and communicating about patrimony requires an investment of time for association members to keep the machinery of social capital running smoothly. The 'network of familial, schooling and professional relations carefully maintained through regular effort' is 'almost a condition of success'.[94] There is another very significant dimension to the practice of distributing prizes and publicising the co-operation between private donors and the State to restore châteaux. It concerns cultural capital.

In accordance with the provisions of the Civil Code artwork and furniture in a privately owned historic monument may be divided up into lots and removed by heirs as a result of successions. Dispersal of artwork and furniture is understood to be a risk in the heritage sector for two reasons. First, it may jeopardise the material conservation of that artwork and furniture. Second, it depletes the attractiveness of the historic monument to tourists when such items are no longer in situ. For tourism the State has an interest in encouraging private owners of châteaux to keep the properties furnished.[95] Any significant change in the physical appearance of a site or monument has pedagogical implications for heritage interpretation.

There is evidence to suggest that the pre-existing ideas people have about a site or monument will influence how they engage with it during a visit. In museums people tend to learn about what they 'almost already know'.[96] Heritage interpreters are obliged to strike a balance between meeting the expectations of visitors by covering points that are already familiar, and introducing new and different points to enrich understanding. To remain commercially viable, heritage sites and monuments must compete in the market for customers who have a wide selection of potential leisure activities to choose from. This places a certain amount of pressure on interpreters to deliver a high-quality experience so as not to discourage visitors from making a return trip or recommending the site or monument to others. A carefully researched presentation that is perceived to depart too 'radically' from a familiar narrative may cause visitors to disengage or even to become hostile to the work of the interpreter.[97]

Halbwachs explained that continuity in frameworks of collective memory does not depend on the survival of individuals belonging to the group, or even the maintenance of their presence in the same physical space. In the absence of any living group members, a framework can still be operating as shared images and meanings collectively held by others.

> Our physical surroundings bear our own and others' imprints ... Our tastes and desires evidenced in the choice and arrangement of these objects are explained in large measure by the bonds attaching us to different groups ... The group not only transforms the space into which it has been inserted, but also yields and adapts to its physical surroundings. It becomes enclosed within the framework it has built. The group's image of its external milieu and its stable relationships with this environment becomes paramount in the idea it forms of itself, permeating every element of its consciousness, moderating and governing its evolution.[98]

In effect, when a family of nobility no longer exists because the bloodline is extinguished, the physical space it once occupied will still carry an imprint of its presence; its patronym may match the name of the château or village or *nom de terre*. A group of tourists entering that physical space will bring to it collectively held images and meanings, yielding and adapting to the surroundings, to learn what may already be partly known. When family portraits of the original owners are on the walls it is all to the benefit of the heritage industry and to the French economy.[99]

Conclusion

Arno Mayer argued that the resilience of *ancien régime* structures meant 'it would take two World Wars and the Holocaust ... to finally dislodge the feudal and aristocratic presumption from Europe's civil and political societies'. His conclusion rests in part on the continued strength of 'venerable elites and institutions bent on prolonging their privileged way of life'. In the 1950s the Earl of Portsmouth expressed that strength, as he perceived it: 'What was, and still is, interesting is that there is a sort of international aristocratic family freemasonry which permeates Europe even now in a one-adult one-vote world.'[100]

Historians and sociologists in the twenty-first century are reopening debate about why members of the middle classes continue patterns of emulation while accepting that prestigious positions in some cultural fields 'should be held by blue bloods'. 'The obvious persistence of the aristocracy calls into question the value of traditional models of "bourgeois" society. Instead of labelling "surviving" nobles exceptions or mere "remnants," we need to think again about the presently accepted conception of a "bourgeois" nineteenth century.'[101]

The determination of nobility to protect noble identity in the France of the Fifth Republic is evident not only in the number of adhesions to the ANF, or in subscriptions to specialist publications on heraldry and genealogy, or even in the high birth rate within their families. There have been multiple avenues for the nobility to maintain social frameworks of collective memory, to safeguard patrimony, and to put its own stamp upon interpretations of the past in France. During the twentieth century, commercialisation of products that could be marketed under aristocratic-sounding names meant that millions of people, on a regular basis in the course of shopping, saw references to patrimony that has long been associated with nobles. Negroni's 'National Aristocratic Universe' is a quirky dramatisation of this phenomenon in the 1970s. But one only has to walk down the aisle of a supermarket that sells wine in the twenty-first century to see that barons, marquis, and châteaux are a part of French *rayonnement*. In Bourdieu's thoughts on the mechanisms of social reproduction: 'usurpations of nobility are a key element … it is because there are people who want to enter into the nobility that the mechanism of nobility works.'[102]

Notes

1 J. de La Bruyère, *Maximes et réflexions* (Paris, 1781), p. 41.
2 For membership of the ANF noble filiation must be in the direct, male line and the application dossier must include an official document to show the candidate has followed the Ministry of Justice procedures to verify noble status. A. Texier, *Qu'est-ce que la noblesse?* (Paris, 1988), pp. 144–7, 214–20,

376, 380–2. The baron Pierre Durye, a conservator at the Archives nationales, served as chair of the ANF's *commission des preuves* before becoming the association's archivist in the 1960s. P. Durye, *La Généalogie* (Paris, 1961).

3 ANF letters 21 June 1946, 1 June 1959, and 27 June 1959 in AD Bouches-du-Rhône 197J/71 Fonds de la famille de Montgrand; ANF, *Receuil des personnes ayant fait leurs preuves de noblesse* 6 vols (Paris, 1950–74). The ANF *Bulletin* no. 115 (January 1968) contains the statutes and internal rules. On the office of *conseiller-secrétaire du roi* in the provinces see Texier, *Qu'est-ce que la noblesse?* p. 563. The hamlet Montgrand is near Vals (Ardèche). The Montgrand family's former *hôtel particulier* in Villeneuve-de-Berg is classed as a historic monument.

4 The edict of 17 April 1760 on *honneurs de la cour* required proof of an ancestor of noble status in 1400. F. Bluche, *Les Honneurs de la cour* 2 ed. (Paris, 2000). Symbols for French people in 1946 were above all 'Marianne' (shown bloodied in front of an execution post in an August 1944 poster) to replace the 'The Marshal' of the Pétainist cult. R. Kedward, *La Vie en bleu: France and the French since 1900* (London, 2005), pp. 252, 305.

5 A.-G. Marsot, 'The crucial year: Indochina 1946', *Journal of Contemporary History* 19 (1984), 337–54; Kedward, *La Vie en bleu*, chs 13–14; I. M. Wall, *French Communism in the Era of Stalin: The Quest for Unity and Integration, 1945–1962* (Westport, 1983); J.-P. Rioux, *The Fourth Republic, 1944–1958* (Cambridge, 1987); W. I. Hitchcock, *France Restored: Cold War Diplomacy and the Quest for Leadership in Europe, 1944–1954* (Chapel Hill, 1998); R. F. Kuisel, *Seducing the French: The Dilemma of Americanization* (Berkeley, 1993); K. Ross, *Fast Cars, Clean Bodies: Decolonization and the Reordering of French Culture* (Cambridge, 1995).

6 C. Duchen, 'Une femme nouvelle pour une France nouvelle?', *Clio, Histoire, Femmes et Sociétés* 1 (1985), 162; C. Duchen, *Women's Rights and Women's Lives in France* (London, 1994), p. 97; M. Pollard, 'Sexing the subject: women and the French Right, 1938–58' in N. Atken and F. Tallett (eds), *The Right in France, 1789–1997* (London, 1998), pp. 231–44; C. Bard, *Les Femmes dans la société française au 20e siècle* (Paris, 2001), pp. 157–60.

7 Texier points out the significance of religion. In an ANF application the candidate's birth certificate, baptism certificate, and where applicable marriage certificate must be submitted as part of the dossier. The ANF internal rules explain that in the area of family life members must not deviate from the moral and spiritual principles upheld by the association. Divorcees who have remarried are precluded from membership. Texier, *Qu'est-ce que la noblesse?* pp. 144–7.

8 C. Grange, *Les Gens du Bottin mondain: y être, c'est en être* (Paris, 1996), pp. 154–5, 160–1, 507. Article 24 of the 1946 Constitution cited in S. Weiner, 'Two modernities: from *Elle* to *Mademoiselle*. Women's magazines in post-war France', *Contemporary European History* 8 (1999), 398.

9   1941 certificate in AD Bouches-du-Rhône 197J/72 Fonds de la famille de
    Montgrand. Among Joseph and Madeleine's children were four sons; each
    of those sons married and established families of between three and five
    children.

10 Texier, *Qu'est-ce que la noblesse?* pp. 383, 386–406; J. Tulard, *Napoléon et
    la noblesse d'Empire* (Paris, 1979), pp. 86–8; J. de Vaulchier, J. Amable de
    Saulieu, and J. de Bodinat, *Armorial de l'Association d'entraide de la Noblesse
    Française* (Paris, 2004).

11 The design appears on the escutcheon (*écu*) and the colour blue (*azur*)
    signifies France. R. Mathieu, *Le Système héraldique français* (Paris,
    1946), pp. 75–87; J. d'Eschavannes, *Traité complet de la science du blason*
    (1880) (Puiseaux, 1994), pp. 16–17; T. Veyrin-Forrer, *Précis d'Héraldique*
    (Montreal, 2004); M. Pastoureau and M. Popoff (eds), *Les Armoiries: lecture
    et identification* (Saint-Aignan-de-Grand-Lieu, 1994); M. Pastoureau, *Traité
    d'héraldique* 4 ed. (Paris, 2003).

12 Duchesse d'Abrantès, *Mémoires de madame la duchesse d'Abrantès* vol. 1
    (Paris, 1830), p. 20; J. Descheemaeker, *Les Titres de noblesse en France et dans
    les pays étrangers* vol. 1 (Paris, 1958), p. 28; P.-M. Dioudonnat, *Encyclopédie
    de la fausse noblesse et de la noblesse d'apparence* (Paris, 1982); M. de Saint
    Martin, *L'Espace de la noblesse* (Paris, 1993), pp. 74–5.

13 Cited in F. de Coustin, *Gens de noblesse* (Paris, 1989), p. 19.

14 *Bulletin de l'ANF* 1 (1933), 2. I have translated and shortened the longer
    quote cited in É. Mension-Rigau and B. Dumons, 'Conserver l'identité
    nobiliaire dans la France contemporaine' in D. Lancien and M. de Saint
    Martin (eds), *Anciennes et nouvelles aristocraties de 1800 à nos jours* (Paris,
    2007), p. 233.

15 E. C. Macknight, *Aristocratic Families in Republican France, 1870–1940*
    (Manchester, 2012), pp. 32–3.

16 W. Z. Silverman, *The Notorious Life of Gyp: Right-Wing Anarchist in Fin-de-
    Siècle France* (Oxford, 1995), chs 13–14; R. Schor, *L'Anti-sémitisme en France
    pendant les années trente: prélude à Vichy* (Brussels, 1992); V. Caron, 'The
    anti-Semitic revival in France in the 1930s: the socioeconomic dimension
    reconsidered', *Journal of Modern History* 70 (1998), 24–73; M. Winock,
    Nationalism, Anti-Semitism, and Fascism in France, translated by J. M.
    Todd (Stanford, 1998); On xenophobia and anti-Semitism in the 1980s,
    É. Mension-Rigau, *Aristocrates et grands bourgeois: éducation, traditions,
    valeurs* (Paris, 1994), pp. 61, 379–80.

17 Mension-Rigau and Dumons, 'Conserver l'identité nobiliaire', p. 238.
    B. Dumons, 'Ainay, le quartier "blanc" de Lyon' in B. Dumons and H. Multon
    (eds), *'Blancs' et contre-révolutionnaires en Europe: espaces, réseaux, cultures
    et mémoires* (Rome, 2011), pp. 105–31; B. Dumons, 'La Nouvelle Revue
    Héraldique, Historique et Archéologique (1917–1947): l'ultime recharge
    royaliste de l'école généalogique lyonnaise' in P. Chopelin and B. Dumons

(eds), *Transmettre une fidelité: la fabrique contre-révolutionnaire du passé (Europe XIXe–XXe siècles)*. See also R. R. Locke, *French Legitimists and the Politics of Moral Order in the Early Third Republic* (Princeton, 1974); R. Bourreau, *Monarchie et modernité: l'utopie restitutionniste de la noblesse nantaise sous la IIIe République* (Paris, 1995).

18 'If aristocracies are never fond of parvenus ... it is primarily because, through their overly rapid success, the necessarily fierce manner in which they achieved it, and the naively ostentatious way they assert or publicize it, these go-getter latecomers call to mind the arbitrary violence at the source of the initial accumulation.' P. Bourdieu, *The State Nobility*, translated by L. C. Clough (Stanford, 1996), p. 318.

19 On types of nobility and terminology, Texier, *Qu'est-ce que la noblesse?*, pp. 530–45; P. du Puy de Clinchamps, *La Noblesse* 5 ed. (Paris, 1996), chs 1–2. On early modern debates, M. Gerber, *Bastards: Politics, Family, and Law in Early Modern France* (Oxford, 2012), pp. 49–71; J.-P. Labatut, *Les Noblesses européennes de la fin du XVe siècle à la fin du XVIIIe siècle* (Paris, 1978), pp. 139–49.

20 On financial problems in the 1920s see Silverman, *The Notorious Life of Gyp*, ch. 13. To compare views of poverty see M. L. Bush, *Rich Noble, Poor Noble* (Manchester, 1988), pp. 6, 7–29, 174; J. Dewald, *The European Nobility, 1400–1800* (Cambridge, 1996), pp. xvi, 22–7; M. Nassiet, *Noblesse et pauvreté: la petite noblesse en Bretagne aux XVe–XVIIIe siècles* (Rennes, 2005).

21 *Bulletin de l'ANF* 1 (1933) cited in Mension-Rigau and Dumons, 'Conserver l'identité', p. 233.

22 R. Encinas de Munagorri, *Introduction générale au droit* Revised ed. (Paris, 2006), pp. 77–80, 85–91; S. Labadi, *UNESCO, Cultural Heritage and Outstanding Universal Value* (Walnut Creek, CA, 2013), p. 11.

23 A. Desvallées, 'A l'origine du mot patrimoine' in D. Poulot (ed.), *Patrimoine et modernité* (Paris, 1998), pp. 89–105; F. Bercé, *Des Monuments historiques au patrimoine, du XVIIIe siècle à nos jours* (Paris, 2000).

24 P. Nora, 'The era of commemoration' in P. Nora (ed.), *Realms of Memory: Rethinking the French Past*, English ed. L. D. Kritzman, translated by A. Goldhammer, 3 vols (New York, 1996–98), vol. 3, pp. 621–6.

25 D. Poulot, *Patrimoine et musées: l'institution de la culture* (Paris, 2003), pp. 152–3.

26 On Franco-Polish connections, J. Dumanowski and M. Figeac (eds), *Noblesse française et noblesse polonaise: mémoire, identité, culture XVI–XXe siècles* (Pessac, 2006).

27 S. Malinowski, 'A counter-revolution d'outre-tombe: notes on the French aristocracy and the extreme right during the Third Republic and the Vichy Regime' in K. Urbach (ed.), *European Aristocracies and the Radical Right 1918–1939* (Oxford, 2007), p. 22.

28 P. Bourdieu, *The Field of Cultural Production: Essays on Art and Literature*,

translated by R. Johnson (New York, 1993); J. Webb, T. Schirato, and G. Danaher, *Understanding Bourdieu* (Crows Nest, 2002), pp. 107–9.

29   Nora, 'The era of commemoration', p. 623.

30   B. L. van Blarcomma and C. Kayahana, 'Assessing the economic impact of a UNESCO World Heritage designation', *Journal of Heritage Tourism* 6 (2011), 143–64; B. S. Frey and L. Steiner, 'World Heritage List: does it make sense?', *International Journal of Cultural Policy* 17 (2011), 555–73; J. Jokilehto, 'World Heritage: observations on decisions related to cultural heritage', *Journal of Cultural Heritage Management and Sustainable Development* 1 (2011), 61–74; L. Meskell, 'UNESCO's World Heritage Convention at 40 challenging the economic and political order of international heritage conservation', *Current Anthropology* 54 (2013), 483–94.

31   In 2017 some of the key bodies are: Centre d'interprétation de l'architecture et du patrimoine (CIAP), Direction régionale des affaires culturelles (DRAC), Institut national du patrimoine (INP); La Fondation du patrimoine; and Laboratoire de recherche des monuments historiques (LRMH).

32   K. Urbach, 'Age of no extremes? The British aristocracy torn between the House of Lords and the Mosley movement' in Urbach, *European Aristocracies*, p. 65.

33   The point is not to track here the educational establishments attended by those nobles whose names are mentioned. The observations I make connect with Bourdieu's findings about education of elites in twentieth-century France, especially the role of *grandes écoles*. See Bourdieu, *The State Nobility*, pp. 285–90, 300–20.

34   Editorial in L. Réau, M. Fleury, and G.-M. Leproux, *Histoire du vandalisme: les monuments détruits de l'art français* (originally published 1959) (Paris, 1994), p. 928. The emphasis on vandalism is also applied in M. Greenhalgh, *Destruction of Cultural Heritage in Nineteenth-Century France: Old Stones versus Modern Identities* (Leiden, 2015).

35   F. Choay, *L'Allégorie du patrimoine* 4 ed. (Paris, 2007), pp. 73–87, 107–8; Poulot, *Patrimoine et musées*, pp. 125–6.

36   N. Adamson, '"Circles of Belief": Patronage, Taste and Shared Creativity in Odilon Redon's Decorative Painting', *Studies in the Decorative Arts* (1996), 107–30; P. Bourdieu, 'The production of belief: contribution to an economy of symbolic goods' in *The Field*, pp. 74–80. See also P. Chaleyssin, *La Peinture mondaine de 1870 à 1960* (Paris, 1993); R. Jensen, *Marketing Modernism in Fin-de-Siècle Europe* (Princeton, 1994), pp. 18–20, 28, 36, 50, 80, 84; B. Whitney Kean, *French Painters, Russian Collectors: The Merchant Patrons of Modern Art in Pre-Revolutionary Russia* (London, 1983), ch. 6; N. J. Troy, *Modernism and the Decorative Arts in France: Art Nouveau to Le Corbusier* (New Haven, 1991), pp. 7–51.

37   Owners' frequency of moving home has complicated the task of reconstructing how the works looked within rooms. The distemper technique

used by Vuillard leads to flaking and dispersion of pigments, hence their fragility. G. Groom, *Edouard Vuillard Painter-Decorator: Patrons and Projects, 1892–1912* (New Haven, 1993), pp. 2–3, 36–9, 59–65, 95–6, 113–19, 139–43, 162–4, 175–7, 195–9.

38 Catalogue and flyers for Galérie Georges Petit in AN AP 31/ 77 Fonds Murat; Kean, *French Painters, Russian Collectors*, pp. 134–5, 154; Troy, *Modernism*, pp. 7–51; Jensen, *Marketing Modernism*, ch. 2; A. Distel, 'Léon Clapisson: Patron and Collector' in C. Bailey (ed.), *Renoir's Portraits: Impressions of an Age* (New Haven, 1997), pp. 77–86; R. B. King, *The Vanderbilt Homes* (New York, 1989).

39 L. Garafola, *Diaghilev's Ballets Russes* (Oxford, 1989), ch. 10, esp. pp. 278, 284; P. Assouline, *Le Dernier des Camondo* (Paris, 1999), ch. 4; D. Wilson, *Rothschild: A Story of Wealth and Power* (London, 1994), pp. 246–8.

40 Assouline, *Le Dernier*, p. 246. For the collection received by the Louvre in accordance with Isaac's will, see pp. 248–9. N. Gasc and G. Mabille, *Le Musée Nissim de Camondo* (Paris, 1997).

41 Letters counter-signed by Pichon and signed by ambassador Jusseraud plus 1 May 1910 from the prince de Béarn to Pichot in AD Charente J 1090 Fonds Galard, Brassac, Béarn, Chalais. J. Descheemaeker, *Les Titres de noblesse en France et dans les pays étrangers* vol. 1 (Paris, 1958), p. 26.

42 D. Poulot, *Une histoire des musées de France XVIII–XXe siècle* (Paris, 2008), p. 7. See also D. J. Sherman, *Worthy Monuments. Art Museums and the Politics of Culture in Nineteenth-Century France* (Cambridge, 1989); F. Haskell, *History and Its Images, Art and the Interpretation of the Past* (New Haven, 1993); R. Thomson, *The Troubled Republic: Visual Culture and Social Debate in France 1889–1900* (New Haven, 2004).

43 D. Mackay Quynn, 'The art confiscations of the Napoleonic wars', *American Historical Review* 50 (1945), 437–60; Tulard, *Napoléon et la noblesse*, pp. 123–6; W. Friedlaender, *David to Delacroix*, translated by R. Goldwater (Cambridge, MA, 1980), pp. 60–6; J. H. Merryman (ed.), *Imperialism, Art and Restitution* (Cambridge, 2006).

44 D. Byrne cited in G. Karskens, 'Engaging artefacts: urban archaeology, museums and the origins of Sydney', *Tasmanian Historical Studies* 7 (2000), 49.

45 R. G. Saisselin, *The Bourgeois and the Bibelot* (New Brunswick, 1984); T. Stammers, 'The bric-à-brac of the old régime: collecting and cultural history in post-revolutionary France', *French History* 22 (2008), 295–315; T. Stammers, 'Catholics, collectors and the Commune: heritage as counter-revolution in Paris, 1860–1909', *French Historical Studies* 37 (2014), 53–87.

46 Mension-Rigau, *Aristocrates*, pp. 134–5.

47 AD Indre-et-Loire 152/82 Fonds de Biencourt for inventories of household items; 152/83 autographs and catalogues; 152/ 84 paintings; 152/85 library; 152/86 porcelains and bronzes.

48 AN AP 86/9 Fonds de la Maison de Jaucourt; AN AP 31/77 Fonds Murat;
    AD Maine-et-Loire 249J/5 Fonds de la famille Montlaur; Macknight,
    Aristocratic Families, ch. 3; Poulot, *Une histoire des musées*, chs 4–6;
    M. Girouard, *Life in the French Country House* (London, 2000), pp. 308–10,
    331.

49 T. Griffiths, 'Social history and deep time', *Tasmanian Historical Studies* 7
    (2000), 27; M. G. Simpson, *Making Representations: Museums in the Post-
    Colonial Era* (London, 1996); S. Barczewski, *Country houses and the British
    Empire, 1700–1930* (Manchester, 2016); Poulot, *Patrimoine et musées*, pp.
    158–9, 202. For cultural histories of empire see, for example, F. Cooper
    and A. L. Stoler, *Tensions of Empire: Colonial Cultures in a Bourgeois World*
    (Berkeley, 1997); E. Ezra, *The Colonial Unconscious: Race and Culture in
    Interwar France* (Ithaca, 2000); T. Chafer and A. Sackur (eds), *Promoting
    the Colonial Idea: Propaganda and Visions of Empire in France* (Basingstoke,
    2002); N. Oulebsir, *Les Usages du patrimoine: monuments, musées et poli-
    tique colonial en Algérie (1830–1930)* (Paris, 2004); M. Evans (ed.), *Empire
    and Culture: The French Experience* (New York, 2004).

50 Mension-Rigau, *Aristocrates*, p. 468; Urbach, 'Age of no extremes?' p. 70.
    Hunting was part of the lifestyle of French nobles and royalty in Africa.
    Letters in AN AP 31/66 Fonds Murat; photographs in Henri, Comte de
    Paris, *Mon album de famille*, text by M. de Grèce (Paris, 1996), pp. 72, 86,
    88–9, 91, 129.

51 Macknight, *Aristocratic Families*, ch. 3; AD Loir-et-Cher 111J/14 Fonds de la
    famille Gilbert-Beauregard; AD Maine-et-Loire 249J/5 Fonds de la famille
    Montlaur. 'L'Hôtel Lambert ravagé par un incendie', *Le Monde*, 11 July 2013;
    'Le Château de Paulhac sous surveillance', *La Montagne* 1 August 2013.

52 On tractors and other aspects of twentieth-century agriculture see G. Duby
    and A. Wallon (eds), *Histoire de la France rurale* vol. 4 *La Fin de la France
    paysanne depuis 1914* by M. Gervais, M. Jollivet, and Y. Tavernier (Paris,
    1977); B. Hervieu, N. Mayer, P. Muller, F. Purseigle, and J. Rémy (eds), *Les
    Mondes agricoles en politique* (Paris, 2010).

53 M. de Saint-Pierre, *Les Aristocrates* (Paris, 1954), pp. 50–9. For photo-
    graphs of châteaux in the 1940s see H. Lemaitre, *Châteaux en France* (Paris,
    1948).

54 P. Mandler, *The Fall and Rise of the Stately Home* (New Haven, 1997),
    p. 325. Submachine guns were in the park at Azay-le-Rideau. J. Vassort, *Les
    Châteaux de la Loire au fil des siècles: art, politique et société* (Paris, 2012),
    p. 307.

55 AD Loir-et-Cher 111J/15 Fonds de la famille Gilbert-Beauregard.
    L. L. Downs, *Childhood in the Promised Land: Working-class Movements and
    the Colonies de Vacances in France, 1880–1960* (Durham, NC, 2002).

56 17 December 1948 in AD Maine-et-Loire 249J/5 Fonds de la famille
    Montlaur.

57 10 February 1944 in AD Loir-et-Cher 111J/13 Fonds de la famille Gilbert-Beauregard.

58 Rioux, *The Fourth Republic*, pp. 18–19.

59 Inventory with photographs AD Manche 138J Chartrier du Chastel; Inventory AD Manche 262J Chartrier du Theré.

60 Exhibition 'Une maison d'enfants au Cluzel' October 2014 at Saint-Eble, Haute-Loire. I am indebted to Madame Simone Sauges for her insights.

61 19 October 1954 in AD Loir-et-Cher 111J/13 Fonds de la famille Gilbert-Beauregard.

62 C. de Bartillat, *Histoire de la noblesse française: de 1789 à nos jours* vol. 2 *Les Nobles du Second Empire à la fin du XXe siècle* (Paris, 1991), pp. 159–61, 531–7; É. Mension-Rigau, *La Vie des châteaux: mise en valeur et exploitation des châteaux privés dans la France contemporaine* (Paris, 1999); Girouard, *Life*, ch. 9.

63 Vassort, *Les Châteaux de la Loire*, pp. 337–40.

64 M. Pinçon and M. Pinçon-Charlot, *Les Ghettos du gotha: au cœur de la grande bourgeoisie* (Paris, 2007), pp. 272–3. On Franco-British contacts and Britain's National Trust see Mandler, *The Fall and Rise*, pp. 300–1, 381–2. On cities see L. Bernie, M. Dormaels, and Y. Le Fur, *Le Patrimonialisation de l'urbain* (Paris, 2012).

65 Nora, 'The era of commemoration', pp. 622, 627–8; S. C. Rogers, 'Natural histories: the rise and fall of French rural studies', *French Historical Studies* 19 (1995), 381–97; P. Daileader and P. Whalen (eds), *French Historians 1900–2000: New Historical Writing in Twentieth-Century France* (Chichester, 2010).

66 Poulot, *Patrimoine et musées*, p. 122; J.-P. Chaline, *Sociabilité et érudition: les sociétés savantes en France, XIXe–XXe siècle* (Paris, 2001), pp. 206–12, 218–20, 242–52, 271. AD Côtes-d'Armor 60J Frotier de La Messelière.

67 Duby and Wallon, *Histoire de la France rurale* vol. 4, pp. 242–309, 383–417; Hervieu et al, *Les Mondes agricoles*, pp. 19–38, 111–29.

68 Texier, *Qu'est-ce que la noblesse?* pp. 142–3.

69 Mandler, *The Fall and Rise*, p. 331.

70 Urbach, 'Age of no extremes?' pp. 53–4. See the editor's preface noting cuts (requested by the owners) in the published version of a manuscript. É. Mension-Rigau (ed.), *Journal de Constance de Castelbajac, marquise de Breteuil 1885–1886* (Paris, 2003).

71 AD Lot 40J/7 Fonds de la famille Vassal et famille alliées. M. Halbwachs, *The Collective Memory* (*La Mémoire collective*, 1950), translated by F. J. Didder Jr and V. Yazdi Ditter (New York, 1980), pp. 134–5.

72 J. Lartigaut, inventory AD Lot 13J Fonds Camy-Gozon.

73 J. Favier (ed.), *La Pratique archivistique française* (Paris, 2008), pp. 70–9; C. de Tourtier-Bonazzi, 'La Loi du 3 janvier 1979 et les archives privées', *La Gazette des Archives* 107 (1979), 261–70; F. Hildesheimer, *Les Archives, pour-*

quoi? comment? (Paris, 1984), pp. 23–37, 119–20; S. d'Huart, 'Les Archives privées aux Archives Nationales', *La Gazette des Archives* 85 (1974), 79–88; J. Sablou, 'Les Archives privées dans les Archives départementales', *La Gazette des Archives* 85 (1974), 89–103.

74 5 October 1970 and 10 October 1970 in AD Loir-et-Cher 97J/13 Fonds Taillevis et familles alliées.

75 J. Descheemaeker, *Les Titres de noblesse en France et dans les pays étrangers* vol. 2 (Paris, 1958), pp. 15–49. On early modern legislation see Labatut *Les Noblesses européennes*, pp. 150–9. On fake titles and Italy's fascist regime see G. Rumi, 'La politica nobiliaire del regno d'Italia 1861–1946' in *Les Noblesses européennes au XIXe siècle* (Rome, 1988), pp. 577–93.

76 Texier, *Qu'est-ce que la noblesse?* p. 148; Saint Martin, *L'Espace*, p. 30; Mension-Rigau, *Aristocrates*, p. 356.

77 Texier, *Qu'est-ce que la noblesse?* pp. 135–7, 144–8; Mension-Rigau and Dumons, 'Conserver l'identité nobiliaire', pp. 239, 241.

78 C. Sowerwine, *France since 1870: Culture, Politics and Society* (Basingstoke, 2001), pp. 274–5.

79 F. de Negroni, *La France noble* (Paris, 1974), p. 70; K. Kete, *The Beast in the Boudoir: Petkeeping in Nineteenth-Century Paris* (Berkeley, 1994), pp. 64–75, 133–4.

80 P. Perrot, *Le Luxe: une richesse entre faste et confort XVIIIe–XIXe siècle* (Paris, 1995); N. Coquery, *L'Hôtel aristocratique: le marché du luxe à Paris au XVIIIe siècle* (Paris, 1998); A. Gerritsen and G. Riello (eds), *Writing Material Culture History* (London, 2014); D. Masseau, *Une histoire du bon goût* (Paris, 2014), P. McNeil and G. Riello, *Luxury: A Rich History* (Oxford, 2016).

81 P. Bourdieu, *Distinction: A Social Critique of the Judgement of Taste*, translated by R. Nice (London, 2000), p. 16, and for analysis of food and drink consumption pp. 179–200; P. P. Ferguson, 'A Cultural Field in the Making: Gastronomy in 19th-Century France', *American Journal of Sociology* 104 (1998), 597–641; E. C. Macknight, 'Dining in aristocratic households in nineteenth-century France: a study of female authority', *Virtus* 23 (2016), 105–23. See also J.-R. Pitte, *Gastronomie française: Histoire et géographie d'une passion* (Paris, 1991); A. B. Trubek, *Haute Cuisine. How the French Invented the Culinary Profession* (Philadelphia, 2000); S. J. Terrio, *Crafting the Culture and History of French Chocolate* (Berkeley, 2000); C. Garnier, 'Les Petits Français à l'école du goût', *The French Review*, 74 (2001), 496–504; M. de Soucy, *Contested Tastes: Foie Gras and the Politics of Food* (Princeton, 2016).

82 Negroni, *La France noble*, pp. 70–1. For expenditure on clothing and beauty products, implications for bodily hexis, and household furnishing see Bourdieu, *Distinction*, pp. 77–9, 200–8.

83 N. Elias, *The Civilising Process* vol. 1 *The History of Manners*, translated by E. Jephcott (Oxford, 1982), p. 38; L. Hunt, *The Family Romance of the*

French Revolution (Berkeley, 1992), pp. 96–7; A. de Baecque, *The Body Politic: Corporeal Metaphor in Revolutionary France 1770–1800*, translated by C. Mandell (Stanford, 1993), pp. 233–46.

84 B. Le Wita, *French Bourgeois Culture* (Cambridge, 1994), p. 68. On 'bourgeois' as a pejorative term see pp. 26–7, 53–6. There are problems of definition associated with use of 'bourgeois' as an adjective: see W. M. Reddy, 'The Concept of Class' in M. L. Bush (ed.), *Social Orders and Social Classes in Europe since 1500: Studies in Social Stratification* (London, 1992), pp. 13–25.

85 M. Lamont, *Money, Morals, and Manners: The Culture of the French and American Upper-Middle Class* (Chicago, 1992), pp. xx, 4–13; Elias, *The Civilising Process* vol. 1, p. 49; M. Lamont and M. Fournier (eds), *Cultivating Difference: Symbolic Boundaries and the Making of Inequality* (Chicago, 1992).

86 Negroni, *La France noble*, p. 71; Bourdieu, *Distinction*, p. xi.

87 Bourdieu, *The State Nobility*, p. 315.

88 Texier, *Qu'est-ce que la noblesse?* pp. 316–17.

89 Kedward, *La Vie en bleu*, p. 486 and ch. 18; Pinçon and Pinçon-Charlot, *Les Ghettos*, pp. pp. 69, 74. On Chirac, 'uses of history', and national identity see Jeremy Ahearne, *Government through Culture and the Contemporary French Right* (New York, 2016), ch. 4.

90 Pinçon and Pinçon-Charlot, *Les Ghettos*, pp. 15, 56–7, 71–3, 239–48, 274.

91 Pinçon and Pinçon-Charlot, *Les Ghettos*, pp. 107, 110–11, 205–15.

92 'La Vie de château', *Propriétés Le Figaro* 163 (2016), pp. 37–40. Code du patrimoine Articles L. 621-1 and L. 621-25; A. de Montgolfier, Senator for Eure-et-Loire, 'Rapport sur la valorisation du patrimoine culturel' Submitted to the President of the Republic 8 October 2010, pp. 2, 3, 29, 33.

93 'La Vie de château', *Propriétés Le Figaro* 163 (2016), pp. 37–40; Fondation pour les monuments historiques, *Rapport annuel d'activité 2015* (Paris, 2015), pp. 21–3.

94 M. de Saint Martin, 'L'Espace de l'aristocratie en France: désagrégation et récomposition(s)' in Lancien and Saint Martin, *Anciennes et nouvelles aristocraties*, pp. 65–80. For the similarities in northern Italy: A. Cardoza, 'Strategies of social reproduction and reconversion within the Piedmontese aristocracy 1880–1940' in Lancien and Saint Martin, *Anciennes et nouvelles aristocraties*, p. 184.

95 Montgolfier, 'Rapport', pp. 2, 3, 29, 33.

96 J. H. Falk and L. D. Dierking, *Learning from Museums: Visitor Experiences and the Making of Meaning* (Lanham, MD, 2000), pp. 137, 150; L. H. Silverman, 'Personalizing the past: a review of literature with implications for historical interpretation', *Journal of Interpretation Research* 2 (1997), 1–12; L. Beck and T. T. Cable, *Interpretation for the Twenty-First Century: Fifteen Guiding Principles for Interpreting Nature and Culture* (Champaign, 2002);

D. M. Knudson, T. T. Cable, and L. Beck, *Interpretation of Cultural and Natural Resources* 2 ed. (State College, PA, 2003).

97 J. Malcolm-Davies, 'Borrowed robes: the educational value of costumed interpretation at historic sites', *International Journal of Heritage Studies* 10 (2004), 277–93; N. Deufel, 'Telling her story of war: challenging gender bias at Culloden Battlefield Visitor Centre', *Historical Reflections: Réflexions historiques* 37 (2011), 72–89.

98 M. Halbwachs, *The Collective Memory* (*La Mémoire collective*, 1950), translated by F. J. Didder Jr and V. Yazdi Ditter (New York, 1980), pp. 129–30.

99 'Les Portraits de famille sont de retour', *La Montagne*, 12 June 2016; J. and A. Cassaigne, *500 châteaux de France: un patrimoine d'exception*, text by S. Bogrow (Paris, 2012); D. Meyer, *Versailles: Visitor's Guide* (Paris, 1997).

100 A. J. Mayer, *The Persistence of the Old Regime: Europe to the Great War* (New York, 1981), p. 329; Earl of Portsmouth cited in Urbach, 'Age of no extremes?' p. 62.

101 E. Wasson, *Aristocracy and the Modern World* (New York, 2006), p. 119; W. D. Godsey, 'Nobles and modernity', *German History* 20 (2002), 504–21; Pinçon and Pinçon-Charlot, *Les Ghettos*; Lancien and Saint Martin, *Anciennes et nouvelles aristocraties*; Urbach, *European Aristocracies*.

102 P. Bourdieu, 'Postface. La Noblesse: capital social et capital symbolique' in Lancien and Saint Martin, *Anciennes et nouvelles aristocraties*, p. 385.

Conclusion

This history opened with a record of the inhabitants of La Malène who in November 1793 looked around at the smouldering remains of their homes. Perhaps a few of those rural people speculated about the fate of the local noble family, the Brun de Montesquiou, when they saw the château de La Malène ablaze. It was impossible to know then whether noble landowners in Gévaudan or any other province might receive compensation for losses or recover property that had been confiscated owing to revolutionary reforms. War and economic problems rumbled on, but there were signs by 1800 that 'after ten years of revolution, after its official suppression, the nobility still had another future'. Michel Figeac cautions against imposing chronological limits when viewing the evolution of the Second Estate. Reflecting on the *longue durée* approach to writing the history of France: 'The interest is precisely to see how the nobility, similar to a phoenix, periodically succeeds in transforming itself to be reborn from its ashes.'[1]

Charles Tilly observed about people migrating from one place to another in nineteenth-century Europe that 'having transferable skills promotes migration, but having a stake in the land impedes it'.[2] While Tilly's assessment holds true for many groups and individuals, who moved either permanently to a new home or on a temporary seasonal basis for work, it is less applicable to nobility who had both a stake in the land and were also migratory. Nobles in early modern France had routinely travelled between estates and towns as well as abroad. This pattern of lifestyle continued across the nineteenth century and into the twentieth as nobles spent the winter and spring in an urban residence, then departed with their household to a landed estate for the summer and autumn.

The Brun de Montesquiou family provides an illustration of real estate ownership characteristic of provincial *petite noblesse*; it held a town-house in Mende, a château by the river Tarn and a sprinkling of lands within Gévaudan. Jean-Baptiste de Brun de Montesquiou, the *émigré*, had reached Paris in 1791 but then returned to his native region, hiding in the mountains of Aubrac on the border of Gévaudan and Rouergue, where he died in June 1794. Jean-Baptiste's father Gabriel, recognising that 'death had put [his eldest son] out of the harm of monsters that burn good people [*les honnêtes gens*] as well as rich ones', set about recovering patrimony for his grandchildren.[3]

In 1795–6 Gabriel repurchased from the nation the properties that had belonged to him and his wife. La Malène was the first, acquired at auction for 14,700 *assignats*. Next was Cauquenas at 5,400 *assignats*, then Récoulettes at 27,787 *assignats*, and finally Mazel at 21,809 *assignats*. There is no evidence that Gabriel was in competition with other buyers for these properties; even the wealthiest of local peasants looking to increase their smallholding may have been hesitant to bid.[4] The land was far from being prime real estate. Récoulettes was a conglomeration of fields set in hollows and valleys, 'subject to fogs because of its position'. Parts of the property were covered in thick undergrowth with a root system that was tangled among boulders making it 'impossible to penetrate and destroy'. Cauquenas and Mazel, positioned on the limestone plateau (*le causse*), consisted of dry rocky terrain that produced meagre amounts of grain, mostly rye and barley. The house at Cauquenas was so dilapidated it had to be propped up with beams and the one at Mazel was 'a ruin'.[5]

A traveller entering the village of La Malène in 1798 would have seen the château still in its burnt-out state for there were insufficient funds for its repair. But one of the houses owned by the family was rebuilt in 1795 and three years later restoration began on a two-storey building beside the gateway to the château. Two carpenters from the nearby village of Sainte Énimie raised the walls, fitted the windows, and laid beams for the new roof; two masons attended to the stonework; labourers cut planks, hammered nails, and lugged sand. It was arduous work that took the better part of a year to complete. According to Gabriel each of the men was given wine twice per day, in addition to wages and food. Since wine was very rarely drunk by the rural poor it may have been an incentive to continue until the work was done. 'All the materials were carried on the men's shoulders since carts and oxen cannot be used in these steep craggy hills.'[6]

In her thoughtful 'allegory of patrimony', Françoise Choay reminds us of the argument advanced by Aloïs Riegl that monuments of stone and wood are not at the time of their building understood to be historic monuments. It is by combining the history of law with social, political, and cultural history that we may trace how changes in attitudes have led people to assign heritage 'value' to sites and structures.[7] Debates about value in the heritage sector are complex, with a long history of transnational discussion and multilateral decision-making. Professionals who specialise in interpretation know that because of those debates it is essential to have self-reflexive thought, qualification, and training to undertake the responsibilities of communicating with the public at heritage sites across the globe today.[8]

The UNESCO Convention for the Protection of the World Cultural and Natural Heritage in 1972 led to the development of the concept of Outstanding Universal Value and its refinement in 2008. The statements produced for World Heritage Sites have to explain the cultural or natural significance that is so exceptional as to transcend national boundaries and be of common importance for present and future generations of all humanity.[9] Among the committee decisions that have generated controversy was the inscription of the Nord-Pas de Calais mining basin, including industrial waste heaps, on the World Heritage List in 2012. In that same year there were 962 sites on the World Heritage List: 745 cultural sites, 188 natural sites and 29 mixed properties. The list in the early twenty-first century remains dominated by sites within Europe but is becoming more representative and inclusive of sites on other continents as well. Most of the sites recognised to be World Heritage in Danger are located in Africa.[10]

The theme for the 2016 Journées du patrimoine in Europe was citizenship. Among a diverse array of cultural heritage sites in France, châteaux constitute just one category with immense variety within that single category. Integral to the promotion of tourism, splendid images of these buildings are ubiquitous in brochures, books, websites, and souvenirs. It is a brilliant stimulus for a debate among students when châteaux are instead photographed as abandoned, weed-infested, condemned structures and the photographs are published together with images of decrepit, junked monuments of industry, transport, and technology.[11] One of numerous ways in which people engage with *le patrimoine* is the practice of donating online via crowdfunding platforms. An average of €6,000 is often raised collectively for a restoration project but for a very iconic structure the total can be much higher, for example €68,565 from 1,183 donors for the Panthéon. In 2013 the Fondation du patrimoine raised funds of €12.2 million, of which €7.5 million came from individuals and the remaining €4.7 million from businesses, associations, and other community collectives. The average amount given by individual donors was €198. With the total funds raised in 2013 the Fondation du patrimoine supported 37,844 projects. Around 2,500 of those projects were small village churches, war memorials, former school buildings, mills, fountains, public statues, and other elements of le petit patrimoine dotted through the French countryside.[12]

As the criteria for classifying heritage evolves in different countries, and categories of 'culture' and 'nature' morph and expand, so new questions are asked about the future of the monuments on paper or other media in the archives. Photographs of damaged archival materials, recoverable with scientific techniques of conservation, capture the vulnerability behind a 'dream of eternity'.[13] Yet parchment, wax, leather, and paper will survive longer than billions of records produced in the digital age, cast into 'trash' as lines are redrawn between archive and ephemera. Archivists' writings highlight concerns over preservation, accountability, access, and other issues of consequence for future research.[14] Now, as in the past, communication between historians and archivists is essential; otherwise we risk 'an ever-growing divide between the multiplicity of interpretive possibilities many historians hope to see the archive yield and the expectations of absolute truth which a variety of more general publics, undergraduates and graduate students included, not only desire but demand'.[15]

David Higgs remarked that 'social and economic historians have perhaps been too often hasty in drawing up single-dimensional views of power in assessing the position of the French nobility in the nineteenth and twentieth centuries'.[16] My approach in this book has been to try to integrate as much as possible the intangibles. 'Power' is understood to encompass not only those expressions of authority that relate to material resources or physical deeds but also more subtle exercises in control deriving from traditions and beliefs underpinned by narratives over the longue durée. Transmission of names and titles, the symbolic capital, plays a key role in social reproduction of nobility. These elements of language, fundamental to social frameworks of collective memory, mean that 'through the generations there continues a totality of well-linked traditions and remembrances'.[17] That is why the history of law is critical for investigations of nobility. It is because of the way linguistic and legal mechanisms intertwine that invisible power can be exercised 'only with the complicity of those who do not want to know that they are subject to it'.[18]

In aiming for radical reversal of 'nobles' disappearance from modern French historical thought' this book has studied nobility not as a group bracketed off in isolation but rather in its relationships with other social groups.[19] There is every reason for historians to continue writing history 'from below' to understand better how dominated groups experience misrecognition and as a consequence adjust to inferior treatment or denial of resources. But when historians trivialise or omit the subject of nobility in teaching and writing modern history the effects may slow down the dismantling of so-called 'natural' distinction in fields where inequality resides. A purpose of research on nobility, in relation to other groups, is to advance the knowledge for identifying arbitrary bases of domination.[20]

In closing this study of nobility and patrimony there are two historiographical issues to address with an eye to future developments in the field. The first issue concerns terminology in writing about class and power. Academic research on nobilities in the Europe of the nineteenth and twentieth centuries is advancing and with the focus on 'noble' identity has come stronger critique of the term 'notable'. Ellis Wasson refers to 'notable' as 'a portmanteau word' that 'may superficially cover a multitude of cases' but clouds the 'vital distinctions' retained by different groups. In modern French history, we have not yet seen nobles or notables or the working class considered to be a myth in the way Sarah Maza argued for the bourgeoisie.[21] If there is a place to use the term 'notable' then it seems to be in the type of study Sylvain Milbach has presented in 2015, very much in the model of Tudesq's fine scholarship. Milbach's exhaustive account of men's parliamentary debates and journalism privileges the *histoire événementielle* approach, and takes as its subject the lay Catholic male with possessions, knowledge, connections, a family, an office that gave him public authority, a name, and often a title.[22]

But when historians consider class and power over a period of time longer than a decade or two, and seek to write history inclusive of women's experiences, then the term 'notables' becomes problematic. David Higgs argued in the 1980s, 'In local as well as in national history it appears necessary to distinguish nobles from notables'.[23] Ralph Gibson found evidence at the regional level that distinctions between noble and non-noble did matter very much, in economic and political terms. Studies by

Adeline Daumard, Jean Tulard, Claude-Isabelle Brelot, Natalie Petiteau, Éric Mension-Rigau, and many others have contributed in various ways to underline a separate 'noble' identity.[24] We have seen that noble families have been strategically preserving patronyms and *prénoms* since the Middle Ages. In nobiliary law the act of the sovereign who creates a title stipulates rules for its transmission to males and/or to females. There is twenty-first-century jurisprudence on titles as a human rights issue, and associations of nobles operate at national and European levels.[25]

The second historiographical issue concerns heritage and historical memory. Sudhir Hazareesingh writes: 'In the modern French context, the language, symbolism and practices of "patriotism" are invariably associated with the republican tradition.'[26] Both Hazareesingh and Malinowski point to a certain amount of forgetting in some history books on modern France about language, symbols, and practices from non-republican traditions. Tangible and intangible heritage from monarchical and imperial regimes provides rich source material from which historians make their interpretations of court politics, international diplomacy, military traditions, knightly and monastic orders, arts and charitable patronage, land-ownership, and law. Nobles were active in these spheres and their ethos of service to France was inspired by faith in God and country that was 'passionate and unshakeable'.[27] Hazareesingh makes an important point that the 'conflation of the genesis of "patriotism" with republican doctrine and sentiment makes little sense. The concept of the "patrie" was used by all mainstream political groups, including republicans, but also liberals, Bonapartists and Bourbon royalists.'[28]

An advantage of a *longue durée* approach is that the multiplicity of traditions and identities in France stands out more clearly. On this point, the nobility serves as a heuristic key. 'To be sure, its history is not the complete history of the nation. But nowhere else is found such continuity of life and thought.'[29] On 19 June 1790 when the deputies of the National Assembly voted to abolish the legal status of nobility, coats of arms were abolished as well. Arms were reintroduced by Napoleon I in article 14 of the 1 March 1808 statute on nobiliary titles and *majorats*. Then by decree of 17 May 1809 towns, communes, corporations, or associations were once again permitted to bear arms as a marker of identity as they had done under the *ancien régime*.

The science of heraldry illustrates the 'deep-seated interdependence' between intangible cultural heritage and tangible cultural heritage.[30] During the 1880s there was a resurgence of heraldry as communities in the departments sought help from archivists to rediscover local arms dating back to the Middle Ages. Under the provisions of the law of 5 April 1884 on municipality, towns reclaimed for use coats of arms with heraldic features such as bees, candlesticks, cows, crocodiles, ducklings, dragons, eagles, flaming hearts, *fleur de lys*, fortresses, gloves, keys, knights, lambs, lions, oak trees, palm trees, sailing ships, sheep, swords, towers, and unicorns. In 1980 the Minister of Culture, Jean-Philippe Lecat, created a Commission nationale d'héraldique presided over by the director general of the Archives nationales de France.[31]

Halbwachs wrote 'Society will abandon its ancient beliefs only if it is assured of finding others'.[32] But there is no such condition that applies in writing history. Nor is it the historian's role to praise or to condemn how and why people hold on to symbols from a very distant, or recent, past. Patrimony across France may be any number of things including tall, dented, harmonic, mossy, bittersweet, zany, muted, illegible, salty, luscious, or austere. Amid twenty-first-century perceptions and celebrations of the nation's heritage there seems to be 'an acceptance of the interplay of opposites' allowing for 'multiple patterns within a single kaleidoscope'.[33]

Notes

1 M. Figeac, *Les Noblesses en France du XVIe au milieu du XIXe siècle* (Paris, 2013), pp. 5–6. For a view across ten centuries see *L'Identité nobiliaire: dix siècles de metamorphoses, IX–XIXe siècle* (Le Mans, 1997).

2 C. Tilly, 'Did the cake of custom break?' in J. M. Merriman (ed.), *Consciousness and Class Experience in Nineteenth-Century Europe* (New York, 1979), p. 37.

3 'Observations sur les domaines' in AD Lozère 7J/7 Fonds de Saint Amand.

4 For a description of auctioning nobles' land in the Ardèche see J. M. Merriman, *The Stones of Balazuc: A French Village in Time* (New York, 2002), pp. 66–9. See also B. Bodinier and É. Teyssier, *L'Événement le plus important de la Révolution: la vente des biens nationaux* (Paris, 2000).

5 'Observations sur les domaines' in AD Lozère 7J/14 Fonds de Saint Amand.

6 'Etat et mémoire des réparations' in AD Lozère 7J/7 Fonds de Saint Amand.

7 F. Choay *L'Allégorie du patrimoine* 4 ed. (Paris, 2007), p. 21; A. Riegl, *Le Culte moderne des monuments: son essence et sa genèse* (Paris, 1984).

8 S. Donaghey, 'What is aught, but as tis valued? An analysis of strategies for the assessment of cultural heritage significance in New Zealand', *International Journal of Heritage Studies* 7 (2001), 365–80; P. Howard, *Heritage Management, Interpretation, Identity* (London, 2003); H. Deacon, 'Intangible heritage in conservation management planning: the case of Robben Island', *International Journal of Heritage Studies* 10 (2004), 309–19; S. von Lewinski (ed.), *Indigenous Heritage and Intellectual Property: Genetic Resources, Traditional Knowledge and Folklore* (The Hague, 2004);

E. Waterton, 'Whose sense of place? Reconciling archaeological perspectives with community values: cultural landscapes in England', *International Journal of Heritage Studies* 11 (2005), 309–25; N. Ndimande-Hlongwa, 'The role of indigenous place names in preserving living heritage of the Zulu people in KwaZulu-Natal', *Proceedings of ICONN* 3 (2015), 533–9.

9 S. Labadi, *UNESCO, Cultural Heritage and Outstanding Universal Value* (Walnut Creek, CA, 2013), p. 11; F. Francioni (ed.), *The 1972 World Heritage Convention: A Commentary* (Oxford, 2008).

10 S. Labadi, 'Representations of the nation and cultural diversity in discourses on World Heritage', *Journal of Social Archaeology* 7 (2007), 147–70; A. A. Arantes, 'Diversity, heritage and cultural politics', *Theory, Cuture and Society* 24 (2007), 290–6; L. Meskell, 'UNESCO's World Heritage Convention at 40 challenging the economic and political order of international heritage conservation', *Current Anthropology* 54 (2013), 483–94.

11 For photographs see A. Goumand, *France interdite et secrète* (Paris, 2015). See also H. l'Huillier, 'Archives, témoignages oraux et histoire des entreprises', *La Gazette des Archives* 139 (1987), 256–9; M. Hamon, 'Les Archives du monde du travail: les enterprises et leurs archives: le temps des mutations', *La Gazette des Archives* 142–3 (1988), 141–71; B. Schroeder-Gudehus (ed.), *La Société industrielle et ses musées: demande sociale et choix politiques, 1890–1990* (Paris, 1992).

12 'Allons enfants du patrimoine', *Le Figaro* 19 January 2014; *Culture et recherche* Special issue 'Patrimoines: enjeux contemporains de la recherche' 133 (2016).

13 *Blessures d'archives, rêve d'éternité: de la conservation préventive à la restauration* (Valence, 2004).

14 In archival science there are some common principles but national variation in approaches to application. See, for example, M. F. Daniels and T. Walch (eds), *A Modern Archives Reader: Basic Readings on Archival Theory and Practice* (Washington, 1984); M. Duchein, 'The history of European archives and the development of the archival profession in Europe', *American Archivist* 55 (1992), 14–24; S. McKemmish and F. Upward (eds), *Archival Documents: Providing Accountability through Record-Keeping* (Melbourne, 1993); L. Duranti, 'The concept of appraisal and archival theory', *American Archivist* 57 (1994), 328–45; T. Cook, 'What is past is prologue: a history of archival ideas since 1898, and the future paradigm shift', *Archivaria* 43 (1997), 17–63; L. Duranti, 'The impact of digital technology on archival science', *Archival Science* 1 (2001), 39–55; L. Craven (ed.), *What Are Archives? Cultural and Theoretical Perspectives* (Burlington, 2008); J. Ridener, *From Polders to Postmodernism: A Concise History of Archival Theory* (Litwin, 2009).

15 A. Burton, 'Introduction' in A. Burton (ed.), *Archives Stories: Facts, Fictions, and the Writing of History* (London and Durham, NC, 2005), p. 13; R. Rosenzweig, 'Scarcity or abundance? Preserving the past in a digital era', *American Historical Review* 108 (2003), 735–62.

16 D. Higgs, 'Social mobility and hereditary titles in France, 1814–1830: the majorats-sur-demande', *Histoire sociale/Social History* 14 (1981), 45.

17 M. Halbwachs, *On Collective Memory* (*Les Cadres sociaux de la mémoire*, 1925), ed. and translated by L. A. Coser (Chicago, 1992), p. 128.

18 P. Bourdieu, *Language and Symbolic Power* (*Ce que parler veut dire*, 1982), ed. J. B. Thompson, translated by G. Raymond and M. Adamson (Cambridge, 1991), p. 164.

19 J. Dewald, 'French nobles and the historians, 1820–1960' in J. M. Smith (ed.), *The French Nobility in the Eighteenth Century: Reassessments and New Approaches* (University Park, 2006), p. 306.

20 P. Bourdieu, *The State Nobility*, translated by L. C. Clough (Stanford, 1996); M. Lamont and M. Fournier (eds), *Cultivating Difference: Symbolic Boundaries and the Making of Inequality* (Chicago, 1992); M. de Saint Martin, *L'Espace de la noblesse* (Paris, 1993); P. Bourdieu, *Masculine Domination*, translated by R. Nice (Cambridge, 2001).

21 E. Wasson, *Aristocracy and the Modern World* (New York, 2006), p. 107; S. Maza, *The Myth of the French Bourgeoisie: An Essay on the Social Imaginary, 1750–1850* (Cambridge, 2003).

22 A.-J. Tudesq, *Les Grands Notables en France (1840–1849): étude historique d'une psychologie sociale* 2 vols (Paris, 1964), vol. 1, p. 457; S. Milbach, *Les Chaires ennemies: L'Église, l'État et la liberté d'enseignement secondaire dans la France des notables (1830–1850)* (Paris, 2015). But see the counter-argument in P. L. R. Higonnet and T. B. Higonnet, 'Class, corruption and politics in the French Chamber of Deputies, 1846–1848', *French Historical Studies* 5 (1967), 204–24. esp. 217, 222.

23 Higgs, 'Social mobility', 45; D. Higgs, *Nobles in Nineteenth-Century France: The Practice of Inegalitarianism* (Baltimore, 1987), pp. xii, xvi, 45, 108, 129.

24 R. Gibson, 'The Périgord: landownership, power and illusion' in R. Gibson and M. Blinkhorn (eds), *Landownership and Power in Modern Europe* (London, 1991), pp. 79–98; R. Gibson, 'The French nobility in the nineteenth century – particularly in the Dordogne' in J. Howorth and P. G. Cerny (eds), *Elites in France: Origins, Reproduction and Power* (London 1981), pp. 7–11; A. Daumard, 'Richesse de la noblesse' in F. Braudel and E. Labrousse (eds), *Histoire economique et sociale de la France* (Paris, 1976), vol. 3, pp. 933–7; J. Tulard, *Napoléon et la noblesse d'Empire* (Paris, 1979); C.-I. Brelot, *La Noblesse réinventée: les nobles de Franche-Comté de 1814 à 1870* 2 vols (Paris, 1992); N. Petiteau, *Élites et mobilités: la noblesse d'Empire au XIXe siècle (1808–1914)* (Paris, 1997), p. 391; É. Mension-Rigau, *Aristocrates et grands bourgeois: éducation, traditions, valeurs* (Paris, 1994).

25 A. Texier, *Qu'est-ce que la noblesse?* (Paris, 1988), pp. 144–8, 214–20, 376, 380–2; M. Guillaume, 'Le Sceau de France, titre nobiliaire et changement de nom' Speech to the Académie des sciences morales et politiques, 3 July 2006. On the legal case mounted by three Spanish noblewomen see S. de Salas, 'A

juste titre: le principe de la primauté de l'homme en matière de transmission de titre nobiliaire est-il contraire à la Convention européenne des Droits de l'Homme?' *Bulletin d'information sur les droits de l'homme* 49 (2000), 20–1.

26 S. Hazareesingh, 'Memory, legend and politics: Napoleonic patriotism in the Restoration era', *European Journal of Political Theory* 5 (2006), 71–84. On politicisation of language and linguistic diversity see, for example, M. Lyons, 'Politics and patois: the linguistic policy of the French Revolution', *Australian Journal of French Studies* 18 (1981), 264–81; P. McPhee, *Living the French Revolution, 1789–99* (New York, 2006), pp. 31–2, 59–60, 156–7, 206–8.

27 W. Z. Silverman, *The Notorious Life of Gyp: Right-Wing Anarchist in Fin-de-Siècle France* (Oxford, 1995), p. 211; Mension-Rigau, *Aristocrates*, pp. 427–31, 455–86; J. M. Smith, *The Culture of Merit: Nobility, Royal Service, and the Making of Absolute Monarchy in France, 1600–1789* (Ann Arbor, 1996), ch. 1; J. M. Smith, *Nobility Reimagined: The Patriotic Nation in Eighteenth-Century France* (Ithaca, 2005).

28 Hazareesingh, 'Memory', 71–2; S. Malinowski, 'A counter-revolution d'outre-tombe: notes on the French aristocracy and the extreme right during the Third Republic and the Vichy Regime' in K. Urbach (ed.), *European Aristocracies and the Radical Right 1918–1939* (Oxford, 2007), ch. 1. See also R. Forster, 'Who is a citizen? The boundaries of "la patrie": the French Revolution and the people of color 1789–91', *French Politics and Society* 7 (1989), 50–64.

29 Halbwachs, *On Collective Memory*, p. 128.

30 UNESCO Convention for the Safeguarding of the Intangible Cultural Heritage (Paris, 2003). The interdependence can also be seen in 'La Marseillaise' and statues of Marianne. M. Agulhon, *Marianne into Battle: Republican Imagery and Symbolism in France, 1789–1880*, translated by J. Lloyd (Cambridge, 1981); L. Mason, *Singing the French Revolution: Popular Songs and Revolutionary Politics in Paris* (Ithaca, 1996).

31 S. de Dainville-Barbiche, 'Les Armoiries des villes et des communes depuis la Révolution: legislation, institutions' and C. Blanc-Riehl, 'L'Héraldique des communes depuis 1870' in *Couleurs et symbolique: armoiries des villes sous le Premier Empire et la Restauration* (Paris, 2010), pp. 5–11, 17–24; J.-J. Lartigue, *Armorial général des communes de France* (Paris, 1995); Texier, *Qu'est-ce que la noblesse?* pp. 392–3; Tulard, *Napoléon et la noblesse d'Empire*, pp. 86–8; J. de Vaulchier, J. Amable de Saulieu, and J. de Bodinat, *Armorial de l'Association d'entraide de la Noblesse Française* (Paris, 2004).

32 Halbwachs, *On Collective Memory*, p. 186.

33 R. Kedward, *La Vie en bleu: France and the French since 1900* (London, 2005), p. 634.

List of families

This is an alphabetical list of nobles' patronymic names that correspond with the archival *fonds* used in primary research. Normally the *fonds* is named after the family or individual who produced it. Some *fonds* are named after a château and contain records for several families; patronymic names have been included in this list for families continuing to produce records after 1789. The province of origin and the type of nobility are given. Where applicable admission to honours of the court and/or membership of the Association d'entraide de la noblesse française (ANF) are also mentioned.

To identify nobles' patronymic names I used the following reference works that contain information on coats of arms and documentary proofs of nobility: Gaston Saffroy, *Bibliographie généalogique, héraldique et nobiliaire de la France* 5 vols (Paris, 1974); Vicomte Albert Révérend, *Les Familles titrées et anoblies au XIXe siècle* (Paris, 1974); Louis d'Izarny-Gargas, Jean-Jacques Lartigue, and Jean de Vaulchier, *Nouveau nobiliaire de France* 3 vols (Versailles, 1997); François Bluche, *Les Honneurs de la cour* 2 ed. (Paris, 2000); Jean de Vaulchier, Jacques Amable de Saulieu, and Jean de Bodinat, *Armorial de l'ANF* (Paris, 2004); Régis Valette, *Catalogue de la noblesse française* (Paris, 2007).

Abbadie (d') Béarn, *extraction*
Albertas (d') Provence, *extraction*, ANF
Alexandry d'Orengiani (d') Savoie, *extraction*, ANF

Andlau (d') Alsace, *extraction, honneurs de la cour*, ANF
Apchier (d') Auvergne, *extraction, honneurs de la cour*

Arlot de Saint-Saud (d') Périgord, *extraction*, ANF

Baillon (de) Paris, *par charge*
Bayly (de) Périgord, *extraction, honneurs de la cour*
Beaumont-Beynac (de) Périgord, *extraction, honneurs de la cour*, ANF
Belot (de) Blésois, *par charge*, ANF
Bigot de la Touanne Berry, *par charge*, ANF
Bizemont (de) Orléanais, *extraction*, ANF
Blacas d'Aulps (de) Provence, *extraction*, ANF
Bodard de la Jacopière Anjou, *par lettres* 19th century, ANF
Bonald (de) Rouergue, *extraction*, ANF
Bonnin de La Bonninière de Beaumont Touraine, *extraction, honneurs de la cour*, ANF
Bot du Grégo (du) Bretagne, *extraction*
Botherel (de) Bretagne, *extraction, honneurs de la cour*, ANF
Briet de Rainvillers Picardie, *par charge*, ANF
Brillet de Candé Anjou, *extraction, honneurs de la cour*
Brochard de La Rochebrochard Poitou, *extraction*, ANF
Brun de Montesquiou (de) Gévaudan, *extraction*
Brunet de Castelpers de Panat (de) Roussillon, *extraction*

Buisson de Bournazel (de) Rouergue, *extraction*

Callières (de) Saintonge, *extraction*
Camy (de) Quercy, *extraction*
Carbonnières (de) Limousin, *extraction, honneurs de la cour*, ANF
Cardon de Sandrans (de) Lyonnais, *par charge*
Castellane (de) Provence, *extraction, honneurs de la cour*, ANF
Chalvet de Rochemonteix Auvergne, *extraction*
Chambrun (de) Bourbonnais, *par charge*
Chanaleilles (de) Vivarais, *extraction, honneurs de la cour*
Chapel d'Espinassoux (de) Gévaudan, *par lettres* 19th century
Chastel de Servières (de) Gévaudan, *extraction*
Châteauneuf-Randon du Tournel (de) Gévaudan, *extraction, honneurs de la cour*, ANF
Chaudruc de Crazannes Saintonge, *par charge*
Chauvelin (de) Vendômois, *par charge, honneurs de la cour*
Chazelles (de) Languedoc, *par lettres* 19th century
Chevigné (de) Bretagne, *extraction, honneurs de la cour*, ANF
Choiseul (de) Champagne, *extraction, honneurs de la cour*, ANF

Clermont-Tonnerre (de) Dauphiné, *extraction, honneurs de la cour*, ANF

Comarmond (de) Lyonnais, *par charge*

Coniac (de) Bretagne, *par lettres*, ANF

Couëssin Bretagne, *extraction*, ANF

Courson (de) Bretagne, *extraction*, ANF

Courtin de Neufbourg Forez, *lettres de relief de dérogeance*, ANF

Croÿ (de) Picardie/Hainaut, *extraction, honneurs de la cour*, ANF

Cugnac (de) Périgord, *extraction, honneurs de la cour*, ANF

Dampierre (de) Picardie, *extraction*, ANF

Decazes Guyenne, *par lettres* 19th century, ANF

Dondel de Kergonano Bretagne, *extraction*

Dufour Normandie, *par charge*

Durfort Civrac de Lorge (de) Languedoc, *extraction, honneurs de la cour*, ANF

Du Teil Velay, *par lettres* 19th century

Emé de Marcieu Dauphiné, *extraction, honneurs de la cour*, ANF

Espagnet (d') Provence, *par charge*, ANF

Espivent de la Villeboisnet Bretagne, *extraction*, ANF

Estienne de Saint-Jean (d') Provence, *par charge*

Estourmel (d') Picardie, *extraction, honneurs de la cour*, ANF

Fabre (de) Languedoc, *par lettres* 19th century, ANF

Faramond (de) Rouergue, *extraction*, ANF

Faure (de) Roussillon, Capitoul de Toulouse, ANF

Fay (de) Normandie, *extraction*

Finiels (de) Languedoc, *par charge*

Fontaines (de) Normandie, *extraction*, ANF

Fontenay (de) Normandie, *extraction*

Forbin (de) Provence, *extraction, honneurs de la cour*, ANF

Forcade (de) États de Béarn

Foresta (de) Provence, *extraction*, ANF

Foucault (de) Berry, *par charge*

Framond (de) Gévaudan, *extraction*

Francheville (de) Bretagne, Scottish origin, recognised noble in France, ANF

Freslon de la Freslonnière (de) Bretagne, extraction, *honneurs de la cour*, ANF

Fresne de Virel (du) Bretagne, *extraction*, ANF

Fretard-d'Ecoyeux (de) Angoumois, *extraction*

Froissard de Broissia (de) Franche-Comté, *par lettres*, ANF

Frotier de La Messelière Poitou, *extraction*, ANF

Galard de Béarn (de) Gascogne, *extraction, honneurs de la cour*, ANF

Gallet (de) Normandie, *extraction*

Geouffre de La Pradelle (de) Limousin, *par charge*

Gérard (de) Périgord, *extraction*, ANF

Gilbert Touraine, *par charge*, ANF

Gontaut-Biron (de) Périgord, *extraction*, ANF

Gontier Toulousain, Capitoul de Toulouse

Gouvello de Keriaval (de) Bretagne, *extraction, honneurs de la cour*, ANF

Goyon de Feltre Gascogne, *par charge*

Grailly (de) Guyenne, *extraction*, ANF

Grasse (de) Provence, *extraction, honneurs de la cour*

Grassis Savoie, *par lettres*

Guillard Paris, *par charge*

Guyon de Montlivault Orléanais, *par lettres*, ANF

Hautpoul (d') Languedoc, *extraction*

Hédouville (de) Île de France, *extraction*, ANF

Hüe de la Blanche Forez, *extraction*

Isoard–Vauvenargues (d') Provence, *par charge*

Jaucourt (de) Bourgogne, *extraction, honneurs de la cour*

Kersaint (de) Bretagne, *extraction*, ANF

La Baume-Le Blanc Touraine, *extraction, honneurs de la cour*

La Borie de Campagne (de) Périgord, *par charge*, ANF

La Bourdonnaye (de) Bretagne, *extraction, honneurs de la cour*, ANF

La Croix de Chevrières Dauphiné, *par charge*, ANF

La Forest d'Armaillé (de) Bretagne, *extraction*, ANF

La Forest Divonne (de) Savoie, *extraction, honneurs de la cour*, ANF

La Haye (de) Bretagne, *extraction*

La Houssaye (de) Normandie, *extraction*

La Monneraye (de) Bretagne, *par lettres*, ANF

La Motte (de) Bretagne, *extraction*

Langlade du Chayla (de) Gévaudan, *extraction*

Langle (de) Bretagne, *extraction*, ANF

La Rochefoucauld (de) Angoumois, *extraction, honneurs de la cour*, ANF

La Rochenégly de Chayla (de) Gévaudan, *extraction*

Laugier de Beaucouse Provence, *extraction*

Le Borgne de Boigne Savoie, *par lettres* 19th century, ANF

Le Chartier de Sédouy Normandie, *par charge*, ANF

Le Chauff de Kerguénec Bretagne, *extraction*

Lecoq de Boisbaudran Angoumois, *par charge*

Le Féron Normandie, *par charge*

Le Forestier Normandie, *extraction*

Le Fournier Normandie, *par lettres*

Le Gonidec de Traissan Bretagne, *extraction*, ANF

Le Gouvello du Timat Bretagne, *extraction*

Le Guennec Bretagne, *extraction*

Lenfernat (de) Bourgogne, *extraction*

Le Ray d'Abrantès Paris, *par lettres* 19th century

Le Roy Normandie, *par lettres* 19th century

L'Escale (de) Lorraine, *extraction*, ANF

Lespinasse (de) Normandie, *extraction*

L'Estourbeillon (de) Bretagne, *extraction*

Le Tellier de Louvois Paris, *par charge, honneurs de la cour*

Le Veneur de Tillières Normandie, *extraction, honneurs de la cour*

Lévesque de Puyberneau Poitou, *extraction*

Lévis Mirepoix (de) Languedoc, *extraction, honneurs de la cour,* ANF

Lezay de Marnesia (de) Franche-Comté, *extraction, honneurs de la cour*

Liebhaber (de) Saxony, French naturalisation

Luppé (de) Armagnac, *extraction, honneurs de la cour*, ANF

Mackau (de) Alsace, Irish origin recognised noble in France

Madaillan Périgord, *lettres de relief de dérogeance*, ANF

Mahuet (de) Lorraine, *par lettres*

Maillard de la Gournerie Bretagne, *extraction*

Maison Paris, *par lettres* 19th century

Maréchal de Longeville Franche-Comté, *par charge*

Marescot (de) Normandie, *par lettres*

Marne (de) Lorraine, *extraction*

Marÿe de Marigny Poitou, *par charge*

Massol (de) Bourgogne, *par charge*, ANF

Metz-Noblat (de) Lorraine, *extraction*, ANF

Milleville Orléanais, *par charge*

Molette de Morangiès (de) Auvergne, *extraction, honneurs de la cour*, ANF

Montrichard (de) Franche-Comté, *extraction*, ANF

Moré de Charaix (de) Gévaudan, *extraction*

Morel (de) Picardie, *par lettres*

Morel de La Colombe Auvergne, *extraction*, ANF

Moucheron (de) Normandie, *extraction*, ANF

Mullot de Villenaut (de) Nivernais, *extraction*

Murat Quercy, *par lettres* 19th century, ANF

Nagu (de) Beaujolais, *extraction, honneurs de la cour*

Narbonne-Lara (de) Languedoc, *extraction, honneurs de la cour*

Nettancourt (de) Champagne/ Lorraine, *extraction, honneurs de la cour*

Orillard de Villemanzy Touraine, *par lettres* 19th century

Passemar de Saint-André Languedoc, *extraction*, ANF

Perrochel de Grandchamp (de) Maine, *par charge*, ANF

Pilliers (des) Lorraine, *extraction*

Pradier d'Agrain (de) Velay/ Bourgogne, *par lettres*, ANF

Quatrebarbes (de) Anjou, *extraction, honneurs de la cour*, ANF

Quentin Normandie, *par lettres*

Quifistre de Bavallan Bretagne, *extraction, honneurs de la cour*

Quillebeuf (de) Normandie, *par lettres*, 19th century

Raymond (de) Rouergue, ANF

Reinach (de) Haut Alsace, *extraction*, ANF

Ripert d'Alauzier Comtat Venaissin, *extraction*, ANF

Rochechouart de Mortemart (de) Limousin, *extraction, honneurs de la cour*, ANF

Rolland du Noday Bretagne, *extraction*, ANF

Rozières (de) Lorraine, *par lettres*, ANF

Sade (de) Comtat Venaissin, *extraction, honneurs de la cour*, ANF

Saint-Astier (de) Périgord, *extraction, honneurs de la cour*

Saint-Blimond (de) Picardie, *extraction*

Saint-Exupéry (de) Périgord, *extraction, honneurs de la cour*, ANF

Salmon de Loiray (de) Orléanais, *extraction*

Sanzillon (de) Périgord, *extraction*

Sarcus (de) Picardie, *extraction*, ANF

Sesmaisons (de) Bretagne, *extraction, honneurs de la cour*, ANF

Suremain (de) Bourgogne, *par charge*

Taillepied Île de France, *par charge*, ANF

Taillevis de Perrigny Blésois, *extraction*

Talleyrand-Périgord (de) Périgord, *extraction, honneurs de la cour*, ANF

Teillard Auvergne, *extraction*

Teillard Rancilhac de Chazelles
Auvergne, *par lettres*, 19th
century

Théas de Caille de Thorenc (de)
Provence, aggregated

Torrilhon de Vacherolles (de)
Velay, *par charge*

Tournemire (de) Auvergne,
extraction, honneurs de la cour,
ANF

Tournier (de) Toulousain,
Capitoul de Toulouse

Tournu de Ventavon Dauphiné,
par charge

Tredecini de Saint-Séverin
Savoie

Treil (de) Languedoc, *extraction*

Vacher de Tournemire Auvergne,
par lettres, 19th century

Vassal (de) Quercy, *extraction*

Vaulchier (de) Franche-Comté,
par charge

Veyre de Soras (de) Vivarais, *par
charge*, ANF

Vigneral (de) Normandie, *par
lettres*

Villardi de Montlaur (de)
Comtat Venaissin, *extraction*,
ANF

Villeneuve (Trans, Flayosc,
Bargemon, Esclapon) (de)
Provence, *extraction, honneurs
de la cour*, ANF

Vincent Lyonnais, *par charge*

Vintimille du Luc (de) Provence,
extraction, honneurs de la cour

Vogüé (de) Vivarais, *extraction,
honneurs de la cour*, ANF

Widranges (de) Lorraine,
extraction

Archival sources

In the course of research archivists brought to my attention *fonds* that had not yet been classed and for which no inventory was available. Where I have cited a document from those collections the corresponding endnote states *fonds 'en vrac'*; for a document from a classed collection the archival box number is given. Papers that were sequestered during the French Revolution can be found in series T at the AN. Those *fonds* were not used for this study because they do not extend into the nineteenth century. I have sometimes checked for information in series M (Administration and economy 1800–1940) and series Q (Property), but predominantly focused on series E, F, and J.

Archives nationales, Paris
AP 22 Fonds Kersaint et Coëtnempren
AP 31 Fonds Murat
AP 86 Fonds de La Maison de Jaucourt
AP 103 Fonds Lucien Bonaparte et ses descendants
AP 156 (I) Fonds Mackau
AP 272 Fonds Ploeuc
BB/11/13391/2 — BB/11/13391/10 Successions aux titres et aux majorats

Archives départementales

AD Ain, Bourg-en-Bresse
15J Fonds Cardon de Sandrans

AD Allier, Yzeure
59J Fonds La Forest Divonne-Boisgelin

AD Alpes de Haute Provence, Digne-les-Bains
28J Archives de la famille Laugier de Beaucouse

AD Alpes Maritimes, Nice
9J Fonds Blacas-Carros
25J Archives du château de Mouans Sartoux

AD Ardèche, Privas
4J Fonds Veyre de Soras
39J Chartrier de Chambonas
61J Fonds du Faure de Satillieu

AD Ariège, Foix
10J Chartrier de Narbonne-Lara
13J Fonds de la famille d'Hautpoul
46J Chartrier de Léran

AD Aveyron, Rodez
9J Fonds du château de Panat
13J Fonds du château de Bournazel
60J Fonds de Faramond
71J Fonds de Bonald de Vielvayssac

AD Bouches-du-Rhône, Marseille, and Aix-en-Provence
3E 241 Fonds de la famille d'Estienne de Saint-Jean
3E 242 Fonds de la famille d'Espagnet
31E Fonds de la famille d'Albertas
19F Fonds de la famille de Grasse
63J Fonds de la famille de Forbin
103J Fonds de la famille d'Isoard–Vauvenargues
140J Fonds de la famille de Foresta
197J Fonds de la famille de Montgrand

AD Cantal, Aurillac
4J Archives familiales Ganilh d'Allanche et Teillard-Nozerolles de Murat
8J Fonds Teillard Rancilhac de Chazelles
17J Fonds de Rochemonteix
19J Fonds Vacher de Tournemire

AD Charente, Angoulême
J1044–1401 Fonds Galard, Brassac, Béarn, Chalais

4J Fonds Lecoq de Boisbaudran
10J Fonds du château de Chalais

AD Charente-Maritime, La Rochelle
19J Chartrier des seigneurs de Clérac
20J Fonds Fretard-d'Ecoyeux
21J Archives de la famille de Grailly
177J Fonds Chaudruc de Crazannes

AD Corrèze, Tulle
54J Fonds Raymond de Geouffre de La Pradelle
1Mi293 Archives du château de Bach

AD Côtes-d'Armor, Saint Brieuc
19J Archives de Courson
60J Fonds Frotier de La Messelière
127J Fonds Goyon de Feltre

AD Côte-d'Or, Dijon
32F Fonds Vogüé
76J Fonds Vogüé
Q 1139 and Q695 fol. 413–21.

AD Deux-Sèvres, Niort
J2535 Fonds du château de Saint-Loup
102J Fonds de la famille Lévesque
126J Fonds de la famille La Rochebrochard

AD Dordogne, Périgueux
3J Papiers Gontier du Soulas
6J Archives du château de Campagne
13J Fonds de Gontaut-Biron
22J Fonds de Beaumont-Beynac
24J Archives du château Lieu-Dieu
62J Fonds Madaillan
74J Fonds de Gérard

AD Finistère, Quimper
23J Fonds Guillard de Kersauzic

AD Gironde, Bordeaux
9J Fonds d'Arlot de Saint-Saud
17J Fonds de Grailly

AD Hautes-Alpes, Gap
70J Fonds Tournu de Ventaron

AD Haute-Loire, Le Puy en Velay
23–24J Archives Langlade du Chayla et familles apparentées
61J Archives Pradier d'Agrain et familles alliées
101J Papiers des familles Chornel, de Chazelles et de Brossac, Eyraud
105J Fonds Morel de La Colombe de La Chapelle d'Apchier

AD Haut-Rhin, Colmar
10J Fonds de Beer
108J Archives de la famille de Reinach

AD Hérault, Montpellier
51J Fonds du marquisat de Murviel-Spinola
72J Fonds Treil de Pardailhan

AD Ille-et-Vilaine, Rennes
13J Fonds de Coniac
14J Fonds Freslon de la Freslonnière
15J Fonds de Langle de La Couyère
19J Fonds de La Motte de Gennes
21J Fonds de Langle des Tesnières
23J Fonds de La Bourdonnaye-Montluc
35J Fonds du comte de Botherel
59J Fonds de La Monneraye

AD Indre et Loire, Tours
4J Fonds Maison
11J Chartrier du Coudray-Montpensier
14J Fonds du château la Vallière
15J Fonds du Breuil
111J Fonds de Orillard de Villemanzy
133J Fonds de Beaumont
152J Fonds de Biencourt

AD Isère, Grenoble
8J Archives du château du Pin
29J Fonds de la famille de La Croix de Chevrières de Pisançon

AD Jura, Lons-le-Saunier
25J Chartrier de Lavigny
35J Chartrier du Deschaux

AD Loire, Saint Etienne
4J Archives de la famille Courtin de Neufbourg
201J Archives de la famille Hüe de la Blanche

AD Loire-Atlantique, Nantes
9J Fonds Régis de L'Estourbeillon
58J Fonds de Fontaines
59J Fonds du marquisat de Becdelièvre
146J Fonds Le Chauff de Kerguénec
185J Fonds de Sesmaisons
186J Fonds du château de l'Escuray
190J Fonds Chevigné
200J Fonds Le Gonidec de Traissan

AD Loir-et-Cher, Blois
83J Fonds du château de Bizemont
97J Fonds de Taillevis
99J Fonds Guyon de Montlivault
111J Fonds du château de Villelouët
113J Fonds du château des Bordes

AD Lot, Cahors
13J Fonds Camy-Gozon
31J Fonds Louis d'Alauzier
40J Fonds de la famille Vassal
44J Fonds du château de Langle
63J Fonds de la famille Valet de Réganhac et des familles alliées

AD Lot-et-Garonne, Agen
1J 1009–13 Fonds Gavini de Campile
25J Fonds Luppé
38J Fonds Durfort
83J Fonds du château d'Arasse

AD Lozère, Mende
F2725–2840 château de Booz
4J Fonds Molette de Morangiès et Moré de Charaix
7J Fonds de Saint Amand
9J Fonds de Villeneuve-Bargemon et Chapel d'Espinassoux
34J Fonds de la famille de Chambrun
38J Fonds Morangiès
56J Papiers Framond de Grèzes

105J Fonds du château de La Vigne
108J Fonds du château de Cauvel

AD Maine-et-Loire, Angers
8J Fonds du chartrier de Jarzé
13J Fonds de la baronnie de Candé
17J Fonds de la famille d'Armaillé
215J Fonds de La Bourdonnaye
249J Fonds de la famille Montlaur

AD Manche, Saint-Lô
138J Chartrier du Chastel
262J Chartrier de Thère
330J Chartrier de la famille Le Chartier de Sédouy

AD Meurthe-et-Moselle, Nancy
2J Archives de la famille de Mahuet
13J Archives de la famille de Lenoncourt
18J Archives de la famille de L'Escale
52J Archives de la famille de Metz-Noblat

AD Meuse, Bar-le-Duc
7J Chartrier de Thillombois
17J Archives de la famille de Metz-Noblat
10J Chartrier de Choiseul-Stainville
29J Collection de l'Escale
38J Chartrier de Nettancourt
39J Archives de la famille de Nettancourt
50J Archives de la famille de Marne

AD Morbihan, Vannes
31J Archives du château de Kerlevénan
34J Archives du château de Trédion
35J Archives du château de Grégo
39J Archives du château de Trémohar
50J Chartrier de Kergonano
55J Archives du château de Penhouët
93J Archives du château de Truscat

AD Nord, Lille
26J E2508 Papiers de la famille de Croÿ

AD Oise, Beauvais
69J Fonds du château de Verderonne

AD Orne, Alençon
34J Chartrier du château de Carrouges
73J Fonds du château de Ri
178J Chartrier du château de Maison-Maugis
242J Fonds du château de Médavy

AD Pyrénées-Atlantiques, Pau
43J Fonds Touaille de Larabrie

AD Rhône, Lyon
8J Fonds comte du Bondy
11J Fonds des familles Comarmond, Baroud et Liebhaber
149J Fonds du château de la Salle

AD Sarthe, Le Mans
4J Chartrier de Grandchamp
14J Archives Bigot de la Touanne, familles de Mondagron, Salmon de Loiray

AD Savoie, Chambéry
29F Fonds d'Alexandry d'Orengiani
46F Fonds Tredecini de Saint-Séverin
8J Fonds de la famille de Boigne
20J Fonds Grassis

AD Seine-Maritime, Rouen
7J Fonds du château de Clères
116J Chartrier de Maulévrier
185J Fonds de Wargemont
203J Chartrier de l'ancien marquisat de la Mailleraye-sur-Seine
229J Fonds Quentin de Gromard

AD Somme, Amiens
2J Archives de la seigneurie de Boismont
3J Fonds Le Couvreur
27J Fonds de Saint-Blimond
36J Fonds de la famille Morel
73J Fonds d'Auguste d'Estourmel
78J Fonds de la famille de Hédouville

AD Tarn, Albi
41J Archives du château de Saint-André
43J Archives du château de Florentin

AD Tarn-et-Garonne, Montauban
29J Fonds Tournier
31J Fonds Cocula
43J Fonds Granié

AD Var, Draguignan
1J 116–120 Famille de Castellane
15J Fonds Villeneuve-Flayosc
16J Fonds Villeneuve-Tourettes
17J Fonds Vintimille
20J Fonds Castellane
23J Chartrier de Villeneuve-Bargemon
51J Fonds Guillaume Barles
62J Chartrier de Beauregard

AD Vaucluse, Avignon
43J Archives de la famille Ripert d'Alauzier

AD Vosges, Épinal
19J Fonds Barbey de Beaumont
41J Fonds de la famille de Rozières
134J Fonds des Pilliers

AD Yonne, Auxerre
3J Fonds Louvois
9J Fonds de Crisenon
12J Fonds de Dampierre
82J Fonds du château de Montillot
87J Fonds du château de Vallery

Index